MARYLAND

MICHAELA RIVA GAASERUD

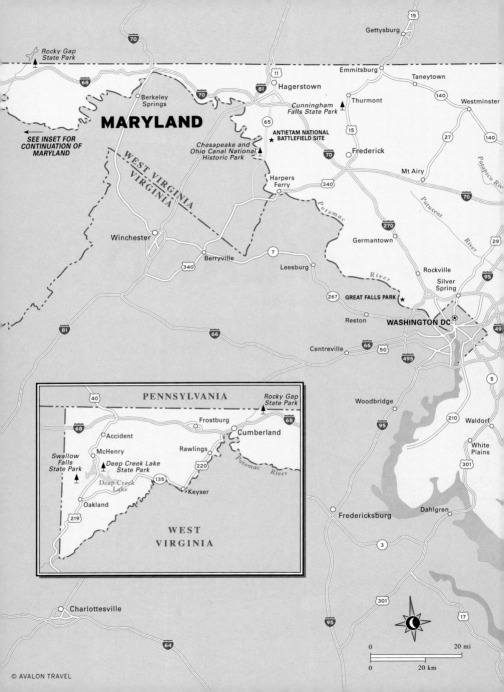

15

Gettysburg

70

Rocky Gap
State Park

68

Berkeley
Springs

70

81

11

Hagerstown

65

Emmitsburg

Thurmont

Taneytown

140

Westminster

MARYLAND

Cunningham
Falls State Park

15

140

27

SEE INSET FOR
CONTINUATION OF
MARYLAND

WEST VIRGINIA
VIRGINIA

Chesapeake and
Ohio Canal National
Historic Park

ANTIETAM NATIONAL
BATTLEFIELD SITE

Frederick

Mt Airy

70

Patapsco River

Harpers
Ferry

340

Potomac

Patuxent

River

Winchester

270

Germantown

29

340

Berryville

7

Leesburg

River

Rockville

Silver
Spring

95

267

GREAT FALLS PARK

81

Reston

66

WASHINGTON DC

49

Centreville

66

50

495

5

PENNSYLVANIA

40

Rocky Gap
State Park

Woodbridge

68

Frostburg

68

210

Waldorf

Accident

Cumberland

McHenry

Rawlings

Swallow
Falls
State Park

Deep Creek Lake
State Park

220

Potomac

River

95

White
Plains

301

Deep Creek
Lake

135

Oakland

Keyser

219

Dahlgren

WEST
VIRGINIA

Fredericksburg

Charlottesville

3

301

95

17

64

0   20 mi

0   20 km

© AVALON TRAVEL

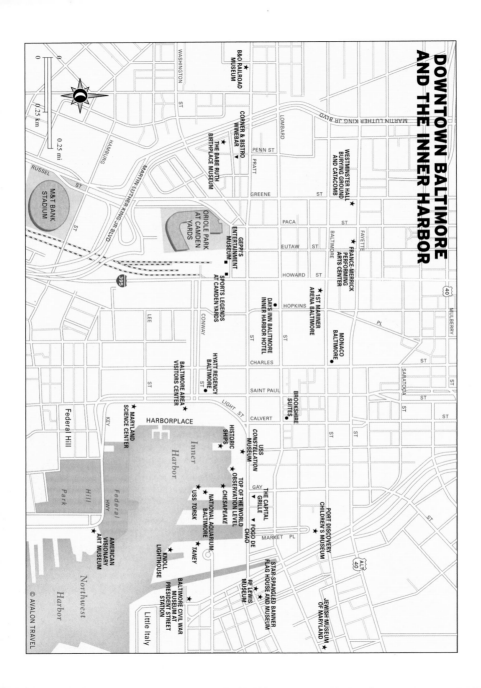

DOWNTOWN BALTIMORE AND THE INNER HARBOR

B&O RAILROAD MUSEUM ★

CORNER & BISTRO WINEBAR ▼

THE BABE RUTH BIRTHPLACE MUSEUM ★

WASHINGTON ST

HAMBURG

RUSSEL ST

M&T BANK STADIUM

MARTIN LUTHER KING JR BLVD

ORIOLE PARK AT CAMDEN YARDS

GEPPI'S ENTERTAINMENT MUSEUM ■

SPORTS LEGENDS AT CAMDEN YARDS ■

395

LEE ST

CONWAY ST

HYATT REGENCY BALTIMORE ●

BALTIMORE AREA VISITORS CENTER ★

KEY HWY

Federal Hill

MARYLAND SCIENCE CENTER ★

HARBORPLACE

HISTORIC SHIPS ★

TOP OF THE WORLD OBSERVATION LEVEL ★

NATIONAL AQUARIUM, BALTIMORE ★

CHESAPEAKE ★

USS TORSK ★

TANEY ★

KNOLL LIGHTHOUSE ★

AMERICAN VISIONARY ART MUSEUM ★

Federal Hill Park

Inner Harbor

Federal HWY

Northwest Harbor

© AVALON TRAVEL

MARTIN LUTHER KING JR BLVD

LOMBARD ST

PENN ST

PRATT ST

GREENE ST

WESTMINSTER HALL BURYING GROUND AND CATACOMB ★

PACA ST

EUTAW ST

HOWARD ST

BALTIMORE ST

FRANCE-MERRICK PERFORMING ARTS CENTER ★

FAYETTE ST

1ST MARINER ARENA BALTIMORE ★

DAYS INN BALTIMORE INNER HARBOR HOTEL ●

MONACO BALTIMORE ●

HOPKINS ST

CHARLES ST

SAINT PAUL ST

BROOKSHIRE SUITES ●

LIGHT ST

CALVERT ST

USS CONSTELLATION MUSEUM ★

GAY ST

THE CAPITAL GRILLE ▼

FOGO DE CHAO ▼

MARKET PL

SARATOGA ST

ST

ST

ST

PORT DISCOVERY CHILDREN'S MUSEUM ★

STAR-SPANGLED BANNER FLAG HOUSE AND MUSEUM ★

RF LEWIS MUSEUM ★

BALTIMORE CIVIL WAR MUSEUM AT PRESIDENT STREET STATION ★

JEWISH MUSEUM OF MARYLAND ★

Little Italy

MULBERRY ST

40

PL

ALT 40

0   0.25 km

0   0.25 mi

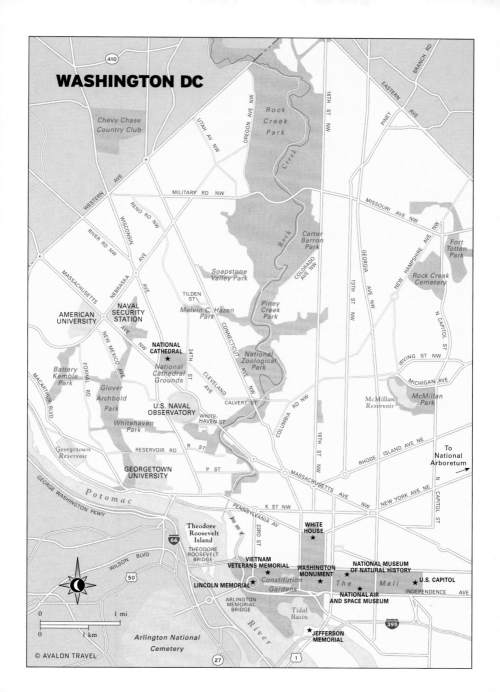

IN THIS TEMPLE
AS IN THE HEARTS OF THE PEOPLE
FOR WHOM HE SAVED THE UNION
THE MEMORY OF ABRAHAM LINCOLN
IS ENSHRINED FOREVER

Contents

DISCOVER
Maryland

Maryland might first attract your attention because of its location on the Chesapeake Bay and its proximity to Washington DC. But there's much more to recommend it than the luck of its geography.

Don't overlook Baltimore, which refracts urban pleasures through its own quirky lens. Long nicknamed "Charm City," it's no longer keeping its charms hidden. It's blossoming into a major mid-Atlantic tourist destination, flaunting its world-class museums, state-of-the-art sports venues, fine dining, and luxury hotels.

The state capital Annapolis is a bit more genteel, with an enchanting historic district and trendy boutiques and taverns. Its busy harbor makes it a launching point for sails on the Bay. It's also home to the U.S. Naval Academy—not to mention an endless supply of blue crabs, oysters, and other delectable seafood.

And then there's the nation's capital. Alongside its monuments and museums, Washington DC offers trendy restaurants and buzzing nightlife.

Clockwise from top left: a basket of blue crabs; a Civil War cannon at Antietam National Battlefield; Washington DC's Martin Luther King, Jr. Memorial by sculptor Lei Yixin; the United States Naval Academy in Annapolis; Potomac River; Baltimore's Inner Harbor.

Not far from these thriving metropolitan areas, you'll find quaint fishing villages, sleepy mountain towns, and an abundance of natural beauty. Wander through glowing fall foliage. Summit the peak of Sugarloaf Mountain. Sail on the Chesapeake Bay before cracking a claw at a waterfront crab house. Hunt for fossils at Calvert Cliffs. Stroll the bustling boardwalks of Ocean City. Relax on the quiet beaches of Assateague Island, where wild ponies roam free.

Maryland has long been both witness and participant in the nation's most historic moments. Today you can tread the hallowed ground at Antietam, the bloodiest battlefield of the Civil War, or see where abolitionist leader Frederick Douglass lived and worked in Baltimore.

Welcome to Maryland, where there's always something new to discover.

Clockwise from top left: detail of a sailboat in Annapolis; Paddleboats Team Chessie in Baltimore; cherry blossoms in Washington DC; cows in a Maryland field.

Planning Your Trip

Where to Go

BALTIMORE

The city of Baltimore, once a rough industrial port, has undergone a series of urban renewal plans over the past few decades. As a result, it has blossomed into a major tourist site of the mid-Atlantic and offers many **fascinating museums, entertainment venues,** professional sporting events such as the **Preakness Stakes,** and the famous **Inner Harbor.** Side trips include **Westminster,** which hosted both Union and Confederate troops during the Civil War, and lovely **Havre de Grace,** sitting at the head of the Chesapeake Bay.

ANNAPOLIS AND SOUTHERN MARYLAND

The nation's sailing capital, **Annapolis,** is the top destination on the mainland banks of the Chesapeake Bay due to its waterfront location, charming historic district, and trendy boutiques and taverns. With a busy recreational harbor, the city features an endless supply of blue crabs, oysters, and other delectable seafood. It is also home to the **U.S. Naval Academy.** Scenic Southern Maryland offers a slower, relaxing pace with idyllic seaside towns such as **Solomons Island** and **Chesapeake Beach** along with historic cities such as **St. Mary's City.**

THE EASTERN SHORE AND ATLANTIC BEACHES

Picturesque fishing towns, blue crabs, and sunsets—these are all traits of Maryland's Eastern Shore. **Chestertown, St. Michaels,** and **Tilghman Island** offer alluring charm and a window into life along the Chesapeake Bay. Maryland's Atlantic beaches are a symphony of contrasts. **Assateague Island** calms your spirits as you share the beaches with wild ponies. **Ocean City** offers an exciting boardwalk and active nightlife. Three neighboring beach communities on the Delaware shore—**Bethany Beach, Rehoboth Beach,** and **Lewes**—are popular vacation spots.

WASHINGTON DC

Washington DC is nestled on the banks of the Potomac River. Best known for politics, government, and **monuments and museums,** the city is also home to universities, nightlife, art, theater,

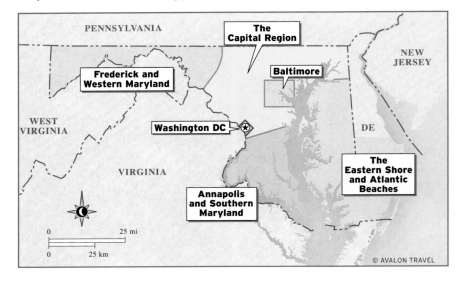

autumn foliage in Maryland

and sports. One of the largest (and cleanest) cities in the country, Washington DC offers **trendy neighborhoods, upscale shopping,** the **National Cathedral,** the **National Zoo,** and professional sports arenas. The nation's capital is easy to navigate, especially with the help of landmarks like the **Washington Monument** and the **U.S. Capitol Building.**

THE CAPITAL REGION

Trendy, sporty, and historical, Maryland's Capital Region is a main suburban area of Washington DC and, as such, is densely populated. **Montgomery County** is sophisticated, urban, and professional with a variety of restaurants, shopping areas, hotels, and upscale neighborhoods. **Prince George's County** is a hub for government agencies including NASA and the Department of Agriculture and is home to the **Washington Redskins.** In addition to offering visitors many interesting attractions, Maryland's Capital Region also serves as a convenient home base for exploring Washington DC.

FREDERICK AND WESTERN MARYLAND

Frederick offers old-town charm, antiques shopping, and terrific food. Some of the region's finest restaurants are tucked into the appealing historic downtown. Western Maryland is the "mountain side" of the state, where the railroad once ruled and the scenery is tranquil and pretty. **Deep Creek Lake** is a popular getaway spot for Washingtonians with its 65 miles of shoreline. Whether your idea of vacation is visiting **Civil War sites,** boating, or riding a steam engine through the mountains, you can find it all in Western Maryland.

When to Go

If you have the luxury of choosing your time to visit, **late spring** (May and June) and **fall** (September and October) are usually the **best times** to explore Maryland. The weather is most pleasant, and there are fewer tourists. Although **summer** is the **prime tourist season,** unless your plans involve some beach time or a stay in a mountain retreat, the humidity can be a bit overwhelming. The fall foliage in the region is some of the most spectacular in the country. If your focus is on historical sites and museums, the **winter** months (with the exception of the holiday season) can mean **short or no wait times** for popular attractions. Just be prepared for some sites to be closed or to have shorter hours.

National Pride and Local Charm

Either **Washington DC** or **Baltimore** makes a good starting point for exploring Maryland. Both cities are centrally located and convenient for air, train, bus, and car travel.

The Best of Washington DC

In addition to monuments and museums, DC boasts trendy neighborhoods and upscale dining and shopping. Although two days isn't enough to cover all the great attractions in the nation's capital, it's enough to experience some of the highlights.

DAY 1

► Put on your walking shoes and start your day on the **National Mall** with a bird's-eye view of the city from the top of the **Washington Monument,** then walk through the **National World War II Memorial** on your way to the **Lincoln Memorial.**

► Choose several of the many beautiful **war memorials** to visit, such as the **Korean War Memorial** and the **Vietnam Veterans Memorial.**

► Pick up lunch at a local food truck and find a nice bench in **West Potomac Park** to rest your feet.

► Ride Metrorail up to Capitol Hill and spend the afternoon on a tour of the **U.S. Capitol.**

► When your feet can take no more, catch a cab to **Vidalia** near Dupont Circle for dinner.

► Walk east on M Street to enjoy some of the city's nightlife at the rooftop bar at **Ozio Restaurant and Lounge.**

► Spend the night in the nearby **Hotel Tabard Inn** or, if you feel like splurging, at the **Hay-Adams Hotel,** overlooking the White House.

the Vietnam Veterans Memorial

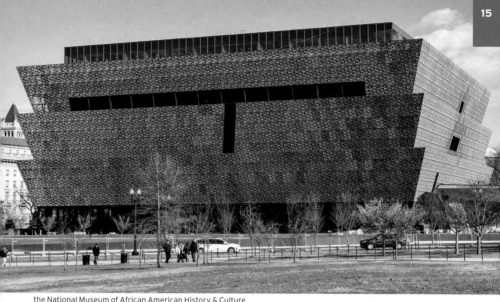

the National Museum of African American History & Culture

DAY 2

▶ After breakfast at the inn, if you're feeling spry, walk the 10 or so blocks down to the National Mall or else take a cab to visit some of the **Smithsonian Institution** museums.

▶ Visit one of the classics, like the **National Air and Space Museum** or **National Museum of Natural History,** or reserve a pass in advance to visit the new **National Museum of African American History & Culture.**

▶ Grab lunch inside one of the museums when you need a break, or sample another one of DC's great food trucks outside.

▶ When you've overloaded on museums, walk to the **P.O.V. Roof Terrace and Lounge** at the W Washington D.C. Hotel and have a cocktail.

▶ End your DC tour with a late dinner at the **Old Ebbitt Grill.**

The Best of Baltimore

Baltimore has flowered into a destination in its own right, with museums, festivals, monuments, and a wide selection of restaurants to call its own; yet it still retains its down-to-earth charm. Use this city as a jumping-off point to explore the rest of the state.

DAY 1

▶ Start in the popular **Inner Harbor,** where you can get around on foot and visit the **National Aquarium** and the **Historic Ships** collection.

▶ Choose one of the restaurants in the busy harbor area for lunch before driving or taking the water taxi to the **Fort McHenry National Monument,** where Baltimore fended off a British attack during the War of 1812 and Francis Scott Key penned the "Star-Spangled Banner."

▶ Jump back on the water taxi or drive over to **Fell's Point** for exploration of its charming waterfront streets before having dinner at the **Red Star Bar and Grill.**

aerial view of Harpers Ferry National Historical Park

Maryland has been both witness and participant in crucial events in the nation's history. Even just one day spent exploring these sites will give you a sense of the depth of history throughout this region.

BALTIMORE

- In Baltimore, **Fort McHenry National Monument and Historic Shrine** (page 40) is the site of the battle that inspired "The Star-Spangled Banner."

- The Inner Harbor is home to one of the most impressive military ship collections in the world (page 29), which includes the sloop-of-war **USS Constellation,** the lightship **Chesapeake,** and the submarine **USS Torsk.**

- The **Frederick Douglass-Isaac Myers Maritime Park** (page 33) chronicles the lives of Douglass, a former slave and abolitionist leader, and Myers, who created the first union for African Americans just after the Civil War. Both men lived and worked in Baltimore.

ANNAPOLIS

- Annapolis is the site of not only the U.S. Naval Academy but many landmarks dating back as far as the 17th century, including **St. John's College, Hammond-Harwood House,** and **St. Anne's Episcopal Church** (pages 83-84). You can also choose to spend the night in any of a number of the city's historic inns.

FREDERICK

- The town of Frederick was spared from burning during the Civil War and became a hospital town for those wounded in battle. Today, it's the site of the **National Museum of Civil War Medicine** (page 252), with exhibits on the practice of medicine during that time.

WESTERN MARYLAND

- **Antietam National Battlefield** (page 271) was the site of the bloodiest single-day battle during the Civil War. Today, the battlefield park grounds are noncommercialized and beautifully maintained. A self-guided tour follows the action of the battle, with 96 monuments and sites such as "Bloody Lane," a sunken road where 5,000 casualties occurred.

- Nearby **Antietam National Cemetery** (page 272) contains the graves of Union soldiers as well as veterans from the Spanish-American War, World War I, and World War II.

- Over the border in Pennsylvania, the **Gettysburg National Civil War Battle Reenactment** (page 263) is held each July. It includes two exciting battles, field demonstrations, live mortar fire demonstrations, living history programs, and all-day activities.

- The historic town of **Harpers Ferry,** just over the West Virginia state line, was the location of abolitionist John Brown's 1859 raid on a national armory, an event that helped trigger the Civil War. **Harpers Ferry National Historical Park** (page 266) features more than 25 historic buildings, including the armory site, which was later converted into a train station.

Antietam National Battlefield

Gettysburg National Military Park

picturesque Fell's Point in Baltimore

► End your evening at the cozy **Cat's Eye Pub** for some blues, jazz, or folk music. Turn in for the night at the **Inn at Hendersons Wharf.**

DAY 2

► Start your day with breakfast at the popular **Blue Moon Café.**

► After breakfast, drive or take a cab to Mount Vernon and visit the **Walters Art Museum,** then climb the 228 stairs of the **Washington Monument** for a great view of the city.

► Grab some pizza at **Joe Squared.** Then continue your cultural tour at the **Baltimore Museum of Art** in Homewood.

► Have dinner at **Woodberry Kitchen** just west of Hampden and finish in time to take in a performance at **Centerstage** in Mount Vernon.

► Finish up your two-day tour with a drink and a wonderful view of the city at the classy **13th Floor** in the historic Belvedere Hotel building.

the view from the top of the Washington Monument

Five Days on the Eastern Shore

The Eastern Shore is a 180-mile-long peninsula that sits east of the Chesapeake Bay and west of the Atlantic Ocean. Historic towns, charming fishing villages, vast natural areas, and abundant seafood make it a prime recreation destination.

Day 1

Begin your trip in the northern part of the region in **Chestertown,** Maryland. This historic colonial waterfront town sits on the banks of the Chester River and is a wonderful place to stroll, eat, and generally relax. You can also take an educational course on the schooner *Sultana.* Stay in a local inn for the night.

Day 2

Drive south for an hour to the charming waterfront town of **St. Michaels** in Maryland. This is one of the loveliest spots on the Eastern Shore and where many Washingtonians have second homes. The town has fine restaurants, shopping, a good museum, and a lot of character. Spend the night in St. Michaels in one of the fine inns or a local bed-and-breakfast.

Day 3

Drive southeast to the Atlantic side of the Eastern Shore to **Assateague Island.** Look for signs of the wild ponies that live there. Enjoy some solitude on the pristine 37-mile beach. Camp overnight on the island.

Day 4

Leave the calm of nature behind and drive north to bustling **Ocean City,** Maryland. This beach town is crazy busy in the summer and offers a wide, active boardwalk, nightlife, and many amusements. Eat some french fries on the boardwalk, ride a Ferris wheel, and then rent a beach umbrella for some downtime on the sand.

Day 5

End your trip with a drive one hour north to the harborfront community of **Lewes,** Delaware. Enjoy a sightseeing cruise from the harbor, spend the afternoon at **Cape Henlopen State Park,** or stroll the enchanting streets of Historic Lewes.

wild ponies on Assateague Island

Best Places to Eat Crab

the Jumbo Lump Crab Cakes from Chick & Ruth's Delly

The slogan "Maryland is for Crabs" is meant to be taken literally. People here know how and where to crack a claw.

- The original "Crab Bomb," with 10 ounces of jumbo lump crabmeat, can be found at **Jerry's Seafood** (page 243) in Bowie.

- The Jumbo Lump Crab Cakes are the calling card of a local Annapolis favorite called **Chick & Ruth's Delly** (page 87). Just a block from the State House, this sandwich shop opened in 1965 under owners Chick and Ruth Levitt, and it has been growing ever since.

- A traditional crab house with huge notoriety in the Annapolis area is **Cantler's Riverside Inn** (page 87). It is situated on a cove right on the water and sells local steamed crabs by the dozen (in all sizes).

- **Buddy's Crabs and Ribs** (page 87) is a lively icon on Main Street in Annapolis. Steamed crabs are the entrée of choice at Buddy's, but the homemade crab cakes are also famous.

- For more suggestions on where to crack a claw, see page 88.

Cantler's Riverside Inn

Baltimore

Look for ★ to find recommended
sights, activities, dining, and lodging.

Highlights

★ **National Aquarium, Baltimore:** The gem of the Inner Harbor, the National Aquarium offers close encounters with sharks, dolphins, and many other sea creatures. Catch a show or sign up for a special slumber party; there's no shortage of awe-inspiring exhibits and activities (page 27).

★ **Historic Ships:** This unique collection on display in the Inner Harbor features four military ships and one lighthouse within easy walking distance of each other (page 29).

★ **Port Discovery Children's Museum:** One of the top children's museums in the country, this educational playground offers three floors of interactive exhibits (page 31).

★ **B&O Railroad Museum:** See the birthplace of the American railroad system and learn about its development in Baltimore. Vintage engines and cars are part of the fun (page 33).

★ **Baltimore Museum of Industry:** Baltimore is the home of many manufacturing firsts. This fascinating museum shares the history of many everyday conveniences (page 38).

★ **Fort McHenry National Monument and Historic Shrine:** This fort dating back to 1802 inspired the poem written by Francis Scott Key that became the U.S. national anthem (page 40).

★ **The Walters Art Museum:** This remarkable collection of 5,000 pieces of work spans 5,000 years and includes a mummy from 1000 BC and two imperial eggs (page 41).

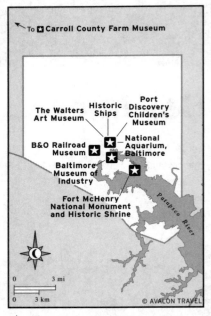

★ **Carroll County Farm Museum:** Glimpse what rural life in the mid-19th century was like on a 142-acre farm (page 74).

Baltimore has been a major port city since the 1700s. The hardworking city is the birthplace of many industries: the first sugar refinery in the country (1796), the first gaslight company (1819), and the first railroad for commercial transportation (1828). Having spent much of its history as a rough industrial seaport, Baltimore managed to keep its treasures to itself. In the 1970s, outsiders started to recognize the city's hidden charm, and the working-class town was nicknamed "Charm City." Today, after a series of successful urban renewal projects, Baltimore has blossomed into a major mid-Atlantic tourist destination. It flaunts world-class museums, state-of-the-art sports venues, fine dining, and luxury hotels—all while retaining its fierce spirit and authenticity.

ORIENTATION

For simplicity's sake, we're going to focus on six primary sections of Baltimore. They are key areas where popular sights are located, as well as trendy neighborhoods where you can find a delightful selection of food, nightlife, and activities.

Downtown and the Inner Harbor

Most of the beauty shots of Baltimore are taken downtown and at the Inner Harbor. The harbor has long been the center of activity in this port city and was once a thriving destination for visitors and supplies arriving by steamship. Although most people think that Baltimore sits on the Chesapeake Bay, the harbor is actually the mouth of the Patapsco River. The river flows into the bay east of the city, which is why this deepwater yet protected harbor has been popular for centuries. After the collapse of the steamship era, the port still saw industrial action, but lapsed into a state of neglect as the city fell off the radar as a vacation destination.

In the 1970s interest in the city was revived as Baltimore underwent extensive innovative redevelopment. The Inner Harbor benefited greatly from the rejuvenation and

---

Previous: the view from Federal Hill Park; row houses on Federal Hill. **Above:** the Washington Monument and Museum at Mount Vernon Place.

Baltimore

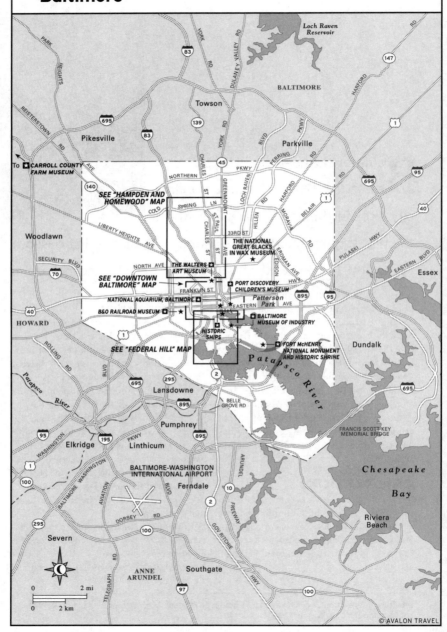

© AVALON TRAVEL

Baltimore's Inner Harbor

became home to many attractions, museums, restaurants, upscale hotels, and a beautiful waterfront promenade. The surrounding downtown area received a boost as well and offers a blend of businesses, historic buildings, and museums.

Fell's Point and Little Italy

Fell's Point is on the harbor to the east of the Inner Harbor. It is about a five-minute drive from the Inner Harbor or can be reached by water taxi. It is one of the oldest neighborhoods in Baltimore, with many historic buildings and trendy eateries. Fell's Point was first settled by William Fell, an English Quaker, in 1726 and many of the 350 historic buildings were constructed before 1800 (200 predate the Civil War). Fell's Point thrived until the need for sailing ships declined in the early 1900s, after which the neighborhood entered a steep decline. The waterfront became a collection of rough saloons, and in the mid-1960s plans for the building of I-95 had it running right through the neighborhood. The community was able to stop the highway, and instead the neighborhood became the first National Historic District in Maryland.

Nearby Little Italy (www.littleitalymd.com)

was settled by Italian immigrants in the mid-1800s, who opened businesses and restaurants in the cozy little area between the Inner Harbor and Fell's Point. The area now boasts almost 30 restaurants and also offers visitors vibrant festivals and a bit of old-world Italy.

Canton

East of Fell's Point on the waterfront is the historic community of Canton, which dates back to the late 19th century. Modern condos and old row houses fuse Baltimore's past and present, and lively **Canton Square** on O'Donnell Street offers bars, restaurants, and endless nightlife for the local partying crowd. The Canton waterfront includes views of navy ships as they dock nearby.

Federal Hill

Federal Hill sits opposite the Inner Harbor on the south side of the harbor. It is named after an imposing hill that boasts a fantastic vantage point for viewing the Inner Harbor and downtown Baltimore. Federal Hill has great shopping, bars, restaurants, and entertainment as well as a thriving residential area. It is home to the famed 120-by-70-foot neon Domino Sugar sign that casts a glow over

Little Italy

the city from its 160-foot perch. The sign is a Baltimore icon and has been a fixture in the harbor since 1951.

Mount Vernon

Mount Vernon, north of downtown Baltimore, is the cultural center of the city. Museums and halls provide endless opportunities to take in a show or listen to the symphony. The neighborhood is full of grand 19th-century architecture, and marble-clad homes originally built for wealthy sea captains surround the first monument to honor our first president.

Hampden and Homewood

Northwest of Mount Vernon is the settlement of Hampden. This 19th-century neighborhood was originally a mill town but is now an eclectic mix of bars, restaurants, thrift stores, galleries, and boutiques. The local residents are both hardworking families and young adults, which gives the area a hip yet grounded feel. To the east of Hampden is the neighborhood of Homewood. Homewood is best known as the home of **Johns Hopkins University,** but it also has nice parks and museums.

PLANNING YOUR TIME

You could easily spend a couple of weeks in Baltimore to really see all the city has to offer, but most people pick and choose sights of particular interest to them and explore the city in a long weekend.

People traveling with children may wish to stay at the Inner Harbor so they can visit the **National Aquarium,** the **Maryland Science Center,** and the **Port Discovery Children's Museum,** and see the **Historic Ships** in the harbor. A visit to **Fort McHenry** is another fun option to pique the little ones' interest in history.

History buffs can pick almost any location in the city as their base and from there take in the **Baltimore Civil War Museum,** the **Star-Spangled Banner Flag House and Museum,** the **Washington Monument, Fort McHenry,** and Edgar Allan Poe's grave site at **Westminster Hall Burying Ground & Catacomb.**

Others come to sample the many restaurants and bars in the busy Fell's Point area or to take in a ball game at Camden Yards. No matter what your interests, there is no shortage of exciting itineraries to create. Baltimore

Fort McHenry

is easy to get around and offers many exciting sights and activities regardless of how long you have to spend there.

If you have time for a full- or half-day excursion from Baltimore, consider putting Westminster or Havre de Grace on your list of places to visit. Westminster, 45 minutes northwest of Baltimore by car, sits in a rural part of the state and has a history of Civil War battles, spies, and ghosts. An hour car ride north on I-95 will take you to the bayside town of Havre de Grace. Its charming seaside atmosphere at the head of the Chesapeake Bay makes the town a rewarding destination for touring and outdoor recreation.

Sights

DOWNTOWN AND THE INNER HARBOR
★ National Aquarium, Baltimore

The **National Aquarium, Baltimore** (501 E. Pratt St., 410/576-3800, www.aqua.org, Mon.-Thurs. 9am-5pm, Fri.-Sat. 9am-8pm, Sun. 9am-6pm, $39.95) is perhaps the most treasured sight in Baltimore's Inner Harbor. Opening in 1981, it was the anchor venue to the redevelopment plan of the Inner Harbor. The aquarium was one of the first large aquariums in the country and remained independent until it joined with the National Aquarium in Washington DC under the blanket name "National Aquarium" in 2003.

Close to 20,000 animals live at the National Aquarium, representing more than 660 species of fish, amphibians, reptiles, birds, and mammals. See the brilliant coral-filled Blacktip Reef exhibit, which mimics Indo-Pacific reefs and offers stunning floor-to-ceiling "pop-out" viewing windows so visitors can get personal with 65 species of animals. Then watch fearsome sharks swim by in their 225,000-gallon ring-shaped tank in Shark Alley, or see divers feed brightly colored fish as you descend the winding ramp through the

Downtown Baltimore and the Inner Harbor

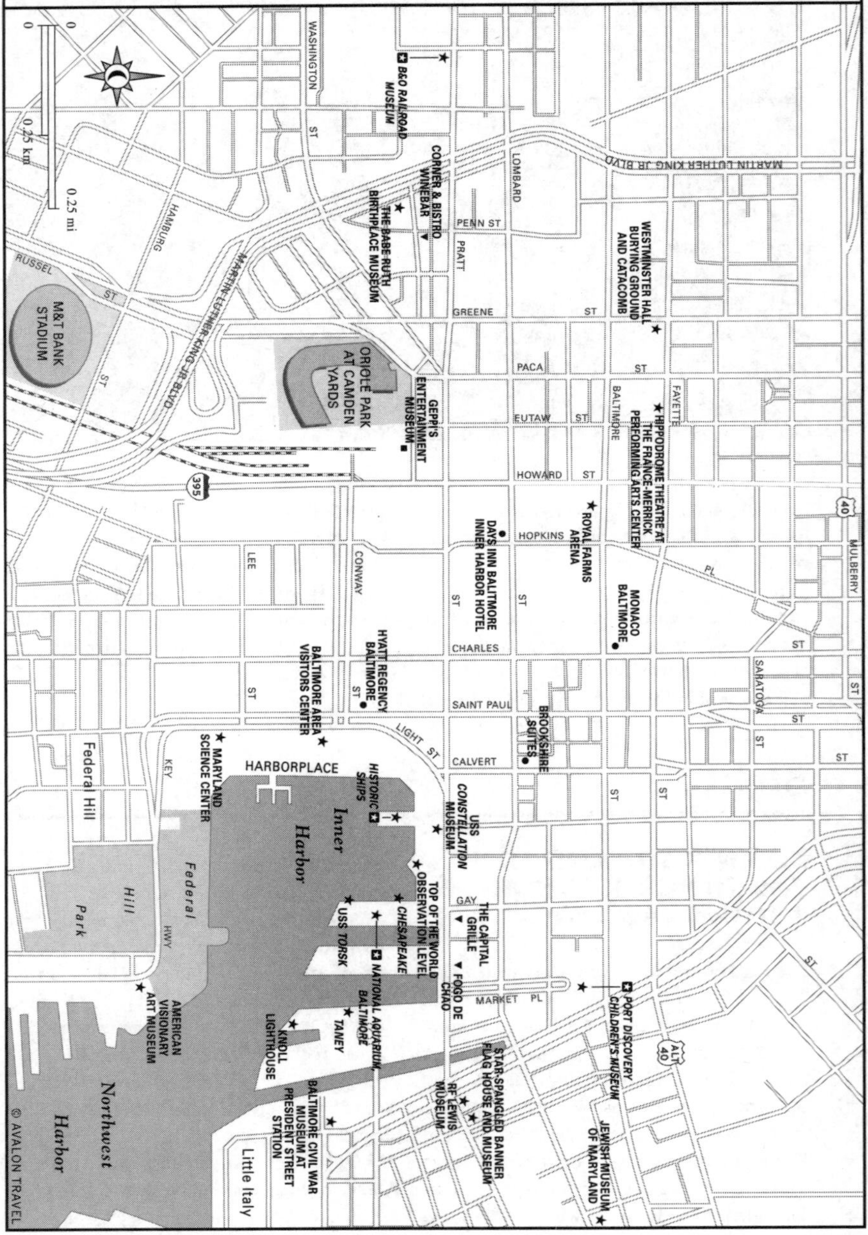

0
0.25 km
0.25 mi

WASHINGTON ST

RUSSEL ST

HAMBURG

MARTIN LUTHER KING JR BLVD

M&T BANK STADIUM

ORIOLE PARK AT CAMDEN YARDS

GEPPI'S ENTERTAINMENT MUSEUM

395

B&O RAILROAD MUSEUM

CORNER & BISTRO WINEBAR

THE BABE RUTH BIRTHPLACE MUSEUM

LOMBARD

PENN ST

PRATT ST

GREENE ST

PACA ST

EUTAW ST

HOWARD ST

BALTIMORE ST

FAYETTE

WESTMINSTER HALL BURYING GROUND AND CATACOMB

HIPPODROME THEATRE AT THE FRANCE-MERRICK PERFORMING ARTS CENTER

MARTIN LUTHER KING JR BLVD

MULBERRY

40

SARATOGA ST

ST

ST

PL

HOPKINS ST

CHARLES ST

SAINT PAUL ST

CALVERT ST

LIGHT ST

CONWAY ST

LEE ST

KEY HWY

DAYS INN BALTIMORE INNER HARBOR HOTEL

HYATT REGENCY BALTIMORE

BALTIMORE AREA VISITORS CENTER

MARYLAND SCIENCE CENTER

HARBORPLACE

ROYAL FARMS ARENA

MONACO BALTIMORE

BROOKSHIRE SUITES

Federal Hill

Federal Hill Park

Inner Harbor

HISTORIC SHIPS

USS CONSTELLATION MUSEUM

TOP OF THE WORLD OBSERVATION LEVEL

CHESAPEAKE

USS TORSK

NATIONAL AQUARIUM BALTIMORE

TANEY

KNOLL LIGHTHOUSE

AMERICAN VISIONARY ART MUSEUM

Northwest Harbor

GAY ST

MARKET PL

THE CAPITAL GRILLE

FOGO DE CHAO

PORT DISCOVERY CHILDREN'S MUSEUM

RF LEWIS MUSEUM

STAR-SPANGLED BANNER FLAG HOUSE AND MUSEUM

BALTIMORE CIVIL WAR MUSEUM AT PRESIDENT STREET STATION

JEWISH MUSEUM OF MARYLAND

ALT 40

Little Italy

© AVALON TRAVEL

Harbor Pass

Many of the popular sights in Baltimore can be accessed with a single ticket that offers discounted entry over individual admission prices. A four-day **Harbor Pass** (877/225-8466, www.baltimore.org, $53.95) includes admission over four consecutive days into four top attractions. Different options are available for the pass, but all include visitation to the National Aquarium and the Top of the World (Observation Level), plus two additional museums such as the Port Discovery Children's Museum, the American Visionary Art Museum, the Reginald F. Lewis Museum of Maryland African American History & Culture, and the Babe Ruth Birthplace Museum.

are expertly designed and instantly engage visitors by drawing them into the world of the animals they feature. They also offer demonstrations such as the Dolphin Discovery where visitors can see dolphins feeding, training, and enjoying playtime.

4-D Immersion films ($5) are shown at the aquarium, and behind-the-scenes tours ($15-220) are available. Overnight dolphin and shark sleepovers, in which guests can spend the night at the aquarium ($115), are two of the more popular activities. Reservations for all the behind-the-scenes activities should be purchased well in advance. Tickets to the aquarium are issued on a timed-entry system (allow at least three hours for your visit), so you can purchase tickets online for the time you'd like to visit. The aquarium is a popular attraction year-round, but can be especially crowded during the hot summer days when school is out of session. Try to avoid this time if your schedule allows for it, or visit late in the day after the crowds have thinned out.

13-foot-deep tropical reef tank in the Atlantic Coral Reef exhibit. Another breathtaking experience can be found in the Upland Tropical Rain Forest. This world-renowned exhibit expertly mimics a real rain forest with live tropical birds, sloths, tamarin monkeys, and even poison dart frogs. A diverse selection of authentic rain forest plant life is also part of this habitat.

The aquarium's award-winning habitats

★ Historic Ships

The **Historic Ships** (Inner Harbor Piers, 301 E. Pratt St., 410/539-1797, www.historicships. org, one ship $11, two ships $15, four ships $18, lighthouse free) in the Inner Harbor form one

National Aquarium, Baltimore

of the most impressive military ship collections in the world. Visitors can not only see four ships and a lighthouse (all within easy walking distance of one another), but also 50,000 photographs, documents, and personal items that relate to the ships. Hours vary between ships and days, but all are open daily March-December (the *Taney* and lighthouse are closed Mon.-Thurs. Jan.-Feb.) 10am-3:30pm at a minimum, with longer hours in the summer months.

The first, the **USS *Constellation*** (Pier 1), was a sloop-of-war ship from 1854 to 1955. The USS *Constellation* was the last all-sail ship built by the U.S. Navy, and it was the flagship of the U.S. African Squadron 1859-1861. Visitors can begin their tour in the museum gallery at the pier to learn about the ship's history through artifacts and personal items that once belonged to the crew. From there, grab a complimentary audio tour wand and go aboard. The "Plan of the Day" will be posted with a list of activities taking place on the day of your visit. If you're lucky, you may get to witness the live firing of the Parrott rifle. Uniformed crew members are on board to answer questions as you explore the ship's four decks.

The second, the submarine **USS *Torsk*** (Pier 3), is the most exciting to visit. It was commissioned in 1944 and was one of just 10 Tench Class submarines to serve in World War II. Visitors can tour the entire boat including the torpedo rooms, operation station, engine room, crew quarters, and navigation station. It is difficult and unnerving to believe that more than 80 navy personnel lived aboard the sub at one time.

The third ship is the lightship ***Chesapeake*** (Pier 3), built in 1930. A lightship is a ship that is moored on a permanent or semipermanent basis and has beacons mounted to it. It is used as a navigational aid. Lightship duty meant long days sitting in place on the water and scary times riding out storms. Visitors can see a unique exhibit on sailors' canine companions.

USS *Constellation*

The fourth ship is the USCG cutter ***Taney*** (Pier 5), built in 1935. A cutter is defined as a Coast Guard ship that is over 65 feet in length and has accommodations for a crew to live aboard. Visitors can tour this authentic cutter that was decommissioned in 1986 and remains pretty much the same as it was when in use.

The **Knoll Lighthouse** (Pier 5), which stands at 40 feet, is one of the oldest Chesapeake Bay-area lighthouses and was erected at the mouth of the Patapsco River on a shallow shoal known as Seven Foot Knoll. It offers a detailed exhibit on how the lighthouse was built back in 1856.

Guided walking group tours of the USS *Constellation* ($14) are available for groups of 10 or more people over age six. Tours include museum admission, presentations, hands-on activities, and a Civil War-era sailor as your guide through the ship. Powder Monkey Tours are offered to children over six. These interactive tours teach the little ones about the young boys (ages 11-18) who served on fighting ships during the Civil War and were responsible for moving gunpowder from the powder magazine of the ship to the artillery pieces. Powder Monkey Tours are available every Saturday and Sunday at 1pm.

The Babe Ruth Birthplace Museum

The **Babe Ruth Birthplace Museum** (216 Emory St., 410/727-1539, www.baberuthmuseum.com, daily 10am-5pm, closed Mondays Sept.-Mar., $7) is located three blocks west from Oriole Park at Camden Yards. It is inside the home where Babe Ruth was born in 1895 (you can even visit the bedroom where he first entered the world). From the west side of the stadium, look down and follow the 60 painted baseballs on the sidewalk, which will lead you to the museum. Babe Ruth memorabilia is on display in the museum, and visitors can learn little-known information on this legend's private life. The museum also screens a film on the Star-Spangled Banner and has a courtyard for events.

★ Port Discovery Children's Museum

The **Port Discovery Children's Museum** (35 Market Pl., 410/727-8120, www.portdiscovery.org, Memorial Day-Labor Day Mon.-Sat. 10am-5pm, Sun. noon-5pm, shorter hours the rest of the year, $14.95) is one of the top five children's museums in the country and is geared toward children up to age 10. The museum offers three floors of interactive exhibits with the goal of connecting learning and play. Exhibits focus on art, science, and health.

Interactive exhibits draw children into a learning adventure. The Adventure Expeditions area is "part physical adventure and part mental obstacle course," in which children decipher hieroglyphics, look for clues, and are eventually led to a lost pharaoh tomb in Egypt. Another fully interactive exhibit is Kick It Up, an indoor soccer and games stadium. In the stadium, children either play soccer or get involved in interactive, electronic games

during which they can compete in a dance competition, ride a bike, and sharpen their balance. Kids and adults can enjoy the KidWorks exhibit together, which is a three-story urban treehouse with rope bridges, slides, and many other exciting surprises. Toddlers (age 2 and up) can "cook" and serve their parents food in Tiny's Diner, a realistic 1950s-style diner.

The museum is geared completely toward children, so adults can take pleasure in the joy on their little ones' faces, but shouldn't expect a lot of exhibits that will capture their own interests. Also, children are free to run through the halls and explore the many fun and entertaining exhibits, so things can get a bit chaotic on busy days. Sneakers are the recommended footwear in order to participate in all the activities. The museum is just north of the Inner Harbor. It gets crowded in the summertime, so going early or late in the day is a good option.

Maryland Science Center

The **Maryland Science Center** (601 Light St., 410/685-2370, www.mdsci.org, Sat.-Thurs. 10am-6pm, Fri. 10am-8pm, shorter hours in winter, $20.95) is a great place to bring the kids for a hands-on learning experience. The Dinosaur Mysteries exhibit is a must-see and will amaze the little ones with life-size models of prehistoric creatures. Your Body: The Inside Story takes kids on an adventure to learn what happens inside a human body in a 24-hour period. In this unique exhibit, visitors can go inside a heart and lungs and feel the heart beat and the lungs breathe. They can also hear a loud concert of digestive noises and interact with germs. Other exhibits include topics such as animal rescue, life on other planets, and a kids' room for children under eight. Other features in the center include Science Encounters, where visitors can see animated data projected on a sphere, or look at the night sky through a telescope in the on-site observatory (free on Fri. nights). There are also a planetarium and an IMAX theater on-site.

The Poe Toaster

Edgar Allan Poe was one of Baltimore's most famous and mysterious citizens. He led a life of tragedy plagued by poverty, illness, and death. Poe was born in 1809 in Boston. The grandson of a Revolutionary War patriot, David Poe Sr., Edgar Allan Poe was orphaned at the age of three. Although he went to live with the Allan family in Richmond, he was never legally adopted and never really accepted fully into the family.

Poe enlisted in the army and after his discharge came to Baltimore to live with his widowed aunt in the neighborhood now known as Little Italy. He left for a brief time to attend West Point, but returned to live with his aunt and a few other family members again, although this time in West Baltimore on Amity Street. It was while here that Poe began writing short stories (prior to that time he had focused primarily on poetry).

Poe was awarded a $50 prize by a Baltimore newspaper for his short story, "MS Found in a Bottle." Many short stories followed including "Berenice," which caused a stir for being too gruesome. In 1835 Poe returned to Richmond. The following year, he married his 13-year-old cousin, Virginia, in Richmond.

In 1847, Virginia died of tuberculosis. Poe only lived another two years before dying a mysterious death back in Baltimore and was buried with his wife and aunt in **Westminster Hall Burying Ground & Catacomb** (519 W. Fayette St., 410/706-2072, www.westminsterhall.org, daily 8am-dusk, free).

The author is still shrouded in mystery, even after death: For 60 years (1949-2009), an unidentified visitor made a yearly trip to Poe's grave in the early hours on his birthday. The visitor was called the "Poe Toaster" because he made a toast of cognac to the grave and left three roses. Although he ended his visits in 2009 for reasons unknown, the Toaster had such an influence that the tradition was resurrected in 2016 with a new Toaster as part of a staged daytime event.

The **Edgar Allan Poe House & Museum** (203 N. Amity St., 410/462-1763, www. poeinbaltimore.org, June-Dec. Sat.-Sun. 11am-4pm, $5) is the house Poe lived in for a short time in West Baltimore. The house itself, which is a 2.5-story, five-room brick duplex (now part of a line of row houses) is the primary attraction of the museum. A few of Poe's personal items including a telescope are featured in the home. The immediate surrounding area is not recommended for sightseeing for safety reasons.

Geppi's Entertainment Museum

Geppi's Entertainment Museum (301 W. Camden St., 410/625-7060, www. geppismuseum.com, Tues.-Sun. 10am-6pm, $10) is a privately owned museum featuring rare collections of American pop culture. The museum showcases a timeline of popular culture and its history in America. Some of the best comic books, cartoons, and memorabilia dating back to the colonial period can be viewed along with posters from 20th-century movies. The museum is in the same building as the Sports Legends Museum at Camden Yards.

Top of the World

For the best view of Baltimore, visit the **Top of the World** (401 E. Pratt St., 410/837-8439, www.viewbaltimore.org, June-Sept. Mon.-Thurs. 10am-6pm, Fri.-Sat. 10am-7pm, Sun. 11am-6pm, reduced hours the rest of the year, $6) on the 27th floor of **Baltimore's World Trade Center.** The Top of the World is a 360-degree observation area with a spectacular view of the city skyline, the harbor, and surrounding areas through expansive windows. Stationary binoculars and photo map guides are available. Visitors are subject to manual searches of personal belongings.

★ B&O Railroad Museum

The **B&O Railroad Museum** (901 W. Pratt St., 410/752-2490, www.borail.org, Mon.-Sat. 10am-4pm, Sun. 11am-4pm, $18) is a National Historic Landmark and the birthplace of the American railroad system. The Baltimore & Ohio Railroad (yes, the one on the Monopoly game board) originated on Pratt Street in Baltimore in 1828. The facility was a station and repair shop that took up 100 acres. Visitors can go inside the 123-foot-tall roundhouse built in the early 1870s that was the turn-around area for large steam engines (they rolled onto a large turntable to reposition). The roundhouse is now a museum for historic train cars. Museumgoers can look at the cars and also take a short ride on the original rail tracks. An exhibition space called the Annex Gallery displays railroad-related artifacts from the museum's collection and those of other institutions such as the Smithsonian. The gallery features small objects such as lanterns, dining car china, tools, fine art, and clocks. Displays on the B&O Railroad's critical role in the Civil War show how the railroad changed the tactics for war and tells personal stories of the people who kept the railroad running during the conflict.

Westminster Hall Burying Ground & Catacombs

What came first, the church or the cemetery? In the case of the **Westminster Hall Burying Ground & Catacombs** (519 W. Fayette St., 410/706-2072, www.westminsterhall.org, daily 8am-dusk, free), the answer is the cemetery by more than 65 years. The cemetery was first used in 1786. Many famous Baltimore residents are interred in the burying ground including Edgar Allan Poe (who was actually buried there twice—his coffin was relocated from his family plot to its current spot near the cemetery gate), General James McHenry, and Francis Scott Key's son, Philip Barton Key. Westminster Hall was built in 1852, at the intersection of Fayette and Greene Streets. The church was constructed above some of the graves on top of brick piers. The result was the creation of catacombs under the church, which visitors can tour. The outside burying ground, where Poe's grave is, is free to tour from 8am-dusk. There is a fee ($5) to tour Westminster Hall and the Catacombs; public tours are offered on the 1st and 3rd consecutive Friday (at 6:30pm) and Saturday (at 10am) of the month, from April to November. At least 15 people are required for a tour.

Baltimore Visitors Center

The **Baltimore Visitors Center** (401 Light St., 877/225-8466, www.baltimore.org, Apr.-Sept. daily 9am-6pm, Oct. 1-Nov. 15 daily 9am-5pm, Nov. 16-Mar. 14 Wed.-Sun. 10am-4pm) is on the waterfront on the Inner Harbor. This large, 8,000-square-foot facility offers information on sights, events, harbor cruises, and other activities to do in Baltimore. Visitors can even purchase tickets here for local attractions. There's a walk-in fountain next to the center where kids of all ages can cool off on hot days.

FELL'S POINT AND LITTLE ITALY
Fell's Point Visitor's Center

A good place to begin exploring Fell's Point and Little Italy is at the **Fell's Point Visitor's Center** (1724 Thames St., 410/675-6750, www.preservationsociety.com/about-us/visitor-center.html, daily 10am-4pm). They offer a great brochure for a walking tour of the neighborhood as well as information on the sights in the area. Seasonal guided historic walking tours also leave from the center, and there is a gift shop.

Frederick Douglass-Isaac Myers Maritime Park

The **Frederick Douglass-Isaac Myers Maritime Park** (1417 Thames St., 410/685-0295, www.douglassmyers.org, Mon.-Fri. 10am-4pm, Sat.-Sun. noon-4pm, $5) is a national heritage site/museum dedicated to African American maritime history. A series of exhibits chronicle the lives of Frederick

Fell's Point and Little Italy

© AVALON TRAVEL

CALVERT

HARBORPLACE

Inner Harbor

USS CONSTELLATION MUSEUM ★
★ HISTORIC SHIPS
★ TOP OF THE WORLD OBSERVATION LEVEL

KEY

Federal Hill

Federal Hill Park

Federal HWY

★ AMERICAN VISIONARY ART MUSEUM

Northwest Harbor

✚ NATIONAL AQUARIUM, BALTIMORE

BALTIMORE MARRIOTT WATERFRONT HOTEL

BALTIMORE
BALTIMORE ST
FAYETTE ST

GAY

MARKET PL

PORT DISCOVERY CHILDREN'S MUSEUM ✚ ★

PRESIDENT

PHOENIX (OLD BALTIMORE) SHOT TOWER ★

ALT 40

VACCARO'S ITALIAN PASTRY SHOP ★

RF LEWIS MUSEUM ★

★ STAR-SPANGLED BANNER FLAG HOUSE AND MUSEUM

JEWISH MUSEUM OF MARYLAND ★

ALBEMARLE ST

HIGH ST

★ AMICCI'S

ST

★ BALTIMORE CIVIL WAR MUSEUM AT PRESIDENT STREET STATION

Little Italy

COURTYARD MARRIOTT BALTIMORE DOWNTOWN/INNER HARBOR

EXETER

CHARLESTON RESTAURANT

CENTRAL

EDEN

LOMBARD ST

BALTIMORE ST

Fell's Point

THE INN AT THE BLACK OLIVE

CAROLINE

ONE-EYED MIKE'S

FLEET

EASTERN ST

PRATT

THE HORSE YOU CAME IN ON SALOON ▼

LANCASTER

ALICEANNA

BOND

▼ THE BLACK OLIVE

BRICK OVEN PIZZA ▼

BLUE MOON CAFE

ADMIRAL FELL INN

CELIE'S WATERFRONT INN

THAMES

▼ MAX'S TAPHOUSE

BROADWAY

PETER'S INN ●

ANN

THAMES STREET OYSTER HOUSE ▼

FELL'S POINT VISITOR'S CENTER

ROBERT LONG HOUSE

WOLFE ST

0
0.25 km

0
0.25 mi

FELL ST

WASHINGTON

▼ RED STAR BAR AND GRILL

The Johns Hopkins Hospital: Pioneering Modern Medicine

The **Johns Hopkins Hospital** (1800 Orleans St.) is known as one of the best hospitals in the world. In the heart of Baltimore, north of Fell's Point and east of Mount Vernon, this teaching hospital and biomedical research facility for the Johns Hopkins University School of Medicine forms with that institution a $5 billion system of physicians, scientists, and students.

Funding for the hospital and school originally came from a wealthy Baltimore banker and merchant, Johns Hopkins, who willed $7 million in 1873 for their founding.

Both the university and hospital set the standard for many modern American medical practices. Numerous specialties were developed here, including endocrinology and neurosurgery. From the beginning, the goal was to combine research, teaching, and patient care. This concept developed into the first model of its kind, and led to unmatched success and an international reputation for excellence.

The Johns Hopkins Hospital is currently ranked third in the nation overall out of more than 4,700 hospitals. For additional information, visit their website at www.hopkinsmedicine.org.

Douglass and Isaac Myers. Douglass was a leader in the abolitionist movement, a former slave, and a successful statesman and orator. He lived and worked on the docks in Baltimore. Myers was a mason and labor leader who created a first-of-its-kind union for African American caulkers just after the Civil War. Union members ultimately formed a cooperative, and that cooperative purchased a shipyard and railroad in Baltimore called the Chesapeake Marine Railway and Dry Dock Company. The site encompasses 5,000 square feet of gallery space and features interactive exhibits, maps, photos, and artifacts that share the history of the African American community and how it influenced Baltimore in the 1800s. Forty-five-minute guided tours are available for parties of 10 or more for $8 per person.

Robert Long House

The **Robert Long House** (812 S. Ann St., 410/675-6750, www.preservationsociety. com, Mon.-Wed. 9:30am-1:30pm, Thurs. 9:30am-2:30pm, Fri. 9:30am-12:30pm, tours daily Apr.-Nov. at 1pm and 2:30pm, $3) is the oldest city row house in Baltimore, having been built in 1765. It is a symmetrical Georgian-style brick row house with a pent roof and now serves as the headquarters for

the Preservation Society of Fell's Point and Federal Hill. The home belonged to Robert Long, who was a quartermaster for the Continental Navy. Visitors can see this restored building and its garden. The interior is furnished as it would have been during the Revolutionary War period.

Baltimore Civil War Museum at the President Street Station

The **Baltimore Civil War Museum** (601 President St., 410/220-0290, Thur.-Mon. 10am-4pm, free) is a great stop for Civil War buffs. The museum is housed in a restored freight and passenger train depot that was known as the **President Street Station.** The depot is the oldest surviving city railroad terminal in the country and was built in 1850. It was an important rail stop during the Civil War and was the location of a famous riot that took place in April 1861 when the first Union troops stopped there on the way to Washington. The altercation marked the first bloodshed of the Civil War and more than a dozen people died in the riot (both soldiers and civilians were among the dead). The museum displays artifacts and pictures that detail Baltimore's involvement in the Civil War. Tours are available by appointment.

Star-Spangled Banner Flag House and Museum

The **Star-Spangled Banner Flag House and Museum** (844 E. Pratt St., 410/837-1793, www.flaghouse.org, Tues.-Sat. 10am-4pm, $8) was the home of Mary Pickersgill, the woman who made the enormous and famous flag that flew over Fort McHenry on September 14, 1814, during the War of 1812 and inspired the poem written by Francis Scott Key that eventually became the U.S. national anthem. The house was built in 1793, and visitors can see what it looked like back when Mary lived there. The museum depicts the daily life in the home (that was also used as a business) around 1812, and living-history staff portray members of the Pickersgill family.

Jewish Museum of Maryland

The **Jewish Museum of Maryland** (15 Lloyd St., 410/732-6400, www.jewishmuseummd.org, Sun.-Thurs. 10am-5pm, $10) offers visitors the opportunity to learn about regional Jewish history, culture, and the community. One of the country's leading museums on regional Jewish history, its displays include photographs, papers, and artifacts that are rotated regularly. The museum does a wonderful job of relating Jewish life in early Baltimore and other small towns in Maryland. The museum oversees a modern museum facility and two historic synagogues: the B'nai Israel Synagogue, built in 1876, and the Lloyd Street Synagogue, built in 1845.

Reginald F. Lewis Museum of Maryland African American History & Culture

The **Reginald F. Lewis Museum of Maryland African American History & Culture** (830 E. Pratt St., 443/263-1800, www.africanamericanculture.org, Wed.-Sat. 10am-5pm, Sun. noon-5pm, $8) is the largest museum on the East Coast dedicated to African American culture. Visitors can learn about the contributions of African Americans in Maryland throughout the

the Star-Spangled Banner Flag House and Museum

state's history. The museum includes galleries, a genealogy center, recording studio, theater, café, and gift shop.

Phoenix Shot Tower

The **Phoenix Shot Tower** (801 E. Fayette St., 410/837-5424, $5), which is also known as the **Old Baltimore Shot Tower,** stands nearly 235 feet tall near the entrance to Little Italy. It was built in 1828 out of one million bricks and, at the time, was the tallest structure in the country. The tower was used from 1828 to 1892 to produce lead shot, done by dropping molten lead from a platform at the top of the tower. The lead ran through a sieve and landed in cold water. It is a National Historic Landmark. Tours of the Shot Tower are offered Sat.-Sun. at 4pm.

CANTON
Patterson Park

Patterson Park (27 S. Patterson Park Ave., 410/276-3676, free) is one of the oldest parks in Baltimore. It encompasses 155 acres and has

Phoenix Shot Tower

the pagoda in Patterson Park

a great view of the harbor. On **Hampstead Hill** inside the park, a pagoda designed in 1890 stands at the site where local residents rallied in 1814 to protect their city from the British. British troops had come up the Patapsco River and attacked Fort McHenry, and on land, they had forces just east of the city at North Point. As they entered Baltimore, the British saw 20,000 troops and a hundred cannons facing them on Hampstead Hill. This caused them to retreat from Baltimore and go back to their ships. The area became a park in 1853, but saw more military activity during the Civil War when a military camp and war hospital were built there.

Today the park offers recreation trails, a lake, pavilions, playgrounds, an ice-skating rink, a public swimming pool, a recreation center, a stadium, and an adult day-care center.

Captain John O'Donnell Monument

The **Captain John O'Donnell Monument** (O'Donnell St. and S. Curley St.) is in the center of Canton Square. John O'Donnell was an Irish sea captain who purchased 1,981 acres in the 1780s in the area that is now Canton. He allegedly named the area after the cargo from his ship, which contained goods from Canton, China. Captain O'Donnell's land included a house near the current-day Boston Street and all the waterfront land east of the northwest branch of the Patapsco River between Colgate Creek and Fell's Point.

SS *John W. Brown*

The **SS *John W. Brown*** (Pier 1, 2000 S. Clinton St., 410/558-0646, www.ssjohnwbrown.org, Wed. and Sat. 9am-2pm, free, donations appreciated) is one of two remaining Liberty ships out of the 2,700 that were produced by the Emergency Shipbuilding Program during World War II. They were designed for swift construction, and the SS *John W. Brown* was built in just 56 days. The ships were used for sealifts of troops, arms, and gear to all war locations.

The SS *John W. Brown* made 13 voyages and was awarded several honors during the war. Oddly, after the war, the ship served as a vocational high school in New York City from 1946 to 1982. It was acquired in 1988 by the current owner, Project Liberty Ship, and fully restored as a museum and memorial. As the only Liberty ship in operation on the East Coast, the boat hosts six-hour Living History Cruises several times a year. During these cruises, it visits other ports on the East Coast. The ship is part of the National Register of Historic Places and also a recipient of the World Ship Trust's Maritime Heritage Award.

FEDERAL HILL
American Visionary Art Museum

The **American Visionary Art Museum** (800 Key Hwy., 410/244-1900, www.avam.org, Tues.-Sun. 10am-6pm, $16) holds a collection of visionary art—slightly different from folk art in nature, but which to the untrained eye can look similar. The museum defines it as "art produced by self-taught individuals, usually without formal training, whose works arise from an innate personal vision that revels foremost in the creative act itself." In a nutshell, it seems like anything goes in this funky, interesting, and inspiring museum. It has art in all mediums—oil, mosaic, watercolor, toothpicks, and even bras.

★ Baltimore Museum of Industry

The **Baltimore Museum of Industry** (1415 Key Hwy., 410/727-4808, www.thebmi.org, Tues.-Sun. 10am-4pm, $12) is housed in the original 1865 Platt Oyster Cannery building, the only remaining cannery structure in the city, and has exhibits on the history of industry and manufacturing in the Baltimore area. Baltimore has traditionally been a key industrial center and was home to the first passenger train, the world's biggest copper refinery, the first traffic light, and the first gas company. Collections include 100,000 artifacts relating to small business, factory workers, and other citizens whose hard work helped shape the country. Featured fields include the garment industry, automobile industry, pharmaceutical industry, newspaper industry, food industry, and the Maryland Lottery. Many of the exhibits are interactive for both adults and children.

The museum is easy to find—just look for the large red crane out front. Be sure to watch the short introductory video near

a cannon in Federal Hill Park

Federal Hill

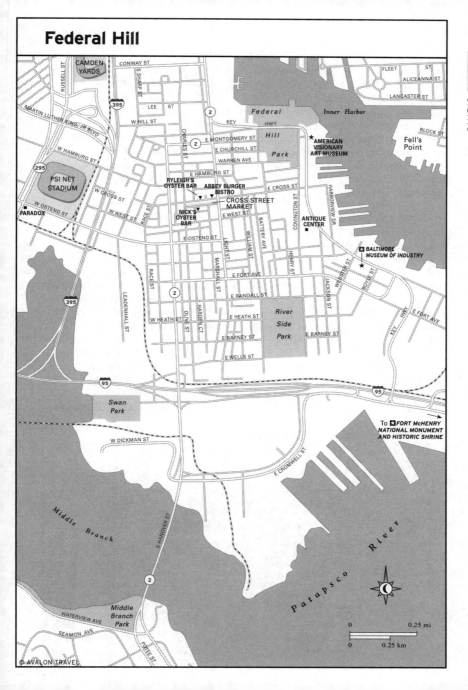

CAMDEN YARDS

RUSSELL ST

CONWAY ST

S SHARP ST

FLEET ST

ALICEANNA ST

LANCASTER ST

LEE ST

MARTIN LUTHER KING JR BLVD

395

W HILL ST

KEY HWY

Federal

Inner Harbor

BLOCK ST

Fell's
Point

295

PSI NET
STADIUM

CHARLES ST

E MONTGOMERY ST

E CHURCHILL ST

WARREN AVE

Hill

Park

AMERICAN
VISIONARY
ART MUSEUM

W HAMBURG ST

E HAMBURG ST

W CROSS ST

RYLEIGH'S
OYSTER BAR

ABBEY BURGER
BISTRO

E CROSS ST

HARBORVIEW DR

W OSTEND ST

PARADOX

W WEST ST

NICK'S
OYSTER
BAR

CROSS STREET
MARKET

E WEST ST

BATTERY AVE

HENRY ST

COVINGTON ST

ANTIQUE
CENTER

E OSTEND ST

LIGHT ST

WILLIAM ST

BALTIMORE
MUSEUM OF INDUSTRY

RACE ST

MARSHALL ST

E FORT AVE

JACKSON ST

WEBSTER ST

BOYLE ST

395

2

E RANDALL ST

LEADENHALL ST

OLIVE ST

HARDEN CT

W HEATH ST

E HEATH ST

River
Side
Park

E BARNEY ST

E BARNEY ST

KEY HWY

E FORT AVE

E WELLS ST

95

95

Swan
Park

To ✚ FORT McHENRY
NATIONAL MONUMENT
AND HISTORIC SHRINE

W DICKMAN ST

E CROMWELL ST

Middle Branch

S HANOVER ST

2

Patapsco River

Middle
Branch
Park

WATERVIEW AVE

SEAMON AVE

POFEE ST

0   0.25 mi

0   0.25 km

© AVALON TRAVEL

the museum entrance; it provides good insight into the background of the museum. Demonstrations are offered on Saturday and include topics such as printing (you can see how a real Linotype machine operates) and the job of a blacksmith. Exhibits aren't limited to the indoors; visitors can also see the coal-fired SS *Baltimore,* a restored and operational steam tugboat from 1906, just outside the museum. Free 45-minute tours of the museum are available. This is an interesting place for both adults and children over age 10. Plan on spending approximately two hours.

Federal Hill Park

Federal Hill Park (300 Warren Ave., 410/396-5828) is a lovely spot right off the harbor that offers great views of the Inner Harbor and downtown from atop Federal Hill. The park is on the south side of the harbor, and the terrain rises steeply. During the colonial era, the grassy hill was a mine for paint pigment, and the drooping hillside and footpaths indicate where old tunnels remain underground. The area has been a park since the late 1700s and remains a nice recreation and picnic area. There is also a playground on-site. On the northern side of the park are cannons from the Civil War that are symbols of those positioned by Union troops to face the city as a warning to Confederate sympathizers.

★ Fort McHenry National Monument and Historic Shrine

The **Fort McHenry National Monument and Historic Shrine** (2400 E. Fort Ave., 410/962-4290, www.nps.gov/fomc, daily 9am-5pm, extended summer hours, free admission to park, $10 fee for Star Fort/historical area) is a 43-acre national park with a historical area that houses Fort McHenry. It is east of Federal Hill and sticks out into the harbor. The fort was built between 1799 and 1802 and named after James McHenry, who was the secretary of war between 1796 and 1800, and constructed in the shape of a star with five points (aka the Star Fort). The star-shaped design was popular at the time since each point was within view of others to the left and right and the entire fort and surrounding area could be guarded with only five sentries.

Fort McHenry is known as the inspiration for the "Star-Spangled Banner." Francis Scott Key wrote the words to the anthem during the War of 1812 when he was held on a truce ship during the British attack on Baltimore. As the battle went on, Key watched from the water

Fort McHenry National Monument and Historic Shrine

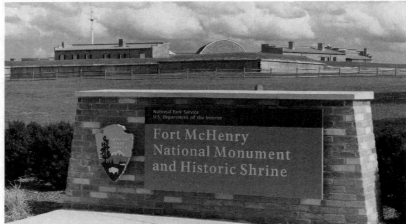

and through a smoke-filled landscape, and at "dawn's early light" on September 14, 1814, he could see the huge 30-by-42-foot American flag still flying above Fort McHenry as a symbol that Baltimore had not surrendered.

Begin your exploration at the visitors center and view the 10-minute video on the fort's history (shown on the hour and half hour). Exhibits on the fort, a gift shop, and restrooms are at the center. Then take a self-guided tour (approximately one hour) of the fort. Inside the fort is a large grassy area, and the rooms of the fort feature displays and authentic artifacts. Continue into the barracks (which include exhibits such as the Enlisted Men's Quarters, weapons, uniforms, Junior Officer's Quarters, the Powder Magazine, Commanding Officer's Quarters, and the 1814 Guard House). Children can participate in the Flag Change Program daily at 9:30am and 4:20pm, when they can assist rangers in raising and lowering a reproduced Star-Spangled Banner flag. Living-history interpreters are available on the weekends in the summer and tell stories about the fort and the people who lived in Baltimore while the facility was active. Allow two hours for your visit. There is no charge to visit the grounds.

MOUNT VERNON
★ The Walters Art Museum

The Walters Art Museum (600 N. Charles St., 410/547-9000, www.thewalters.org, Wed.-Sun. 10am-5pm, Thurs. until 9pm, free) showcases the personal art collection of two men: William Thompson Walters, an American industrialist and art collector, and his son, Henry Walters. Both collected paintings, antiques, and sculptures. Upon Henry Walters's death, their joint collection of more than 22,000 works of art was left to the city of Baltimore for the benefit of the public.

The Walters Art Museum houses a fascinating collection that spans 5,000 years and five continents. It includes pieces from ancient Egypt, Roman sarcophagi, Renaissance bronzes, Chinese bronzes, and art nouveau jewelry. Some must-see items are an ancient Egyptian mummy from 1000 BC, two Fabergé eggs, and one of the best collections of armor in the country (including a child's set of armor).

Be sure to visit the Chamber of Wonders, where the museum has brought to life an intricate scene from a 1620 painting that came from the area that is now Belgium. The scene replicates the painting in detail and

The Walters Art Museum

Mount Vernon

Washington Monument and Museum at Mount Vernon Place

The **Washington Monument and Museum at Mount Vernon Place** (699 N. Charles St., 410/962-5070, www.mvconservancy.org, Wed.-Fri. 2pm-5pm, Sat.-Sun. 10am-1pm and 2pm-5pm, free) is the site of the first monument planned to honor George Washington. Completed in 1829, the white marble monument stands 178 feet tall and has a rectangular base, a relatively plain column, and a statue of Washington on the top. The monument looks even more imposing than its 178 feet because it sits on a hill. It was a landmark for boats making their way up the river from the Chesapeake Bay. Today, visitors can climb 228 narrow stone stairs to the top and enjoy a great view of Baltimore ($6.35). There is a little museum at the base of the monument.

Baltimore Streetcar Museum

The **Baltimore Streetcar Museum** (1901 Falls Rd., 410/547-0264, www.baltimorestreetcar.org, Sun. Mar.-Dec. noon-5pm, Sat. June-Oct. noon-5pm, $10) details the history of streetcars in the city and their evolution

is a re-creation of a chamber of natural history wonders that taps into human ingenuity from all over the globe. A highlight of the room is a 12-foot stuffed alligator. Although general admission to the museum is free, purchased tickets are required for special exhibits.

the Baltimore Streetcar Museum

from horse-drawn transportation to an electricity-driven system. The fun part of this interesting little museum is that a number of original historic streetcars have been salvaged and visitors can actually ride in them (accompanied by volunteer conductors) down the old tracks. Unlimited rides are included with the admission fee. For a taste of what you'll find in the museum, visit the website and click on "Streetcar Memories."

Basilica of the Assumption

The **Basilica of the Assumption** (409 Cathedral St., 410/727-3565, www.baltimore-basilica.org, Mon.-Fri. 7am-4pm, Sat.-Sun. 7am to the conclusion of mass at 5:30pm and 4:30pm respectively, $2 donation for tours) was the first Catholic cathedral built in the United States after the Constitution was ratified, and the building quickly became a symbol of the new country's religious freedom. It was constructed between 1806 and 1821 and the design and architecture were overseen by John Carroll, the first bishop in the country (and later archbishop of Baltimore), and Benjamin Henry Latrobe, who designed the U.S. Capitol. The basilica sits on a hill above the harbor and features a grand dome and what was considered cutting-edge neoclassical architecture to match that of the new federal city of Washington DC. Great effort went into creating an architectural symbol of America rather than using a European gothic design. At the time the cathedral was built, its only architectural rival in terms of scale and size was the U.S. Capitol, and the basilica was considered the most architecturally advanced structure in the country.

The full name of the cathedral is the Basilica of the National Shrine of the Assumption of the Blessed Virgin Mary, in Baltimore. It is ranked as a minor basilica, but is also a national shrine. The basilica is a cultural institution in Baltimore and offers services, tours, concerts, and lectures. It also has a prayer garden nearby on the corner of Franklin and North Charles Streets. The basilica recently underwent an extensive

two-year restoration. Forty-five minute tours are offered Monday-Saturday at 9am, 11am, and 1pm, although Saturday tours are sometimes not possible due to weddings and special services. Tours are not required for visitation, but sightseeing is not permitted during mass.

Brown Memorial Presbyterian Church

The **Brown Memorial Presbyterian Church** (1316 Park Ave., 410/523-1542, www.browndowntown.org, daily 9am-6pm, free) is a historic gothic revival-style Presbyterian church that was built in 1870. A unique feature is its 11 Tiffany stained glass windows representing scenes from the Bible, several of which are nearly three stories tall. The windows were added in the early 1900s, which made the church a local art treasure.

The National Great Blacks in Wax Museum

The **National Great Blacks in Wax Museum** (1601 E. North Ave., 410/563-3404, www.greatblacksinwax.org, hours vary throughout season, $13) is the first wax museum in Baltimore and the first African American-oriented wax museum in the country. It was established in 1983 and displays more than 100 figures. The museum does a nice job of telling the history behind each figure through audio and text displays. Several famous Baltimore residents are depicted in the museum, including Frederick Douglass and singer Billie Holiday.

The Maryland Historical Society

The **Maryland Historical Society** (201 W. Monument St., 410/685-3750, www.mdhs.org, Wed.-Sat. 10am-5pm, Sun. noon-5pm, museum only with no library hours on Sun., $9) is a great starting point for discovering Baltimore. You can view more than one million objects on display in two museum buildings including photographs, paintings, manuscripts, and lithographs. It also includes a huge library with more than 7 million items, including the most treasured: the historical manuscript to the "Star-Spangled Banner." Exhibits cover a diversity of topics including the War of 1812, African American history, women's history, maritime history, the history of Fell's Point, immigration, furniture, and mining. The Historical Society is easy to spot—the 1,700-pound, 14-foot statue of Nipper the RCA Dog sits on its rooftop facing Park Street.

HAMPDEN AND HOMEWOOD
Druid Hill Park

Druid Hill Park (2600 Madison Ave., 443/281-3538, www.druidhillpark.org, daily dawn to dusk, free) is a 745-acre park developed in 1860. It is approximately two miles from Hampden. It is one of the country's oldest landscaped public parks, along with Central Park in New York City and Fairmount

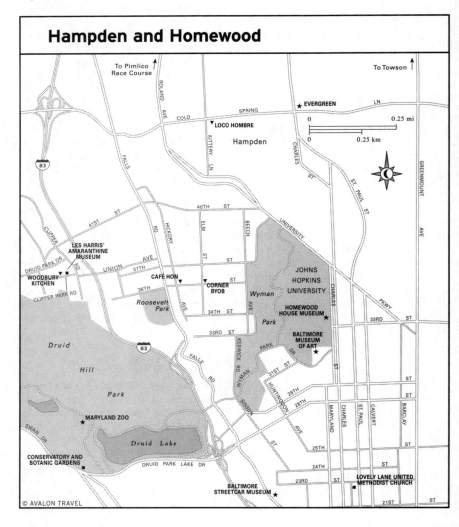

Hampden and Homewood

To Pimlico Race Course

To Towson

★ EVERGREEN

▼ LOCO HOMBRE

Hampden

LES HARRIS' AMARANTHINE MUSEUM

WOODBURY KITCHEN ▼

CAFÉ HON ▼

▼ CORNER BYOB

JOHNS HOPKINS UNIVERSITY

Wyman

HOMEWOOD HOUSE MUSEUM ★

Roosevelt Park

Druid

Hill

Park

Park

BALTIMORE MUSEUM OF ART ★

MARYLAND ZOO ★

Druid Lake

CONSERVATORY AND BOTANIC GARDENS ■

DRUID PARK LAKE DR

BALTIMORE STREETCAR MUSEUM ★

LOVELY LANE UNITED METHODIST CHURCH ■

© AVALON TRAVEL

Park in Philadelphia. Druid Park has something else in common with Central Park: It was formed at the northern edges of the city at the time it was established. To this day, the northern end of the park features forest that is some of the oldest in Maryland. The southern end of the park, however, has always been a popular area for those living in the city. Druid Hill Lake was built in 1863 and is one of the biggest earthen dammed lakes in the nation. Many fountains and artificial ponds that were original features in the park have been drained and reclaimed by nature, although their remains can still be found. The park also features tennis courts, a pool, disc golf, and workout equipment. There is also a zoo in the middle of the park, accessible only through the official zoo entrance. Safety can be a concern in the park at any time, but mostly after dark. Be aware of your surroundings, and if you feel uncomfortable, cut your visit short.

THE MARYLAND ZOO IN BALTIMORE

The Maryland Zoo in Baltimore (Druid Park Lake Dr., 410/396-7102, www. marylandzoo.org, Mar.-Dec. daily 10am-4pm, shorter hours Jan.-Feb., $18) is inside the large Druid Hill Park to the west of Hampden. The zoo opened in 1876 and is one of the oldest zoos in the country. It houses more than 1,500 animals. One of the premier exhibits in the zoo is the Polar Bear Watch, where visitors can take a large viewing buggy (like they use on the tundra) to watch three polar bears in their habitat. The zoo also offers other hands-on experiences such as camel rides and a Children's Zoo, where the little ones can pet certain animals. A family camping experience is also available in the spring.

HOWARD PETERS RAWLINGS CONSERVATORY AND BOTANIC GARDENS

The **Howard Peters Rawlings Conservatory and Botanic Gardens** (3100 Swan Dr., Druid Hill Park, 410/396-0008, www.rawlingsconservatory.org, Wed.-Sun. 10am-4pm, free) within Druid Hill Park is the only remaining public conservatory in Baltimore. The complex dates back

Howard Peters Rawlings Conservatory and Botanic Gardens

The Dog Who Found His Way Home

You'll find Nipper on the roof of the Maryland Historical Society.

The 14-foot, 1,700-pound RCA Dog, known as Nipper, that sits atop the Maryland Historical Society roof has a long history of adventure. The original Nipper was a stray terrier adopted in the 1880s by a man named Mark Barraud. He named the little black-and-white dog Nipper because he nipped at people's legs. When Barraud passed away, his brother, Francis, who was a painter, adopted the dog.

At the time, the phonograph was the latest technology. Nipper was captivated by the sound of the machine and would sit with his head tilted near its trumpet, listening. Francis thought this would make a great advertisement, and he painted a picture of Nipper and sold it to the Gramophone Company (which made phonographs). A United States patent was issued for the trademark of the image, and after two sales of the company, RCA ended up with the image in 1929.

In 1954, The Triangle Sign Company of Baltimore made the statue of Nipper, and it was placed on top of the D&H Distributing building. D&H Distributing was an RCA distributor. But when the company moved in 1976, they left the statue behind.

A collector from Fairfax, Virginia, wanted the statue and after he spent six years trying to convince D&H Distributing to let him buy it, they finally sold it to him for $1. Baltimore residents and officials were outraged. They felt Nipper was a Baltimore landmark, but a sale is a sale, and Nipper left Baltimore and was moved to Virginia where he sat on the collector's front lawn for 20 years.

In 1996, the collector decided to move, and he sold Nipper to the Baltimore's City Life Museum for $25,000. Two years later, the museum closed, and the Maryland Historical Society took over its collections and, in turn, inherited Nipper and placed him on the roof. Today visitors can still enjoy the 1,700-pound pooch, who found his way home to Baltimore and seems to be here to stay.

to 1888 and consists of two buildings from the Victorian era. There are also three newer buildings. Five different climates are represented in the buildings and there are also beautiful outdoor gardens. The Palm House is one of the most interesting buildings. The Palm House was built in 1888 and was designed by George Frederick (who also designed Baltimore's City Hall). Towering palms reach the upper windows of the impressive five-story house and block some of the natural sunlight in the conservatory.

Les Harris' Amaranthine Museum

It would be a challenge to find another museum comparable to **Les Harris' Amaranthine Museum** (2010 Clipper Park Rd., 410/456-1343, www.amaranthinemuseum.org, Sun. noon-3pm and by appointment, closed July-Aug., $5). This unusual museum, which is open during very limited hours, takes visitors through a maze of the late Baltimore artist Les Harris's work while telling the history of art in chronological order, starting with prehistoric times and going out into the future. The museum is a labyrinth of art history and the creative process, made up of rooms, chambers, and passages, decorated from floor to ceiling with Harris's art. The Amaranthine Museum (the word *amaranthine* means eternally beautiful) itself is a unique art form and a fun deviation from traditional museums.

Baltimore Museum of Art

The **Baltimore Museum of Art** (10 Museum Dr., 443/573-1700, www.artbma.org, Wed.-Fri. 10am-5pm, Sat.-Sun. 11am-6pm, free) is a cultural destination in Baltimore and one of two great art museums in the city (the other is the Walters Art Museum in Mount Vernon). The museum is adjacent to the Homewood campus of Johns Hopkins University.

The museum was founded in 1914 and grew from housing one single painting to offering 90,000 pieces on display. Its collection of 19th-century, modern, and contemporary art is internationally known and includes the famous Cone Collection of over 3,000 pieces by world-famous artists donated by wealthy socialite sisters Claribel and Etta Cone. The Cone Collection is worth approximately $1 billion. The Cone Collection includes the largest single collection of works by Henri Matisse in the world (500 total); 42 oil paintings, 18 sculptures, and 36 drawings are among the Matisse pieces. It also amasses work by Cézanne, Picasso, Degas, Manet, Van Gogh, and Gauguin.

In addition to the Cone Collection (housed in the Cone Wing), the museum features many other galleries. The West Wing for Contemporary Art contains 16 galleries with 20th- and 21st-century art including abstract expressionism, minimalism, conceptual art, and works by Andy Warhol. American galleries feature paintings, sculptures, decorative arts, and works on paper. There is also an African art collection of more than 2,000 pieces with works spanning from ancient Egypt to contemporary Zimbabwe.

The museum also offers visitors two lovely outdoor gardens with 20th-century sculptures.

Johns Hopkins University

Johns Hopkins University (410/516-8000, www.jhu.edu) is a private not-for-profit research university that was founded in 1876 and named for philanthropist Johns Hopkins, its benefactor. The university maintains two main campuses in Baltimore: the Homewood Campus (3400 N. Charles St.) and the Medical Institution Campus (600 N. Wolfe St.). There are secondary campuses in Washington DC, Italy, Singapore, and China. Johns Hopkins developed the concept of a modern research university in the United States and is known throughout the world as one of the best. At least 37 Nobel Prize winners are affiliated with Johns Hopkins.

The Homewood Campus has a parklike setting even though it is located in a large city, with lovely old trees, large grassy areas, stately brick academic buildings, and red-brick residence halls. The Medical Institution Campus is located north of Fell's Point in east Baltimore.

HOMEWOOD HOUSE

The **Homewood House** (3400 N. Charles St., 410/516-5589, www.museums.jhu.edu, Tues.-Fri. 11am-4pm, Sat.-Sun. noon-4pm, $8) on the eastern side of Johns Hopkins University is a wonderful example of federal architecture. Completed in 1808, the house is decorated with well-researched colors, patterns, and furniture from the period, much of it original. The country home was owned by wealthy Baltimore residents during the colonial era and then by the son of Charles Carroll, a signer of the Declaration of Independence.

EVERGREEN MUSEUM & LIBRARY

The **Evergreen Museum & Library** (4545 N. Charles St., 410/516-0341, www.museums.jhu.edu, Tues.-Fri. 11am-4pm, Sat.-Sun. noon-4pm, $8) is a beautiful mansion that was built in the mid-19th century and purchased by the president of the B&O Railroad, John W. Garrett, in 1878. This wonderful exemplar of the Gilded Age sits surrounded by Italian-style gardens on 26 acres. The museum and library hold a collection of rare books, manuscripts, and artwork. The estate's 48 rooms, housing more than 50,000 items from the Garrett family (including a 24K gold-leafed toilet), can be viewed by the public only on guided tours. Tours begin every hour on the hour with the last tour starting at 3pm. Concerts and lectures are also given on the property. The museum is 4.5 miles north of the Inner Harbor.

WALKING TOURS

Historic walking tours around Baltimore are given by the **Preservation Society of Fell's Point and Federal Hill** (410/675-6750, www.preservationsociety.com).

Entertainment and Events

NIGHTLIFE

Whether you're looking for delicious cocktails, a large wine selection, or a wild night of dancing, Baltimore has it all.

One block from the Inner Harbor is a great collection of bars and clubs in an entertainment complex called **Power Plant Live!** (34 Market Place, www.powerplantlive.com). The complex opened in sections between 2001 and 2003 and was named for a neighboring former power plant on Pier 4 that faces the Inner Harbor. Restaurants, bars, and nightclubs line an outdoor plaza where free music is offered May-October on the plaza stage. A popular venue in the complex is **Rams Head Live** (20 Market Pl., 410/244-1131, www.ramsheadlive.com). This general admission, standing-room-only venue features five full-service bars and two food kiosks. A wide variety of groups have played here including Patti Smith, Big Head Todd and the Monsters, They Might Be Giants, and Citizen Cope.

Two blocks north of the Inner Harbor near Power Plant Live! is a slightly upscale nightclub that caters to an older crowd. The **Havana Club** (600 Water St., 410/468-0022, www.havanaclub-baltimore.com, Wed.-Sat. 6pm-2am) is above Ruth's Chris Steak House and features a more intimate atmosphere with leather seating areas, private seating options, an extensive wine list, and a notable cigar selection. They also offer salsa dancing on Friday nights. The dress code is business casual.

Hidden in an industrial warehouse area southwest of the Inner Harbor is a thriving dance club called **Paradox** (1310 Russell St., 410/837-9110, www.thedox.com). People come from all over the region to be part of the serious parties that take place on the wooden dance floor. They feature all types of dance music and do not serve alcohol.

Those looking for a terrific place to catch live jazz won't be disappointed by **An Die Musik Live** (409 N. Charles St., 2nd Fl., 410/385-2638, www.andiemusiklive.com), downtown on the second floor of a town house. This intimate concert venue is for true music lovers. The cool renovated building offers great acoustics, comfortable seating, and a high caliber of artists. There is no elevator, so be prepared to climb some stairs.

Not far away is a popular old-school drinking establishment called **Club Charles** (1724

N. Charles St., 410/727-8815, www.club-charles.us, Mon.-Sun. 6pm-2am). This art deco bar is dark and crowded, but the bartenders are fantastic and the drinks are strong. There's even a resident ghost that plays pranks at the bar.

A classy place to linger over a drink and soak in a gorgeous view of the city is the **13th Floor** (1 E. Chase St., 410/347-0880, www.13floorbelvedere.com, Tues.-Wed. 5pm-10pm, Thurs. 5pm-11pm, Fri.-Sat. 5pm-1am). This Mount Vernon establishment is housed in the historic Belvedere Hotel building, which was known during the early part of the 20th century as the premier hotel in the city; it hosted U.S. presidents, foreign dignitaries, and movie stars. Today, the newly renovated restaurant and bar feature dark hardwood floors, white tabletops, live jazz, and a 360-degree view of the city. This is another place with a dress code, so be prepared so you're not disappointed.

One of the first modern lounges in the city, Mount Vernon's **Red Maple** (930 N. Charles St., 410/547-0149, www.930redmaple.com, Tues.-Fri. 5pm-2am, Sat. 6pm-2am) is still a popular hot spot. It features Asian-inspired tapas and other small plates, and guests can relax in lounge-style seating on the first floor or table seating on the second floor. The indoor dance floor and outdoor patio are popular nightspots.

A local landmark in Fell's Point is the **Cat's Eye Pub** (1730 Thames St., 410/276-9866, www.catseyepub.com, daily noon-2am). It is known for nightly live music despite the close and often crowded space. Music at this cozy pub includes blues, jazz, and folk.

A charming little wine bar on the waterfront in Fell's Point is **V-NO** (905 S. Ann St., 410/342-8466, www.v-no.com, Mon.-Wed. 4:30pm-9pm, Thurs. noon-10pm, Fri.-Sat. noon-midnight, Sun. noon-6pm). They offer indoor and outdoor seating and a lovely wine list with enough of a selection to keep things interesting. This is a great place to unwind away from the crowds.

The Horse You Came In On Saloon

(1626 Thames St., 410/327-8111, www.the-horsebaltimore.com, open daily at 11:30am, $8-15) is America's oldest continuously operated saloon (it operated before, during, and after Prohibition). It first opened in 1775 and is allegedly the last place Edgar Allan Poe was seen alive. It may be where Poe had his last drink, and it's been rumored that his ghost haunts the saloon. The saloon originally had hitching posts out back to park horses. Menu items include traditional bar food, and there's nightly live entertainment (rock and roll). The saloon's slogan is "Where no one's ugly at 2am." It also has Maryland's only Jack Daniel's club (Old No. 7), where members purchase their own bottles of Jack Daniel's and the saloon stores them in a coveted space in their custom Jack Daniel's case. The saloon sells more Jack Daniel's than any other bar in Maryland.

The Horse You Came In On Saloon

PERFORMING ARTS
Hippodrome Theatre at France-Merrick Performing Arts Center

The **Hippodrome Theatre at France-Merrick Performing Arts Center** (12 N. Eutaw St., 410/837-7400, www.france-merrickpac.com) is a well-known circa 1914 stage performance theater on the west side of Baltimore. In the 1940s, this part of town had a flourishing arts scene and saw big-time acts such as Frank Sinatra, Bob Hope, and Benny Goodman, but the neighborhood declined in the following decades. This performing arts center is part of the rebirth of the area, and the Hippodrome Theatre was beautifully restored as part of that project. The center now offers musicals, holiday performances, and many other types of performances.

Centerstage

Centerstage (700 N. Calvert St., 410/332-0033, www.centerstage.org) in Mount Vernon is a historic venue with two intimate performance spaces, two rehearsal halls, and three lobbies. The six-story building is a local landmark that has roots as the former Loyola College and High School. It offers a close-up theater experience for classical and contemporary performances and lends itself well to audience interaction. There are no bad seats in the house.

Royal Farms Arena

The **Royal Farms Arena** (201 W. Baltimore St., www.royalfarmsarena.com) is showing its age a bit (it was built in the 1960s), but still hosts musical artists such as Carrie Underwood, well-known shows such as Cirque Du Soleil and Disney on Ice, and sporting events.

Patricia & Arthur Modell Performing Arts Center at the Lyric

The **Patricia & Arthur Modell Performing Arts Center at the Lyric** (140 W. Mount Royal Ave., 410/900-1150, www.

lyricoperahouse.com) is a music hall that originally opened in 1894. Today it plays host to a wide variety of talent from kids' shows to top musical artists.

Arena Players

The longest continuously running African American community theater in the country is the **Arena Players** (801 McCulloh St., 410/728-6500, www.arenaplayersinc.com). Founded in 1953, this respected theater supports local actors and writers.

Joseph Meyerhoff Symphony Hall

The **Joseph Meyerhoff Symphony Hall** (1212 Cathedral St., 410/783-8000, www.bsomusic.org) is a 2,443-seat music venue in the Mount Vernon neighborhood. The venue is named for a former president of the Baltimore Symphony, Joseph Meyerhoff, who made a sizable donation for the construction of the hall. The venue is currently home to the **Baltimore Symphony Orchestra.**

EVENTS

The **Baltimore Fun Guide** (www.baltimorefunguide.com) is a great online resource that lists local events throughout the city.

Hundreds of boats (both power and sail) can be found at the **Baltimore Convention Center** (1 W. Pratt St., 410/649-7000, www.bccenter.org) for four days in mid to late January during the **Baltimore Boat Show** (www.baltimoreboatshow.com, $14). The show features exhibits and activities for all ages.

April brings the **Preakness Crab Derby** (400 W. Lexington St, 410/685-6169) to the Lexington Market where fans can watch Baltimore celebrities race crabs for charity. The winner is awarded $500 for donation to their favorite charity.

For something completely different, attend the American Visionary Art Museum's annual **Kinetic Sculpture Race** (www.avam.org/kinetic-sculpture-race/), which takes place on a Saturday in early May. This race showcases completely human-powered works of art that can travel on the land, water, and through mud. These "machines" are often made of old bicycle parts, gears, etc. and can be "driven" by one person or a team. Fun awards are given out such as the "Grand Mediocre East Coast Champion Award (to the vehicle finishing in the middle of the pack)," the "Next to Last Award," and the "Best Bribe" award.

A more serious race that also takes place in May is the **Preakness Stakes** (www.preakness.com). With more than a 140-year history, this second leg of the Triple Crown of Thoroughbred Racing (which consists of the Kentucky Derby, the Preakness Stakes, and the Belmont Stakes) is a big deal in Baltimore and in horse racing overall.

Honfest (www.honfest.net) in Hampden is a major city festival that started out as a neighborhood celebration and blossomed to an international following. The festival takes place in mid-June along 36th Street. The "Hon" is short for "honey" ("hon" is a commonly used term of endearment in Baltimore) and refers to a ladies fashion that evolved in the 1960s. The style included large, brightly colored horn-rim glasses, loud prints, spandex and leopard-print pants, thick makeup, and beehive hairdos. The festival features many Hons in full attire and one is crowned "Miss Hon." There is also the running of the Hons. Hair and makeup can be done by vendors right in the street.

Baltimore's **Fourth of July** celebration (www.baltimore.org) is an annual favorite in the Inner Harbor. It features live music and a fireworks display. The fireworks celebration can be viewed from many vantage points around the city including, Federal Hill, Fell's Point, and Canton.

America's largest free arts festival, **Artscape** (Mount Royal Avenue, www.artscape.org) is held for three days each July and attracts more than 350,000 people. The festival is a rare opportunity for visitors and people from all neighborhoods in Baltimore to interact. More than 150 artists display their craft at this well-known event that began in the early 1980s.

Miracle on 34th Street (www.christmasstreet.com) is the premier holiday extravaganza in Hampden. Throughout December, one block of 34th Street becomes a magical, although somewhat over-the-top display of lights, reindeer, and really any type of decoration you can think of. It's quite the spectacle, but also quite festive, and definitely worth checking out if you don't mind sitting in traffic with the other spectators.

The **Night of 100 Elvises** (www.nightof100elvises.com) is actually a two-day event held in the beginning of December that benefits the Johns Hopkins Children's Center and the Guardian Angels. This ticketed party held at Lithuanian Hall (851-3 Hollins St.) features a dozen bands and multiple Elvis tribute performances.

Shopping

DOWNTOWN AND THE INNER HARBOR
Harborplace

Harborplace (201 E. Pratt St., 410/332-4191, www.harborplace.com, Mon.-Sat. 10am-9pm, Sun. 11am-7pm) is the premier shopping market in downtown Baltimore. It was created in 1980 as a main attraction during the rebirth of the Inner Harbor. The market consists of two pavilions, the **Pratt Street Pavilion** and the

Light Street Pavilion. National stores and restaurants are abundant at Harborplace, but specialty shops such as **Life in Charm City** (Pratt Street Pavilion, 410/230-2652, Mon.-Sat. 10am-9pm, Sun. noon-6pm), which sells Baltimore-related merchandise; **Sock It To You** (Pratt Street Pavilion, 443/286-8889, Mon.-Sat. 10am-9pm, Sun. noon-6pm), which sells socks; and **Destination Baltimore** (Pratt Street Pavilion, 443/727-5775, Mon.-Sat.

10am-9pm, Sun. noon-6pm), which sells apparel, gifts, and seasonal items, are some of the independent stores located in the market.

The Gallery

The Gallery (200 E. Pratt St., 410/332-4191, www.thegalleryatharborplace.com, Mon.-Sat. 10am-9pm, Sun. noon-6pm) opened a few years after Harborplace in a glass building across Pratt Street (attached to the Renaissance Hotel). The two shopping areas are connected by a skywalk. Many upscale national stores and restaurants are located in the four-story structure, but local merchants running Maryland-themed shops can also be found there.

FELL'S POINT

Some of the most charming shops in Baltimore can be found in Fell's Point. Whether you're in the market for jewelry, home items, music, or clothing, you should turn up plenty to keep you interested if you poke around the historic streets and venture up some side alleys. **B'More Betty** (1500 Thames St., 443/869-6379, www.onlybetty.com, Wed.-Sun. 11am-7pm) is a trendy buyer and seller of designer handbags, shoes, and accessories. **Killer Trash** (602 S. Broadway, 410/675-2449, daily 11am-7:30pm) is a vibrant vintage shop with an eclectic selection of jewelry and clothes for wearing and for costumes. If you are looking for a special piece for your home, or just need a lamp rewired, **Brasswork Co., Inc.** (1641 Thames St., 410/327-7280, www.baltimorebrassworks.com, Mon.-Fri. 8:30am-5pm, Sat. 10am-6pm, Sun. noon-6pm) is the place to go. They offer gifts, lighting, timepieces, candleholders, and many other brass merchandise.

For all types of hats, visit **Hats in the Belfry** (813 S. Broadway, 410/342-7480, www.hatsinthebelfry.com, Mon.-Thurs. 10am-6pm, Fri.-Sat. 10am-8pm, Sun. 10am-7pm).

FEDERAL HILL

Charles Street and Light Street are the best areas in Federal Hill to do some window browsing. Small boutiques and shops selling clothes and home goods are scattered through the charming neighborhood. Favorites include **Phina's for the Home** (919 S. Charles St., 410/685-0911, www.phinas.com, Tues.-Sat. noon-6pm, Sun. noon-3pm), a boutique linen store selling home and spa items and gifts; and **Brightside Boutique & Art Studio** (1133 S. Charles St., 410/244-1133, www.shopbrightside.com, Mon.-Sat. 11am-7pm, Sun.11am-5pm), selling clothes, accessories and home items.

HAMPDEN

The "happening place" in Hampden is 36th Street, known locally as "The Avenue." This is especially true for shoppers since there are four blocks of retail stores offering clothing, furniture, antiques, beauty supplies, and some funkier items. The stores are locally owned, and the merchants are helpful if you're looking for a specific item. For starters, visit **Atomic Books** (3620 Falls Rd., 410/662-4444, www.atomicbooks.com, Sun.-Tues. 11am-7pm, Wed.-Thurs. 11am-9pm, Fri. 11am-10pm, Sat. 11am-9pm, Sun. 11am-7pm) to find unique titles and comics, or visit **Ma Petite Shoe** (832 W. 36th St., 410/235-3442, www.mapetiteshoe.com, Mon.-Thurs. and Sat. 11am-7pm, Fri. 11am-8pm, Sun. noon-5pm) for designer shoes and artisan chocolate.

Sports and Recreation

SPECTATOR SPORTS

Oriole Park at Camden Yards

Oriole Park at Camden Yards (333 W. Camden St., 888/848-2473, http://baltimore. orioles.mlb.com) is the home of Major League Baseball's **Baltimore Orioles.** The park opened in 1992 in downtown Baltimore, just a short walk from the Inner Harbor. Camden Yards is consistently rated one of the top professional baseball parks in the country. The train station at the intersection of Howard and Camden Streets services the stadium for the Baltimore Light Rail.

M&T Bank Stadium

A stone's throw from Camden Yards is the **M&T Bank Stadium** (1101 Russell St., 410/261-7283, www.baltimoreravens.com), home to the **Baltimore Ravens** of the National Football League. The multipurpose venue opened in 1998. The Hamburg Street Station of the Baltimore Light Rail services the stadium.

Royal Farms Arena

The **Royal Farms Arena** (201 W. Baltimore St., www.royalfarmsarena.com) is the location for the **Baltimore Blast** (www.baltimore-blast.com) professional indoor soccer team's home games. The team was founded in 1992 and is part of the Major Indoor Soccer League.

BIKING

Baltimore has a large biking community that is working hard to make the city more bike-friendly. Since 2006, 42 on-street bike lane miles have been created in the city, and there are 39 miles of off-road trails.

The **BWI Bike Trail** (www.bikewashington.org) is a 11-mile, asphalt surface, loop trail that circles BWI Airport. It has short sections on city streets, but is mostly level with a few bridge hills and one tougher hill. The trail runs past a light-rail station where a drinking fountain, restrooms, and vending machines are accessible. Parking is available in several spots including the **Dixon Aircraft Observation**

Pimlico Race Course

The second leg of the famed Triple Crown horse races, **The Preakness Stakes,** is held on the third Saturday in May at **Pimlico Race Course** (5201 Park Heights Ave., 410/542-9400, www. pimlico.com), northwest of Hampden. The historic racecourse is the second-oldest in the country, having opened in 1870. The course was built after the governor of Maryland, Oden Bowie, made a proposition over dinner in 1868 to racing gurus in Saratoga, New York. The proposition included a race, to be held two years after the dinner, between horses that were yearlings at the time of the dinner. The American Jockey Club wanted to host the race, but Bowie pledged to build a state-of-the-art racetrack in Baltimore if the race was held there. After the pledge was made, plans were put in place for the birth of Pimlico.

Pimlico (originally spelled "pemblicoe") was a name given to the area west of the Jones Falls, an 18-mile-long stream that runs through the city of Baltimore and into the Inner Harbor, during the colonial era. The Maryland Jockey Club bought 70 acres in the area for $23,500 and constructed the racetrack for $25,000. Race day was always a big event at Pimlico, and horse-drawn carriages made their way through Druid Hill Park toward the course before additional roads were built directly to the track.

Pimlico quickly became an institution. It has survived wars, recession, the Great Depression, fire, and storms. The first Preakness Stakes was held here in 1873 and remains a time-honored tradition.

Area (Route 176 on Dorsey Road) and at the light-rail station (on the west side of Route 648).

The **Baltimore and Annapolis Trail** (410/222-6244) is a 15.5-mile paved trail that runs along a railroad route from Dorsey Road (near BWI Airport) and ends at the Annapolis waterfront. At the north end of the trail is a short connector to the BWI Bike Trail.

The **Gwynns Falls Trail** (www.gwynnsfallstrail.org) covers 15 miles between the I-70 Park and Ride trailhead and the Inner Harbor. The trail connects 30 neighborhoods in west and southwest Baltimore.

Bikes can be rented at **Light Street Cycles** (1124 Light St., 410/685-2234, Mon.-Fri. 10am-7pm, Sat. 10am-6pm, hybrids $30 per day, mountain bikes and road bikes $60 per day).

PADDLEBOATS

Most kids get wide-eyed when they see the lineup of brightly colored "Chessie" the sea monster paddleboats at **Paddleboats Team Chessie** (301 E. Pratt St., www.baltimorepaddleboats.org, Memorial Day-Labor Day daily 11am-10pm, mid-Apr.-day before Memorial Day and day after Labor Day-mid-Nov. daily 11am-6pm, $20 per half hour) on the waterfront. Renting a paddleboat for a half hour or

an hour is a fun way to get a new perspective on the harbor. Regular paddleboats are also available for rent ($12 per half hour).

CRUISES
Urban Pirates

Bring the family on a unique 1.5-hour adventure in the harbor. The **Urban Pirates** (Ann Street Pier, Fell's Point, 410/327-8378, www.urbanpirates.com, $22-25) offers pirate cruises out of Fell's Point. Three pirates lead an interactive adventure where guests can dress up, get their faces painted, get a tattoo, and then depart on a cruise complete with songs, games, water cannons, and treasure. Adult cruises are also offered.

Paddle Wheeler Cruise

The Black-Eyed Susan (2600 Boston St., 410/342-6960, www.baltimorepaddlewheel.com) is an authentic paddle wheeler that is docked in Canton but can board passengers at the Maryland Science Center, Pier 5 Hotel, and Broadway Pier in Fell's Point. It is designed for entertainment and can be chartered for corporate or private events, but public events (such as murder mystery dinner cruises for $70) are also offered.

Paddleboats Team Chessie

Food

DOWNTOWN AND THE INNER HARBOR
American
The Capital Grille (500 E. Pratt St., 443/703-4064, www.thecapitalgrille.com, Mon.-Thurs. 11:30am-10pm, Fri. 11:30am-11pm, Sat. 5pm-11pm, Sun. 4pm-9pm, $29-50) on Pratt Street is part of a national chain of restaurants, but still offers a superb dining experience in a great location on the Inner Harbor. Steak and seafood make up the bulk of the menu in this traditional steak house, but the good service and pleasant atmosphere add to its overall appeal.

The **Corner & Bistro Winebar** (213 Penn St., 410/727-1155, www.cbwinebar.com, lunch Tues.-Thurs. 11am-2pm, Fri. 11:30am-2:30pm, dinner Sun. 4pm-10pm, Mon.-Thurs. 5pm-midnight, Fri. 5pm-10pm, Sat. 4pm-1am, $10-17) is a casual little bistro and wine bar that serves a bar menu of tasty appetizers and a small lunch and dinner menu of salads, burgers, and ciabattas. Try the Chesapeake, a ciabatta with grilled marinated chicken breast, crab dip, and grilled tomato and a side of sweet potato fries. The bistro is easy to walk to from attractions such as the Babe Ruth Birthplace Museum and is about a half block off Pratt Street.

Asian
Ban Thai Restaurant (340 N. Charles St., 410/727-7971, www.banthai.us, Mon.-Thurs. 11am-10:30pm, Fri.-Sat. 11am-11pm, Sun. noon-9:30pm, $13-21) opened in 1993, and the same chefs that were here then are still cooking delightful Thai dishes in the kitchen today. The modest restaurant is known for its made-to-order food. They do a nice job with spices and can make each dish as hot or mild as you like. The menu includes a variety of classic and more daring dishes so both beginners and those experienced with Thai cuisine should have no problem finding a suitable dish. Vegetarian dishes are on the menu as well, but some have fish sauce. Try for a seat by the window so you can people-watch on Charles Street.

Brazilian
For die-hard carnivores, it's hard to beat the Brazilian steak house **Fogo De Chao** (600 E. Pratt St., 410/528-9292, www.fogodechao.com, lunch Mon.-Fri. 11:30am-2pm, dinner Mon.-Thurs. 5pm-10pm, Fri. 5pm-10:30pm, Sat. 4pm-10:30pm, Sun. 4pm-9pm, lunch $34.95, dinner $51.95). This dining experience includes a large salad bar with more than 30 items, then an onslaught of 15 cuts of fire-roasted meats brought tableside. Each guest has a card to turn to green when you'd like more meat offered or red when you are taking a break or have had enough. This is a fun place to bring business guests (if they are not vegetarian) and a good place for groups. Although this restaurant is part of a small chain out of Dallas, Texas, this is the only location in Maryland.

Turkish
Cazbar (316 N. Charles St., 410/528-1222, www.cazbar.pro, Mon.-Thurs. 11am-11pm, Fri.-Sat. 11am-midnight, Sun. 4pm-11pm, $16-27) is Baltimore's first authentic Turkish restaurant. They offer consistently good food, a warm and pleasant atmosphere, and friendly staff. As one person sitting close by commented, "I will eat here until my mouth burns like the fires of hell. It's that good." Although the food isn't generally that spicy, it's always good to know someone will take one for the team. The servers know the menu well and can help with tough decisions. Try their hummus or Mohamra walnut dip for a starter. They also have Turkish beer and sangria. On Friday and Saturday nights there are free belly dancing shows—not many places can say that.

FELL'S POINT
AND LITTLE ITALY
American

Peter's Inn (504 S. Ann St., 410/675-7313, www.petersinn.com, Tues.-Sun. 6:30pm-10pm, Fri.-Sat. 6:30pm-11pm, $11-30) is a casual contemporary eatery that is known for its innovative dishes and fresh ingredients. It is housed in a farmhouse built in 1799 and the owners live upstairs. The restaurant was mainly known as a biker bar throughout the 1980s and early 1990s but has since transformed into a great food-focused restaurant. The menu changes weekly (look for the chalkboard next to the men's washroom) with the exception of salad, steaks, and garlic bread, which are staples. The restaurant is crowded on weekends so expect a wait (perhaps at their bar). They do not take reservations.

Beer lovers will think they've won the lottery after stepping inside ★ **Max's Taphouse** (737 S. Broadway, 410/675-6297, www.maxs.com, daily 11am-2am $10-12.50). With 140 rotating drafts, 102 taps, 5 casks, and 1,200 bottles in stock, you could spend a lifetime here searching for your favorite beer. This beer-lover's institution is Baltimore's premier beer pub and has been featured in countless magazines and "best of" lists. The friendly owner, expert "beertenders" (many of whom have been here for more than a dozen years), and delicious pub menu make this well-known establishment in the heart of Fell's Point not just a great drinking spot, but also a great place to eat and hang out with new and old friends. For the sports minded, they offer numerous televisions, pool tables, foosball, and dartboards. Private rooms are available with large-screen TVs, custom beer lists, and great sound systems with iPod connections. Weekday specials such as "Monday sucks happy hour" and "Friday big ass draft happy hour" occur weekly in addition to great annual events such as Max's Annual German Beer Fest and the Hopfest.

If you are looking for a classy restaurant with a lovely atmosphere and delicious food, and you don't mind paying for it, then make a reservation at the acclaimed ★ **Charleston Restaurant** (1000 Lancaster St., 410/332-7373, www.charlestonrestaurant.com, Mon.-Sat. 5:30pm-10pm, $79-212). They offer an extensive prix fixe tasting menu with three to six courses and an award-winning wine list of more than 800 labels. Chef Cindy Wolf has been a James Beard Award finalist for best chef, mid-Atlantic, on multiple occasions, and as recently as 2016. She is one of the best-known chefs in the city. Wolf's cooking is a blend of French fundamentals and South Carolina's Low Country cuisine. The restaurant is in Harbor East near Fell's Point. A jacket and tie are recommended but not required.

The **Blue Moon Café** (1621 Aliceanna St., 410/522-3940, www.bluemoonbaltimore.com, daily 7am-3pm, weekends 24 hours, $5-16) is a well-known breakfast café that was featured on Guy Fieri's show *Diners, Drive-Ins and Dives*. Open 24 hours on weekends, this small eatery inside a converted row house has a line out the door on the average Saturday or Sunday. The reason couldn't be that they're serving Captain Crunch—or could it? Captain Crunch french toast is one of their most popular dishes, but Maryland Eggs Benedict and delightful homemade biscuits and gravy are other very convincing reasons.

Exposed brick and beams, high ceilings, and dark wood add to the charm of the **Red Star Bar and Grill** (906 S. Wolfe St., 410/675-0212, www.redstarbar.us, Mon.-Thurs. 11:30am-midnight, Fri. 11:30am-2am, Sat. 10am-2am, Sun. 10am-midnight, $7-20). This fun eatery is a little off the beaten path in Fell's Point but still within easy walking distance of all the action. They serve great sandwiches, pizza, and burgers and also offer a nice selection of beer. This is a fun, casual place with a good vibe and tasty menu. They also have full bar, which is a comfortable place to stop in for a drink or meet friends.

A unique find is **One-Eyed Mike's** (708 S. Bond St., 410/327-0445, www.oneeyedmikes.com, Mon.-Fri. 11am-2am, Sat.-Sun. 10am-2am, $7-35). This lovely little treasure is one of the oldest operating taverns in Baltimore. It's housed in a tiny space on the edge of Fell's Point in an off-the-beaten-path row house. Walk through the bar and to the lovely little restaurant in the back, where they serve delicious crab cakes and stuffed filet. The staff is fun, the atmosphere is comfortable, and the food is good. The backbar was hand-carved, and they still have the original tin ceiling, both of which were put in during the 1860s. They also offer courtyard seating in nice weather. Ask about their Grand Marnier Club, the world's first.

British Pub

The **Wharf Rat** (801 S. Ann St., 410/276-8304, www.thewharfrat.com, daily 11am-2am, $9-20) harkens back to a day when old seaport taverns were filled with visiting sailors. The name itself is a term used in the 18th century for seafarers and pirates when they came ashore. This is a fun place for great beer and pub food (their specialty is crab dip pizza and fish-and-chips). The bartenders are also the cooks, so be patient with your food. The atmosphere is friendly and inviting, and the pub is allegedly haunted.

Seafood

Thames Street Oyster House (1728 Thames St., 443/449-7726, www.thamesstreetoysterhouse.com, lunch Wed.-Sun. 11:30am-2:30pm, dinner Sun.-Thurs. 5pm-9:30pm, Fri.-Sat. 5pm-10:30pm, raw bar open until 1am, $12-27) is a slightly upscale gem amid the bar scene in Fell's Point. They offer a fun staff and a lively nighttime atmosphere, but can also be a great place for a romantic seafood dinner if you reserve a table early in the evening. This is a classic oyster house with a great raw bar. There's a large bar area, and a water view from the upstairs.

Italian

There is no shortage of great Italian restaurants in Little Italy and the surrounding area. ★ **Amiccis** (231 S. High St., 410/528-1096, www.amiccis.com, Sun.-Thurs. 11am-11pm,

Fri.-Sat. 11am-midnight, $14-19) has been a tradition in Baltimore since 1991. It's a self-proclaimed "Very Casual Eatery" whose mission is to provide great homemade Italian comfort food in a relaxed environment. All the menu items are wonderful, but first-timers should try the signature appetizer, the Pane' Rotundo. People in the know call it "that great shrimp and bread thing," and you'll see why after you try it. Amiccis also has a nice bar area that was added as the restaurant expanded from 25 seats to 300, and the original two friends who bought it are still running it today. The atmosphere is lively, and the patrons are a mix of locals and visitors.

★ **Vaccaro's Italian Pastry Shop** (222 Albemarle St., 410/685-4905, www.vaccarospastry.com, café menu $5-10) is *the* place to go in Baltimore for Italian pastries. They are widely known for their incredible cannoli filling but also offer many other delectable baked goods such as rum cake, biscotti, and cheesecake. They also offer a café menu of salads and

Amiccis

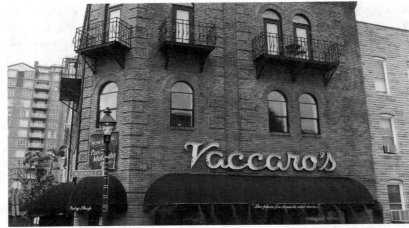

Vaccaro's Italian Pastry Shop

sandwiches and make cakes, cookie trays, and other items such as tiramisu for parties and other occasions. There are three additional locations throughout the Baltimore area (2919 O'Donnell St., 118 Shawan Rd., and 696A Bel Air Rd.).

For a great slice of pizza pie, stop in **Brick Oven Pizza** (800 S. Broadway, 410/563-1600, www.boppizza.com, Sun.-Thurs. 11am-11pm, Fri.-Sat. 11am-3am, $9-24), another fun, casual restaurant that was featured on *Diners, Drive-Ins and Dives*. The crispy-crust pizza and the list of more than 40 toppings including crab, gyro meat, and even Spam are reason enough dine here, but they also offer wraps, pasta, and salads.

Greek

The Black Olive (814 S. Bond St., 410/276-7141, www.theblackolive.com, $27-40) serves authentic organic Greek food in a cozy section of Fell's Point. This elegant restaurant is family-owned and uses organic produce, dairy, flours, and sugars in all dishes. They have relationships with local farms and also serve fresh fish from all over the world including black sea bass, barbouni, and turbo. They boast the largest wine list in Baltimore. The wine cellar and dining rooms are available for private parties.

CANTON
American

The raven handrails are just one of many "Poe" details at **Annabel Lee Tavern** (601 S. Clinton St., 410/522-2929, www.annabelleetavern.com, Mon.-Sat. 4pm-1am, Sun. 3pm-midnight, $11-25). Baltimore is a natural setting for a restaurant and bar done in "Edgar Allan Poe." This unique little restaurant is a warm, funky place to have a good meal or a house cocktail off the Poe-themed drink list. The walls are inscribed with Poe's work. The tavern serves affordable upscale comfort food from an interesting but not over-the-top menu (try the rosemary beef tenderloin gyro or the roasted orange roughy tacos). They offer many daily specials and nice vegetarian options, but are known for their duck fat fries, which are worth a try if you've never had them.

The **Blue Hill Tavern** (938 S. Conkling St., 443/388-9363, www.bluehilltavern.com, brunch Sat.-Sun. 10:30am-2:30pm, lunch Mon.-Fri. 11:30am-2:30pm, dinner Mon.-Wed. 5pm-9pm, Thurs.-Sat. 5pm-10pm, Sun. 4pm-9pm, $13-29) is a great little modern tavern a few blocks off O'Donnell Street in Canton. Presentation is key in this trendy restaurant, and the food tastes as good as it looks. The menu includes a variety of American food with a heavy lean toward seafood. Try the mushroom Wellington, surf and turf, or yellowfin tuna and shrimp roulade. They also offer a hearty burger and salads. There's a rooftop patio for summertime dining that is one of the best in the city, even though it isn't on the water. They offer free valet parking.

Greek

The **Sip and Bite Restaurant** (2200 Boston St., 410/675-7077, www.sipandbite.com, open 24/7, $5-28) is a Baltimore landmark that was featured on *Diners, Drive-Ins and Dives*. This 1948 original between Fell's Point and Canton is owned by a husband-and-wife team that are the third generation in one family to run this diner. They offer a huge menu of breakfast, lunch, and dinner with a slant toward Greek dishes. They serve classic Greek specialties like gyros, but also have killer crab cakes made from a 60-year-old family recipe.

Seafood

Mama's on the Half Shell (2901 O'Donnell St., 410/276-3160, www.mamasmd.com, Mon.-Fri. 11am-2am, Sat.-Sun. 9am-2pm, $23-35) opened in 2003 and quickly became a tradition in Canton. This classic seafood house sits on the corner of O'Donnell Street and South Linwood Avenue in the heart of the neighborhood. They specialize in large, succulent oyster dishes (oyster stew, fried oysters, grilled oysters—you get the picture) but also have wonderful crab dishes, other seafood favorites, and a filet mignon selection. The two-story restaurant has a dark wood interior, a long bar on the first floor, and patio seating. The staff is warm and friendly, and they offer daily specials.

Mediterranean

The **Speakeasy Saloon** (2840 O'Donnell St., 410/276-2977, Mon.-Thurs. 4:30pm-11pm, Fri.-Sat. 11:30am-11pm, Sun. 10am-10pm, bar daily until 2am, $12-22) is a an elegant saloon with a throwback decor to the Roaring Twenties. A 150-year-old staircase, large murals, mirrors, and a tin ceiling help visitors visualize what things were like when

gangsters and flappers frequented the original corner establishment. The upstairs patio boasts beautiful ironwork railings accented with flower boxes and a redbrick exterior. The food is surprisingly good for the reasonable prices they charge, with both seafood and Mediterranean dishes (examples include Mediterranean chicken, veal marsala, lamb scampi, and pork Athena). If you're looking for a quiet spot, sit on the patio, since it can get loud inside on a busy night.

Mexican

If you like good Mexican food and you can put up with a few house rules, such as "Report any Elvis sightings to server," "Be nice or leave," and "Don't feed kitchen staff," then take a table at **Nacho Mama's** (2907 O' Donnell St., 410/675-0898, www.nachomamas-canton.com, Mon.-Sat. 11am-2am, Sun. 9am-2am, $11-30) in the heart of Canton. Nacho Mama's has been a hot spot in Baltimore since it opened on Elvis's birthday in 1994. The decor is a mix of the King, Natty Boh,

Mama's on the Half Shell

Speakeasy Saloon

the Orioles, the Baltimore Colts, and everything else Baltimore. The food is delicious, the portions are large, and they have more than a dozen kinds of margaritas. This is a great place to bring visitors to share some Baltimore tradition.

FEDERAL HILL
American
Peanut butter burgers, waffle fry nachos, pretzel roll buns, and homemade chips are just some of the items to try at **The Abbey Burger Bistro** (1041 Marshall St., 443/453-9698, www.abbeyburgerbistro.com, kitchen hours Tues.-Sun. 11:30am-midnight, Mon. 5pm-midnight, $6-17.50). This burger-and-beer-focused eatery has a great menu for both, including a build-your-own burger section and a rotating beer list (they even take requests online). This is a great place to stir your creativity, fill your burger appetite, and wash it all down with a cold brew.

Hull Street Blues Cafe (1222 Hull St., 410/727-7476, www.hullstreetblues.com, lunch Tues.-Sat. 11am-5pm, Mon. 11am-10pm, Sun. brunch 10am-2pm, dinner Tues.-Thurs. 5pm-10pm, Fri.-Sat. 5pm-11pm, Sun. 4pm-9pm, $16-29) has a long history. It got its start as a saloon back in 1889 and is now a lovely neighborhood café. Nestled amid the blocks of row

houses in Locust Point, the café is named for its side street address on Hull Street (which was named after a naval hero of the War of 1812, Isaac Hull). The restaurant has two sides: one is a casual barroom (where bar fare is served) with a 40-foot-long bar, and the other is the nautical-themed Commodore Room, where guests can enjoy gourmet meals off linens and stemware in front of the fireplace. Seafood, beef, and poultry are at the heart of the menu, but other options such as the chipotle-lime barbecue pork loin are local favorites.

Seafood
When you're craving good seafood and aren't looking for an upscale atmosphere, **Nick's Oyster Bar** (1065 S. Charles St., 410/685-2020, www.nicksoysterbar.com, Sun.-Thurs. 11am-7pm, Fri. 11am-10pm, Sat. 11am-9pm, $10-22) is the place to go. It is in the west end of the Cross Street Market area and has been in business since 1972. It has cement floors, bottles of beer on ice, televisions tuned to sports, and all the local seafood favorites (including a raw bar). The menu includes steamed shrimp, crab, fish-and-chips, mussels, and the famous crab soup. They also have a sushi bar. Pull a stool up to the counter, order a beer, and chat with the crowd that forms on weekends.

Natty Boh

The one-eyed, handlebar-mustached Mr. Boh pictured on a gold-and-white National Bohemian Beer can is not just the symbol for **National Bohemian Beer** (aka "Natty Boh"), but also a treasured icon in Baltimore. National Bohemian Beer was first brewed in Baltimore in 1885 by the National Brewing Company. After Prohibition, National Bohemian introduced Mr. Boh, who wears a distinctive smile that has delighted the people of Baltimore for decades.

Now make no mistake, Natty Boh is a cheap, domestic beer (think Pabst Blue Ribbon and Miller High Life); in fact the brand is now owned by Pabst Brewing Company. The beer's slogan is "From the Land of Pleasant Living," which refers to the Chesapeake Bay.

In 1965, Natty Boh became the Baltimore Orioles' official sponsor, and the beer was served at their former home, Memorial Stadium, as "the official beer of Baltimore."

The brand has been sold several times (the first in 1979 to Heileman Brewing Company), and in 1996 its production was moved out of the state. The beer was no longer available on tap in Baltimore. Disappointed fans went for years without their favorite beer being offered fresh from the keg (almost 90 percent of Natty Boh sales are in Baltimore), but in 2011, good news came. Pabst Blue Ribbon announced the return of the famous brew to Baltimore and the rest of Maryland on tap.

Nacho Mama's in Canton was one of the first to tap the newly available kegs, and did so on February 3, 2011. A packed house welcomed Natty Boh back. A total of eight official keg-tapping parties were held throughout the area, and it looks like the people of Baltimore can enjoy their beer on tap for the foreseeable future.

Another great seafood restaurant is **Ryleigh's Oyster Bar** (36 E. Cross St., 410/539-2093, www.ryleighs.com, Mon.-Sun. 11am-10pm, $8-29). The atmosphere is more upscale than a bar scene, and they offer really fresh oysters on their old slate oyster bar. There is a gourmet seafood menu with items such as crab cakes, tuna, and shrimp and grits. The crab pretzels are a great way to start, and they also offer salads and sandwiches and other items that aren't seafood.

MOUNT VERNON

Afghan

The Helmand (806 N. Charles St., 410/752-0311, www.helmand.com, Sun.-Thurs. 5pm-10pm, Fri.-Sat. 5pm-11pm, $13-17) looks like a simple restaurant but has been serving incredible Afghan food since 1989. It is one of a handful of eateries owned by a prominent Afghan family that helped bring the cuisine to the United States. Considered by many to be a local treasure, the *kaddo borawni*, a pumpkin appetizer, is a must-try before making the difficult entrée decision.

American

The tuxedoed servers, stuffed leather seats, live piano music, and stiff drinks haven't changed a bit at ★ **The Prime Rib** (1101 N. Calvert St., 410/539-1804, www.theprimerib. com, Mon.-Thurs. 5pm-10pm, Fri.-Sat. 5pm-11pm, Sun. 4pm-9pm, $28-63) since its opening in 1965. Jackets are required, and the place looks like an establishment Sinatra would have frequented. The best part, however, is the food. The Prime Rib has been named one of the best in the country by *Esquire* magazine for its steaks, and it is easy to believe. This is a place to come when you want first-class food and service to match, and you don't mind paying for it.

The funky little pizza shop **Joe Squared** (33 W. North Ave., 410/545-0444, www.jo-esquared.com, Sun.-Wed. 11am-midnight, Thurs.-Sat. 11am-2am, $11-25) offers coal-fired square pizza, 17 varieties of risotto, an extensive rum list, good beer, and free live music (funk, soul, jazz, old time, etc.). Featured on *Diners, Drive-Ins and Dives,* the restaurant is family-owned, and the food is delicious. The clientele is mainly college-aged, and the area isn't ideal after dark. There is also a location in the Inner Harbor (30 Market Pl.).

Italian

A great choice for pizza in Mount Vernon is **Iggies** (818 N. Calvert St., Ste. 1, 410/528-0818, www.iggiespizza.com, Tues.-Thurs. 11:30am-9pm, Fri.-Sat. 11:30am-10pm, Sun. 11:30am-8pm, $10-18). The pizza has a thin, crispy crust and a multitude of interesting topping options (think peaches, gorgonzola, rosemary, etc.). The place is very casual, and you must BYOB if you'd like to drink. When you enter, wait to be seated. Once seated, leave your plate on the table and get in line to order. When your food is ready, the staff will call your name and order number. The pizza is excellent, and the crowd is young and lively. It's a great place to grab a bit before heading to Centerstage.

HAMPDEN AND HOMEWOOD
American

★ **Woodberry Kitchen** (2010 Clipper Park Rd., 410/464-8000, www.woodberrykitchen. com, brunch Sat.-Sun. 10am-2pm, dinner Mon.-Thurs. 5pm-10pm, Fri.-Sat. 5pm-11pm, Sun. 5pm-9pm, $15-48) is a hip little restaurant in the historic Clipper Mill west of Hampden. They serve local meats and seafood and use fresh organic ingredients. The menu is based on what is seasonal and includes many regional dishes (think brined pork chops and oysters roasted in a wood-burning oven). The atmosphere is contemporary in design, and the space, a renovated 19th-century industrial mill, offers the warm ambience of exposed brick, wood, and soft lighting. On nice evenings, diners can also enjoy patio seating under market umbrellas and white lights. Reservations are a must on weekends and should be made weeks in advance if possible.

The **Corner Charcuterie Bar** (850 W. 36th St., 443/869-5075, www.cornerchar-cuteriebar.com, lunch Wed.-Fri. at 11 am, dinner daily at 4pm, brunch Sat.-Sun 11am-2:30pm, $9-19) is a treasure in Hampden. They offer Belgium-influenced fare with interesting dishes such as roasted bone marrow and ostrich tartare and a great selection of meats and cheeses. A chef's $20 meal option changes daily as does the discount cocktail of the day. They have a convenience charge on credit card sales.

It's hard to find a more local dining institution in Hampden than **Café Hon** (1002 W. 36th St., 410/243-1230, www.cafehon. com, Mon.-Thurs. 11am-9pm, Fri. 11am-10pm, Sat. 9am-10pm, Sun. 9am-8pm, $7-19), and it's hard to miss the two-story pink flamingo that stands over its front door. The café name is a tribute to the "hon" culture in Hampden (see Honfest in the events section of this chapter), and the café serves a mix of comfort food and seafood. The adjoining Hon Bar offers live music and oyster shucking. This purely Baltimore establishment even has a Baltimore, Maryland, dictionary (or Bawlmer, Murlin, if you will) on the website.

Café Hon is a local institution in Hampden.

Accommodations

$100-200

If you want to be where the action is in Fell's Point, book a room at the **Admiral Fell Inn** (888 S. Broadway, 410/522-7380, www.admiralfell.com, $169-289). This historic European-style hotel includes seven buildings, some of which date back to the 1770s. Many stories surround the inn, as the building has served many purposes such as a ship chandlery, boardinghouse, theater, and YMCA. No two rooms are alike at the inn but each is decorated in modern furnishings with a cozy decor. Two specialty rooms are available, one with two levels and the other with a balcony overlooking the waterfront. The Tavern at the Admiral Fell Inn is open Wednesday-Saturday evenings to serve beer, wine, cocktails, and traditional spirits.

Travelers looking for a charming boutique hotel near bustling O'Donnell Street in Canton will be thrilled with the **Inn at 2920** (2920 Elliott St., 410/342-4450, www.theinnat2920.com, $175-215). This five-room inn is inside a rather regular-looking row house on Elliott Street. Look for the pale-green door on the corner. Once inside, the rooms are lovely, unique, and contemporary. They have exposed brick walls and modern furnishings. This hip little hotel is definitely something special, and you'll feel like a local stepping out onto the street. The water is within walking distance, but Fell's Point is a good 15-20 minutes by foot.

Budget-conscious travelers can have a great stay at the **Brookshire Suites** (120 E. Lombard St., 410/625-1300, www.brookshiresuites.com, $107-199) just a block away from the Inner Harbor on Lombard Street. The 11-story, 97-room hotel has a distinct exterior with a large black-and-white geometric pattern that can't be missed. The interior is contemporary with traditional-style rooms. The hotel caters to business travelers and offers a nice business center and laundry facilities, but its central location makes it a good choice for pleasure travel as well.

$200-300

The **Monaco Baltimore** (2 N. Charles St., 443/692-6170, www.monaco-baltimore.com, $209-309) is consistent with other Kimpton Hotels as a top-notch choice for accommodations. This warm and friendly hotel is housed in the restored B&O Railroad building on Charles Street a few blocks northwest of the Inner Harbor. The personal service and attention to detail they offer is hard to beat. The hotel has Tiffany stained glass windows, a marble staircase, and vaulted ceilings. The rooms are large and modern with high ceilings and a hint of funky styling that's unique to Kimpton. The staff is wonderful, and the location is convenient to many restaurants and attractions even though it's not right on the water. They offer bikes and bike route maps to guests and a hosted wine hour in the evenings. They have 24-hour valet parking with in-and-out services for $38. The hotel is pet friendly.

The ★ **Hyatt Regency Baltimore** (300 Light St., 410/528-1234, www.baltimore.hyatt.com, $239-439) offers one of the best locations in the Inner Harbor. Situated right across Light Street from Harborplace and connected to it by two skywalks, the hotel offers tremendous harbor views. The rooms are modern and comfortable with large bathrooms and contemporary furniture. The building's lit-up, glass-enclosed elevators seem to shoot through the lobby roof and along the outside of the hotel. They are beautiful to look at and afford incredible views to the people inside. The hotel staff is also extremely helpful and pleasant. Bistro 300 on the third floor serves breakfast, lunch, and dinner (and has a nice bar). There is a small gift shop on-site, a fitness room, and pool. Ask for a harbor-view room on an upper floor; the corner rooms

Traveling with Fido

Baltimore is surprisingly pet friendly for such a large and industrial city. Many hotels throughout the city allow your best friend to accompany you in your room. Additional fees and rules may apply to your four-legged friend, so ask when you make a reservation. Some hotels that allow dogs include:

- **Admiral Fell Inn** (888 S. Broadway, 410/522-7380)
- **Biltmore Suites** (205 W. Madison St., 410/728-6550)
- **Brookshire Suites** (120 E. Lombard St., 410/625-1300)
- **Four Seasons Hotel Baltimore** (200 International Dr., 410/576-5800)
- **Hilton Baltimore Convention Center Hotel** (401 W. Pratt St., 443/573-8700)
- **Holiday Inn Express Baltimore—Downtown** (221 N. Gay St., 410/400-8045)
- **Holiday Inn Inner Harbor Hotel** (301 W. Lombard St., 410/685-3500)
- **Hotel Monaco** (2 N. Charles St., 443/692-6170)
- **Intercontinental Harbor Court Hotel** (550 Light St., 410/234-0550)
- **Pier 5 Hotel** (711 Eastern Ave., 410/539-2000)
- **Lord Baltimore Hotel** (20 W. Baltimore St., 410/539-8400)
- **Residence Inn Downtown Baltimore/Inner Harbor** (17 Light St., 410/962-1220)
- **Sheraton Inner Harbor Hotel** (300 S. Charles St., 410/962-8300)
- **Sheraton Baltimore North** (903 Dulaney Valley Rd., 410/321-7400)
- **Sleep Inn & Suites Downtown Inner Harbor** (301 Fallsway, 410/779-6166)

offer spectacular floor-to-ceiling windows overlooking the water.

The ★ **Inn at Hendersons Wharf** (1000 Fell St., 410/522-7777, www.hendersonswharf.com, $197-325) is a lovely boutique hotel sitting directly on the water on the eastern side of Fell's Point. The hotel is located in a large brick building dating back to 1893, which it shares with condos and a conference center. The inn's 38 cozy rooms have exposed brick walls, colonial décor, feather beds, and 30-inch televisions with satellite service. There's a pretty interior courtyard. Rooms include a continental breakfast, access to a fitness center and pools, and high-speed Internet. Self-parking is available for $10 per night. The hotel is close to restaurants and shops in Fell's Point but far enough away to filter the noise. Ask for a harbor view.

The **Courtyard Marriott Baltimore Downtown/Inner Harbor** (1000 Aliceanna St., 443/923-4000, www.marriott.com, $249-304) has 195 rooms and 10 suites not far from the waterfront. The staff at this hotel is exceptionally friendly and helpful. They also offer great packages for family members of patients at Johns Hopkins Hospital, which include a discounted room rate, breakfast, and cab vouchers to and from the hospital. There is a small indoor swimming pool, a small fitness room, and an on-site restaurant and bar serving breakfast, lunch, and dinner. High-speed Internet is included. Ask for an upper-floor room on the harbor side of the hotel, where limited water views are available.

For a less expensive stay that is still convenient to the Inner Harbor, the **Days Inn**

Baltimore—Inner Harbor Hotel (100 Hopkins Pl., 410/576-1000, www.daysinnerharbor.com, $199-229) is the ticket. Just a few blocks from the stadiums and Inner Harbor, the 250 rooms are clean and convenient. Although the rooms aren't large, this is a well-located hotel with an affordable price tag.

OVER $300

The **Inn at the Black Olive** (803 S. Caroline St., 443/681-6316, www.innattheblackolive.com, $289-439) is a boutique organic hotel offering 12 luxury guests suites along the waterfront on the border of Fell's Point and the harbor. All the suites are modern, with water views and spa bathrooms. Rooms include a basic organic breakfast. Other room amenities include balconies or sitting porches, king-size beds with organic mattresses, Sanijet pipeless hydrotherapy tubs, and high-speed Internet. All rooms are cleaned with natural chemical-free cleaners. There's an organic market and rooftop restaurant on-site called The Olive Room that serves Greek cuisine and has a large wine list. The Inn at the Black Olive is a LEED Platinum Inn.

A good choice on the waterfront in the Harbor East area of Baltimore between Fell's Point and the Inner Harbor is the **Baltimore Marriott Waterfront Hotel** (700 Aliceanna St., 410/385-3000, www.marriott.com, $269-489). This towering 31-story hotel is on the water's edge and offers stunning harbor views and great access to many of the best attractions. There are 733 modern rooms and 21 suites. Harbor-view rooms and city-view rooms are available.

Right near the Baltimore Marriott Waterfront Hotel is the **Four Seasons Hotel Baltimore** (200 International Dr., 410/576-5800, www.fourseasons.com, $509-2,500), which offers great views of the harbor and an elegant interior. There are 256 rooms and suites with views including the harbor, city, and marina. The rooms offer generous space, and the stunning Presidential Suite is more than 2,800 square feet. The corner suites offer stunning views. The service is on par with other Four Seasons hotels, which is to say much above average.

Information and Services

Helpful tourist information on Baltimore can be found on the **Baltimore Area Convention and Visitors Association** website at www.baltimore.org. The website has details on events and attractions throughout the city and answers many common questions. Special offers are also available through the website. The **Baltimore Area Visitor Center** (401 Light St., 877/225-8466, Apr.-Sept. daily 9am-6pm, reduced hours the rest of the year) in the Inner Harbor is a great place to begin any trip to Baltimore. The 8,000-square-foot center offers information on nearly everything the city has to offer.

The most widely read paper in the city is the *Baltimore Sun* (www.baltimoresun.com).

It is also Maryland's largest daily newspaper and covers local and regional news. The Baltimore *City Paper* (www.citypaper.com) is a free alternative weekly paper that is distributed on Wednesday. It is known for having good coverage of clubs, concerts, restaurants, and theater. It also has political articles and covers subjects not featured in mainstream publications.

There are 31 hospitals in the metropolitan area of Baltimore. Top-ranking facilities include **Johns Hopkins Hospital** (1800 Orleans St., 410/955-5000, www.hopkinsmedicine.org) and the **University of Maryland Medical Center** (22 S. Greene St., 410/328-8667, www.umm.edu).

Getting There

AIR

The **Baltimore Washington International Thurgood Marshall Airport (BWI)** (410/859-7111, www.bwiairport.com) is just 10 miles south of Baltimore and a short 15-minute car ride from downtown Baltimore. This busy regional airport is a hub for Southwest Airlines and offers some of the best fares in the Washington DC/Baltimore area. Most other major airlines offer flight service to BWI as well. Parking is available at the airport by the hour or day, and there is a free cell phone lot for those who are picking up arriving passengers.

Car rentals are available at the airport from numerous national car rental companies, and courtesy shuttles run between the airport and major downtown hotels. The **SuperShuttle** (www.supershuttle.com, approximately $15 for a shared van) runs 24-hour service from the airport to locations throughout Baltimore and has a reservation counter on the lower level of the airport near baggage claims 1 and 10.

Cab service is also available from the airport, but this can be a costly option with fares running upward of $40 to downtown Baltimore.

Train service is available from the airport to downtown Baltimore through the Maryland Transit Administration (MTA) on their **Light Rail** (410/539-5000, www.mta.maryland.gov/light-rail, Mon.-Fri. 5am-11pm, Sat. 6am-11pm, Sun. 11am-7pm, $1.60). The BWI Marshall Light Rail station can be found outside the lower lever of the terminal near Concourse E.

CAR

Baltimore is a very accessible city. Strategically located right on I-95, it can be reached easily by car from both the north and south. The drive from major cities such as New York (3.5 hours, 188 miles), Philadelphia (2 hours, 100 miles), Washington DC (1 hour, 39 miles), and Richmond (2.75 hours, 152 miles) is a straight shot and takes between one and four hours. I-83 also runs into the city from the north.

TRAIN

Pennsylvania Station (1515 N. Charles St., 800/872-7245, www.amtrak.com) is centrally located on Charles Street near Mount Vernon and is less than two miles from the Inner Harbor. The stately 1911 building is nicely restored, and the station is one of the busiest in the country. Amtrak runs dozens of trains through Penn Station daily from all corners of the country. They offer ticket discounts for seniors, children, students, veterans, and conference groups.

A commuter rail service called **Maryland Area Rail Commuter (MARC)** (410/539-5000, www.mta.maryland.gov) operates trains on weekdays between Washington DC and Baltimore ($8 one way). This is another option for visitors traveling during the week.

BUS

Just south of downtown Baltimore in an industrial section of the city is the **Greyhound** bus station (2110 Haines St., 800/231-2222, www.greyhound.com). Bus service runs daily from multiple destinations. It is advisable to take a cab from the station to points around Baltimore. Walking near the station is not advisable after dark.

A number of private bus lines provide service between cities in the mid-Atlantic and offer reasonable fares from cities such as Washington DC, Philadelphia, and New York City. An example is **Peter Pan Bus Lines** (800/343-9999, www.peterpanbus.com, $14 one-way from DC). Additional service can be found on www.gotobus.com.

Getting Around

Although walking is a viable option for getting to many of the sights in Baltimore, depending on where you are staying, it is often easiest (and safest at night) to move around the city by car. Public transportation does provide other alternatives; however, most public transportation is geared toward commuters and isn't the most convenient for visitors wishing to explore major attractions.

The exception to this is the **Charm City Circulator** (www.charmcitycirculator.com, year round Mon.-Thurs. 7am-8pm, Fri. 7am-midnight, Sat. 9am-midnight, Sun 9am-8pm). This free, eco-friendly shuttle service has a fleet of 30 Hybrid electric shuttles that serve four routes in Baltimore City. The Green Route offers transportation from City Hall to Fell's Point and to Johns Hopkins. The Purple Route serves locations from 33rd Street to Federal Hill. The Orange Route runs between Hollins Market and Harbor East and the Banner Route goes from the Inner Harbor to Fort McHenry. Shuttles stop every 10-15 minutes at each designated stop.

CAR

Downtown Baltimore is divided by two main streets. Baltimore Street runs east to west, and Charles Street runs north to south. All streets north of Baltimore Street (or above Baltimore Street if you're looking at a map) have the "north" designation (such as N. Highland Street). Likewise, those south (or below) Baltimore Street have a "south" designation. The same is true for the streets east and west of Charles Street (which is a one-way street running north downtown). Those streets to the east of Charles Street (or to the right) have "east" designations. Those to the west (left) have "west" designations.

When driving, it is very important to be aware that there are many one-way streets in Baltimore. Parking isn't too difficult in most parts of the city on weekends; however, garages right around the Inner Harbor can be expensive. Parking during the week is more of a challenge when commuters are in town and spaces are in short supply. There is on-street parking in many areas and pay lots are scattered throughout town. Be sure to read parking signs carefully, as many neighborhoods have resident-only parking and time restrictions.

Overall, driving in Baltimore is much as it is in other big cities. Drive with purpose and have a plan as to where you are headed. Sightseeing out the window in the middle of traffic can result in some less-than-friendly gestures from those in cars around you. When in doubt, or if you miss a turn, just drive around the block; it's difficult to get too lost if you keep an eye on the harbor.

BUS

Bus service provided by the **Maryland Transit Administration (MTA)** (410/539-5000, www.mtamaryland.com, $1.60) includes 73 routes in Baltimore. Forty-seven of these routes are local routes inside the city. Bus routes primarily serve commuters on weekdays and are more limited on weekends, but it pays to check out the latest schedule online.

RAIL

Two public rail systems serve Baltimore, although each only has one rail line. The first, called **Light Rail** (410/539-5000, www.mtamaryland.com, Mon.-Fri. 5am-12am, Sat. 6am-12am, Sun. 11am-7pm, $1.70), runs from BWI Airport north to Hunt Valley Mall (in northern Baltimore County). This is only a good option if you are traveling between two specific points on the line, such as Camden Yards to Mount Vernon (there are no east/west stops). The second is the **Metro Subway** (410/539-5000, www.mtamaryland.com, Mon.-Fri. 5am-12am, Sat.-Sun. 6am-12am, $1.70) that runs from the suburbs northwest of town and into downtown and Johns Hopkins. The line is 15.5 miles, and has 14 stations. Trains run every 8-10 minutes

All Aboard the Water Taxi

Baltimore Water Taxi

For decades residents and visitors to Baltimore have enjoyed an alternative form of public transportation around the city. The **Baltimore Water Taxi** (410/563-3900, www.thewatertaxi.com) is a fun, easy way to travel between some of the best attractions, shopping areas, and restaurants in town. The famed blue-and-white boats can be seen zipping between 17 well-placed landings along the waterfront. The taxi service shuttles thousands of commuters and visitors alike on a daily basis, and local businesses rely on the service to bring their customers.

During the summer months, the taxi runs 10am-11pm Monday-Saturday and 10am-9pm Sunday. Hours are shorter during the remainder of the year. All-day adult passes are $14, and trip times range 10-20 minutes. Tickets can be purchased online with a credit card or on board with cash or a personal check. Landing areas are as follows:

- Landing 1: Aquarium
- Landing 2: Harborplace
- Landing 3: Science Center
- Landing 4: Rusty Scupper
- Landing 5: Pier Five
- Landing 7: Harbor East
- Landing 8: Maritime Park

- Landing 9: HarborView
- Landing 10: Locust Point
- Landing 11: Fell's Point
- Landing 14: Captain James Landing
- Landing 16: Canton Waterfront Park
- Landing 17: Fort McHenry

during rush hour, every 11 minutes on weekday evenings, and every 15 minutes on weekends. Again, this line is geared toward commuters and isn't too helpful for visitors wishing to move around town between sights.

TAXI

Taxi service is available through three providers: **Yellow Cab** (410/685-1212), **Diamond** (410/947-3333), and **Royal** (410/327-0330). Hailing a cab on the street can be an impossible feat on busy nights in the city, so it's best to bring their phone numbers and try calling from your cell phone. Metered rates in Baltimore are $1.80 for the first one-eleventh of a mile or fraction thereof. Each additional one-eleventh of a mile is $0.20; $0.20 is also charged for each 30 seconds of wait time.

WATER TAXI

Water taxi service (410/563-3900, www. thewatertaxi.com) is available around the harbor between many of the popular sights. This is a great service for visitors. The little boats with the blue awnings that can be seen scooting around the harbor are the taxi boats. They move between 17 stops that include all the prime waterfront destinations (including Fell's Point, Canton, and Fort McHenry in the summer). The boat captains are often chatting and make excellent tour guides.

BIKE

Biking in Baltimore as a mode of transportation is becoming more popular. Many attractions have iron bike racks that look like bicycles stationed out front, so cyclists have a convenient place to lock up their bikes (yes, lock your bike). New bike lanes are being added around the city to encourage biking, although narrow roads and hills will always be a factor and riding in traffic can be risky when the streets are crowded.

Excursions

If you have extra time and want to venture outside of Baltimore for a half- or full-day excursion, Havre de Grace and Westminster are two very different, yet equally alluring towns to visit. Havre de Grace provides the attractions of a historic bayside community, while Westminster offers Civil War history and a wonderful farm museum.

HAVRE DE GRACE

Havre de Grace is a beautiful little town in Harford County that sits at the head of the Chesapeake Bay and the mouth of the mighty Susquehanna River. Its name in French means "Harbor of Beauty" or "Harbor of Grace."

The city was once seriously considered for the location of the nation's capital. Havre de Grace was incorporated in 1785 and has a population of around 13,000. Its seaside-like atmosphere makes it a popular tourist and outdoor recreation destination.

Havre de Grace is halfway between Baltimore and Philadelphia. It was, at one time, a popular stop for stagecoaches traveling between the two cities. Between 1912 and 1950, it was home to the Havre de Grace Racetrack, a popular horse-racing track. Famous horses such as Man o' War, his son War Admiral, Seabiscuit, and Challedon raced here during its heyday. For years, the Havre de Grace Handicap was one of the most highly regarded races in the northeast. The track was sold in 1951 to the owners of two other Maryland racetracks (Pimlico Race Course and Laurel Park Racecourse). The new owners closed the Havre de Grace course and moved the track's racing allotment dates to their own facilities.

Havre de Grace shelters well over 100 historic structures, and the town is designated a National Historic District. The town was first mapped in 1799, and the structures that

Havre de Grace

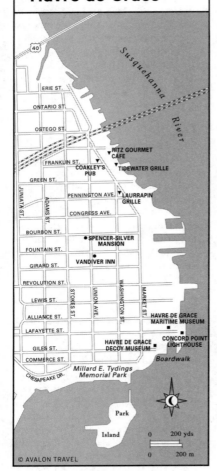

© AVALON TRAVEL

Wed.-Sat. 10am-5pm, Sun. 1pm-5pm, Oct. 15-Mar. 31 Sat. 10am-5pm, Sun. 1pm-5pm, $3) is a small window into the history of the upper Chesapeake Bay and lower Susquehanna River. Exhibits explore topics such as fishing, waterfowl hunting, lighthouses, navigation, the Native Americans who lived in the region, European settlers, and wooden boat building.

CONCORD POINT LIGHTHOUSE

The **Concord Point Lighthouse** (corner of Concord and Lafayette Sts., 410/939-3213, www.concordpointlighthouse.org, Apr.-Oct. Sat.-Sun. 1pm-5pm, free, donations appreciated) is a pretty little piece of history on the waterfront in Havre de Grace. The lighthouse was built in 1827 out of local granite and is one of the oldest lighthouses on the East Coast that has operated continuously. Now fully restored, it stands on a scenic stretch of the promenade. The climb up the 30-foot lighthouse tower is fairly short (as lighthouses go), so it's a fun activity to do with children (but they must be at least 42 inches tall). The lighthouse offers terrific views of the Susquehanna River and the Chesapeake Bay. There are a few informative exhibits at the Keeper's House (which used to be a bar) that give details on the lighthouse's first keeper, John O'Neil, and the history of the lighthouse. There is a gift shop.

HAVRE DE GRACE DECOY MUSEUM

The **Havre de Grace Decoy Museum** (215 Giles St., 410/939-3739, www.decoymuseum. com, Mon.-Sat. 10:30am-4:30pm, Sun. noon-4pm, $6) is more than a showcase for wooden birds. Decoys have been part of the culture on the Chesapeake Bay for centuries. Originally, they were not considered art, but were made purely to lure waterfowl within hunting range. Today decoys are an art form. Carvers create sophisticated reproductions of birds using century-old skills. This pretty little museum is home to one of the best collections of functional and decorative Chesapeake Bay decoys in existence. Visitors can learn the history of waterfowling on the upper Chesapeake Bay

remain today are of many different ages and architectural designs. Simple Victorian duplexes stand side by side with single-family homes and Queen Anne estates built by wealthy residents.

Sights
HAVRE DE GRACE MARITIME MUSEUM

The **Havre de Grace Maritime Museum** (100 Lafayette St., 410/939-4800, www.hdgmaritimemuseum.org, April 1-Oct.14

the Concord Point Lighthouse

The Susquehanna Museum at the Lock House (817 Conesteo Street, 410-939-5780, www.thelockhousemuseum.org, mid-April-Oct. Fri.-Sun. 1pm-5pm, free) is a museum inside a historic house, which was built in 1840 and home to one of the lock tenders for the Susquehanna and Tidewater Canal (which ran 45 miles between Havre de Grace and Wrightsville, Pennsylvania). It also served as the office for the Toll Collector. The two-story brick building was almost twice the size of other lock houses on the Canal (there were 29 locks total). Exhibits in the museum recreate life along the canal and provide details on Havre de Grace's role in the growth of the country.

Recreation

There are several **boat launch sites** in Havre de Grace. The first two are at the mouth of the Susquehanna River. One is north of the train bridge at the intersection of Otsego and Union Streets (on Water Street at Jean Roberts Memorial Park). The second is just downstream, off of Franklin Street by the Tidewater Grille (this is just for cartop boats since there is no ramp). A third launch site is at Tydings Park off Commerce Street, on the south side of town. This site is right on the Chesapeake Bay. It is important to know that boating near the Aberdeen Proving Ground south of the city is strictly forbidden. In addition to getting a fine for trespassing, landing anywhere on the proving grounds can be very dangerous because there are live munitions. Obey all signage in the area and respect the buoy markers.

Three miles northwest of Havre de Grace is the beautiful **Susquehanna State Park** (410/557-7994, www.dnr.state.md.us, daily 9am-sunset, Nov.-Feb. weekends only, $4). The park offers boating ($12 launch fee), hiking, mountain biking, kayaking, fishing, a playground, and picnicking. There are also several historic buildings on-site such as a 200-year-old gristmill (visitors can tour its four floors), a stone mansion, a barn, a tollhouse, and a miller's house. All buildings are

and also how decoys are made through exhibits, lectures, tours, and demonstrations. More than 1,200 decoys are on display. Annual festivals are held at the museum, and there is a nice little gift shop with decoys, books, and other waterfowl-related items.

TYDINGS PARK

Tydings Park (350 Commerce St. at the southern end of Union Ave., 410/939-1800) is a 22-acre park on the waterfront in Havre de Grace. It is situated at the head of the Chesapeake Bay and is the site of several annual festivals and concerts. The park facilities include a fishing pier, boat ramp, picnic area, tennis courts, gazebos, and a playground. It is also the starting point of the half-mile **Havre de Grace Promenade,** a waterfront walkway that goes past the Maritime Museum and continues to the Concord Point Lighthouse. The park is also known as the **Millard E. Tydings Memorial Park.**

open on weekends between Memorial Day and Labor Day from 10am-4pm. A section of the former **Susquehanna and Tidewater Canal** can be seen in the park. This canal was built in 1836 and connected Havre de Grace with Wrightsville, Pennsylvania. Mule-drawn barges made this an important commercial route for more than 50 years. To reach the park, take I-95 to exit 89, and then proceed west on Route 155 to Route 161. Turn right on Route 161 and then right again on Rock Run Road.

Food

Cold beer, good pub food, and friendly service can be found at **Coakley's Pub** (406 St. John St., 410/939-8888, www.coakleyspub.com, Mon.-Sat 11am-10pm, Sun. 11am-9pm, $4-24) on St. John Street. This cozy spot offers quality fare with a Chesapeake Bay flair (try the crab pretzel). The food and service are consistent, and the atmosphere is casual and inviting.

The ★ **Laurrapin Grille** (209 N. Washington St., 410/939-4956, www.laurrapin.com, Mon.-Thurs. 4pm-10pm, Fri. 4pm-2am, Sat. 11am-2am, Sun. noon-6:30pm, $11-25) is a contemporary American restaurant that specializes in seasonally inspired food. They take fresh local ingredients and turn them into delicious and creative items that take advantage of the bounty of the surrounding area. The result is a wonderful menu with dinner entrées that include crab cakes, lamb, pasta, salmon, and steak. It is obvious that great care goes into developing each menu item, and the result is fresh and tasty. The atmosphere has a bit of a bar feel, but the back room is quieter.

The **Havre de Grace Ritz Gourmet Café** (421 St. John St., 410/939-5858, www.havredegraceritzgourmetcafe.com, Mon.-Sat. 11am-9pm, Sun. 11am-4pm, $9-14) makes superb sandwiches and panini. Kate's Kickin' Cajun Shrimp Panino, the New Yorker Deli Sandwich, and the prime rib tartine are just a few of the delectable choices. They also offer salads, seasonal selections, and breakfast on weekends.

A popular waterfront restaurant is the **Tidewater Grille** (300 Franklin St., 410/939-3313, www.thetidewatergrille.com, Mon.-Fri. 11am-10pm, Sat.-Sun. 9am-10pm, $8-44). They offer a traditional seafood menu with a great view of the Susquehanna and Chesapeake headwaters. Ask for a seat by the window or sit on the patio when it's nice out. Free docking is available for those coming by boat.

Accommodations

The elegant **Vandiver Inn** (301 S. Union Ave., 410/939-5200, www.vandiverinn.com, $145-165) offers 18 guest rooms in three beautifully restored Victorian homes. Eight are in the Vandiver Inn mansion (built in 1886), and an additional 10 are in the adjacent Kent & Murphy Guest Houses. All have private bathrooms. Each guest is treated to a lovely breakfast, free in-room wireless access, and in-room cable television. The inn is within blocks of the Chesapeake Bay and within the city of Havre de Grace. Many special events are held at the inn, so if you are looking for a quiet stay with little activity, ask about events during your stay when you make a reservation.

The only Victorian mansion built of the stone in Havre de Grace is the **Spencer Silver Mansion** (200 Union Ave., 410/939-1485, www.spencersilvermansion.com, $85-160). This nicely restored 1896 home offers four guest rooms and a lovely carriage house for rent. A full breakfast is served each morning until 10:30am. The mansion is a short walk to the Chesapeake Bay and is near the attractions in downtown Havre de Grace. It is also pet friendly.

Five miles south of Havre de Grace is the **Hilton Garden Inn Aberdeen** (1050 Beards Hill Rd., 410-/272-1777, www.hiltongardeninn3.hilton.com, $179-189) in Aberdeen, Maryland. This modern hotel offers a fitness center and indoor pool. All rooms have 32-inch HD flat-screen televisions, microwaves, refrigerators, and complimentary wireless Internet.

Camping

Camping is available at **Susquehanna State Park** (888/432-2267, www.dnr.state.md.us, Apr.-Oct., $22.49-51.49 plus $4 park fee and a nightly park facility fee $4.51-4.61). They have 69 sites (six have electric and six have camper cabins). There are two comfort stations with hot showers.

Information and Services

For additional information on Havre de Grace, stop by the **Havre de Grace Office of Tourism & Visitor Center** (450 Pennington Ave., 410/939-2100) or visit www.explorehavredegrace.com.

Getting There

Havre de Grace is approximately one hour by car (37 miles) north of Baltimore. It is off I-95, on the southern side of the M. E. Tydings Memorial Bridge. Exit onto Route 155 and follow that road past the Susquehanna Museum and into the historic district of Havre de Grace.

WESTMINSTER

Westminster is the seat of Carroll County and has a population of around 18,000. It was founded in 1764 and incorporated in 1838. This picturesque town surrounded by primarily farmland and rolling terrain saw a cavalry battle known as Corbit's Charge fought right on the downtown streets during the Civil War. It was also the first locale in the country to offer rural mail delivery.

Westminster is also the home of the late Whittaker Chambers's farm. He hid the "pumpkin papers," which were the key to a controversial case concerning espionage during the Cold War, in a hollowed-out gourd here. The papers resulted in the 1950 conviction of former State Department official Alger Hiss. This evidence confirmed Hiss's perjury in front of Congress when he denied being a Soviet spy.

Westminster is also known for its above-average number of tornadoes. No fewer than four major tornadoes have touched down in Westminster in its recorded history, resulting in varying degrees of destruction.

Today, Westminster is a lovely little city with many artists and art galleries. It is also home to **McDaniel College** (2 College Hill, 410/848-7000, www.mcdaniel.edu), a private liberal arts and sciences college founded in 1867 with just under 3,000 students.

Sights
DOWNTOWN WESTMINSTER

Downtown Westminster offers a lovely historic district along Main Street with many old buildings and stories to surround them. The area is friendly to pedestrians and shelters many independent shops, galleries, and restaurants. Large trees line the streets, and there is plenty of parking in two parking decks and outdoor lots.

Many buildings on Main Street in Westminster have a long history, but none as varied as **Odd Fellows Hall** (140 E. Main St.). This plain, three-story brick building was erected in 1858 for $9,000 by the Salem Lodge No. 60 of the Independent Order of Odd Fellows. It was a central location for gatherings in Westminster.

Prior to the Civil War, the building was used by a local militia with Southern sympathies. Not long after the war, a comedian from Alabama performed at the hall and made jokes about President Grant and other officials in the government. As legend has it, the patrons did not appreciate the jokes and threw rocks at him. After being hit in the neck, the performer became upset and left the stage. The local sheriff offered him protection for the night, but the performer refused and went out back to saddle his horse. He was found dead behind the hall shortly after, having had his throat slit. Shortly after that day, and from then on, reports of people seeing a ghost behind the hall of a man engaged in monologue have been common. The building later became a town library, a saloon, a concert hall, and a newspaper office.

In 1912, the building was known as the Opera House, when the Odd Fellows created an opera room that became the first movie theater in town. In recent years it was home to the Opera House Printing Company, but at the time of writing, it was empty.

HISTORICAL SOCIETY OF CARROLL COUNTY

The **Historical Society of Carroll County** (210 E. Main St., 410/848-6494), on the east end of Westminster's downtown area, has exhibits on the heritage of Carroll County and the surrounding Piedmont area.

★ CARROLL COUNTY FARM MUSEUM

The **Carroll County Farm Museum** (500 S. Center St., 410/386-3880, www.ccgovernment.carr.org, Mon.-Sat. 9am-4:30pm, Sun. noon-4pm, adults $5, family $10) offers visitors a unique opportunity to see what rural life in the mid-19th century was like. Part of a 142-acre complex, the museum demonstrates how families had to be self-sufficient by producing everything they needed (food, household items, soap, yarn, etc.) right on their own land.

The museum features a three-story brick farmhouse and authentic farm buildings built in the 1850s, including a log barn, smokehouse, saddlery, broom shop, springhouse, and wagon shed. A guided tour conducted by costumed interpreters of the farmhouse's seven rooms is included with admission, as is a self-guided walking tour of the various exhibit buildings. The wagon shed houses the buggy that was used for the first rural mail delivery route. The route ran between Westminster and Uniontown. Although the route signaled the development of a sophisticated mail delivery system, many residents were not happy about it because they felt cut off from the rest of the community when they were no longer forced into taking regular trips into town to get news and socialize.

There are also public buildings on-site such as a firehouse, schoolhouse, and general store. Artifacts and antiques from the period (many

of which were donated by local families) are also on display. There are many live animals at the museum such as sheep, geese, pigs, goats, and horses, which make this a great place to bring children. There is also a gift store.

ART GALLERIES

At the west end of the downtown area, the **Carroll Arts Center** (91 W. Main St., 410/848-7272, Mon., Wed., Fri., and Sat. 10am-4pm, Tues. and Thurs. 10am-7pm) houses two locally focused art galleries, the **Tevis Gallery** and the **Community Gallery.** It also has a 263-seat theater where it hosts concerts, plays, lectures, recitals, and films year-round. In addition, there are a handful of independent galleries along Main Street and Liberty Street.

The **Esther Prangley Rice Gallery** (410/857-2595), in Peterson Hall at McDaniel College, features work by students and local artists.

WALKING TOURS

Walking tours are popular in Westminster, and brochures with self-guided tours are available at the **Visitor Center** (210 E. Main St., 410/848-1388). One of the most popular is the Ghost Walk brochure that tells tales of local hauntings. The **Carroll County Public Library** (50 E. Main St., 410/386-4488) also offers guided one-hour ghost tours.

Shopping

Many national stores and chain restaurants can be found along Route 140, but the historic downtown area offers a mix of locally owned retail shops and restaurants. Westminster blends cultural experiences with the atmosphere of a small town.

The **Downtown Westminster Farmers Market** (Conaway Parking Lot, Railroad Avenue and Emerald Hill Lane) is held on Saturday mid-May through mid-November (8am-noon). It is a "producers-only" market and offers fresh produce, baked goods, flowers, and local honey.

Food

AMERICAN

A nice and cozy casual neighborhood restaurant is **Rafael's** (32 W. Main St., 410/840-1919, www.rafaelsrestaurant.com, Mon.-Thurs. 11am-9:30pm, Fri. 11am-10:30pm, Sat. noon-10:30pm, Sun. noon-9pm, breakfast Sat.-Sun. 8am-1pm, $7-19). They have good food and reasonable prices and are especially known for their hamburgers. They serve lunch and dinner daily and breakfast on weekends. The staff is friendly, and the food is consistent.

A popular local eatery with homebrewed beer is **Johansson's Dining House** (4 W. Main St., 410/876-0101, www.johanssons-dininghouse.com, Mon.-Thurs. 11am-10pm, Fri.-Sat. 11am-11pm, Sun. 10am-10pm, $8-31). This casual restaurant serves a varied menu (filet mignon, seafood, pizza, and sandwiches) and homemade desserts. The place has a lot of character, a good decor, and is in the heart of Westminster. The 1913 building opened as a restaurant in 1994.

IRISH

O'Lordans Irish Pub (14 Liberty St., 410/876-0000, www.olordansirishpub.com, Sun. and Tues.-Thurs. 11am-10pm, Fri.-Sat. 11am-11pm, $8-30) is a lively spot on Liberty Street. The pub has a traditional Irish pub feel with a fireplace, murals, dark wood, plank floors, and a stone facade. The bartenders are witty, and the food portions are ginormous and delicious. The pub offers a great happy hour menu and has developed a loyal fan base.

MEXICAN

Papa Joe's Mexican Restaurant (250 Englar Rd., 410/871-2505, www.papajoeswestminstermd.com, Mon.-Sat. 11am-10pm, $9-18) is the local favorite for Mexican food. They offer traditional Mexican dishes in a friendly, colorful atmosphere. The restaurant is family owned and operated, and they have fun specials such as a salsa bar night on Monday. The fajitas are a signature dish and come smothered in a wonderful cream sauce, which is a little different from traditional fajitas. Seating is limited, but there is outdoor seating when the weather is nice.

TEAROOM

The best tearoom in Westminster (okay, maybe it's the only tearoom in Westminster, but it's a good one) is **Gypsy's Tearoom** (111 Stoner Ave., 410/857-0058, www.gypsystearoom.com, Tues.-Sat. 10am-5pm, $9-30) in the oldest home in Westminster, which was built by town founder William Winchester. This English-style tearoom serves everything from tea with hors d'oeuvres to full-service dinners. They also offer event planning for special occasions. The tearoom is located in a rural setting near town. It also has a gift shop.

Accommodations

Accommodations right in Westminster are mainly limited to chain hotels such as the **Westminster Days Inn** (25 S. Cranberry Rd., 410/857-0500, www.daysinn.com, $79-89), and the **Best Western Westminster Catering and Conference Center** (451 WMC Dr., 410/857-1900, www.book.bestwestern.com, $113-117).

Eight miles southwest of town on the way to New Windsor is the **Yellow Turtle Inn Bed and Brunch** (111 S. Springdale Ave., New Windsor, 410/635-3000, www.yellowturtleinn.net, $120-199). This lovely bed-and-breakfast sits on three acres in the country and offers eight guest rooms with private bathrooms and two whirlpool suites.

Information and Services

Additional information on Westminster can be found at the **Carroll County Visitor Center** (210 E. Main St., 410/848-1388, www.carrollcountytourism.org, Mon.-Sat. 9am-5pm, Sun. 10am-2pm).

Getting There

Westminster is 35 miles northwest of Baltimore and 56 miles north of Washington DC. Route 140 runs through Westminster from east to west and Route 97 runs north to south.

Annapolis and Southern Maryland

Capital city Annapolis has been the crown jewel of Maryland throughout its rich history. The city is known as the sailing capital of the world, as the birthplace of American horse racing, and for having more 18th-century buildings than any other city in the United States. Annapolis has remained extremely well preserved as a colonial-era town despite its popularity with tourists and businesses. It is a fun place to visit, a great place to people-watch, and a fantastic place to eat seafood.

Southern Maryland offers a relaxed atmosphere compared to the bustle of Annapolis. The cities along the western shore of the Chesapeake Bay vary from sleepy seaside towns to active sailing communities. Crisscrossed with scenic roadways and state and national parks, this area makes for a lovely excursion.

PLANNING YOUR TIME

Annapolis and Southern Maryland can be explored in a long weekend or over several day trips from Baltimore. The distance between Annapolis and Point Lookout is approximately 82 miles (about two hours by car). Annapolis and Solomons Island are good choices for overnight stays or for boating on the Chesapeake Bay.

The closest airport to Annapolis is **Baltimore Washington International Thurgood Marshall Airport (BWI)** (410/859-7040, www.bwiairport.com), but parts of Southern Maryland are actually closer to **Ronald Reagan Washington National Airport (DCA)** (703/417-8000, www.metwashairports.com), just outside Washington DC in Arlington, Virginia (Point Lookout is 79 miles from DCA and 99 miles from BWI). Normally, the lowest airfares can be obtained by flying into BWI, so it pays to explore both options. Once you arrive in the region, it is best to explore by car. Parking is plentiful except for right in downtown Annapolis, but even there, most hotels have parking available and public garages can be found.

Previous: the docks at Sandy Point State Park; Maryland State House. **Above:** Annapolis Harbor.

Look for ★ to find recommended
sights, activities, dining, and lodging.

Highlights

★ **Annapolis City Dock:** This public waterfront boasts beautiful scenery, impressive yachts, and many shops and restaurants (page 80).

★ **U.S. Naval Academy:** More than 60,000 men and women have graduated from this prestigious school and gone on to serve in the U.S. Navy and Marine Corps (page 80).

★ **Calvert Marine Museum:** This wonderful museum shares the whole history of the Chesapeake Bay, focusing on prehistoric times, the natural environment, and the bay's unique maritime heritage (page 94).

★ **Calvert Cliffs State Park:** More than just a beautiful sandy beach with stunning cliffs, this park offers superb fossil hunting (page 96).

★ **St. Mary's City's Outdoor Museum of History and Archaeology:** This living re-creation teaches visitors about life in Maryland's original capital city during colonial times (page 98).

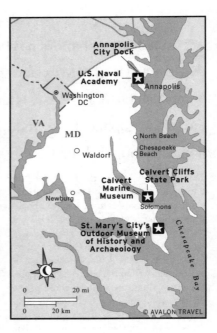

Annapolis and Southern Maryland

Silver Spring
College Park
WASHINGTON DC
Largo
Suitland
Upper Marlboro
Oxon Hill
Clinton
VIRGINIA
Accokeek
White Plains
Waldorf
POPLAR HILL RD
Malcolm
Indian Head
Pomfret
White Plains Park
Bryantown
Smallwood State Park
Marbury
La Plata
Hughesville
Port Tobacco
Mallows Bay
Welcome
Charlotte Hall
Mechanicsville
Popes Creek
Newburg
Chaptico
Tompkinsville
Cobb Island
St. Clement's Island
Coltons Point
Piney Point
St. George Island
VIRGINIA

ANNAPOLIS
U.S. NAVAL ACADEMY
ANNAPOLIS CITY DOCK

North Beach
Chesapeake Beach
King's Landing Park
Huntingtown
Prince Frederick
Chesapeake Bay
St. Leonard
Flag Ponds Nature Park
Broomes Island
Lusby
Jefferson Patterson Park And Museum
Greenwell State Park
CALVERT CLIFFS STATE PARK
Loveville
Hollywood
Solomons
CALVERT MARINE MUSEUM
Leonardtown
Lexington Park
Great Mills
Valley Lee
St. Mary's City
ST. MARY'S CITY'S OUTDOOR MUSEUM OF HISTORY AND ARCHAEOLOGY
Wynne
Ridge
Point Lookout State Park

Patuxent River
Potomac River

0   10 mi
0   10 km

© AVALON TRAVEL

Annapolis

Maryland's capital city of Annapolis is a picturesque and historic seaport on the Chesapeake Bay. It is widely known as the "Sailing Capital of the World," due to its popularity as a sailing port for both resident and international vessels. Literally hundreds of sailboats cruise the surrounding waters year-round, with regular races being held several times a week during the summer.

In 1649, a settlement named Providence was founded on the northern shore of the Severn River by Puritans exiled from Virginia. The settlement was later moved to the southern shore and renamed several times before finally becoming Annapolis, a tribute to Princess Anne of Denmark and Norway, who was in line to be the queen of Great Britain. The city was incorporated in 1708. Annapolis prospered as a port and grew substantially during the 18th century. It even served as the temporary capital of the United States in 1783.

From its earliest days more than 300 years ago, Annapolis was known as a center for wealth, social activities, and a thriving cultural scene. It was also known for its cozy pubs and abundant seafood restaurants, which welcomed prosperous visitors from all over the globe. Annapolis was also the birthplace of American horse racing—several of the original stock of the American Thoroughbred line entered through its port, and people came from all over the colonies to watch and bet on horse races. George Washington is even said to have lost a few shillings at the local track.

Annapolis is a great place to visit and explore. It has a vibrant waterfront with many shops and restaurants, and is quaint and historical, yet welcomes an international crowd. The city was designed more like the capital cities in Europe with a baroque plan, rather than the grid layout customary to U.S. cities. Circles with radiating streets highlight specific buildings, such as St. Anne's Episcopal Church (one of the first churches in the city)

and the State House. Numerous magnificent homes were built in the city's early days and hosted many of the founders of our country for lavish social events. Today Annapolis it is home to the U.S. Naval Academy and St. John's College.

The most popular neighborhood for visitors is the Historic Downtown area. This is where the scenic waterfront and City Dock are located, as well as charming boutiques, fabulous restaurants, and historic homes. Another popular tourist area is Eastport, just south of Historic Downtown. This area is home to "Restaurant Row" and offers sweeping Chesapeake Bay views and a fun-loving, slightly funky atmosphere.

SIGHTS
★ Annapolis City Dock

The **Annapolis City Dock** (Dock Street on the waterfront) is the heart of the downtown area. Annapolis boasts more 18th-century buildings than any other American city, and many of these charming structures line the dock area. Locally owned shops, boutiques, and souvenir stands beckoning shoppers off the busy streets and waterfront restaurants help fuel the energy of this hot spot. The public waterfront is where visitors can take in the beautiful scenery while getting a good look at many expensive yachts. The waterfront area is also known as **Ego Alley,** since a steady parade of high-end sailing and motor vessels can be seen going by on nearly every weekend and evening.

★ U.S. Naval Academy

The **U.S. Naval Academy** (121 Blake Rd., 410/293-1000, www.usna.edu) was founded in 1845 by the secretary of the navy. Since that time, more than 60,000 men and women have graduated from this prestigious school and gone on to serve in the U.S. Navy or the U.S. Marine Corps. The student body is referred

Annapolis

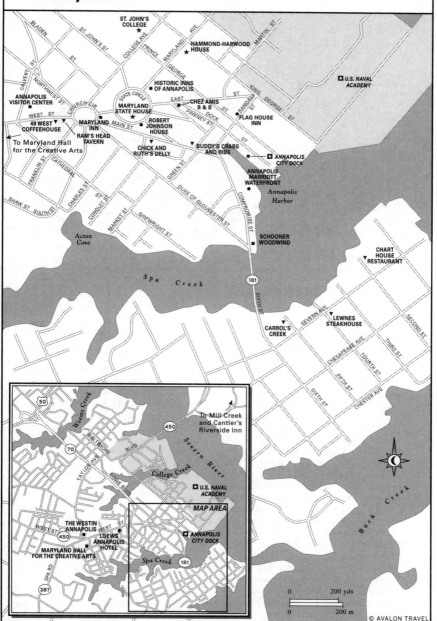

© AVALON TRAVEL

Annapolis City Dock

The Chesapeake Bay

The Chesapeake Bay is the largest estuary in the country. Its drainage basin includes more than 64,000 square miles with more than 150 tributaries. The bay is approximately 200 miles long, starting at the mouth of the Susquehanna River on the northern end and the Atlantic Ocean on the southern end. At its widest point it is 30 miles across, and at its narrowest point it is 2.8 miles.

The Chesapeake Bay is part of the **Intracoastal Waterway,** a 3,000-mile navigable inland water route that runs along the Atlantic and Gulf coasts. The bay links the Delaware River with the Albemarle Sound in North Carolina.

More than 300 species of fish and countless shellfish live in the Chesapeake Bay. Maryland is known for its abundant local seafood, especially the famed blue crab, which can be found on nearly every menu in the region.

Many shorebirds live all or part of their lives on the Chesapeake Bay or in the bordering wetlands, including bald eagles, great blue herons, ospreys, peregrine falcons, and piping plovers.

The Chesapeake Bay is a prominent feature in Maryland. During the second half of the 19th century and the first half of the 20th, the bay was a vital link between major cities in Maryland and Virginia, such as Baltimore and Norfolk, and was home to passenger steamships and packet boats (boats that kept regular schedules and were originally designed to transport mail, passengers, and freight). When road crossings were built in the late 20th century, making the steamboat industry obsolete, the bay became known for its seafood production, with a focus on the blue crab and oyster industries. By the mid-20th century, nearly 9,000 full-time watermen worked on the bay. Plentiful oyster harvests were the inspiration for Maryland's state boat, the **skipjack,** which remains the only type of working boat in the country that operates under sail.

Today, the Chesapeake Bay produces less seafood than it did in the last century due to runoff from many mainland areas, overharvesting, and the invasion of foreign marine species. The **Chesapeake Bay Foundation** (www.cbf.org), headquartered in Annapolis, is the largest conservation organization dedicated to the well-being of the Chesapeake Bay watershed.

to as the "Brigade of Midshipmen." The academy is directly northeast of downtown Annapolis at the confluence of the Severn River and the Chesapeake Bay. Guided walking tours of the more than 300-acre campus led by professional guides are offered to visitors through the **Armel-Leftwich Visitor Center** (52 King George St., 410/293-8687, www.usnabsd.com, Mar.-Dec. daily 9am-5pm, Jan. and Feb. Mon.-Fri. 9am-4pm, Sat.-Sun. 9am-5pm, $10.50). Tours are 1.25 hours and are offered throughout most of the day while the visitors center is open; they cannot be booked in advance. Tours provide a close-up look at the imposing marble buildings and monuments on campus, and cover topics such as history, architecture, traditions, and life as a midshipman.

Access to the Naval Academy grounds is limited. Government-issued photo identification is required for admission. Parking is available at the stadium on Rowe Boulevard inside the Noah Hillman Parking Garage (enter from Duke of Gloucester or Main Street). There are also parking meters around City Dock.

Maryland State House

The **Maryland State House** (100 State Circle, 410/260-6445, www.msa.maryland. gov, daily 9am-5pm, free, donations appreciated) is the oldest legislative house in the country that has been in continual use. It is also the oldest peacetime capitol. The State House was built in the 1770s, and the first Maryland legislature meeting was held here in 1779. The building is architecturally significant—its dome is the largest wooden dome constructed without nails in the United States.

During 1783 and 1784, when Annapolis served as the U.S. capital, the State House was home to the U.S. government. It was there that two significant events took place. The first was that George Washington resigned his commission before the Continental Congress on December 23, 1783, and the second was that the Treaty of Paris ending the Revolutionary War was ratified here on January 14, 1784. Self-guided tour information is available on the first floor of the State House.

St. John's College

St. John's College (60 College Ave.,

the Maryland State House

410/263-2371, www.sjca.edu) is the oldest college in town, despite the misconception that this distinction belongs to the U.S. Naval Academy. The school was founded in 1696 as the King William's School. It is the third-oldest college in the country behind Harvard and William & Mary. One block from the State House (across King George Street from the Naval Academy), the school sits on 32 scenic acres adorned with stately brick buildings, tree-lined paths, and sprawling lawn. It is also a National Historic Landmark with several 18th-century buildings.

St. John's College offers a liberal arts curriculum. Because of its location at the confluence of the Chesapeake Bay and the Severn River, the school offers strong sailing, crew, and rowing opportunities. Each April, St. John's College and the Naval Academy play each other in a highly anticipated croquet match on the front lawn of the St. John's campus. Both teams dress for the event, which has become a spirited spectacle.

St. John's College adopted the "Great Books" program of study in 1937. This mandatory four-year program requires students to read Western civilization's prominent authors in philosophy, theology, math, science, poetry, music, and literature. Classes are then discussion based. The school uses a series of manuals in place of textbooks, lectures, and exams. Grades are only released at the student's request and are based on papers and class participation.

Hammond-Harwood House

There are many historic homes in Annapolis. If you can only choose one to visit, the **Hammond-Harwood House** (19 Maryland Ave., 410/263-4683, www.hammondharwoodhouse.org, Apr.-Dec. Tues.-Sun. noon-5pm, Jan.-Mar. appointment only, $10) should be it. It is one of the most superb British colonial homes in the country and the most impressive in Annapolis. Designed in the Anglo-Palladian style (a variation of the classical Roman revival style), construction began on the house in 1774. It was completed

sometime after 1776, but the exact year is unknown. The home is special because it offers perfectly preserved architecture and one of the best collections of furniture and decorative art from the 18th century in Maryland. It is a National Historic Landmark.

Fifty-minute walk-in tours begin at the top of each hour and provide insight into the history of the house, information on its architect and the people who lived in the home, and the opportunity to learn about the collections, such as a large collection of the works of Charles Willson Peale, a painter well known for his Revolutionary War period portraits. Visitors can also tour the garden at no extra cost. In-depth, two-hour architectural tours of the home are offered by appointment for $20.

St. Anne's Episcopal Church

St. Anne's Episcopal Church (1 Church Circle, 410/267-9333, www.stannes-annapolis.org, free) was the first church in Annapolis. The original structure was established in 1692 and completed in 1704 and was one of 30 original Anglican parishes in Maryland. Its bell was donated by Queen Anne. The original 65-foot-by-30-foot structure was razed in 1775 to make way for reconstruction of the second St. Anne's Episcopal Church on the same grounds. Building of the new church was delayed due to the Revolutionary War but was finally finished in 1792. The new church was larger and more structurally sound, but burned down on Valentine's Day in 1858 due to a furnace fire. The church that stands in Church Circle today was built in 1858 (although the steeple was finished in 1866). Its design incorporated part of the old tower. The clock in the church steeple actually belongs to the city due to a special agreement it made with the church when a city clock was needed. Visitors to St. Anne's can examine the church's Romanesque revival architecture with its original archways, pews, and stained glass windows. They can also visit the first cemetery in the city, which is located on the grounds. Four Sunday worship services are held weekly at 8am, 9:30am, 11:15am, and 5:30pm.

ENTERTAINMENT AND EVENTS

Nightlife

Annapolis harbors one of the best little venues in the mid-Atlantic for intimate concerts with big-name artists. **Rams Head on Stage** (33 West St., 410/268-4545, www.ramsheadonstage.com) is the performance venue at the popular **Rams Head Tavern** (www.ramsheadtavern.com), which has been a fixture in Annapolis for more than two decades. Rams Head on Stage is a reserved-seating venue with food and drink service during the shows. Nearly all shows at this venue are 21 and older. There are no bad seats in the house, and the bands play right in front of the tables. Samples of recent performances include the Smithereens, Cowboy Junkies, The English Beat, and Los Lobos.

The **49 West Coffeehouse, Winebar & Gallery** (49 West St., 410/626-9796, www.49westcoffeehouse.com) is a great place to kick back and enjoy coffee or a great martini (depending on the time of day) and listen to jazz. They host live music most nights and jazz for brunch on Sunday. The establishment is also an art gallery and features different artists monthly. They offer a neighborhood feel near the downtown area and serve breakfast, lunch, and dinner daily.

Performing Arts

The **Maryland Hall for the Creative Arts** (801 Chase St., 410/263-5544, www.marylandhall.org) is an active center for the performing arts. Resident companies include a symphony, opera, ballet, and chorale, offering performances throughout the year in the 800-seat theater.

Events

The **Maryland Renaissance Festival** (1821 Crownsville Rd., Crownsville, 410/266-7304, www.rennfest.com) is a long-standing tradition in Maryland. After passing through the entry gates to the festival, visitors become part of a wooded, 25-acre 16th-century English village named "Revel Grove." There are plenty of activities to keep the entire family busy, with shows on 10 major stages, a jousting arena, games, crafts, five pubs, and of course, tons of delicious food. The festival is open on Saturday, Sunday, and Labor Day Monday from the end of August through late October. The festival is held in Crownsville, eight miles northwest of Annapolis.

Many events are scheduled throughout the year in Annapolis, including several footraces such as the **Annapolis Ten Miler** (www.annapolisstriders.org), festivals, food celebrations, and art shows. For a list of events, visit www.downtownannapolis.org.

SHOPPING

There are many boutiques and locally owned shops in downtown Annapolis. Maryland Avenue, Main Street, and West Street are great places to start a shopping adventure. Some examples of the types of stores you can browse include jewelry stores, maritime stores, home furnishings shops, women's boutiques, antiques stores, glass shops, and fine-art galleries.

They'll Scare Ya Sober

Sometimes referred to as "a drinking town with a sailing problem," Annapolis has long known how to get its drink on. The city is filled with all kinds of history, including tales of hair-raising hauntings at local watering holes. **Annapolis Tours and Crawls** (443/534-0043, www.toursandcrawls.com, $18) offers a great two-hour haunted pub crawl through the downtown area. They take guests through some of the most haunted taverns, pubs, and bars while telling stories that are sure to give you goose bumps. Each stop is about 30 minutes and can be different each time. This drinking tour is a great way to learn the history of some of the best taverns in town, with an added twist. Tours meet at the top of Main Street and are for people 21 and over.

SPORTS AND RECREATION

Two-hour sailing cruises can be booked on two beautiful, 74-foot wooden schooners through **Schooner *Woodwind* Annapolis Sailing Cruises** (410/263-7837, www.schoonerwoodwind.com, mid-Apr.-late Oct. daily, $44). Cruises depart from the **Annapolis Waterfront Hotel** (across from the City Dock) and sail by the U.S. Naval Academy and into the Chesapeake Bay. Private cruises can also be booked.

Pirate Adventures on the Chesapeake (311 3rd St., 410/263-0002, www.chesapeakepirates.com, mid-Apr.-Memorial Day and Labor Day-Oct. Sat.-Sun., Memorial Day-Labor Day daily, sail times at 9:30am, 11am, 12:30pm, 2pm, 3:30pm, and 5pm, $22) is a children's adventure aboard a pirate ship. Kids quickly become part of a pirate tale with face painting, costumes, and a lot of imagination. Once aboard, they learn the rules of the ship, read treasure maps, and find a message in a bottle. They even engage in battle using water cannons. Cruises leave from the company's office in Annapolis. Face painting and dress-up begin 30 minutes prior to departure; sailing time is 75 minutes.

The **Baltimore & Annapolis Trail** (www.traillink.com/trail/baltimore-and-annapolis-trail.aspx) is a 13-mile paved rail trail that is part of the former route of the Baltimore & Annapolis Railroad. It opened in 1990 and runs from Boulters Way in Annapolis to Dorsey Road in Glen Burnie. The southern part of the trail is primarily residential and winds through pleasant suburban neighborhoods. The northern part of the trail is much more urban.

An extremely popular nearby park right on the Chesapeake Bay is **Sandy Point State Park** (1100 E. College Pkwy., 410/974-2149, www.dnr.state.md.us, daily Jan.-Oct. 7am-sunset, Nov.-Dec. 7am-5pm, boating 24 hours year-round, $7). This lovely 786-acre park, 10 miles northeast of Annapolis at the western terminus of the Chesapeake Bay Bridge, used to be the site of a ferry that shuttled people and cars between the mainland and the Eastern Shore prior to completion of the bridge. Today it offers a wide sandy beach, swimming area, bathhouse, boat landing, picnic areas, and stunning view of the Chesapeake Bay. It is also a great place for bird-watching. The park is off Route 50 at exit 32.

FOOD

American

The premier steak house in Annapolis is ★ **Lewnes Steakhouse** (401 4th St., 410/263-1617, www.lewnessteakhouse.com, Sun. 4pm-10pm, Mon.-Thurs. 4pm-10pm, Fri.-Sat. 4pm-10:30pm, $19-44). This independent restaurant opened in 1921 and is still owned by the same local family. They serve prime steak that is properly prepared to sear in the flavorful juice while browning the exterior. Their menu includes filet, prime rib, porterhouse, New York strip, rib eye, and some non-beef selections such as tuna steak and lobster. They also have an extensive, well-selected wine list. The food and wonderful staff are the lure of this restaurant, and the atmosphere is well suited for a romantic evening. This is a restaurant that really cares whether the guests are satisfied.

A local institution, the **Rams Head Tavern** (33 West St., 410/268-4545, www.ramsheadtavern.com, Sun. 10am-2am with brunch, Mon.-Sat. 11am-2am, $9-30) has been serving tasty pub food since 1989. This friendly, multiroom tavern (including the original space in the cozy downstairs) serves sandwiches, burgers, and pub favorites such as shepherd's pie, brats and mash, chicken stuffed with crab imperial, and shrimp and grits. They have a terrific brunch menu on Sunday with a wonderful variety of entrées that are beautifully presented. They also serve beer from the Fordham Brewing Company, which used to be on-site. The atmosphere is classically "pub" with warm, friendly service and convivial patrons. This can be a busy place on concert nights at the adjoining Rams Head on Stage.

Quarter-pound crab cakes with no filler,

seasoned to perfection, are the calling card of a local favorite named ★ **Chick & Ruth's Delly** (165 Main St., 410/269-6737, www.chickandruths.com, daily 6:30am-11:30pm, $6-33). Just a block from the State House, the sandwich shop was opened by Chick and Ruth Levitt in 1965, and it has been growing ever since. Specialty sandwiches named after politicians augment the traditional Jewish deli fare, along with seafood, pizza, wraps, burgers, and tasty ice-cream treats. This is a touch of New York with an Annapolis flair. They are open for breakfast, lunch, and dinner.

Vin 909 Winecafe (909 Bay Ridge Ave., 410/990-1846, www.vin909.com, $12-19) is a wine-tasting café. They offer more than 35 types of wine by the glass and an extensive selection of beer. The café is in what once was a private residence, a bit off the beaten path south of the historic area of Annapolis (across Spa Creek). Prices for wine and food are reasonable, and there is frequently a wait for a table. They specialize in pizza, panini, and plates to share. The ambience is cozy and modern with wooden floors and low lighting. There is an outdoor patio with seating when the weather is nice.

Crab Houses

If you like seafood, you can't visit Annapolis without eating local blue crabs. *The* place to go for the authentic crab house experience is ★ **Cantler's Riverside Inn** (458 Forest Beach Rd., 410/757-1311, www.cantlers.com, Sun.-Thurs. 11am-10pm, Fri.-Sat. 11am-11pm, $8-32), a short distance from the downtown area and accessible by both car and boat. It is situated on a cove right on the water in a mostly residential neighborhood and sells local steamed crabs by the dozen (in all sizes) as well as offering other fresh seafood like crab cakes, shrimp, and oysters. They also serve pizza and sandwiches for non-seafood eaters. This is not a fancy place; it is a place to relax, get messy picking crabs, and meet new friends. They have indoor seating, a covered deck, and outdoor picnic tables. This used to be where the locals went, but in recent years it has become a popular tourist restaurant also. They also have a large bar inside the dining room. Word of warning: Don't rub your eyes with Old Bay seasoning on your hands.

Another popular crab house right in the historic downtown area is **Buddy's Crabs and Ribs** (100 Main St., 410/626-1100, www.buddysonline.com, Mon.-Thurs.

the Reuben sandwich at Chick & Ruth's Delly, made with freshly baked rye bread

Feeling Crabby?

Cantler's Riverside Inn in Annapolis offers an authentic crab house experience.

Maryland is known for its blue crabs, and the full "crab" experience can be enjoyed at a number of traditional crab houses throughout the bay region. For those new to the authentic crab experience, be prepared that this is a casual event, but not necessarily a cheap one. Traditional crab houses will often have long tables spread with brown paper and equipped with wooden mallets, claw crackers, and picks. Cold beer can accompany the appetizer, main course, and dessert. Patrons bring a lot of time, good cheer, and their appetites. Eating crabs is a social and messy event, but it is also one of the best experiences on the Chesapeake Bay.

Where to crack a claw:

- **Abner's Crab House** (3748 Harbor Rd., Chesapeake Beach, 410/257-3689, www.abnerscrabhouse.com)

- **Bo Brooks Crab House** (2780 Lighthouse Point, Baltimore, 410/558-0202, www.bobrooks.com)

- **Cantler's Riverside Inn** (458 Forest Beach Rd., Annapolis, 410/757-1311, www.cantlers.com)

- **Captain James Crab House** (2127 Boston St., Baltimore, 410/327-8600, www.captainjameslanding.com)

- **Hamilton's Canton Dockside** (3301 Boston St., Baltimore, 410/276-8900, www.cantondockside.com)

- **Mike's Restaurant and Crab House** (3030 Riva Rd., Riva, 410/956-2784, www.mikescrabhouse.com)

- **Thursday's Steak and Crabhouse** (4851 Riverside Dr., Galesville, 410/867-7200)

11:30am-9:30pm, Fri. 11:30am-10pm, Sat. 11am-11pm, Sun. 9:30am-9pm, $11-39). This lively icon on Main Street is a family-owned restaurant and also the largest restaurant in Annapolis. They specialize in serving large groups and also give special pricing to kids. Steamed crabs are the entrée of choice at Buddy's, but the homemade crab cakes are also a front-runner. Buddy's has a wide menu for both the seafood lover and the non-seafood eater and offers three all-you-can-eat buffets. The first is their soup, salad, and pasta bar for $8.95 (offered Mon.-Fri. 11:30am-3pm), the second is their seafood dinner buffet for $22.95 (Fri. 4pm-9pm and Sat. 11am-9pm), and the third is their Sunday brunch for $14.95 (Sun. 9:30am-1:30pm).

Italian

If you're looking for good pizza in a family atmosphere and want to get away from the crowds of the downtown area, go to **Squisito Pizza and Pasta** (2625 Riva Rd., 410/266-1474, www.squisitopizzaandpasta. com, Sun.-Thurs. 11am-10pm, Fri.-Sat. 11am-11pm, $7-16). This casual restaurant serves delicious pizza, pasta, and sandwiches at very reasonable prices. They are a small franchised chain with a handful of locations (all in Maryland). Order at the main counter and then take a seat. A server will bring you your meal. This is a very casual restaurant that is popular with families with children.

Seafood

A great place for local seafood and waterfront dining is **Carrol's Creek** (410 Severn Ave., 410/263-8102, www.carrolscreek.com, Mon.-Thurs. 11:30am-9pm, Fri.-Sat. 11:30am-10pm, Sun. 10am-8:30pm, $7-34). A short walk from the historic area across the Spa Creek Bridge, the bright-red building is easy to spot along Restaurant Row in Eastport. The menu offers local seafood, fresh fish, steak, chicken, and vegetarian dishes. Their Southwestern scallops are to die for. They also have a large wine list. The restaurant is locally owned and run, and much of the staff has been there

for decades. There is plenty of free parking. Reservations are recommended (ask for a seat by the windows).

The **Chart House Restaurant** (300 2nd St., 410/268-7166, www.chart-house.com, brunch Sun. 10am-2pm, dinner Mon.-Thurs. 4:30pm-9pm, Fri.-Sat. 4:30pm-10pm, Sun. 2pm-9pm, $20-43) offers fantastic waterfront views of the City Dock and is within walking distance of the historic district. The restaurant is a part of an upscale national chain and is housed in a nice historic building. The menu is heavily weighted toward seafood and steak, with fresh fish, crab, lobster, filet, and surf and turf. They also offer chicken and salads. The food and decor are above average, which is reflected in the prices, but the restaurant has a great location and the service is excellent. Reservations are recommended.

Another lovely waterfront restaurant is the **Severn Inn** (1993 Baltimore Annapolis Blvd., 410/349-4000, www.severninn.com, Sun. brunch buffet 10am-2pm, $36; lunch Mon.-Sat. 11:30am-2:30pm, dinner Mon.-Sat. 5pm-close, closed Mon. Jan.-Mar., $14-45), situated on the east side of the Naval Academy Bridge, overlooking Annapolis and the Severn River. They describe themselves as a "modern American seafood house" and serve local and nonlocal seafood and other dishes such as a wonderful filet mignon. They have a pleasant decor inside with white tablecloths and a comfortable, yet airy feel to the dining room as well as a large waterfront deck with pretty blue market umbrellas (open after April). Sunset is especially scenic, and if you're an oyster lover, grabbing a drink and a few oysters while watching the sun go down is a combination that's hard to beat.

ACCOMMODATIONS
$100-200

If you are looking for charming accommodations in a historic property, the **Historic Inns of Annapolis** (58 State Circle, 410/263-2641, www.historicinnsofannapolis. com, $120-270) offers three boutique hotels housed in 17th- and 18th- century buildings.

The **Maryland Inn** (16 Church Circle) has 44 guest rooms within view of the State House, Main Street, and the waterfront. The inn was built in the late 1700s and has hosted presidents, statesmen, and political dignitaries. The decor includes Victorian-era furnishings. It has a fitness center on-site, a restaurant, and a Starbucks. The **Governor Calvert House** (58 State Circle) is across the street from the Maryland State House and is one of the oldest buildings in Annapolis (built in 1695). It has 51 guest rooms, a colonial garden, meeting space, Internet, cable television, and views of the State House. Rooms are small, but this was originally a private home and was even the residence of two former Maryland governors. This property is where guests for all three historic properties check in. The **Robert Johnson House** (23 State Circle) is a smaller hotel with 29 guest rooms. This brick home was built in 1773 and has views of the Governor's Mansion and the State House. The house has Georgian-style architecture and is furnished with 19th-century furniture.

An alternative in this price range is the

Hampton Inn & Suites Annapolis (124 Womack Dr., 410/571-0200, www.hamptoninn3.hilton.com, $109-134). The hotel is in a business park four miles from the historic area of Annapolis. The 117 rooms are comfortable and come with complimentary wireless Internet, a mini fridge, 37-inch television, and free breakfast. The hotel is pet friendly.

$200-300

For a comfy bed-and-breakfast stay, the lovely ★ **Chez Amis Bed and Breakfast** (85 East St., 410/263-6631, www.chezamis.com, $202-228) offers four beautiful rooms and wonderful service. Each room in this 1890s home has a private bathroom, a television, and free wireless Internet. A delicious three-course breakfast is served each day at 9am, and cookies and refreshments are available all day. The bed-and-breakfast is within walking distance to downtown Annapolis, but a complimentary shuttle is offered to restaurants. The owners live in the bottom floor of the home.

The **Flag House Inn** (26 Randall St., 410/280-2721, www.flaghouseinn.com,

Governor Calvert House

$189-350) is a wonderful bed-and-breakfast with off-street parking in historic Annapolis. Just a half block from the City Dock, this comfortable, friendly inn is a great home base for exploring Annapolis. They offer four guest rooms and a two-room suite with private bathrooms and a full hot breakfast each morning.

Over $300

Fabulous waterfront views can be found at the **Annapolis Waterfront Hotel** (80 Compromise St., 888/773-0786, www.annapoliswaterfront.com, $335-599). This Marriott hotel is the only waterfront hotel in Annapolis, and many of the rooms overlook the Chesapeake Bay and some have balconies (other rooms view Annapolis Harbor and the downtown area). The hotel is walking distance to historic attractions, shopping, restaurants, and the Naval Academy. Allergy-free rooms are available. The hotel offers standard amenities such as a fitness center and meeting facilities. Valet parking and Internet service are available for an additional fee. Their waterfront restaurant, **Pusser's Caribbean Grille,** is a popular dining spot for seafood and also offers great views. This premium location doesn't come cheap, but if you are after a room with a view, it delivers.

The **Westin Annapolis** (100 Westgate Circle, 410/972-4300, www.westinannapolis.com, $299-459) is an immaculate, top-notch hotel a short distance from all the action in downtown Annapolis. The 225 guest rooms are spacious and modern, and there's a lovely, well-stocked bar in the lobby. Free shuttle service is available to the downtown area, and there is parking on-site. There are an indoor pool and fitness center, and the hotel is pet friendly.

The **Loews Annapolis Hotel** (126 West St., 410/263-7777, www.loewshotels.com, $309-409) is a lovely hotel in downtown Annapolis within walking distance to many attractions (10 minutes to the City Dock). The bright, nautical decor is perfect for the hotel's location, and the 216 guest rooms are

luxurious and large (there are also 18 suites). Parking is available on-site for an additional fee ($18 for self-parking and $22 for valet), and there is a complimentary local shuttle service operating throughout the historic district. There are a fitness room and spa (no pool) for hotel guests, and wireless Internet service is available in guest rooms for an additional fee. There is also a restaurant on-site.

INFORMATION AND SERVICES

For additional information on Annapolis, stop in the **Annapolis & Anne Arundel County Conference and Visitors Bureau** (26 West St., 410/280-0445, daily 9am-5pm) or visit www.visitannapolis.org.

GETTING THERE

Most people arrive in Annapolis by car. The city is a quick 45-minute drive east from Washington DC (32 miles) via U.S. 50 and about 30 minutes (26 miles) south of the Inner Harbor in Baltimore (via I-97).

Annapolis is 22 miles from **Baltimore Washington International Thurgood Marshall Airport (BWI)** (410/859-7040, www.bwiairport.com). Private shuttle service can be arranged from the airport to Annapolis through **Annapolis Airport Shuttle** (410/971-8100, www.annapolisairportshuttle.com) or by limousine through **Lighthouse Limousine** (410/798-8881, www.lighthouselimousines.com).

GETTING AROUND

Parking can be challenging in the downtown area but **The Circulator** (410/216-9436, www.parkannapolis.com, every 10 minutes Sun.-Thurs. 6:30am-midnight, Fri.-Sat. 6:30am-2:30am) is a great way to move around Annapolis. It is a trolley service that provides free transportation around the central business district and stops at four downtown parking garages. The four garages are **Gotts Court Garage** (25 Northwest St., 410/972-4726, first hour $2, $15 maximum), the **Noah Hillman Garage** (150 Gorman St.,

410/267-8914, $2 an hour, $20 maximum), the **Knighton Garage** (corner of Colonial Ave. and West St., 410/263-7170, $1 first hour, $10 maximum), and the **Park Place Garage** (5 Park Pl., $1 an hour, $10 maximum). Stops are located along the trolley's loop route from Westgate Circle to Memorial Circle and start at the Westin Annapolis Hotel at Park Place. Trolleys also stop at popular areas such as Church Circle and City Dock. If you aren't at a stop but want to get on the trolley, simply raise your hand when one drives by and it will pull over to pick you up.

There is also metered parking at City Dock near Spa Creek, and there is a parking lot at the Navy Marine Corps Memorial Stadium (off Rowe Blvd. on Taylor Avenue). Trolley rides from the stadium lot cost $2 since it is not within the central business district.

Two free shuttle buses also run from the stadium to downtown. The **Navy Blue Shuttle** runs to the historic area and west Annapolis with stops at the Naval Academy Main Gate and Church Circle. It leaves the stadium parking lot every half hour Monday-Friday 9am-6pm, and Saturday and Sunday 10am-6pm. The **State House Shuttle** operates on a loop between the stadium and the State Legislative Buildings. It leaves the stadium every 15 minutes (every 5 minutes during rush hour) Monday-Friday 6:30am-8pm.

Southern Maryland

Southern Maryland contains a thousand miles of shoreline on the Chesapeake Bay and the Patuxent River. The region includes Calvert, Charles, and St. Mary's Counties and is a boater's playground, a bird-watcher's paradise, and a seafood lover's dream. Traditionally a rural agricultural area connected by steamboat routes, today Southern Maryland is traversed by scenic byways that connect charming towns and parks. The communities in the region have grown tremendously in recent decades and welcome tourists and those seeking outdoor recreation such as boating, fishing, crabbing, hiking, and biking.

CHESAPEAKE BEACH

Chesapeake Beach is on the mainland in Calvert County about 45 minutes south of Annapolis (29 miles). The town was founded in 1894 by the Chesapeake Bay Railway Company and was intended to be a vacation destination for Washingtonians. The town thrived as such during the early 1900s when visitors arrived by train. Today, long after the railroad days, visitors can still enjoy nice views of the Chesapeake Bay, beach access, and charter fishing.

Sights

A nice little museum that does a good job of presenting local history is the **Chesapeake Beach Railway Museum** (4155 Mears Ave., 410/257-3892, www.cbrm.org, hours vary by season, free). The small, three-room museum is housed in a restored train depot and provides information on the train that once ran between Chesapeake Beach and Washington DC. Artifacts, photos, maps, equipment, and postcards are on exhibit, and the volunteers are very friendly and helpful. The museum hosts many family events throughout the year.

If you're looking for summer fun and a break from the heat, bring the kids to the **Chesapeake Beach Water Park** (4079 Gordon Stinnett Blvd., 410/257-1404, www.chesapeakebeachwaterpark.com, daily mid-June-mid-Aug. Mon. 11am-6pm, Tues.-Sun. 11am-7pm, $21). It features eight waterslides, pools, fountains, waterfalls, and giant floating sea creatures to climb on. There are even "adult" swim times.

Surfing enthusiasts will enjoy spending an hour or two at **Bruce "Snake" Gabrielson's Surf Art Gallery and Museum** (Route 261, three miles south of Chesapeake Beach,

240/464-3301, www.hbsnakesurf.com, open evenings by appointment on Mon., Wed., and Thurs., free). Maryland's only surfing museum opened in 2012 and showcases the personal treasures collected by its founder, surfing legend Bruce Gabrielson, over the course of 60 years. Featured items include antique surfboards, photographs, and posters signed by various surfing legends. It is a little off the beaten path in the offices of the National Surf Schools and Instructors Association.

Food

The two restaurants within the **Chesapeake Beach Hotel and Spa** (4165 Mears Ave., 410/257-5596, www.chesapeake-beachresortspa.com) are a couple of the best dining options in Chesapeake Beach. The **Rod 'N' Reel** (410/257-2735, daily 8am-2am, $10-33) serves breakfast, lunch, and dinner. They have a nice selection of sandwiches and seafood entrees and items from the land. They also have an extensive wine list. **Boardwalk Cafe** (Fri. 4pm-midnight, Sat. 11am-midnight, Sun. 11am-9pm, $8-25) is a casual restaurant on the resort boardwalk. They serve soup, salads, and casual seafood. It is a great spot to grab a drink and enjoy the scenery.

Another choice in Chesapeake Beach is the family-owned **Trader's Seafood Steak and Ale** (8132 Bayside Rd., 301/855-0766, www.traders-eagle.com, Sun. 7am-9pm, Mon.-Thurs. 8am-9pm, Fri.-Sat. 7am-10pm, $8-24), offering seafood, burgers, and other entrées for lunch and dinner and many traditional options for breakfast. The atmosphere is friendly and casual and they have a deck bar. They also have a breakfast buffet on Sunday (7am-1pm).

Accommodations and Camping

The **Chesapeake Beach Resort and Spa** (4165 Mears Ave., 410/257-5596, www.chesapeakebeachresortspa.com, $169-382) is a well-maintained property with 72 guest rooms. The hotel is on the Chesapeake Bay waterfront, and some rooms have balconies overlooking the water. A full-service spa is on-site, and there is also a marina. There are two waterfront restaurants at the hotel, a fitness room, sauna, game room, and an indoor swimming pool. Complimentary continental breakfast is served on weekdays. Fishing charters can be arranged through the hotel.

Breezy Point Beach and Campground (5300 Breezy Point Rd., 410/535-0259, www.co.cal.md.us, May-Oct., $50 per night) is a public beach and campground six miles south of Chesapeake Beach at **Breezy Point Beach** (410/535-0259, May-Oct. daily 6am-dusk, $10). The half-mile beach has a swimming area, bathhouse, picnic area, playground, and a 300-foot fishing pier. The camping available May-October includes water and sewage. Multiple-night minimums may be required on certain days. No pets are allowed on the beach or in the campground.

Information and Services

For additional information on Chesapeake Beach visit www.chesapeake-beach.md.us.

SOLOMONS ISLAND

Solomons Island sits at the southern tip of Calvert County at the confluence of the Chesapeake Bay and the Patuxent River. It is about a 1.5-hour drive southeast from Washington DC (61 miles), a 1.75-hour drive south of Baltimore (81 miles), and an 80-minute drive (58 miles) south from Annapolis. It is connected to St. Mary's County by the **Governor Thomas Johnson Bridge,** a 1.5-mile bridge over the Patuxent River on Route 4.

Solomons was first settled by tobacco farmers, but a surge in the oyster industry following the Civil War led it into the oyster processing and boatbuilding trades. The town quickly became a shipbuilding, ship repair, and seafood harvesting stronghold. In the 1880s, the local fishing fleet counted more than 500 boats, and many of them had been built right in Solomons. Among these were "bugeyes," which were large, decked-over sailing canoes, mostly built from shaped logs. The

Solomons Island

HILTON GARDEN INN SOLOMONS → To ■ CALVERT CLIFFS STATE PARK

NEWTON RD

DOWELL RD

2
4

ANNMARIE SCULPTURE GARDEN ★

PATUXENT ADVENTURE CENTER
HOSPITALITY DR
HOLIDAY ST

LORE RD

Back Creek

Dowell

■ CALVERT MARINE MUSEUM

DRUM POINT LIGHTHOUSE ★

DOWELL RD

Mill Creek

4
SOLOMONS ISLAND RD
LANGLEY ST
CALVERT ST
SEDWICK AVE
C ST
DRY DOCK RESTAURANT

Johnstown

CD CAFE
WOODBURN ST
POINT ST

Creek

BACK CREEK B & B

ALEXANDER

The Narrows

Turkey Bar

Ship Point

Janes Point

Ma Leg Island

Patuxent River

2
LOTUS KITCHEN
BLUE HERON INN
SOLOMONS VICTORIAN INN
CHARLES ST
SOLOMONS ISLAND TIKI BAR

Solomons

0   500 yds
0   500 m

Sandy Point

© AVALON TRAVEL

recreation play an important role in Solomons' economy. It houses countless marinas, boat suppliers, charter boat companies, a pilot station, and other types of water-related business such as kayaking outfitters. Many restaurants and inns serve the influx of tourists to this beautiful waterside town.

Sights

★ CALVERT MARINE MUSEUM

The **Calvert Marine Museum** (14200 Solomons Island Rd., 410/326-2042, www.calvertmarinemuseum.com, daily 10am-5pm, $9) does a wonderful job of sharing the story of the Chesapeake Bay, with exhibits on prehistoric times, the natural environment, and the bay's unique maritime heritage. There are three exhibit galleries totaling 29,000 square feet, including a discovery room with fossils, live animals (such as otters, fish, and rays), and a paleontology exhibit.

Behind the museum is a marsh walk that enables visitors to stroll over the salt marsh flats. Wildlife is abundant in the marsh, and you can expect to see signs of inhabitants such as raccoons, opossums, water snakes, crabs, herons, and ducks. This great natural exhibit is a living study of the local plant and animal life.

On the museum's waterfront is the iconic **Drum Point Lighthouse,** a "screwpile," cottage-style lighthouse that is one of only three that still stand out of an original 45 on the bay. The lighthouse is fully restored and houses early 20th-century furniture. Guided tours are available.

The museum's small-craft collection is housed in a 6,000-square-foot building that is open toward the boat basin. The collection has 19 boats in a range of sizes. Some boats are displayed on land, and others are in the water.

Those wishing to see an original seafood-packing house can visit the **Lore Oyster House** (May and Sept. weekends 1pm-4pm, June-Aug. daily 1pm-4pm, free). This restored National Historic Landmark is a little more than half a mile south of the museum campus on Solomons Island Road. It was built in 1934

city soon became the dominant commercial center in Calvert County.

By the late 1920s, oyster harvests began to decline. This was followed by the Great Depression and the worst storm to ever hit the island (in 1933), which left the lower half of it under water. World War II brought better times when the island became a staging area for training troops readying for amphibious invasions.

Today, tourism, boating, and outdoor

Pirates of the Chesapeake

Although Blackbeard the pirate was best known for his ruthless handiwork in the Caribbean and his eventual beheading in Ocracoke, North Carolina, he often retreated to the Chesapeake Bay to repair his ship and prepare her for sea. He was not alone on the bay. The tobacco industry thrived along its shores for nearly 200 years (between roughly 1600 and 1800), bringing with it explorers from all parts of Europe as well as large populations of pirates.

Initially pirates settled in the southern part of the bay, but later they spread through most of the area. Although pirates often attacked colonial ships, the outlaws were tolerated by the colonies and in some ways helped them become independent from England. Pirates often sold goods to colonists that they could not purchase from England.

Despite their success, pirate life was very difficult, and most died young. Entire crews could be wiped out by disease, as living conditions were filthy on board their ships. Many also suffered fatal wounds during battle. Although some did go on to enjoy the riches they stole, this was the minority.

and now shares exhibits that explain oyster processing.

Sightseeing sailing cruises on the river leave from the museum dock weather permitting. They are one hour long and go through the inner harbor, underneath the Governor Thomas Johnson Bridge, and turn around at the Naval Recreation Center. The cost is $7. Trips can accommodate 40 passengers and leave the dock at 2pm Wednesday-Sunday (May-Oct.). On Saturday and Sunday in July and August additional 12:30pm and 3:10pm

cruises are offered. Call 410/326-2042, ext. 41. Tickets can be purchased at the museum the day of the cruise.

The museum also has a woodworking shop and a reference library.

ANNMARIE SCULPTURE GARDEN AND ARTS CENTER

The **Annmarie Sculpture Garden and Arts Center** (13480 Dowell Rd., 410/326-4640, www.annmariegarden.org, sculpture garden daily 9am-5pm, arts building daily

Calvert Marine Museum

10am-5pm, $5) features a lovely sculpture garden accessed by a quarter-mile walking path. The path goes through a wooded garden where sculptures both on loan and part of the center's permanent collection can be viewed. More than 30 sculptures are on loan from the Smithsonian Institution and National Gallery of Art. The Arts Building features a rotating exhibit space and a gift shop. The center offers many family activities throughout the year and also hosts annual festivals. This is a peaceful place to walk or bring the kids.

★ CALVERT CLIFFS STATE PARK

One of the prime recreation attractions in Calvert County is **Calvert Cliffs State Park** (10540 H. G. Trueman Rd., Lusby, 301/743-7613, www.dnr.state.md.us, daily sunrise to sunset, $5 per vehicle). This day-use park is about 7 miles north of Solomons Island, right on the Chesapeake Bay, and offers a sandy beach, playground, fishing, marshland, and 13 miles of hiking trails. The main attraction in this park, however, is fossil hunting along the beach. At the end of the Red Trail (1.8 miles from the parking lot), the open beach area gives rise to the dramatic Calvert Cliffs. More than 600 species of fossils have been identified in the cliff area, dating back 10 to 20 million years. The most common types of fossils found include oyster shells from the Miocene era and sharks teeth. Visitors can use sieves and shovels to look through the sand, but it is illegal to hunt fossils beneath the cliffs for safety reasons (dangerous landslides can occur). Swimming off the beach is allowed at your own risk, as there are no lifeguards on duty.

Sports and Recreation

Those wishing to rent a kayak or paddleboard (starting at $35 for three hours) or take a guided kayak tour ($75 per person), can do so from **Patuxent Adventure Center** (13860 C Solomons Island Rd., 410/394-2770, www.paxadventure.com). They also sell bikes and kayaks and other outdoor gear and accessories.

Nightlife

The **Solomons Island Tiki Bar** (85 Charles St., 410/326-4075, www.tikibarsolomons.com, mid-Apr.-mid-Oct.) is a local institution in Solomons. This well-known shack/tiki village near the harbor makes a killer mai tai and caters to pretty much anyone over 21 looking for a good time, good drink, and a fun island atmosphere. Visitors come by land and sea for this "adventure." Just be sure to decide ahead of time who is driving or sailing you home.

Food

Relaxed waterfront dining can be found at **The Dry Dock Restaurant** (C St., 410/326-4817, www.zahnisers.com, hours vary by season, $19-32). This harborfront restaurant specializes in steaks and seafood and prides itself on using as much local produce and sustainable seafood as possible. Large windows overlook the harbor, and there is outside deck seating in the warmer months. This is a small, intimate establishment that has been part of the marina for many years. There is an interesting collection of antique wooden decoys around the bar that were part of a private collection.

The ★ **CD Café** (14350 Solomons Island Rd., 410/326-3877, www.cdcafe.info, Sun. lunch 11am-3:30pm, dinner 5:30pm-9pm, Mon.-Sat. lunch 11:30am-3:30pm, dinner 5:30pm-9:30pm, $9-26) is a small, 11-table restaurant with a large menu of simply delicious food. They are open daily and serve lunch (pasta, burgers, salad) and dinner (seafood, steak, pasta, burgers). This is a popular restaurant, so expect to wait at prime times (there is a nice bar and waiting area), but the atmosphere is warm and inviting, the staff is genuinely helpful and friendly, and the food keeps residents and tourists coming back. Try the hummus, the cheesecake appetizer, and the salmon.

The **Lotus Kitchen** (14618 Solomons Island Rd., 410/326-8469, www.lotuskitchen-solomons.com, Wed.-Thurs. 9am-8pm, Fri. 9am-10pm, Sat. 9am-6pm, Sun. 9am-4pm, under $10) offers healthy food and a scenic view in a charming converted house right in town. The offering includes breakfast sandwiches, deli sandwiches, quiche, soup, meat and cheese boards, beer, wine, and coffee drinks. With menu items with names such as the Good Karma, the Garden Unicorn, and the Pot of Gold, half the fun is picking out your order. They are also known for their famous Kim's Key Lime Pie.

Accommodations

There is no shortage of wonderful bed-and-breakfasts in Solomons Island. The ★ **Back Creek Inn Bed and Breakfast** (210 Alexander Ln., 410/326-2022, www. backcreekinnbnb.com, $115-225) is a beautiful waterfront inn with seven clean and spacious guest rooms. They have two deepwater boat slips on their 70-foot pier (at mile marker 5 on Back Creek) and two bicycles for guest use. The inn is in a quiet part of town and can accommodate small business groups with indoor and outdoor meeting space. They also have free wireless Internet throughout the property. A full gourmet breakfast is served Monday-Saturday between 8:30am and 9:30am. Coffee, tea, juice, and coffee cake are available starting at 8am.

Another lovely waterfront bed-and-breakfast is the ★ **Blue Heron Inn** (14614

Solomons Island Rd., 410/326-2707, www. blueheronbandb.com, $179-249). The two suites have king-size beds, and the two guest rooms have queens. All rooms have private bathrooms and a water view (with either a private balcony or access to a common balcony). Wireless Internet and cable are included with all rooms.

Guests are treated to a gourmet breakfast each morning in a sunny breakfast room with access to the balcony (where breakfast can be served on nice days). A complimentary glass of wine is available each evening.

Solomons Victorian Inn (125 Charles St., 410/326-4811, www.solomonsvictorianinn. com, $135-250) offers great harbor views and a lush garden, and is within a short walk of shops and restaurants. At the southern tip of Solomons Island, on the western Chesapeake Bay shore, this gracious inn was built in 1906 and was the home of a renowned yacht builder. Several of the rooms are named after his boats. Six guest rooms and one carriage house with a separate entrance are available to rent, and each includes a private bathroom, television, wireless Internet, and a full breakfast. Most rooms have a harbor view.

A good option for hotel accommodations in Solomons Island is the **Hilton Garden**

Lotus Kitchen

Inn Solomons (13100 Dowell Rd., 410/326-0303, www.hiltongardeninn3.hilton.com, $159-195), which is a half mile from the downtown attractions. They have clean, comfortable rooms, a fitness center, indoor pool, seasonal outdoor pool, business center, and complimentary wireless Internet.

Information and Services
For additional information on Solomons Island, visit www.solomonsmaryland.com or stop by the **Solomons Island Visitor Center** (14175 Solomons Island Rd., 410/326-6027).

ST. MARY'S CITY
St. Mary's City is a small community an hour and 45 minutes south of Annapolis (73 miles) and two hours south of Baltimore (96 miles) in extreme Southern Maryland. It sits on the western shore of the Chesapeake Bay and the eastern shore of the St. Mary's River (a Potomac River tributary). Established in 1634, the area is the fourth-oldest permanent settlement in the country and is widely known as the "birthplace of religious tolerance."

St. Mary's City is in St. Mary's County, a beautiful rural area with abundant farmland and water access. St. Mary's County has many Amish and Mennonite communities, and

motorists are warned to be alert for horse-drawn carriages along the highways. Amish farms dot the landscape and are recognizable by their windmills and the lack of power lines running along their properties.

St. Mary's was Maryland's capital for 60 years. Roman Catholics founded the city in their quest for religious freedom. When the state capital moved to Annapolis, St. Mary's went into deep decline and had dropped out of existence by 1720. In 1840, St. Mary's College was developed by Maryland legislature to celebrate the state's founding site. In 1966, the state of Maryland started the process of preserving the site and created the Historic St. Mary's City Commission. Today the city is still home to St. Mary's College and the outdoor museum of history and archaeology known as Historic St. Mary's City. Today, St. Mary's City is home to **St. Mary's College of Maryland** (Route 5, www.smcm.edu).

Sights
★ ST. MARY'S CITY'S OUTDOOR MUSEUM OF HISTORY AND ARCHAEOLOGY
Maryland's premier outdoor living-history museum, the **St. Mary's City's Outdoor Museum of History and Archaeology**

an Amish buggy near St. Mary's City

(18559 Hogaboom Ln., 240/895-4990, www.hsmcdigshistory.org, hours change by season, $10) is a re-creation of colonial St. Mary's City. The complex includes the *Dove* ship that first brought settlers to the area, an early tobacco plantation, the State House of 1676 (47418 Old State House Rd.), and a woodland Native American hamlet.

Although visitors should not expect the living museum to be on the same scale as Williamsburg, Virginia, the park is still a wonderful place to visit and has costumed interpreters, archaeological discoveries, a visitors center (18751 Hogaboom Ln.), outdoor living-history exhibits (where you can watch new buildings being erected in the town center, learn about Native American culture, and see the people and livestock at a tobacco plantation), reconstructed colonial buildings, the St. John's site museum, and a working 17th-century farm.

Visitors to St. Mary's City can participate in many hands-on activities and special events during the open season, such as a workshop on dinner preparation at the plantation and a hands-on pirate experience. Professional archaeologists are actively working to rediscover the city's past, and

excavation sites can be seen throughout this National Historic Landmark.

POINT LOOKOUT

Point Lookout State Park (11175 Point Lookout Rd., Scotland, 301/872-5688, www.dnr.state.md.us, daily 6am-sunset, $7) encompasses 1,042 acres at the southern tip of St. Mary's County near Scotland, Maryland. The park is two hours (82 miles) south of Annapolis on a beautiful peninsula at the confluence of the Chesapeake Bay and the Potomac River. It is managed by the Maryland Department of Natural Resources.

Captain John Smith was the first to explore the peninsula in 1612, but the park is best known as the location of a prison camp during the Civil War. In the years leading up to the war, the area was a thriving summer resort thanks to its sandy beaches and stunning location. The coming of the war brought financial hardship, and the area was leased by the Union army as the site of a hospital facility, and then later the largest Confederate prison camp.

Conditions were horrible at the camp, which was primarily for enlisted men, and many of the prisoners froze to death during the winter months. Those who survived

Point Lookout State Park

were plagued by filth. It is said that more than 52,000 Confederate soldiers were held at the camp during the war, and between 3,000 and 8,000 died there. There are two monuments and an on-site museum that recall this part of the park's past.

Whether or not you believe in ghosts, the park boasts countless incidents of unexplained phenomena and firsthand encounters with "ghosts" of soldiers. The most haunted location is said to be the lighthouse, which is no longer in use.

Today the park is primarily known as a wonderful recreation spot. It has several boat launch locations ($12), canoe rentals, a camp store, fishing, hiking trails, picnic areas, a playground, beaches, swimming, and a nature center. The park is also pet friendly.

In addition to being surrounded by water, there is a large lake in the center of the park (Lake Conoy), which is a perfect spot for boating and fishing. A water trail guide for the park is available for purchase at the park headquarters.

Camping is offered in the park April-October on 143 wooded sites ($21.49). Twenty-six have full hookups ($38.49) and 33 provide electricity (33.49). There are also a half-dozen four-person camper cabins for rent ($50.49) on a nightly basis. Off-season camping is available with limited services. Call 888/432-2267 for reservations.

The Eastern Shore and Atlantic Beaches

Look for ★ to find recommended sights, activities, dining, and lodging.

Highlights

★ **Schooner *Sultana*:** This amazing replica of a British Royal Navy ship serves as an educational center and the site of the annual Chestertown Tea Party (page 106).

★ **Historic District in St. Michaels:** Beautiful churches, colonial homes, interesting shops, and great restaurants charm in this elegant downtown area (page 112).

★ **Chesapeake Bay Maritime Museum:** This wonderful museum in St. Michaels fills 18 acres with all things Chesapeake Bay (page 112).

★ **Pickering Creek Audubon Center:** This 400-acre farm in Easton includes forest, marsh, meadow, a freshwater pond, wetlands, and more than a mile of shoreline (page 117).

★ **Blackwater National Wildlife Refuge:** This beautiful waterfowl sanctuary features 27,000 acres of protected freshwater, brackish tidal wetlands, meadows, and forest (page 124).

★ **Assateague Island National Seashore:** These 37 miles of protected coastline are a haven for migrating birds and home to a herd of wild ponies (page 128).

★ **Ocean City Boardwalk:** Along three miles of wood-planked boardwalk sit dozens of hotels, motels, restaurants, shops, and amusement parks (page 131).

★ **Ocean City Life-Saving Station Museum:** Learn the history of rescues at sea along the Maryland coast (page 131).

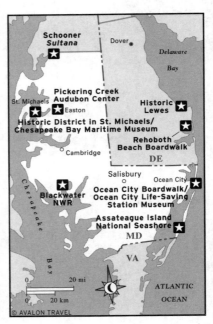

★ **Rehoboth Beach Boardwalk:** This mile-long walkway offers stunning views of the Atlantic and enough activity and food to keep a family busy for days (page 143).

★ **Historic Lewes:** Victorian homes, upscale restaurants, and cozy inns are the trademark of this relaxing little coastal town (page 147).

Maryland is blessed with thousands of miles of shoreline along the Chesapeake Bay and Atlantic Ocean. One of the most scenic areas in the state, the Eastern Shore is made up of a series of bayside towns that retain the charm of yesteryear and are still partly supported by the local fishing industry.

Most travelers are welcomed to the Eastern Shore in the seafood haven of Kent Island after crossing the Chesapeake Bay Bridge. From there they head north to historic towns such as Chestertown and Rock Hall, or south to upscale St. Michaels or the quaint towns of Tilghman Island and Oxford. Easton and Cambridge offer their own special charm with bustling downtown areas and ample sports and recreation.

Maryland and Delaware share a thin strip of barrier island along the Atlantic coast, offering beachgoers many choices for a sun-filled vacation. On the very southern end, the Assateague Island National Seashore, which is shared with Virginia, is a quiet place to calm your spirits, view wildlife, and enjoy a long, pristine beach. Its northern neighbor is the bustling beachfront community of Ocean City. With its exciting boardwalk, active nightlife, and plentiful activities, Ocean City never sleeps. Three popular Delaware beaches, Bethany, Rehoboth, and Lewes, stretch to the north.

PLANNING YOUR TIME

The Eastern Shore of the Chesapeake Bay can be explored in a day or two, but many people choose to go there for extended relaxation and to spend a little downtime. Getting around by car is the best option, as public transportation is sparse. Route 301 is the major north/south route in the northern part of the Eastern Shore, while U.S. 50 is the major route in the middle and southern regions.

A good plan of action is to choose one or two towns to explore and spend a weekend enjoying them and learning about the Chesapeake Bay. The distance between Chestertown and Cambridge is about 52 miles, so the distances are not too cumbersome when traveling by car. Be aware,

Previous: Rehoboth Beach Boardwalk; Cambridge waterfront. **Above:** a sandpiper on Rehoboth Beach.

The Eastern Shore and Atlantic Beaches

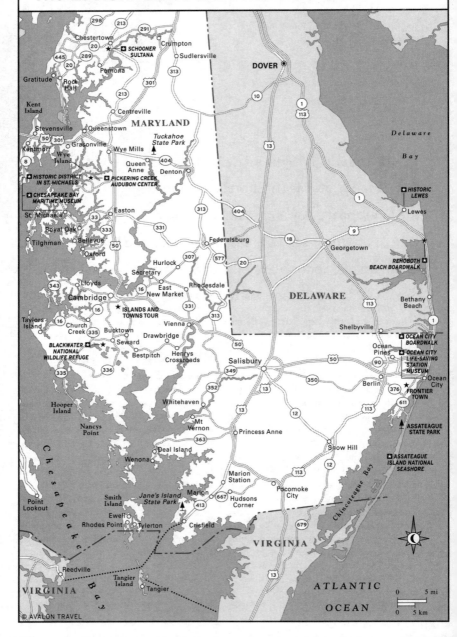

© AVALON TRAVEL

however, if you are traveling during the busy summer months, especially on a weekend, that traffic can back up on Route 50. Friday evening drives over the Bay Bridge (toll $4) can mean long wait times and bumper-to-bumper traffic.

The Atlantic beaches in Maryland and Delaware can be explored individually over a weekend, but they are often destinations that people spend a week at a time at over the summer months for a relaxing vacation. In the high season—generally, mid-June until Labor Day—many accommodations have minimum stays. The off-season is a great time to go if you don't have school constraints. Spring and fall offer cooler temperatures and fewer crowds at the beaches, and generally, prices for accommodations are reduced.

If you plan to just visit one of the beaches, keep in mind they all have unique characteristics. If you seek excitement, activity, and the bustling hubbub of a busy boardwalk, then Ocean City is a good choice. If you prefer the charm of a quaint, harborside historic town with close access to the beach, then Lewes, Delaware, may be a better option. If it's something in between that you are looking for, perhaps a more family-oriented beach scene with fewer hotels and more beach house rentals, then Bethany Beach is a good choice. Finally, if you seek the activity of a boardwalk, but a scaled-down version is more your style, then Rehoboth Beach may suit you.

Regardless of where you end up, you will find good seafood and many excellent choices for restaurants at all the beaches. Keep in mind, "Maryland is for Crabs," and delicious blue crab dishes are available in many places. This is *the* place to eat them.

The vast majority of visitors to the Maryland and Delaware beaches drive there. Once you arrive, it's difficult to get too lost as long as you know where the beach is. One main road, the Coastal Highway, runs along the coast; it goes by Route 528 in Maryland and Route 1 in Delaware.

The **Ocean City Municipal Airport** (12724 Airport Rd., Berlin, 410/213-2471) is three miles west of the downtown area of Ocean City and can accommodate general aviation and charter aircraft. Commercial air service is provided at the **Salisbury-Ocean City Wicomico Regional Airport** (5485 Airport Terminal Rd., Salisbury, 410/548-4827) five miles from downtown Salisbury on Maryland's Eastern Shore.

the beach at Ocean City

The Eastern Shore

The Eastern Shore holds a special place in many Marylanders' hearts. The wide peninsula between the Chesapeake Bay and the Atlantic Ocean contains endless miles of shoreline, beachfront resorts, nature preserves, and small seaside towns. Water is everywhere on the Eastern Shore and so are the culinary delights fished right from the bay. Amazing restaurants with million-dollar views, cozy inns, and plentiful outdoor activities welcome visitors nearly year-round.

KENT ISLAND AND KENT NARROWS

The Chesapeake Bay Bridge stretches from Sandy Point near Annapolis on the mainland to Kent Island. Kent Island is the largest island in the Chesapeake Bay and the gateway to the Eastern Shore. The island is bordered on the east by a narrow channel called the Kent Narrows.

Kent Island welcomes Bay Bridge drivers to a gathering of easily accessible waterfront restaurants. Visitors traveling Route 50 are immediately thrown into a seaside atmosphere, and the urge to stop and sample some of the local cuisine is hard to resist.

Food

The **Narrows Restaurant** (3023 Kent Narrows Way South, Grasonville, 410/827-8113, www.thenarrowsrestaurant.com, lunch Mon.-Sat. 11am-4pm, Sun. brunch 11am-2pm, dinner Mon.-Sat. 4pm-close, Sun. 11am-close, $10-36) is one of the most popular seafood restaurants on the island. It has a nice atmosphere and a great view. Patio seating is available.

Another local favorite is **Harris Crab House** (433 Kent Narrows Way, Grasonville, 410/827-9500, www.harriscrabhouse.com, daily lunch and dinner from 11am, $11-68). They have two levels of waterfront dining and outdoor seating. The views are great, and the

seafood is plentiful. This is a casual place with a crab house atmosphere.

The **Fisherman's Inn & Crab Deck** (3116 Main St., 410/827-8807, www.fishermansinn.com, daily 11am-10pm, $19-40) serves great seafood and also has a seafood market.

CHESTERTOWN

Chestertown is a pretty waterfront colonial town with less than 5,000 residents. It is 40 minutes (29 miles) northeast of Kent Island on the Chester River, a tributary of the Chesapeake Bay. It is about 35 miles northeast of the Chesapeake Bay Bridge.

The town's history dates back to 1706, and it was known as one of Maryland's six "Royal Ports of Entry" (second only to Annapolis as a leading port). The town was a spot for the wealthy in its heyday, which is reflected in the numerous brick mansions and row houses that line the waterfront. The port is still a popular location for sailing ships and tourists. It is also home to **Washington College** (www.washcoll.edu), a private liberal arts college of which George Washington was a founding patron. The school was established in 1782, making it the tenth-oldest college in the country.

Sights
HISTORIC CHESTERTOWN

Chestertown is worth exploring on foot. The state's second-highest concentration of colonial homes (after Annapolis) can be found in Chestertown, and there is a scenic waterfront promenade.

★ SCHOONER *SULTANA*

The schooner *Sultana* (107 S. Cross St. on the waterfront, 410/778-5954, www.sultana-education.org) is a replica of a British Royal Navy ship that sailed during the 18th century and patrolled the North American coastline just before the Revolutionary War. The ship lives in the Chestertown Harbor and is used to

William Preston Lane Jr. Memorial Bay Bridge

Once upon a time, Marylanders had to depend on boats to cross the Chesapeake Bay. The first plan to connect the mainland to the Eastern Shore came in 1927 but was abandoned first until 1938 and then again until 1947. Finally, under the leadership of Governor William Preston Lane Jr. the State Roads Commission began building the "Bay Bridge" in 1949.

The original span of the bridge, which is used for eastbound traffic today, cost $45 million and became the longest continuous over-water steel structure in the world at 4.3 miles. It first opened to traffic on July 30, 1952. The bridge is part of U.S. Routes 50 and 301 and quickly became an important connection to the Baltimore/Washington DC area from the Eastern Shore and Ocean City, Maryland.

The second span, which currently carries westbound traffic, was started in 1969 at a cost of $148 million. This span opened in 1973. This architectural marvel has a vertical clearance of 186 feet, and the suspension bridge towers are 354 and 379 feet tall. The bridge starts on the mainland next to Sandy Point State Park and stretches to Kent Island. The bridge can accommodate 1,500 vehicles per lane per hour.

teach students about the Chesapeake Bay history and environment. Two-hour public sails are held on weekends from the end of April to the beginning of November ($30). Many events are offered throughout the season on the ship; a list is available on the website.

Events

The biggest annual event in Chestertown is the **Chestertown Tea Party** (www.chestertownteaparty.org), held at the end of May. In May 1774, five months after the famous Boston Tea Party when the British closed the port of Boston, residents of Chestertown resolved to prohibit the purchase, sale, or drinking of tea. Legend has it that they then held their own version of the Boston Tea Party staged on the schooner *Sultana* on the Chester River to show their colonial defiance. The annual festival celebrates this heritage through a reenactment of the tea party and a weekend of family events.

Aviation enthusiasts won't want to miss the annual **Potomac Antique Aero**

Squadron's Antique Fly-In (www.fly-ins. com, free but donations appreciated). This wonderful one-day antique aircraft show is held in June at the **Massey Aerodrome** (33541 Maryland Line Rd., Massey, www. masseyaero.org), approximately 17 miles northeast of Chestertown. It is sponsored by the Potomac Antique Air Squadron. More than 200 antique and rare aircrafts make up this impressive show. Visitors can see the airplanes up close, speak with the owners, and enjoy delicious food.

Shopping

A dozen or so art galleries, studios, and shops feature the work of local, regional, and international artists in the historic waterfront district of Chestertown.

From April to December a local farmers market is held on Saturday mornings in the heart of the downtown area between Spring Avenue and Cross Street. It features fresh bakery items, produce, plants, herbs, and local artwork.

Food

The most well-known eatery in town is the **Kitchen at the Imperial** (208 High St., 410/778-5000, www.imperialchestertown. com, Mon., Wed.-Sat. 11:30am-9pm, Sun. brunch 10am-3pm, dinner 3pm-9pm, $9-33). This wonderful restaurant was formerly located in Rock Hall but is now located in the Imperial Hotel, which first opened in 1903 and still offers three rooms for rent. The restaurant is open for lunch and dinner and offers a Bloody Mary brunch on Sunday. Their fresh menu varies seasonally but they usually have terrific local seafood dishes and meat from local farms.

Seafood, comfort food, and sophisticated choices can all be found at the **Lemon Leaf Café** (337 High St., 443/282-0004, www. thellcafe.com, Mon.-Wed. 11am-8pm, Thurs. 11am-9pm, Fri.-Sat. 7:30am-9pm, Sun. 7:30am-8pm, $7-30). This clean little gem has a signature dish of chicken and dumplings but also serves incredible authentic Maryland

Tiki Bar Boat Stop

If you are exploring the Chesapeake Bay by boat and could use a taste of the islands and a party-hardy atmosphere, stop in **Jellyfish Joel's Tiki Bar** (22170 Great Oak Landing Rd., Chestertown, 410/778-5007, www.mearsgreatoaklanding.com, in-season Fri. starting 2pm and Sat.-Sun. starting 11am). This waterside bar sits on a peninsula by the beach on Fairlee Creek nine miles west of Chestertown and is a favorite boating stop. It offers a sandy beach, palm trees, and sunset beach parties every Friday during the summer. Boats can anchor or tie up on the floating docks. The bar is the main attraction, with cold beer and colder tropical drinks with names such as "Painkillers" and "Pain n'de Ass." They have live entertainment on the weekends and sell snacks and sandwiches.

crab soup, great crab cakes, and a delicious lemon meringue pie. The friendly service really makes diners feel like part of the "family," and makes for a relaxed dining experience even though the restaurant is usually full.

Right next door to the Lemon Leaf Café, and accessible through the restaurant or off the street, is **JR's Past Time Pub** (337 High St., 443/282-0055, www.jrspub.net, daily 11am-1am, $7-30). This 60-year-old pub has the same owner as its popular neighbor. It has a unique vintage clock motif and is decorated with signs from businesses in Chestertown's past. They serve traditional pub fare and share some dishes with their sister restaurant. The food menu is printed on paper grocery bags and their drink menu on wine bags. The pub is popular with students from Washington College and also has a piano bar with live music on Sunday evenings.

If you're looking for a water view with your meal, the only game in town is **The Fish Whistle** (98 Cannon St., 410/778-3566, www. fishandwhistle.com, Mon.-Wed. 11am-8pm, Thurs. 11am-8:30pm, Fri.-Sat. 11am-9pm, Sun. 11am-7pm, late-night bar menu daily until

11pm, $10-29). The location is excellent, right on the Chester River, and they serve a nice seafood menu with good daily specials. They have a large menu with bar food, sandwiches, and land and seafood entrées. Try the catfish fingers or the oyster potpie. Their slogan is, "It's all about the food," and they mean it.

Phenomenal oyster fritters are among the menu items at the **Blue Heron Café** (236 Cannon St., 410/778-0188, www.blueheron-cafe.com, dinner Mon.-Sat. from 5pm, $16-30). This consistently good restaurant serves regional American cuisine such as crab cakes, filet, and lamb. The desserts are amazing. Reservations are a must on weekend nights.

A great place to grab a drink in the summer and watch the sun set is at **The Sandbar at Rolph's Wharf** (1008 Rolph's Wharf Rd., 410/778-6389, www.rolphswharf.com). This is a small outdoor bar that is primarily open on weekends. It offers wonderful views of the Chester River, cold beer, and snacks.

The **Chestertown Farmers Market** is held every Saturday (late March-late December) from 8am to noon at **Fountain Park** (220 High St.).

Accommodations

A pre-Revolutionary War landmark, the **White Swan Tavern** (231 High St., 410/778-2300, www.whiteswantavern.com, $150-280) is a cozy bed-and-breakfast in the historic district of Chestertown. The inn was built in 1733 and has been used for a number of purposes throughout its history, including a private home and a tavern. A special room in the inn houses many artifacts that were found when the building was restored in 1978. There are six guest rooms, one of which was the original one-room dwelling that housed shoemaker John Lovegrove prior to 1733. The rooms are large and comfortable, and the location of this inn couldn't be any better if you are looking to explore the downtown area and waterfront. A continental breakfast and afternoon tea are served to guests. The bed-and-breakfast can accommodate small weddings and conferences. Two additional apartments are available for long- or short-term stays near the inn.

A cute home away from home very convenient to Washington College (it's 100 yards from campus) and within a 15-minute walk to the riverfront is **Simply Bed and Bread** (208 Mount Vernon Ave., 410/778-4359, www.simplybedandbread.com, $129-149). They offer two allergy-friendly guest rooms in a 1947 Cape Cod-style home. One room has a queen bed, and the other has a

White Swan Tavern

king. Each clean, cozy room has ample space. The innkeepers do a great job of making guests feel welcome. A continental breakfast is served each morning, and guests are treated to welcome sweets upon arrival.

One mile outside of Chestertown is the lovely **Brampton Bed and Breakfast Inn** (25227 Chestertown Rd., 410/778-1860, www. bramptoninn.com, $180-380), a restored plantation house built in 1860. It now has 13 guest rooms, suites, and cottages available to visitors. All accommodations have private bathrooms, sitting areas, fireplaces, flat-screen televisions with DVD players (no cable), bathrobes, and bath amenities. The estate is well cared for with beautiful gardens and a large front porch. A full à la carte breakfast is served in the dining area daily between 8:30am and 10am, although guests may opt to have breakfast delivered to their rooms. One cottage on the property is pet friendly.

A few chain hotels are options near the historic district in Chestertown. The **Holiday Inn Express Hotel & Suites Chestertown** (150 Scheeler Rd., 410/778-0778, www.ihg.com, $95-122) has 81 guest rooms, complimentary breakfast, and free wireless Internet, and the adjacent **Comfort Suites** (160 Scheeler Rd., 410/810-0555, www. choicehotels.com, $110-120) has 53 guest rooms, complimentary continental breakfast, and an indoor pool.

Information and Services

For additional information on Chestertown visit www.chestertown.com or stop by the **Kent County Visitor Center** (corner of Rte. 213 and Cross St., www.townofchestertown. com, Mon.-Fri. 9am-5pm, Sat.-Sun. 10am-2pm).

ROCK HALL

Fourteen miles southwest of Chestertown is the small waterfront town of Rock Hall. Rock Hall sits directly on the Chesapeake Bay and has a population of less than 1,500 people. Sometimes referred to as the "Pearl of the

Simply Bed and Bread

Chesapeake," this quaint maritime town has a history of fishing and boating and during the colonial era was a stop for passenger boats and shipping boats transporting tobacco and seafood. Today Rock Hall still has a working harbor and a fleet of professional watermen.

Sights

There are three small museums in Rock Hall. **The Rock Hall Museum** (at the Municipal Building on S. Main Street, www.rockhallmd. com, Sat.-Sun. 11am-3pm, free, donations appreciated) is a two-room facility a short walk from the town center housing artifacts from the town's history and focusing on the lifestyle, economy, and traditions of the community. **The Waterman's Museum** (in the Haven Harbour Marina, 20880 Rock Hall Ave., 410/778-6697, www.havenharbour. com, daily 10am-4pm, free) features a unique collection of vintage photographs taken during the watermen era, as well as boats and local carvings. The third museum, **Tolchester Beach Revisited** (Main St.

behind the Shoppes at Oyster Court, www. rockhallmd.com, Sat.-Sun. 11am-3pm), is a unique little place with artifacts and memorabilia from a former amusement park that was at a nearby steamboat landing. In its prime, it included 155 acres of amusement space and brought in as many as 20,000 visitors during a weekend by six steamships and one ferry. The park included a dance hall, bowling alley, bingo parlor, roller coaster, pony carts, a roller-skating rink, and numerous vendors. The park closed for good in 1962.

A warm and friendly local theater, **The Mainstay** (5753 Main St., 410/639-9133, www.mainstayrockhall.org) is a cultural and artistic center in Rock Hall. It occupies a building that was constructed more than a century ago. With just 120 seats, this is an intimate theater that offers more than 50 blues, folk, classical, and jazz concerts every year. They sell beer, wine, soft drinks, and home-baked treats during performances.

Food

The **Osprey Point Inn Restaurant** (20786 Rock Hall Ave., 410/639-2194, www. ospreypoint.com, dinner Wed.-Sun. starting at 5pm, Sunday brunch May-Sept. 10:30am-2pm, $18-25) features great water views from the Osprey Point Inn. The setting is comfortable and relaxing, and the young but highly skilled chef is truly passionate about his work. They have a fresh, seasonal menu with seafood and land-borne choices.

Another good choice in Rock Hall is **Uncle Charlie's Bistro** (834B High St., 410/778-3663, www.unclecharliesbistro.com, Mon.-Thurs. 11am-8pm, Fri. 11am-9pm, Sat., noon-9pm, $8-27). They offer American dishes, including seafood, salads, burgers, and sandwiches. The atmosphere and staff are very pleasant despite a not-so-impressive exterior.

Accommodations

The serene waterfront setting of the ★ **Inn at Huntingfield Creek** (4928 Eastern Neck Rd., 410/639-7779, www.huntingfield. com, $185-325) is hard to beat. Guests can literally swim, kayak, and bike right from the front door of this beautiful farm estate that was once a high-end hunting club and horse racing track. Four guest rooms in the manor house and four private cottages allow for a variety of accommodations (pets are allowed in the cottages). The estate is a blend of old-world charm and modern conveniences. It has lovely grounds, a view of the Chesapeake Bay, a saltwater pool, wireless Internet, and a library. Gourmet breakfasts are served daily in the gorgeous manor house.

The **Osprey Point Inn** (20786 Rock Hall Ave., 410/639-2194, www.ospreypoint.com, $180-280) offers luxurious accommodations in three settings. There are seven guest rooms in the main inn, three rooms in the farmhouse, and five rooms at the marina annex. Guests in all three locations can enjoy the amenities at the inn, including a pool and daily continental breakfast. A marina provides boat access, docks, and a bathhouse. There is also a lovely on-site restaurant that features delicious food in a waterfront setting (dinner Wed.-Sun. starting at 5pm, Sunday brunch May-Sept. 10:30am-2pm).

Information and Services

Additional information on Rock Hall can be found at www.rockhallmd.com or by stopping by the **Rock Hall Visitor's Center** (5585 Main St., 410/639-7611, www.rockhallmd. com, open daily).

ST. MICHAELS

The historic waterfront town of St. Michaels is approximately one hour (51 miles) from Annapolis (from Route 50, exit on Route 322 and follow the signs for Route 33 to St. Michaels). This charming vintage port is a popular tourist destination and features manicured colonial, federal, and Victorian homes, stunning churches, and a scenic shopping area with specialty stores, restaurants, exclusive inns, and bed-and-breakfasts. Seafood lovers can eat their fill of local crab, fish, and oysters, and those looking to go out on the water can take a cruise or launch a kayak.

St. Michaels was founded in the mid-1600s as a trading stop for the tobacco and trapper industries. The town's name came from the Christ Episcopal Church of St. Michael Archangel parish that was founded in 1677. The historic center of St. Michaels, known as St. Mary's Square (between Mulberry Street and E. Chestnut Street), was created in 1778 when a wealthy land agent from England purchased 20 acres and created 58 town lots. Many of the homes in St. Michaels that were built in the late 1700s and 1800s still stand today.

St. Michaels earned the nickname "the town that fooled the British" during the War of 1812, when residents protected their town from British gunfire using trickery as their defense. Warned of a nighttime attack from British barges positioned in their waters, the townspeople strung burning lanterns in the treetops above the town to fool the attackers into overshooting their targets. The plan worked, and only one house, still known today as the "cannonball house," was hit in the attack.

In the late 1800s and early 1900s, St. Michaels's economy was primarily supported by seafood processing and shipbuilding. Slowly, toward the end of the 20th century, the town became a popular tourist destination and a weekend getaway spot for Washingtonians and other regional residents.

Sights
★ HISTORIC DISTRICT IN ST. MICHAELS

The charming and historic downtown area of St. Michaels is a cornucopia of churches, colonial homes, shops, restaurants, and galleries. This elegant district was added to the National Register of Historic places in 1986 and is a destination for many tourists and area residents. The area includes a scenic harbor on the Miles River. South Talbot Street (Route 33) is the main artery through town, just a few blocks from the waterfront.

★ CHESAPEAKE BAY MARITIME MUSEUM

The **Chesapeake Bay Maritime Museum** (213 N. Talbot St., 410/745-2916, www.cbmm.org, daily May-Oct. 9am-5pm, Nov.-Apr. 10am-4pm, $15) is an 18-acre learning center for all things Chesapeake Bay. There are 10 exhibit buildings, a large display of traditional

Chesapeake Bay Maritime Museum

bay boats, and the Hooper Strait Lighthouse built in 1879.

The museum is a wealth of information on Chesapeake Bay history and the people who live there. Instead of relying on tour guides or reenactors to teach visitors about the bay, the Chesapeake Bay Maritime Museum employs real people of the Chesapeake who live and work on the bay and share their actual experiences. Examples include master decoy carvers, retired crab pickers, and ship captains. Visitors can also witness a boat restoration in progress in the museum's working boatyard or climb a lighthouse.

The museum offers scenic 45-minute cruises on the Miles River on a replica buyboat (May-Oct. Fri.-Mon. at noon, 1pm, 2pm, and 3pm). Buyboats were used to buy catches off watermen's boats and take them directly to market. Cruises depart from the lighthouse (tickets are sold in the Admissions Building, $10).

Both self-guided tours (by map) and guided tours are available with admission to view the museum's many exhibits, including art and maritime displays.

Recreation

St. Michaels is all about water. Those looking for an upscale sailing adventure can charter the *Selina II,* a vintage catboat, through **Sail Selina** (101 N. Harbor Rd., 410/726-9400, www.sailselina.com, May-Sept.). Passengers are limited to just six per two-hour outing and are offered a personal sailing experience/tour through the harbor and on the Miles River. Guests are invited to help sail the vessel or to just sit back and relax. The boat is docked at the Harbor Inn and Marina. Outings start at $65 per person.

Narrated cruises up the Miles River are also available through **Patriot Cruises** (410/745-3100, www.patriotcruises.com, early spring-late fall, $24.50). This two-level, 49-passenger cruising boat is climate-controlled and offers 60- to 70-minute tours. It leaves from 301 N. Talbot Street.

If you long to sail aboard an authentic

skipjack, the **Skipjack *H. M. Krentz*** (800/979-3370, www.oystercatcher.com, Apr.-Oct. daily, $40) offers two-hour narrated cruises aboard a 70-foot working skipjack from the 1950s. Sailing cruises leave from the Chesapeake Bay Maritime Museum.

Kayaks ($30 per hour), stand-up paddleboards ($30 per hour), and bikes ($10 per hour) can be rented from **Shore Pedal & Paddle** (store: 500 S. Talbot St., dock: 125 Mulberry St., 410/745-2320, www.shorepedalandpaddle. com). They also offer guided two-hour kayak tours in St. Michaels Harbor on weekends and by appointment during the week. Bikes can also be rented from **TriCycle & Run** (929 S. Talbot St., 410/745-2836, www.tricycleand-run.com, Sun. 10am-2pm, Mon. 10am-5pm, Thurs.-Sat. 10am-5pm, $10 for 2 hours).

Shopping

Talbot Street is the place to start your shopping adventure in St. Michaels. For unique gifts, stop by **The Preppy Redneck** (310 S. Talbot St., 410/829-3635, www.thepreppyredneck.com), a fun gift shop; **NETime Designs** (404 S. Talbot St., 410/745-8001) for home decor, gifts, and jewelry; and **Ophiuroidea** (609 S. Talbot St., 410/745-8057) for coastal-inspired furnishings and gifts.

Food
AMERICAN
Good food with a romantic atmosphere and modern ambience can be found at **Theo's Steaks, Sides, and Spirits** (407 S. Talbot St., 410/745-2106, www.theossteakhouse.com, Wed.-Sun. for dinner at 4:30pm, $15-55) on Talbot Street. This popular eatery offers a small but diverse menu of pub fare and steaks, expertly prepared and presented.

Another good date-night spot is **208 Talbot** (208 N. Talbot St., 410/745-3838, www.208talbot.com, Wed.-Sun for dinner at 5pm, tavern menu $12-23, dining room menu $28-36). They offer delicious steak and seafood dishes such as pan-seared grouper, grilled ribeye, and seared sea scallops in the dining room and a casual menu with items

The Preppy Redneck gift shop

such as pizza, burgers, and shrimp and grits in their tavern. Reservations are recommended.

A good bet for casual American fare any day of the week is **Mike and Eric's Front Street Restaurant & Bar** (200 S. Talbot St., 410/745-8380, www.mikeandericsfrontstreet. com, Mon.-Sat. 11am-10pm, Sun. 9am-10pm, $13-27). They serve sandwiches, flatbread, and an eclectic selection of entrees that includes pasta, lamb, chicken potpie, salmon, and oysters.

ITALIAN

Theo's sister restaurant, **Ava's Pizzeria and Wine Bar** (409 S. Talbot St., 410/745-3081, www.avaspizzeria.com, daily 11:30am-9:30pm, $8-24) serves exceptional pizza, pasta, and sandwiches. They also have an extensive wine and beer menu. The atmosphere is fun and inviting with an outdoor patio, fireplaces, and even a waterfall. They do not take reservations, although they do have a call-ahead list. They are known for pizza, but the meatballs are out of this world.

MEXICAN

Feeling funky? Then try **Gina's Cafe** (601 Talbot St., 410/745-6400, Wed.-Mon. noon-10pm, $11-28). This tiny, 1,000-square-foot Southwestern eatery on the corner of Talbot Street and East Chew is barely large enough to be termed a restaurant, but they serve up interesting, south-of-the-border goodness with a nod to fresh seafood. They offer fish tacos, drinks, and house-made tortilla chips, in addition to a host of other unique favorites. This is the place to come when your taste buds need a break from the usual restaurant fare. People either love it for its uniqueness or dislike it for its quirkiness. Try the soft-shell tacos with crab and guacamole or the crab nachos.

SEAFOOD

A great view and a harbor atmosphere are the calling cards of the **Town Dock Restaurant** (125 Mulberry St., 410/745-5577, www.town-dockrestaurant.com, Sun. 11am-8pm, Thurs. 4pm-9pm, Fri.-Sat. 11:30am-9pm, $15-30). This waterfront restaurant specializes in seafood, but also offers steak, ribs, and seasonal menu items. The atmosphere is casual, but it's best to come on a nice day so you can enjoy the harbor-side porch.

Another waterfront seafood house is the **St. Michaels Crab and Steakhouse** (305 Mulberry St., 410/745-3737, www.stmichaelscrabhouse.com, Thurs.-Mon. at 11am for lunch and dinner, $9-30). They offer a large menu of seafood favorites along with sandwiches, steak, pasta, and salad. All meals are made to order, and they pride themselves on being flexible in accommodating requests. The atmosphere is fun and lively. This is a good place to grab a drink and enjoy the local food and a good view.

ICE CREAM

Mouthwatering ice cream in a friendly atmosphere can be found at **Justine's Ice Cream Parlour** (106 N. Talbot St., 410/745-0404, www.justinesicecreams.com, Sun.-Thurs. 11am-8pm, Fri.-Sat. 11am-10pm, under $10) on North Talbot Street. They have been a staple in St. Michaels for more than 25 years. They serve ice cream, floats, shakes, and malts.

Accommodations
$100-200

There is no shortage of comfortable bed-and-breakfasts and inns in St. Michaels. The **Cherry Street Inn** (103 Cherry St., 410/745-6309, www.cherrystreetinn.com, $155-180) is one good option, with its convenient location, great breakfasts, and friendly, down-to-earth hosts. Just a short walk from the downtown area, this Victorian inn offers two suites with queen beds and private bathrooms. The inn was built in the 1880s by a steamboat captain and has been fully renovated.

$200-300

Bring your kayak or fishing rod to the **Point Breeze Bed and Breakfast** (704 Riverview Ter., 410/745-9563, www.pointbreezebandb. com, $205, minimum stays may be required). This lovely home has 400 feet of waterfront on the harbor, a pier, and complimentary kayaks, canoes, and bicycles for guest use. There are several guest rooms, all decorated with family heirlooms from five generations. Breakfast is included with each stay.

An additional nice bed-and-breakfast option is the **Snuggery Bed and Breakfast** (203 Cherry St., 410/745-2800, www. snuggery1665.com, $200-250), with two guest rooms in the oldest residence in St. Michaels.

OVER $300

Also located on Cherry Street is the ★ **Dr. Dodson House Bed and Breakfast** (200 Cherry St., 410/745-3691, www. drdodsonhouse.com, $290-385). This charming bed-and-breakfast is steps from Talbot Street and a stone's throw from the harbor. The inn was built in 1799 for use as a tavern and also served as the first post office in town. The home still has many of its original features, such as the fireplaces, woodwork, doors, and glass. It is considered to be one of the best-preserved examples of federal architecture in St. Michaels. The interior is modern but keeps with the character of its time. There are three guest rooms: two with queen beds and one with a king or two twins. All have fireplaces (either wood-burning or electric) and private bathrooms. There are large sofas on the first floor and a second-floor porch for guests to relax on. A wonderful breakfast is served each morning in the elegant dining area.

The lavish **Inn at Perry Cabin** (308 Watkins Ln., 410/745-2200, www.belmond. com/inn-at-perry-cabin-st-michaels/, $615-1,035) is a grand old resort and spa formerly owned by Sir Bernard and Lady Laura Ashley. It sits on the Miles River and has nice views of the water. The hotel was built around 1816 and is surrounded by antique gardens from the same period. Docking facilities (free for guest use), a fitness center, heated outdoor pool, and complimentary bicycles are part of the property amenities. There are 78 guest rooms and the resort is pet friendly. Ask for a room on an upper floor with a view of the water.

The **St. Michaels Harbour Inn Marina & Spa** (101 N. Harbor Rd., 410/745-9001, www. harbourinn.com, $279-729) is also located on the Miles River and offers 46 guest rooms and a full-service marina. This is a lovely property in a good location.

Information and Services

For additional information on St. Michaels, visit www.stmichaelsmd.org.

TILGHMAN ISLAND

Tilghman Island is one of the few remaining working watermen's villages in the mid-Atlantic. It provides an unvarnished look at life on the Chesapeake Bay. Tilghman Island is home to the last commercial sailing fleet in North America. The fleet is known as the Skipjacks in honor of the classic oyster boat (and Maryland's state boat), which visitors can see at **Dogwood Harbor,** on the east side of the island. Tilghman Island is in the middle Chesapeake Bay region and is separated from the Eastern Shore by Napps Narrows, but is easily accessed by driving over a drawbridge. Tilghman Island is three miles long and reachable via Route 33, 11 miles west of St. Michaels. It has a population of less than 800 people.

Sights

The **Phillips Wharf Environmental Center** (6129 Tilghman Island Rd., 410/886-9200, www.pwec.org, Apr.-mid-Oct. Thurs.-Mon. 10am-4pm, free, donations appreciated) is a wonderful place for children and adults to learn about creatures living in the Chesapeake Bay. The center gives visitors the opportunity to see, touch, and learn about the wildlife such as horseshoe crabs, turtles, and oysters.

The **Tilghman's Watermen's Museum** (6031 Tilghman Island Rd., 410/886-1025, www.tilghmanmuseum.org, Apr.-Dec. Sat.-Sun. 10am-3pm, free) features exhibits on the heritage of the local watermen. It houses a collection of artifacts, boat models, and artwork by local artists.

Recreation

Boat tours and charters are available on Tilghman Island through **Harrison House Charter Fishing** (21551 Chesapeake House Dr., 410/886-2121, www.chesapeakehouse. com, starting at $125). They have a charter fleet of 14 boats that can carry 6-40 passengers. They tout the "complete charter experience," regardless of the size of your party.

Lady Patty Classic Yacht Charters (6176 Tilghman Island Rd., 410/886-1127, www.

ladypatty.com, $42) offers seasonal two-hour charters in the waters surrounding Tilghman Island. Beer, wine, and cocktail service is available on all charters. Private charters can be arranged.

Charters aboard the oldest working skipjack on the Chesapeake Bay can be arranged on the **Skipjack *Rebecca T. Ruark*** (410/829-3976, www.tilghmanisland.com, $30). This beautiful boat was built in 1886, and the wonderful captain helps make this a great two-hour sail. Sailing charters leave from **Dogwood Harbor** (21308 Phillips Rd.).

Several **Tilghman Island Water Trails** (410/770-8000, www.dnr2.maryland.gov/boating/Pages/eastern_north.aspx) are available for kayaking. The **East Tilghman Island Trail** is 10.2 miles and explores the eastern portion of the island, while the **Tilghman Island Trail** tours the entire island. Maps can be downloaded at the trail website. **Tilghman Island Marina** (6140 Mariners Ct., 410/886-2500, www. tilghmanmarina.com) rents kayaks and canoes.

Food

Two If By Sea Restaurant (5776 Tilghman Island Rd., 410/886-2447, www.twoifbysearestaurant.com, breakfast Mon., Tues., Thurs. 8am-11am, breakfast and lunch, Wed., Fri.-Sun. 8am-2pm, dinner Thurs. and Sun. 6pm-8:30pm, Fri. and Sat. 6pm-9pm, $15-24) is a cozy little restaurant serving breakfast, lunch, and dinner. They have wonderful traditional breakfasts, sandwiches, salads, fresh seafood, and homemade pastries. This is a delightful choice for a casual meal at a reasonable price.

The **Marker Five Restaurant** (6178 Tilghman Island Rd., 410/886-1122, www. markerfive.com, $11-27) offers a casual waterfront dining experience. They serve soup, sandwiches, local seafood, and other items such as barbecue and house-smoked ribs. They have an outdoor bar with more than 30 beers on tap.

If you're looking for a great view, laid-back atmosphere, and an interesting take on casual fare, grab a seat on the deck at the **Characters**

Bridge Restaurant (6136 Tilghman Island Rd., 410/886-1060, www.charactersbridgerestaurant.com, daily 11am-10pm, $8-29). The menu offers staples like local seafood, burgers, and steak, but also includes interesting dishes such as oyster pie and Cajun burgers. This is a great place to watch the boats on Knapps Narrows and the activity at the drawbridge.

Accommodations

For peace and serenity, stay a few nights at the ★ **Black Walnut Point Inn** (4417 Black Walnut Point Rd., Tilghman, 410/886-2452, www.blackwalnutpointinn.com, $150-350). This charming bed-and-breakfast is at the southern point of Tilghman Island and bounded by water on three sides. The main house is meticulously maintained and offers four rooms with private baths. Two nicely appointed cabins right on the Choptank River provide a larger, more private space, and one is wheelchair accessible. The innkeepers are extremely friendly and knowledgeable about the long history of the property. Full breakfast is served each morning in the dining room, and the beautiful grounds offer a swimming pool, hot tub, pier, bird-watching trails, and unrivaled views of the Chesapeake Bay.

The **Knapps Narrows Marina and Inn** (6176 Tilghman Island Rd., 410/886-2720, www.knappsnarrowsmarina.com, $120-260) is a wonderful little waterfront inn, restaurant, and tiki bar that offers 20 guest rooms and great views of the Chesapeake Bay. Each room has a private waterfront patio or balcony. The inn is three stories, and each room is nicely furnished but not overstuffed. The staff is truly accommodating and friendly. The inn is adjacent to the Knapps Narrows Bridge (the entrance to the island). There is an outdoor pool on-site.

The Lazy Jack Inn on Dogwood Harbor (5907 Tilghman Island Rd., 410/886-2215, www.lazyjackinn.com, $185-305) has two rooms and two suites with private bathrooms. This charming waterfront inn has watched over Dogwood Harbor for more than 150 years. It is within walking distance of several restaurants and activities in the harbor. Nicely restored, the current owners have owned and run the inn for more than 20 years. A full gourmet breakfast is included. This is a great place for a peaceful getaway with wonderful views.

Information and Services

For additional information on Tilghman Island, visit www.tilghmanisland.com.

EASTON

Easton is a wonderful small town on the Eastern Shore that was founded in 1710. It is an hour's drive (42 miles) southeast of Annapolis. Easton is the largest town in Talbot County, with a population of around 16,000. It offers residents and visitors a beautiful downtown area with colonial and Victorian architecture, casual and fine restaurants, shopping, antiques, and galleries, while also providing ample opportunities for recreation such as golf and water sports on the Chesapeake Bay.

Sights
ACADEMY ART MUSEUM

The **Academy Art Museum** (106 South St., 410/822-2787, www.academyartmuseum.org, Mon. and Fri.-Sun. 10am-4pm, Tues.-Thurs. 10am-8pm, $3) is a little museum near downtown Easton that has five studios. It is housed in a charming building was built in 1820 and was the location of the first chartered school in Easton. It is now a historic landmark. The museum offers both regional and national exhibits; hosts concerts, lectures, and educational programs; and offers performing arts education for adults and children. More than 70,000 visitors come to the museum each year. Past exhibits have included original works by Ansel Adams, Roy Lichtenstein, and N. C. Wyeth.

★ PICKERING CREEK AUDUBON CENTER

The **Pickering Creek Audubon Center** (11450 Audubon Ln., 410/822-4903, www.

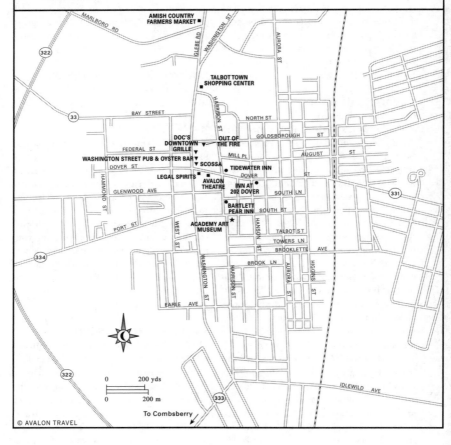

Easton

pickeringcreek.audubon.org, trails and viewing areas daily dawn-dusk, free) is a 400-acre working farm next to Pickering Creek in Talbot County. The property is a natural habitat of forest, marsh, meadow, a freshwater pond, wetlands, more than a mile of shoreline, and farmland. More than 3.5 miles of walking trails are available as well as gardens, a canoe and kayak launch, and 100 acres of hardwood forest. Trails and viewing areas are open to the public from dawn until dusk every day, and there is no admission fee. The center is great for bird-watching and features viewing platforms, a bluebird trail, and 90 acres of wetlands. Office hours at Pickering Creek are Monday-Friday 9am-4pm. The center is north of Easton: Take Route 662 north past the airport. Turn left on Sharp Road (west) and go right at the Y. Turn right (north) on Presquille Road and then right again on Audubon Lane.

THE AMISH COUNTRY FARMERS MARKET
The Amish Country Farmers Market (101 Marlboro Ave., 410/822-8989, www. amishcountryfarmersmarket.com, Thurs.

9am-6pm, Fri. 9am-7pm, Sat. 9am-3pm) is a tradition on the Eastern Shore. The market features numerous authentic Amish vendors from Pennsylvania selling a great variety of produce, dairy products, baked goods, meats, candy, furniture, and crafts. Many locals do their regular grocery shopping at the market, but it is a popular stop for tourists wishing to purchase fresh foods and handmade products.

Recreation and Entertainment

Easton is home to the popular **Hog Neck Golf Course** (10142 Old Cordova Rd., 410/822-6079, www.hogneck.com, $55). The facility offers an 18-hole championship course and a 9-hole executive course.

Visitors can catch a show at the **Avalon Theatre** (40 E. Dover St., 410/822-7299, www. avalontheatre.com). This cozy little theater has a full schedule of entertainment including theatrical performances, symphonies, bluegrass, jazz, comedians, and art festivals.

The largest annual event in Easton, and one of the best known on the Eastern Shore, is the **Waterfowl Festival** (www.waterfowlfestival. org, $15 for all three days). Taking place over three days in November, this event began in the early 1970s and now hosts 17,000 visitors, 300 of the best wildlife artists, craftspeople, and vendors, and 1,500 volunteers. This is a citywide event that closes several streets and prompts businesses to decorate their buildings with natural greens. The festival is a leader in promoting conservation of waterfowl and natural habitat.

Shopping

Downtown Easton is a shopper's delight, with many gift stores, antiques shops, crafts, clothing, and shops with collectibles. Two of the prime streets to include on your shopping journey are Harrison and Washington, although many lovely stores may be found on various side streets. The **Talbot Town Shopping Center** on North Washington Street offers national retail chains.

Food

Good Northern Italian food is served at **Scossa** (8 N. Washington St., 410/822-2202, www.scossarestaurant.com, lunch Thurs.-Sun. 11:30am-3pm, dinner Mon.-Thurs. 4pm-9pm, Sun. 4pm-8pm, Fri.-Sat. 4pm-10pm, $15-35) in the heart of the downtown

downtown Easton

area on North Washington Street. The owner/chef was born in northern Italy and has an impressive culinary résumé. The modern dining room is the perfect place to meet with friends, business associates, and family. The dinner menu is a step above traditional Italian with creative combinations, fresh ingredients, and daily specials that offer something new each visit. They also offer a prix fixe menu for $40. Lunch is a completely different experience and features wonderful salads and sandwiches. The bar area is very inviting and serves top-shelf wine and liquor. They have a large specialty drink menu. Sunday brunch is also served.

Another excellent choice for Italian food is **Out of the Fire** (22 Goldsborough St., 410/770-4777, www.outofthefire.com, lunch Tues.-Sat. 11:30am-2pm, dinner Tues.-Thurs. 5pm-9pm, Fri.-Sat. 5pm-10pm, $14-28) on Goldsborough Street. They serve gourmet pizza and other creative entrées made from high-quality ingredients procured from mostly local farmers and vendors (try the mussels). The wraps and sandwiches are delicious, and they offer organic and gluten-free choices. The atmosphere is very warm and relaxing with tile floors and soft lighting.

For a good pub-style meal in Easton, go to the **Washington Street Pub & Oyster Bar** (20 N. Washington St., 410/822-1112, www.washingtonstreetpub.com, Mon.-Thurs. 11am-2am, Fri.-Sat. 11am-2am, Sun. 11am-2am, $10-17). The trendy decor and lively atmosphere rival the food at this cozy pub and raw bar. They also have a good selection of beer on tap. Try the Chesapeake chicken sandwich (crab imperial and cheese on top of chicken); it is decadent to say the least.

The **Bartlett Pear Inn** (28 S. Harrison St., 410/770-3300, www.bartlettpearinn.com, Wed.-Sun. 5:30pm-10pm, $26-44) has a lovely upscale American bistro serving delicious entrées such as Alaskan halibut, New York strip steak, and curry-dusted sea scallops. They also offer a five-course tasting menu for $75 and a seven-course tasting menu for $95. The

Washington Street Pub & Oyster Bar

food is very flavorful, and the presentation is exquisite. The restaurant is part of a working inn with seven guest rooms.

For a fun atmosphere or to watch your favorite sports event, dine at **Doc's Downtown Grille** (14 N. Washington St., 410/822-7700, daily 11am-2am, $11-30). They serve traditional pub food and delicious local seafood (crab cakes, shrimp po'boy, fried oysters, etc.). The restaurant is family owned and operated and their passion for their business is evident in the friendly service.

Accommodations

The ★ **Bartlett Pear Inn** (28 S. Harrison St., 410/770-3300, www.bartlettpearinn.com, $234-289) is a beautiful property on South Harrison Street in downtown Easton. This lovely inn dates back to the late 1700s and offers seven individually decorated guest rooms named for different types of pears. The handsome brick building with white covered porches is on a quiet street within walking distance to shopping and restaurants. The husband-and-wife owners are very gracious hosts, and they pay attention to the small details that make their guests feel welcome. The inn is pet friendly and can even accommodate large dogs. Ask for a room on the upper floor; this will provide the most quiet and privacy. There is an on-site restaurant that is open Wednesday-Sunday for dinner.

Luxurious accommodations can be found on Dover Street at the ★ **Inn at 202 Dover** (202 E. Dover St., 410/819-8007, www.innat-202dover.com, $289-525). This grand, beautifully renovated home is truly a work of art. From the stately exterior of this historic 1874 mansion to the inviting common areas and the themed rooms and suites, every last detail is attended to. An example of this is the Safari Suite, which has an elephant vanity, exotic lamps, and themed details down to the bath soap. Each of the five rooms is furnished with antique and reproduction items, pillow-top mattresses, and comfortable linens. Air jet tubs, steam showers, high-speed Internet, and cable television are also standard. The upscale

Peacock Restaurant serves delightful cuisine with Eastern Shore influence prepared by a Cordon Bleu-trained executive chef. They also have wonderful martinis.

The gracious **Tidewater Inn** (101 E. Dover St., 410/822-1300, www.tidewaterinn.com, $189-289) is the landmark lodging property in Easton. This elegant downtown hotel opened in 1949 and is known as a romantic getaway. The inn has 89 guest rooms with yesterday's charm and some modern conveniences such as wireless Internet and flat-screen televisions. The hotel does not have some of the amenities many travelers are used to such as a fitness room and on-site pool, although many of the rooms underwent renovations in early 2016. If you are looking for a comfortable manor house atmosphere with good service, this is a lovely choice. There is a good restaurant (the Hunter's Tavern) on-site and many more within walking distance.

Information and Services

For additional information on Easton, visit www.eastonmd.org or stop by the **Talbot County Visitors' Center** (11 S. Harrison St., 410/770-8000).

Bartlett Pear Inn

Getting There and Around

Most people arrive in Easton by car. There is a small public airport, the **Easton Airport** (29137 Newnam Rd., 410/770-8055, www.eastonairport.com), two miles north of Easton.

OXFORD

The small waterfront town of Oxford, 10 miles southwest of Easton, is a fun day-trip destination. Oxford was settled in the mid-1660s on just 30 acres and is one of the oldest towns in Maryland. It was selected shortly after its settlement to be one of only two ports of entry for the Maryland Province (the other was Anne Arundel, which later became Annapolis). What followed was a period of prominence for the little town, and it became known as an international shipping center and home to many thriving tobacco plantations. After the Revolutionary War, when British ships stopped visiting its waters for trade, the town declined. Today, Oxford has a population of less than 1,000 people, but it remains a scenic and inviting place.

Oxford-Bellevue Ferry

The **Oxford-Bellevue Ferry** (27456 Oxford Rd., 410/745-9023, www.oxfordbellevueferry. com, mid-Apr.-mid-Nov. daily, one-way/round-trip $12/20 car and driver, $6/9 motorcycle, $4/7 bike, $3/5 pedestrian) is one of the oldest privately run ferries in the country, dating back to 1683. It runs between Oxford and Bellevue, Maryland, across the Tred Avon River. The trip is less than a mile and takes approximately 10 minutes. The ferry accommodates cars, motorcycles, bikes, and pedestrians and has a capacity of nine vehicles. This is a popular connection for cyclists biking a circular route from St. Michaels.

Food and Accommodations

Overnight visitors to Oxford can enjoy a stay at the **Oxford Inn** (504 S. Morris St., 410/226-5220, www.oxfordinn.net, $50-190). This lovely bed-and-breakfast is on a charming street across from a small marina. The exterior of the building is white with a green roof, covered porches, and seven dormer windows. The seven guest rooms are quaintly decorated in a country style, and the inn has a wonderful European bistro, **Pope's Tavern** ($24-34), that offers elegant dinner space for 40 guests. They serve entrées such as chicken, crab cakes, beef tenderloin, and pasta. There is also a cozy teak bar with seating for 12. A note at

the Oxford Inn

the bottom of their menu states "unattended children will be given a double espresso and a puppy."

The ★ **Robert Morris Inn** (314 N. Morris St., 410/226-5111, www.robertmorrisinn.com, $145-240), near the ferry landing, is another wonderful choice for accommodations in Oxford. This historic building with a yellow exterior and large patio dates back to 1710 and was once the home of a prosperous merchant and famous financier of the American Revolution, Robert Morris. A close friend of George Washington's, Morris entertained Washington at his home on multiple occasions. In later years, author James Michener spent time at the inn while working on his novel *Chesapeake*. The rooms offer a choice of cozy period furniture and canopy beds or more modern furnishings.

The inn contains a great restaurant, **Salter's Tavern and Tap Room,** that serves breakfast ($4-12), lunch ($14-21), and dinner ($17-31). The ambience is warm and inviting with slate floors, redbrick walls, and timber beams. The casual menu is centered on the local seafood treasures found in the bay such as crab, oysters, and fresh fish, but also features land-based menu items such as burgers and salads. The restaurant is overseen by Mark Salter, a well-known British master chef.

Information and Services

For additional information on Oxford, visit www.oxfordmd.net.

CAMBRIDGE

Cambridge is 17 miles south of Easton off Route 50. It is the largest town in Dorchester County and one of the oldest colonial cities in Maryland, having been settled in 1684. It sits directly on the Choptank River (which was the setting for James Michener's book *Chesapeake*) near the Chesapeake Bay. The town was originally a trading center for tobacco.

In the late 19th century, Cambridge opened food processing businesses that canned foods such as oysters, tomatoes, and sweet potatoes. At its peak, the primary packing concern, Phillips Packing Company, employed 10,000 people. By the 1960s the decline in the canning industry had led to the closure of the company and left behind a struggling city that is still fighting to prosper.

Today Cambridge offers a pretty downtown area with historic 18th- and 19th-century

the Cambridge waterfront

EASTERN SHORE THE EASTERN SHORE

homes and scenic waterfront parks and marinas.

Sights

HARRIET TUBMAN MUSEUM & EDUCATIONAL CENTER

The **Harriet Tubman Museum & Educational Center** (424 Race St., 410/228-0401, www.visitdorchester.org/harriet-tubman-museum-educational-center, Tues.-Fri. noon-3pm, Sat. noon-4pm, tours by appointment only, free) is a tribute to Harriet Ross Tubman (1822-1913), a freedom fighter and former slave who was known for leading many slaves to freedom through the Underground Railroad. This small museum is dedicated to telling stories of this heroine's life and features exhibits on her work helping dozens of slaves. Tubman was a Dorchester County native.

J. M. CLAYTON COMPANY

Pay a visit to the market at the world's oldest working crab house, **J. M. Clayton Company** (108 Commerce St., 410/228-1661, www.jmclayton.com, Mon.-Fri. 8am-5pm) on Commerce Street. This historic crab house is still operated by the same family that started it back in 1890. They even have an 80-year old canning machine. Their market is open daily where visitors can purchase local crabmeat and crab-related items.

RICHARDSON MARITIME MUSEUM

Visitors can learn about the lost tradition of wooden boatbuilding at the **Richardson Maritime Museum** (401 High St., 410/221-1871, www.richardsonmuseum.org, Sat. 10am-4pm, Sun. 1pm-4pm, $3). This historic brick building on the corner of High and Locust Streets housed a bank for almost a hundred years. One step into the museum takes visitors into the world of wooden sailing vessels and their role on the Chesapeake Bay. Boat models, building tools, and original artifacts are just some of the items on display. The rich wooden boat history includes everything from crabbing skiffs to dovetails to clipper ships and even schooners.

★ BLACKWATER NATIONAL WILDLIFE REFUGE

Blackwater National Wildlife Refuge (2145 Key Wallace Dr., 410/228-2677, www. friendsofblackwater.org, daily dawn-dusk, vehicles $3, pedestrians $1, cyclists $1) was established in 1933 as a sanctuary for waterfowl migrating along the **Atlantic Flyway** (a migration route along the Atlantic coast). The refuge 12 miles south of Cambridge encompasses 27,000 acres including freshwater, brackish tidal wetlands, meadows, and forest. It is open year-round.

More than 250 species of birds live in the refuge, and it is home to the largest breeding population of bald eagles on the East Coast north of Florida. The eagle population swells in the winter months, when many birds migrate here from northern areas. During the winter, the refuge is also home to more than 35,000 geese and 15,000 ducks. Fall (Sept.-Nov.) is the best time to see migrating waterfowl and songbirds.

A wide variety of mammals also live in the refuge. Delmarva fox squirrels, southern flying squirrels, voles, shrews, nutria, gray foxes, red foxes, river otters, mink, skunks, deer, and beavers all call the refuge home.

There is a wonderful visitors center on Key Wallace Drive (year-round Mon.-Fri. 8am-4pm, Sat.-Sun. 9am-5pm) with wildlife exhibits, nature books, birding guides, a butterfly garden, maps, restrooms, and a gift shop. The prime attraction in the refuge is the Wildlife Drive, a four-mile paved road where visitors can drive, bike, and walk through the refuge to view wildlife. There is also a great viewing platform over the marsh. In addition to the Wildlife Drive, the refuge has four land trails and three paddling trails. Visitors can also hunt, fish, and crab. Environmental education programs are also offered for young people.

Recreation and Events

One-hour **Historic High Street Walking Tours** (410/901-1000, $8) are offered by the West End Citizens Association. Reservations are not required but they are recommended. Tours meet at 11am on Saturday April-October at Long Wharf (High Street and Water Street).

One- or two-hour cruises on the skipjack **Nathan of Dorchester** (Long Wharf on High St., 410/228-7141, www.skipjack-nathan.org, most Saturdays May-Oct., two-hour sails $30, call for reservations) offer an authentic Chesapeake Bay experience. Tours go out on the Choptank River and teach the history of oystering.

There are two lovely parks in Cambridge that offer nice views of the Choptank River. **Great Marsh Park** (at the end of Somerset Ave. on the Choptank River, www.choosecambridge.com) has a boat launch, fishing pier, playground, and picnic tables. **Sailwinds Park East** (2 Rose Hill Pl., 410/228-1000, www.tourdorchester.org) is next to the Dorchester County visitors center. There is a playground, and the park is known as a good spot to fly kites.

Cambridge is the site of many endurance events including the **Ironman 70.3 Eagleman Triathlon** (www.ironman.com) in June, **Ironman Maryland** (www.ironman.com) in early October, and the **Six Pillars Century** bike ride (www.6pillarscentury.org) in early May.

Blackwater Paddle & Pedal (2524 Key Wallace Dr., 410/901-9255, www.blackwaterpaddleandpedal.com) offers guided three-hour bike tours and two-hour kayak tours. Bike tours depart from the Hyatt Regency, and kayak tours leave from the Hyatt Beach. They also offer rentals for bikes, kayaks, and paddleboards (call for pricing).

Food

★ **The High Spot** (305 High St., 410/228-7420, www.thehighspotgastropub.com, Mon.-Thurs. 11am-11pm, Fri.-Sat. 11am-midnight, Sun. 11am-10pm, $7-25) is a trendy gastropub serving lunch and dinner. Their food is innovative and tasty, and they have a great beer list and full bar. They also offer special events such as beer pairing dinners. This is a fun

place to eat, with delicious food, a hip atmosphere, and cute little terrariums with cacti on the tables. The only drawback is that it is sometimes very loud inside, but that is due in part to its popularity.

An unexpected French treat in Cambridge is the ★ **Bistro Poplar** (535 Poplar St., 410/228-4884, www.bistropoplar.com, Thurs.-Sun. starting at 5pm, $24-30). They serve traditional French cuisine infused with local seafood flavors such as scallops and flounder. The restaurant is housed in a historic building constructed in 1895. The interior is unmistakably French with ornate floor tiles, dim lighting, a dark-framed bar, and red velvet cushions. The food is artfully presented by servers well versed in the menu. This is a special find in Cambridge and has won many awards.

The **Blue Point Provision Company** (100 Heron Blvd. at Rte. 50, 410/901-6410, www.chesapeakebay.hyatt.com, Wed.-Sun. 5pm-9pm, $20-45) at the Hyatt Regency is a waterfront restaurant with a great seafood menu and a wonderful deck overlooking the

The High Spot

Choptank River. The restaurant is at the far end of the resort, a short walk down the beach from the main complex. The interior is inviting with nautical touches and soaring ceilings, beautiful ceiling fans, parquet floors, and wooden furniture. There is also a large bar area. The menu offers goodies such as Maryland crab dip, Asian barbecued salmon, fried oysters, and the famous Drunkin' Dancin' Jumbo Shrimp. They also have fresh fish selections daily based on the local catch at area fish markets. For landlubbers, they offer steak and chicken.

For good beer and pub fare, stop in **RaR Brewing** (504 Poplar St., 443/225-5664, www.rarbrewing.com, Mon.-Thurs. 2pm-midnight, Fri. 2pm-2am, Sat.-Sun. noon-midnight, under $15). Located inside a former billiards hall, this friendly brewery is a local favorite. They serve a casual menu with pizza, crab dip, hummus, hot dogs, sandwiches, and more than a dozen delicious beers.

Good diner food at a reasonable price can be found at the **Cambridge Diner and Restaurant** (2924 Old Rte. 50, 410/228-8898, daily 6am-10pm, $10-15). They serve traditional comfort food in large portions.

Accommodations

At first glance, ★ **The Hyatt Regency Chesapeake Bay Golf Resort, Spa & Marina** (100 Heron Blvd. at Rte. 50, 410/901-1234, www.chesapeakebay.hyatt.com, $399-469 per night) seems a bit "glam" for the quiet town of Cambridge, but it does quite well in providing a self-contained oasis of luxury for both golfing and non-golfing visitors. One of the premier hotels on the Eastern Shore, it sits on 400 acres along the Choptank River and has beautiful views of the water and surrounding marsh. The resort offers elegant rooms and enough activities that visitors can easily park their car and never leave the compound during their stay. The resort is known for its golf course, the River Marsh Golf Club, but is also family friendly, with planned children's activities and many amenities (two pools, hot tub, mini golf, game room, fitness center, spa, water sports, etc.). It is also dog friendly on the first floor.

Guests can grab a drink or a bottle of wine and relax in one of the big rocking chairs that line the patio. The centerpiece is a large open fireplace where guests can toast marshmallows or gather for happy hour. There

The Hyatt Regency Chesapeake Bay Golf Resort, Spa & Marina

are several dining options at the hotel that are nice but not as exquisite as might be expected. Book a room with a view and/or balcony; it costs more but makes a big difference. Opening your curtains in the morning to look out at the water is worth the added expense. Rooms are clean and spacious, and the beds are comfortable. The staff does a good job of making guests feel welcome, and the hotel can also make arrangements for activities both on and off the property.

A wonderful waterfront bed-and-breakfast is the **Lodgecliffe on the Choptank Bed and Breakfast** (103 Choptank Ter., 866/273-3830, www.lodgecliffe.com, $180-200). This gorgeous mansion was built in 1898 and sits on a bluff with wonderful views of the lower Choptank River. The establishment was the first bed-and-breakfast in Dorchester County when it opened in 1986 and has remained a family business. There are four guest rooms, each with an individual personality. A glorious three-course breakfast is served each morning. This is a relaxing retreat with wonderful water views and matching service.

Another lovely inn in the historic area of Cambridge is the **Mill Street Inn** (114 Mill St., 410/901-9144, www.millstinn.com, $179-229). This beautiful Victorian-style home was built in 1894 and offers three individually decorated guest rooms. Each features high-quality linens and towels, specialty soaps, fresh flowers, cable television, DVD players, and free wireless Internet. It is a half block from the Choptank River and within walking distance to restaurants. The innkeepers,

who are retired organic growers and bakers, pride themselves in serving delicious breakfasts, complete with locally grown produce and some unusual items from their yard such as figs and pecans.

Additional accommodations in Cambridge include large chain hotels such as the **Holiday Inn Express Cambridge** (2715 Ocean Gtwy., 877/859-5095, www.ihg.com, $117-135), which is clean, quiet, and well-located on Route 50. This hotel has 85 guest rooms, an indoor pool, wireless Internet, and a fitness room. Each room comes with a refrigerator. Another similar option is the **Comfort Inn and Suites** (2936 Ocean Gtwy., 410/901-0926, www. choice hotels.com, $190-210). This hotel is also on Route 50 and has 65 guest rooms. It also offers an indoor pool, fitness room, free breakfast, and free wireless Internet.

Information and Services

Additional information on Cambridge can be found at the **Visitors Center at Sailwinds Park East** (2 Rose Hill Pl., daily 8:30am-5pm) or online at www.visitdorchester.org/about-dorchester/visitor-center/.

Getting There

Most travelers arrive in Cambridge on U.S. Route 50. This east-west route runs from Ocean City, Maryland, to Sacramento, California. The road is known locally as the Ocean Gateway. The **Cambridge-Dorchester Airport** (5263 Bucktown Rd.) is southeast of Cambridge. It is a general aviation airport with one runway.

Assateague Island

Assateague Island sits opposite Ocean City across the Ocean City Inlet. It is considered part of both Virginia and Maryland. The inlet didn't always exist: It was formed during the Chesapeake-Potomac Hurricane in 1933, which created a nice inlet at the south end of Ocean City, and the Army Corps of Engineers decided to make it permanent.

In its southern reaches, Assateague Island borders Chincoteague Island. Both Assateague and Chincoteague are known for their resident herds of wild ponies and the famous **Wild Pony Swim** (www.chincoteaguechamber.com) that takes place each year in late July, when the herd is taken for a swim from Assateague Island across the channel to Chincoteague Island.

SIGHTS
★ Assateague Island National Seashore

Assateague Island National Seashore (www.nps.gov, year-round in Maryland, 24 hours, $5) was established in 1962. It is managed by three agencies: the National Park Service, U.S Fish & Wildlife Service, and the Maryland Department of Natural Resources. The island includes a beautiful 37-mile beach, dunes, wetlands, and marsh. The island is protected as a natural environment, and many opportunities exist for wildlife viewing. Assateague Island is a stopover for migrating shorebirds and provides important areas for feeding and resting. More than 320 bird species can be viewed here during the year, including the piping plovers, great egrets, and northern harriers.

Assateague Island is also known for its wild ponies. It is widely believed that the ponies originally came to the island years ago when a Spanish cargo ship loaded with horses sank off the coast and the ponies swam to shore. In 1997, a Spanish shipwreck was discovered off the island, which supports this theory.

Other mammals in Assateague include rodents as small as the meadow jumping mouse,

wild ponies on Assateague Island

along with red fox, river otters, and deer. Several species of whales feed off the island's shore, along with bottlenose dolphins.

There are two entrances to the national seashore. One is eight miles south of Ocean City at the end of Route 611. The second is at the southern end of the island at the end of Route 175, two miles from Chincoteague, Virginia. Visitors to Assateague Island mostly stay in Chincoteague or Ocean City since there are no hotel accommodations on the island, but camping is allowed and quite popular.

Park hours and fees are different in Virginia and Maryland and also vary by month in Virginia. Consult www.assateagueisland.com for specific information for the time of year and location you wish to visit.

The **Assateague Island Visitor Center** (Maryland District of Assateague Island, on the southern side of Route 611, 410/641-1441, Jan.-Feb. Thurs.-Mon. 9am-5pm, rest of the year daily 9am-5pm) offers a film on the wild ponies, brochures, aquariums, a touch tank, maps, and other exhibits.

Assateague Island Lighthouse

The red-and-white-striped **Assateague Island Lighthouse** (www.assateagueisland. com, 0.25 mile from Chincoteague Island and accessible from Chincoteague by car in approximately five minutes and from Maryland in an hour, 757/336-3696, Apr.-Nov. weekends 9am-3pm, free but donations encouraged) is on the Virginia side of Assateague Island. There is a trail that connects Chincoteague with Assateague Island that can be walked or accessed by bicycle. The original lighthouse was built in 1833 but was replaced by a taller, more powerful lighthouse in 1867. The lighthouse is still in operation and features twin rotating lights that sit 154 feet above sea level. The U.S. Coast Guard maintains the light as a working navigational aid, but the Chincoteague National Wildlife Refuge is responsible for the lighthouse preservation efforts. The top of the lighthouse can be visited by the public.

RECREATION

Due in part to its relative isolation, Assateague Island has one of the nicest beaches on the East Coast. Visitors can enjoy the area by kayaking, beach walking, swimming, fishing, biking, and bird-watching.

The **Maryland Coastal Bays Program** (www.mdcoastalbays.org/rentals) operates a kayak ($15 per hour), canoe ($22 per hour), paddleboard ($25 per hour), and bike rental ($6 per hour) stand at Assateague Island National Seashore (13002 Bayside Dr., Berlin, 410/726-3217, mid-Apr.-Memorial Day weekends 10am-4pm, Memorial Day-Labor Day daily 9am-6pm, Labor Day-mid-Oct. weekends only 10am-4pm). To find the stand, take the second right after the park tollbooth. A 3.5-mile paved bike path leads from Route 611 through the parks.

CAMPING

Camping is allowed on the Maryland side of the national seashore through the **National Park Service** (410/641-2120, $30). Oceanside and bayside campsites are available all year. Sites do not have hookups but can accommodate tents, trailers, and RVs. There are also horse sites ($50) and group tent sites ($50). Cold showers and chemical toilets are available on-site. Camping is also permitted in **Assateague State Park** (7307 Stephen Decatur Hwy., 410/641-2918, late Apr.-Oct., $30), also on the Maryland side of the island. There are 300 campsites here. Each site has a picnic table, fire ring, room for one car, and access to a bathhouse with warm showers. Backpackers and kayakers can also take advantage of backcountry camping. Camping information can be found at www. assateagueisland.com.

GETTING THERE

There are two entrances to Assateague Island National Seashore. One is eight miles south of Ocean City at the end of Route 611. From Ocean City, cross the bridge on Route 50 heading west. Turn left at the third traffic light onto Route 611. Follow the brown signs to the park. The second is at the southern end of the island at the end of Route 175, two miles from Chincoteague, Virginia. There are no hotel accommodations on the island; visitors to Assateague Island can stay in Chincoteague or Ocean City.

Ocean City

For many people, the quintessential summer vacation is a trip to the beach. Ocean City, the most popular destination in Worcester County, stretches for 10 miles along the Atlantic Ocean between Delaware and the Ocean City Inlet. It offers enough stimulation to keep kids of all ages entertained for days. The three-mile wooden boardwalk is packed with shopping, restaurants, games, and amusements and is open all year. Seemingly every inch of real estate is claimed along the strip, and more than 9,500 hotel rooms and 21,000 condominiums provide endless choices for accommodations.

Ocean City's history dates back to the 1500s, when Giovanni da Verrazano came through the area while surveying the East Coast in service of the King of France. By the 17th century, British colonists had settled the area, after moving north out of Virginia. Ocean City took off as a beach community in 1900 when the first boardwalk was built. Back then, the boardwalk was a seasonal amenity that was taken apart each winter, plank by plank, and stored until the following season.

Today, Ocean City is bustling, to say the least. It is a major East Coast destination for people who enjoy the beach, company, entertainment, and a lot of activity. Visitors can get a good taste for the town in a weekend, but many people stay for a week or more. Approximately eight million people visit Ocean City each year.

Ocean City is a family town but also a party town. Unlike its northern neighbor, Atlantic City, it lacks casinos and has limited development options and, as such, is able to keep the beach as its main focus. Although the city refers to itself as "The East Coast's Number One Family Resort," it is also a popular area for high school seniors letting off steam after graduation at what is traditionally known as

Ocean City Boardwalk

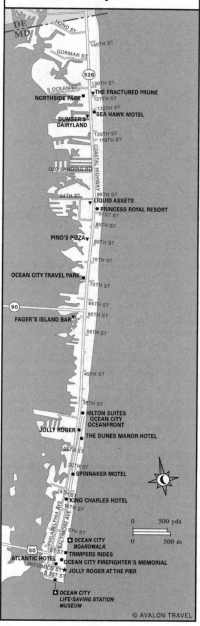

Ocean City

(map labels:)

DE
MD
142ND ST
140TH ST
GORMAN ST
528
130TH ST
S. OCEAN ST
NORTHSIDE PARK
THE FRACTURED PRUNE
127TH ST
125TH ST
SEA HAWK MOTEL
DUMSER'S DAIRYLAND
120TH ST
118TH ST
COASTAL HIGHWAY
OLD LANDING RD
94TH ST
95TH ST
LIQUID ASSETS
PRINCESS ROYAL RESORT
91ST ST
85TH ST
PINO'S PIZZA
80TH ST
75TH ST
OCEAN CITY TRAVEL PARK
70TH ST
65TH ST
90
60TH ST
FAGER'S ISLAND BAR
55TH ST
45TH ST
35TH ST
HILTON SUITES OCEAN CITY OCEANFRONT
JOLLY ROGER
THE DUNES MANOR HOTEL
26TH ST
20TH ST
SPINNAKER MOTEL
16TH ST
KING CHARLES HOTEL
10TH ST
PHILADELPHIA AVE
BALTIMORE AVE
5TH ST
0   500 yds
0   500 m
OCEAN CITY BOARDWALK
TRIMPERS RIDES
ATLANTIC HOTEL
WICOMICO ST
OCEAN CITY FIREFIGHTER'S MEMORIAL
JOLLY ROGER AT THE PIER
50
3RD ST
OCEAN CITY LIFE-SAVING STATION MUSEUM
© AVALON TRAVEL

"Senior Week" or "Beach Week." Keep this in mind if you plan to visit in June. You will have a lot of young, unchaperoned company (the average number graduating seniors visiting in June is 100,000). Some rental complexes even cater specifically to high school and college groups.

SIGHTS
★ Ocean City Boardwalk

The primary attraction in Ocean City is the three-mile-long boardwalk. It begins at the south end of the beach at the Ocean City Inlet. The boardwalk is lined with dozens of hotels, motels, condos, shops, restaurants, and entertainment venues. There is 24-hour activity on the boardwalk and many attractions and establishments orient visitors by their proximity to this popular landmark. During the summer season the boardwalk is very crowded, so if you like hearing the ocean, smelling french fries, and listening to the sounds of vacationers enjoying themselves, then this is the place to go.

Ocean City Beach

The beach in Ocean City is wide and sandy. Brightly colored umbrellas are lined up like soldiers in the sand in front of most hotels and are available for rent. Lifeguards are on duty throughout the season and go through a vigorous training program. The beach is swept every night so it remains in fairly clean condition. It is also patrolled regularly by the local police force. In peak season, the beach and water can get very crowded, so visitors should be prepared for a lot of company.

★ Ocean City Life-Saving Station Museum

The **Ocean City Life-Saving Station Museum** (813 S. Atlantic Ave., 410/289-4991, www.ocmuseum.org, May and Oct. daily 10am-4pm, June-Sep. daily 10am-6pm, Apr. and Nov. Wed.-Sun. 10am-4pm, Dec.-Mar. weekends 10am-4pm, $3) preserves the history of Ocean City and the U.S. Life-Saving Service (a predecessor of

Ocean City Life-Saving Station Museum

the coast guard that conducted marine rescues). Several fascinating historical exhibits, including one on rescue equipment used to save people who were shipwrecked, and aquariums housing local marine life are on display in a beautifully renovated historic building at the extreme southern end of the Ocean City Boardwalk. Visitors can learn about the history of the boardwalk and its lifeguards, how sailors were rescued at sea, and see examples of old-fashioned bathing suits. This well-maintained, one-of-a-kind museum offers an inexpensive learning experience, powerful exhibits, and great views of the beach. There is a gift store on-site and parking in the municipal lot next door.

Northside Park

Northside Park (125th-127th Sts. on the Bay, 410/250-0125, www.ococean.com) is a beautiful 58-acre park at the end of 125th Street. It has ball fields, a fishing lagoon, paths for walking or biking, a playground, a pier, a picnic shelter, an indoor gym, conference facilities, and a 21,000-square-foot sports arena. Regular events such as Sundaes in the Park (entertainment and make-your-own sundaes) are held regularly.

Amusement Parks

There are two famous amusement parks on the boardwalk in Ocean City. **Trimpers Rides** (S. 1st St. and the Boardwalk, 410/289-8617, www.trimpersrides.com, outdoor rides: summer starting in June, weekdays 3pm-midnight, weekends noon-midnight; indoor rides: year-round daily noon-midnight, unlimited rides during the day $26) is a historical icon in Ocean City. This amusement park was built in 1893 at the southern point of the boardwalk near the inlet. There are three outdoor amusement lots and a year-round indoor facility. A historic carousel, the Herschel-Spellman merry-go-round, dating back to 1902, is also at Trimpers Rides.

The **Jolly Roger at the Pier** (at the pier at the south end of the Boardwalk, 410/289-3031, www.jollyrogerpieroc.com) is home to the tallest Ferris wheel in town, a double-decker carousel, a coaster called Crazy Dance, and many other amusements. The view from the Ferris wheel is phenomenal. A second Jolly Roger Park is at 30th Street. There is no admission fee to the parks; the rides are "pay-as-you-go," and costs vary between rides.

There are several other amusement parks in Ocean City including the **Frontier Town**

Western Theme Park (Rte. 611, www. frontiertown.com, Apr.-Nov.), and **Baja Amusements** (12639 Ocean Gtwy./Rte. 50, www.bajaoc.com, June-Aug. 9am-midnight, shorter hours Apr.-May and Sept.).

Ocean City Firefighter's Memorial

The **Ocean City Firefighter's Memorial** (Boardwalk and N. Division St., www.ocvfc. com) is a six-foot-tall bronze statue of a firefighter that stands on a black granite base. The memorial honors "firefighters of the world, the Ocean City firefighters of the past, present, and future, as well as the 343 FDNY firefighters lost on 9/11." The memorial stands in a 2,500-square-foot plaza, surrounded by engraved brick pavers. A recovered piece of twisted steel from the World Trade Center also stands as a memorial to the firefighters who lost their lives on 9/11. A memorial event is held at the site each year on September 11.

ENTERTAINMENT
Nightlife

There's no shortage of nightlife in Ocean City. One of the premier hot spots is **Seacrets** (117 W. 49th St., 410/524-4900, www.seacrets. com), a Jamaican-themed entertainment complex featuring 14 bars and a dance club with nightly music (DJ and live). It is open all year and has an artificial beach and real palm trees. It is one place where people of different ages can mingle together. There is a dress code, so consult the website if you think your attire might be questionable.

The **Purple Moose Saloon** (on the Boardwalk between Talbot and Caroline Sts., 410/289-6953, www.purplemoose.com) is a nightclub on the boardwalk that offers nightly live rock and roll mid-May-August. It is one of the few places to walk into and have a drink on the boardwalk.

Fager's Island Bar (201 60th St. on the Bay, 410/524-5500, www.fagers.com) is a good place to have a drink on the bay. They offer nightly entertainment with dancing and DJs. Jazz and bluegrass music is featured early with

pop and dance music taking over after 9pm. The establishment has a bit of a split personality. The restaurant side has an upscale feel to it, while the nightclub side caters to the younger dance crowd.

SPORTS AND RECREATION
Fishing

Ocean City is known as the "White Marlin Capital of the World." A large fishing tournament called the **White Marlin Open** (www. whitemarlinopen.com) is held there each year at the beginning of August. Anglers of all abilities will find plenty of places to cast a line, whether it be off a boat, pier, or in the surf. For starters, try the public fishing piers at **Inlet Park** (S. 2nd St.), the **Third Street Pier** (bayside), **Ninth Street Pier** (bayside), and **Northside Park** (125th Street, bayside). Fishing charter companies include **Fin Chaser Sportfishing Charters** (12806 Sunset Ave., 443/397-0315, www.finchasersportfishing.com, $800-2,550) and **Ocean City Girl** (302/448-4184, www.oc-girl.com, starting at $266).

Boating

There are several public boat ramps in Ocean City including ones at **Assateague State Park** (Rte. 611 at the Assateague Island Bridge), **Gum Point Road** (off Rte. 589), and **Ocean City Commercial Harbor** (Sunset Ave. in West Ocean City).

Kayaking, Paddleboarding, and Windsurfing

For some hands-on action on the water, rent a kayak or paddleboard from **48th Street Watersports** (4701 Coastal Hwy., 410/524-9150, www.48thstreetwatersports.com, starting at $15). This bayfront facility has a wonderful beach and is a great location to try out a number of water sports. Learn to sail, try out sailboarding—they have just about every type of water toy you can dream of. They will even deliver kayaks to your location and pick them up at no extra charge. Kayak rentals and tours are also available from **Ayers Creek**

Adventures (8628 Grey Fox Ln., Berlin, 443/513-0889, www.ayerscreekadventures. com, starting at $15) in nearby Berlin.

Boat Tours

Take a dolphin and nature excursion with **The Angler** (312 Talbot St. bayside, 410/289-7424, www.angleroc.net) aboard a 65-foot boat to explore the shores of Assateague Island and catch a glimpse of the resident ponies on land and dolphins at sea. Tours originate at the Ocean City Inlet. The Angler also offers deep-sea fishing ($65) and 45-minute scenic evening cruises.

Surfing

If surfing like a local is more your style, rent a board from **Chauncey's Surf Shop** (2908 Coastal Hwy., 410/289-7405, www. chaunceyssurfshop.com, $25). They also rent paddleboards.

Biking

Bike rentals are available from **Dandy Don's Bike Rentals** (1109 Atlantic Ave., 410/289-2289, www.dandydonsbikerentals.com, starting at $7). They rent beach cruisers, "Boardwalk Cars," banana bikes, and surreys. **Bike World** (6 Caroline St., 410/289-2587, www.bikeworldoc.com) also rents bikes and surreys near the boardwalk.

Miniature Golf

Ocean City boasts a wide selection of mini golf courses. Try one or two or a new one every day. **Old Pro Golf** (outdoor locations 23rd St. and 28th St., indoor locations 68th St. and 136th St., 410/524-2645, www.oldprogolf. com, $8.50) has four locations in Ocean City. The indoor golf course and arcades on 68th Street and 136th Street are open all year. **Lost Treasure Golf** (13903 Coastal Hwy., 410/250-5678, www.losttreasuregolf.com, open Mar.-Nov.) offers 18 holes dedicated to noted explorer Professor Duffer A. Hacker.

FOOD
American
Liquid Assets (9301 Coastal Hwy.,

410/524-7037, www.la94.com, Sun.-Thurs. 11:30am-11pm, Fri.-Sat. 11:30am-midnight, $13-34) is a surprisingly trendy little restaurant hidden within a strip mall, inside a liquor store. Guests pick their wine right off the shelf with or without the help of the staff and pay a corking fee to drink it with dinner. The menu is wide-ranging, the food is delicious, and the presentation is appealing. This unusual little gem is geared toward adults and does not serve a children's menu. The bar area is rustic with oak barrels, and the bistro has couches and tables that are well spaced so you aren't sitting on top of your neighbor. There's normally a long wait for seating, but they do not take reservations.

Italian
For good pizza, try **Pino's Pizza** (8101 Coastal Hwy., 410/723-3278, open daily in summer season, hours vary by month, $8-37). This joint has terrific pizza with a zesty sauce and is open until 4am. They offer pick-up and delivery only—no dining in. They are very generous with their cheese (both mozzarella and white cheddar) and toppings, and the slices are delicious and filling. They have reliable, friendly service and often offer coupons on their website. Be aware when ordering the really large pizzas that sometimes the price of two smaller ones is much cheaper.

Seafood
★ **The Shark on the Harbor** (12924 Sunset Ave., 410/213-0924, www.ocshark. com, Sunday brunch 10:30am-3pm, lunch daily 11:30am-4:30pm, dinner daily 4:30pm-10pm, $12-35) offers an ever-changing menu of fresh seafood, dictated by what is available and fresh on that day. They serve lunch and dinner daily and have a happy hour and a kid's menu. The restaurant is on a commercial fishing harbor and is known for having great views of the harbor and Assateague Island. The owners describe the style of food offered as "globally influenced seasonal cuisine," which allows them to be creative in

their daily menu offerings. Local seafood is prominently featured on the menu, and they also serve organic produce and natural dairy and meat products. Don't let the plain exterior fool you; the inside of this restaurant is hip and comfortable and has large windows. The large bar is the primary internal feature, with seating on three sides. The full menu can be ordered at the bar, at pub-style tables, or at regular dining tables. The clientele is good mix of vacationers and locals, and the owners are extremely friendly.

The **Captain's Galley Restaurant and Lounge** (12817 Harbor Rd., 410/213-2525, www.captainsgalleyoc.com, daily 11:30am-10pm, upstairs $6-14, downstairs $14-33) is on the waterfront in the harbor and offers free boat docking for customers. They specialize in seafood and are known for having some of the best crab cakes in Ocean City, which is a steep claim given the overwhelming competition. They also have a variety of steaks on the menu. The restaurant has two levels and two menus. The downstairs menu is a dinner menu (starting at 4:30pm), and the upstairs menu is casual (starting at 11:30am) with sandwiches, seafood baskets, steamed

seafood, and individual sides. You can't mix menus, so choose which floor to dine on based on what you want to eat. Enjoy a great view of the harbor from the inside or dine outside on the large deck, which is a great place for digging into a pile of freshly steamed crabs. The interior is a bit dated, but the food and view compensate.

For great local crab cakes visit the **Crabcake Factory** (12000 Coastal Hwy., 410/250-4900, www.crabcakefactoryonline.com, Mon.-Thurs. 11am-9pm, Fri.-Sat. 9am-11pm, Sun. 9am-9pm). They specialize in local seafood, including their signature crab cakes, peel-and-eat shrimp, and crab pizza. They are also known for their breakfasts and Bloody Marys. Breakfast is served Friday-Sunday at the Ocean City location, and the second location in Fenwick Island (37314 Lighthouse Road, 302/988-5000) serves breakfast daily and has great views of the bay.

Doughnuts
The Fractured Prune (127th St. and Coastal Hwy., 410/250-4400, www.fracturedprune.com) is a well-known doughnut shop that was featured on the Food Network's *Unwrapped.*

The Shark on the Harbor

It is hidden in the North Bay Shopping Center near Ledo Pizza. The specialty is "hot-dipped, made to order" doughnuts, and they're home to the "create your own donut." Guests can select from 15 doughnut glazes and multiple toppings to create their dream doughnut. Standard Fractured Prune flavors include interesting names such as "Black Forest" and "Sand." This small shop turns out 840 yummy cake doughnuts each hour and has become an icon at the beach. The shop doesn't offer prune toppings; it was named after an iconic lady named Prunella, who lived in Ocean City in the early 1900s and traveled around competing against men in different sports. She was always on crutches from getting hurt, so the shop is named the Fractured Prune after her. There are five additional locations in West Ocean City (9636 Stephen Decatur Hwy.), on the boardwalk (Boardwalk and 14th Street), on 81st Street (81st and Coastal Hwy) at 28th Street (2808 Philadelphia Ave.) and 56th Street (5601 Coastal Hwy.).

Classic Beach Food

The beach and ice cream go hand in hand. **Dumser's Dairyland** (124th St. and Coastal Hwy., 410/250-5543, www.beach-net. com, Memorial Day-Labor Day daily 7am-11:30pm), which was established in 1939, offers beachgoers an ice-cream parlor and restaurant that is open late in the summer (hours are shorter in the off-season). They also have locations at 49th Street and Coastal Highway plus three stands on the boardwalk.

Another longtime favorite is **Thrasher's French Fries** (www.thrashersfrenchfries. com, under $5). They've been making french fries on the boardwalk since 1929. With three locations in Ocean City—at the Pier, 2nd Street and Boardwalk, and 8th Street and Boardwalk—the aroma of Thrasher's is one of the defining smells of the boardwalk.

Dolle's (500 S. Boardwalk at Wicomico St., 410/289-6000, www.dolles.com, daily 10am-6pm, Fri.-Sat. 10am-8pm) has been a staple on the boardwalk since 1910. They make mouthwatering saltwater taffy, fudge, popcorn, and other candy.

Fisher's Popcorn (200 S. Boardwalk, www.fisherspopcorn.com, 410/289-5638) is another Ocean City icon. This family-owned and operated business opened in 1937 and offers many flavors of mouthwatering popcorn. They are especially known for their caramel popcorn.

ACCOMMODATIONS
$100-200

A good value is the **Sea Hawk Motel** (12410 Coastal Hwy., 410/250-3191, www. seahawkmotel.com, $178-210). This older motel is a half block from the beach and offers 60 motel rooms and efficiencies with kitchens. Sleeping areas are separated from living areas. The rooms are spacious and clean, and there's an outdoor pool.

The **King Charles Hotel** (1209 N. Baltimore Ave., 410/289-6141, www. kingcharleshotel.com, $114-189) is a small hotel a block from the boardwalk. The 22 rooms are modest but competitively priced and clean. They are available with one queen bed or two double beds. There are small refrigerators and microwaves in the rooms. The hotel owners are very friendly and make it feel more like a bed-and-breakfast (minus the breakfast) than a hotel.

The **Atlantic Hotel** (oceanfront on the Boardwalk and Wicomico St., 410/289-9111, www.atlantichotelocmd.com, $160-250) was the first boardwalk hotel in Ocean City. It was built in 1875 and was considered one of the finest hotels on the East Coast. It burned down in a devastating fire in 1925 but was rebuilt the following year. Today, the hotel is still going strong and offers guests a central location on the boardwalk and a rooftop deck overlooking all the action and the ocean. They offer 100 rooms with one or two queen beds, and there are also two apartments for rent on a weekly basis. The rooms are small and cozy but clean. They feature dark wood furniture and small private bathrooms. There is an outdoor pool for guests. The staff is very friendly, and the location is ideal for those wanting to stay on the boardwalk.

$200-300

The ★ **Atlantic House Bed and Breakfast** (501 N. Baltimore Ave., 410/289-2333, www. atlantichouse.com, $200-250) is a diamond in the rough in a town packed with imposing hotels and motels. This little Victorian-style treasure built in the 1920s sits right on North Baltimore Street and is conspicuously different from the surrounding accommodations. The nine guest rooms (seven with private baths and two with semiprivate) are small since the home was originally a boardinghouse, but they are immaculate and tidy. Second-story room decor is mostly floral and wicker, while the third-floor rooms have paneling. The grounds are nicely maintained, and there is a wonderful front porch where guests can watch the bustle of activity on the busy street. The location is central to the Ocean City attractions, just one street back from the boardwalk. The innkeepers are extremely warm and helpful and are a great asset to the establishment. Breakfast is delicious and plentiful with egg dishes, meats, fruit, and waffles. Snacks are also offered each afternoon. This bed-and-breakfast gets a lot of repeat business.

The **Dunes Motel** (2700 Baltimore Ave., 410/289-4414, www.ocdunes.com, $269-309) is an older motel at the end of the boardwalk offering 49 oceanfront rooms and 62 poolside rooms. The decor is older, but the motel is a good value for budget-minded travelers and the rooms are clean. There's an outdoor pool and direct beach access. The motel's sister property, **The Dunes Manor Hotel** (2800 Baltimore Ave., 410/289-1100, www.dunes-manor.com, $449-469), is next door. It offers 174 rooms and an indoor pool that can be used by guests of both establishments.

The **Spinnaker Motel** (18th St. and Baltimore Ave., 410/289-5444, www.ocmotels. com, $242-346) offers 100 clean guest units within a short walk to the boardwalk (about a half block). Although not fancy, the rooms are reasonably priced and many have good views of the ocean. There is parking on-site, an outdoor pool, and free wireless Internet. This hotel is a good value for families on a budget.

Over $300

The **Hilton Suites Ocean City Oceanfront** (3200 N. Baltimore Ave., 410/289-6444, www. oceancityhilton.com, $579-659) is one of the nicest hotels in Ocean City. All 225 modern rooms are oversize, luxurious suites on the oceanfront and offer nicely sized balconies. Each suite has a kitchen. There are both an indoor pool and a lovely outdoor pool overlooking the ocean that has a swim-up bar. There is also a children's pool with a waterslide and a lazy river. The hotel is about five blocks from the boardwalk (10-minute walk). The hotel offers live music, movie nights, and children's activities. It is very family-oriented. Parking right at the hotel is limited, but there is additional parking across the street. This is a beautiful hotel with nice amenities, as it should be for the price.

The **Princess Royal Resort** (91st St. Oceanfront, www.princessroyale.com, $299-399) is an oceanfront hotel with 310 two-room suites and 30 condos. They offer pleasant rooms with kitchenettes, comfortable beds, and great views. Ask for a room with a good view; the staff will often do their best to accommodate the request. The hotel has a large indoor pool and scheduled activities such as movie night on the beach and live music by the outdoor bar. The furniture is a bit dated, but otherwise this is good choice for oceanfront accommodations. Their prime rib and seafood buffet is a tasty option for dinner.

Condos

There are many condos for rent in Ocean City. **Summer Beach Condominium** (410/289-0727, www.summerbeachoc.com) and **Holiday Real Estate** (800/638-2102, www. holidayoc.com) are management companies that offer weekly rentals.

the Princess Royal Resort

Camping

Frontier Town (Rte. 611 and Stephen Decatur Hwy., Berlin, 410/641-0880, www.frontiertown.com, Apr.-Nov., starting at $32) in nearby Berlin offers tent and RV facilities. They are open seasonally and only five minutes from Ocean City.

INFORMATION AND SERVICES

For additional information on Ocean City, visit www.ococean.com or stop by the **Ocean City Visitor Information Center** (12320 Ocean Gateway, 410/213-0552).

GETTING THERE

Ocean City is a 2.5-hour drive from Annapolis (109 miles). Most people arrive by car via Route 50 or Route 113 (the two primary routes to the area). **Greyhound** (12848 Ocean Gtwy., 410/289-9307, www.greyhound.com) bus service is also available to Ocean City.

GETTING AROUND

Route 528 is the only major road running north-south in Ocean City. It is called Philadelphia Avenue at the southern end and the Coastal Highway everywhere else. Streets running east-west in Ocean City are numbered beginning in the south, and run up to 146th before the Delaware border. Locations are normally explained by the terms "oceanside" (east of the Coastal Highway) or "bayside" (west of the Coastal Highway).

The **Boardwalk Tram** (410/289-5311, June-Aug. daily 11am-midnight, shorter hours spring and fall, $3 per ride or $6 unlimited daily pass) is a seasonal tram that runs the entire length of the boardwalk from the inlet to 27th Street. The tram stops at most locations along the boardwalk. It takes 30 minutes to ride the entire length of the boardwalk.

The Coastal Highway **Beach Bus** (410/723-2174, www.oceancitymd.gov, $3 all-day pass) is a municipal bus service that runs 24/7 along the Coastal Highway. Free parking is available at the two bus transit centers at South Division Street and at the West Ocean City Park and Ride.

Delaware Beaches

Just north of Ocean City, along the Coastal Highway, is the Delaware state line and some of the nicest beach resort areas in the mid-Atlantic. Three main areas—Bethany Beach, Rehoboth Beach, and Lewes—attract visitors year-round. They offer first-class restaurants, historic beach charm, and lovely accommodations in all price ranges. Although not as busy as their southern neighbor, they each offer their own attractions and have sights of historical interest.

GETTING THERE

DART First State and the Delaware Transit Corporation (www.dartfirststate.com) offers public bus transportation between Ocean City and the Delaware beaches. A parking lot ($8) is north of Rehoboth Avenue on Shuttle Road. With the price of parking, you receive four free unlimited-ride daily bus passes. Stops are located throughout the resort areas.

BETHANY BEACH

Bethany Beach is located in southeastern Delaware, 15 miles north of Ocean City, Maryland. It is part of a seven-mile stretch of beach referred to as the "Quiet Resorts," along with South Bethany Beach and Fenwick Island. Bethany Beach is small and much lower-key than nearby Ocean City and Rehoboth Beach. It is mostly residential, and there is a small shopping area at its heart.

Since 1976, visitors to Bethany Beach have been greeted by **Chief Little Owl,** a 24-foot totem pole that was donated to the town as part of a project by sculptor Peter Wolf Toth, who carved more than 50 wooden works of art in honor of famous Native Americans and gave one to every state. The current totem is actually the third version of the sculpture to stand in Bethany Beach. The first two were destroyed by decay. The current version was created in 2002 of red cedar and is expected to last 50-150 years.

EASTERN SHORE
DELAWARE BEACHES

downtown Bethany Beach

Sights

BETHANY BEACH

The beach at **Bethany Beach** is wide, sandy, and family-oriented. Although it would be a stretch to say it's empty during the season, it is mostly quiet at night and offers a relaxing atmosphere during the day. Visitors will need to pay to park (there are meters near the beach entrance on Garfield Street).

BETHANY BEACH BOARDWALK

The **Bethany Beach Boardwalk** is a pleasant family area with less fanfare than the boardwalk in nearby Ocean City. It is basically a nice walkway made of wooden planks. The boardwalk entrance is at the end of Garfield Street, and the boardwalk itself stretches between 2nd and Parkwood Streets. There is plenty to do and see with shops, restaurants, and free concerts at the bandstand on weekends during the summer.

BETHANY BEACH NATURE CENTER

The **Bethany Beach Nature Center** (807 Garfield Pkwy., Rte. 26, 302/537-7680, www.inlandbays.org, mid-June-Oct. Tues.-Fri. 10am-3pm, Sat. 10am-2pm, donations appreciated) offers interactive exhibits that enable visitors to explore the Inland Bays watershed and learn about local flora and fauna. It is housed in a beautiful cottage built around 1901. Nature trails on the 26-acre grounds take visitors through wetlands and forest. There is also a play area for children.

THE FENWICK ISLAND LIGHTHOUSE

The **Fenwick Island Lighthouse** (146th St. and Lighthouse Ave., http://fenwickislandlighthouse.org, end of May-June weekends 9am-noon, July-Aug. Fri.-Mon. 9am-noon, Sept. weekends 9am-noon, free) stands 87 feet above Fenwick Island. It was built in 1859 after an increase in shipwrecks near the Fenwick Shoals (a shallow area 6 miles offshore). The operational lighthouse tower is closed to visitors, but there is a small museum at its entrance that is run by the New Friends of the Fenwick Island Lighthouse. Visiting hours are Friday-Monday 10am-2pm during the summer. Admission is free but donations are appreciated.

DISCOVERSEA SHIPWRECK MUSEUM

The **DiscoverSea Shipwreck Museum** (708 Coastal Hwy., Fenwick Island, 302/539-9366, www.discoversea.com, June-Aug. daily 11am-8pm, free) is a dynamic museum that recovers and preserves the area's maritime history. Exhibits are centered on shipwreck artifacts dating back to the colonial era (gold, coins, cannons, personal items, even old rum). The museum is run by public donations and owner contributions. Exhibits change with the discovery and acquisition of new artifacts, but the average number of items on display is 10,000. Many additional items are rotated through exhibits around the world. Check the website for hours during the off-season.

Recreation and Entertainment

Delaware Seashore State Park (Rte. 1 between Bethany Beach and Dewey Beach, 302/227-2800, www.destateparks.com, daily 8am-sunset, $10) is to the north of Bethany Beach along the coast. The park of more than 2,800 acres covers a thin strip of land between the Atlantic and Rehoboth Bay. The primary attraction in the park is the beach itself—a six-mile-long beach lover's paradise—where visitors can swim and relax along the shore. There are modern bathhouses with showers and changing rooms, and lifeguards are on duty during the day in the summer. There are also snack vendors and beach equipment rentals such as chairs, rafts, and umbrellas. Fishing is popular in the park and can be done in the surf in designated locations or from the banks of the Indian River Inlet. There is also a special-access pier for the elderly or people with disabilities.

Just north of the inlet on the beach in Delaware Seashore State Park is a designated surfing and sailboarding area. The shallow bays are also good areas for sailboarding and sailing. A boat ramp for nonmotorized craft is also available.

Holt's Landing State Park (302/227-2800, www.destateparks.com, daily 8am-sunset, $10) is on the southern shore of the Indian River Bay (take Route 26 West from Bethany Beach and turn right on County Road 346 to the park entrance). Clamming, fishing, and crabbing are possible in the park, along with facilities such as a picnic pavilion, playground, horseshoe pit, and ball fields. Two great kayaking trails start in the park. The first is a 10-mile paddle to the **Assawoman Wildlife Area** (allow five hours), and the second is to Millsboro, which is just under 10 miles.

Mini golf is a staple at the beach, and **Captain Jack's Pirate Golf** (21 N. Pennsylvania Ave., 302/539-1122, www.captainjackspirategolf.com, seasonal daily 9am-11:30pm, $8.50) is the place to go in Bethany Beach. It has eye-catching features such as a large skeleton pirate and pirate's ship, rock and water features, and palm trees. The course is well maintained and a fun place for the entire family. There's a small gift shop on-site.

If you're visiting in early September, check out the one-day **Annual Bethany Beach Boardwalk Arts Festival** (Bethany Beach Boardwalk, 302/539-2100, www.bethany-beachartsfestival.com). More than 100 artists exhibit their work on the boardwalk and surrounding streets. Local and national artists partake in this anticipated event that draws more than 7,500 visitors. Admission is free.

Food

★ **Off The Hook** (769 Garfield Pkwy., 302/829-1424, www.offthehookbethany.com, Sun.-Thurs. 11:30am-9pm, Fri.-Sat. 11:30am-10pm, $8-27) offers excellent seafood in an off-the-beaten-path location. The seafood and the atmosphere are both fresh, with creative dishes and specials. They are known for the cioppino (a fish stew with shellfish, finfish, garlic confit, chorizo, and pesto in a tomato broth). The restaurant prides itself in supporting local farmers and anglers. They do not take reservations, so there can be a long wait time.

A local favorite is the **Cottage Café Restaurant** (33034 Coastal Hwy., 302/539-8710, www.cottagecafe.com, daily 11am-1am, $10-29). This is a good family restaurant serving local seafood. The staff is kind and patient,

Off The Hook

and the menu is wide enough to satisfy most tastes. Menu selections include crab cakes, fried oysters, stuffed flounder, pot roast, pasta, and meat loaf. The food is not fancy, but it is consistent and reasonably priced.

For fresh crepes, visit **Sunshine Crepes** (100 Garfield Pkwy., 302/537-1765, summer daily 8am-2pm, under $10). This casual and affordable breakfast stop in downtown Bethany Beach by the boardwalk makes fresh savory and sweet crepes with a nice selection of fillings. You can even watch the kitchen staff at work. The atmosphere is not fancy, but the portions are large and the food is tasty. This is a nice alternative to regular bacon and eggs. If you like bananas, try the banana crepe. This is a wonderful local business offering something a little different coupled with friendly service.

Accommodations

Meris Gardens Bed & Breakfast (33309 Kent Ave., 302/752-4962, www.merisgardensbethany.com, $139-169) is a small, affordable bed-and-breakfast that used to be the Westward Pines Motel. They offer 14 comfortable rooms and are located in a quiet area of Bethany Beach. All rooms have private bathrooms and they are dog friendly ($20 charge). It is convenient to the beach (four blocks), and downtown Bethany Beach is within walking distance. Breakfast is included. This property offers simple, friendly accommodations with personal service.

The **Addy Sea** (99 Ocean View Pkwy., 302/539-3707, www.addysea.com, $175-375) is a renovated oceanfront Victorian home and guesthouse that is now an adults-only bed-and-breakfast. The home offers 13 guest rooms and is furnished with antiques, tin ceilings, and original woodwork. The rooms are comfortable, the staff is friendly, and the location is wonderful. The breakfasts are also plentiful with good choices. Book a room with an ocean view for the best experience. Not all rooms have private baths, and Room 12 is the only one with a television.

The **Sea Colony Resort** (Rte. 1,

888/500-4261, www.wyndhamvacationrentals.com) is a large and well-known condominium resort in Bethany Beach with 2,200 units. Condo rentals are available through a number of management companies. Amenities include tennis courts, a fitness center, a small shopping area, and pools. The beaches around Sea Colony are some of the busiest in Bethany Beach due to the large number of condos in the complex; however, the half-mile stretch of beach is for guests and visitors of the resort only, which does make it somewhat private. Units of different sizes are available for rent. Additional information can be obtained at www.resortquestdelaware.com.

Information and Services

For additional information on Bethany Beach, visit www.bethanybeachde.com or stop by the **Bethany-Fenwick area visitor information center** (daily Mon.-Fri. 9am-5pm, Sat. 9am-3pm) on the Coastal Highway between Fenwick Island State Park and Lewes Street.

REHOBOTH BEACH

Rehoboth Beach is 14 miles north of Bethany Beach. It is the happy medium among the Maryland and Delaware beaches. It is larger and more commercial than Bethany Beach, yet smaller and less commercial than Ocean City.

Rehoboth Beach was founded in 1873 as a Methodist Episcopal Church beach camp. Today, the town is known as "the Nation's Summer Capital," since so many visitors come from Washington DC each year. The town is also noted for its eclectic shops, wonderful eateries, artistic appeal, and the large number of gay-owned businesses. Downtown Rehoboth Beach is one square mile and has more than 200 shops, galleries, and spas, 40 hotels and bed-and-breakfasts, and more than 100 restaurants.

Just south of Rehoboth is **Dewey Beach,** which is known as a party town for young adults during the summer months. The two towns share a beautiful strand of sandy white

Rehoboth Beach

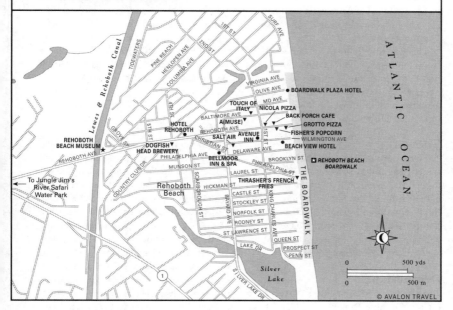

beach that continues to be the main attraction despite all the built-up distractions.

Dogs are not permitted to run loose on the beach in Rehoboth. They are prohibited from the beach and boardwalk 24 hours a day between May 1 and September 30, but they are allowed on the beach in Dewey prior to 9:30am and after 5:30pm (although they still must be leashed and have a Dewey Beach license). There is a strict leash law, and owners must pick up after their dogs.

Sights
★ REHOBOTH BEACH BOARDWALK

The easiest public access to the mile-long boardwalk in Rehoboth Beach is from Rehoboth Avenue. Less crowded than Ocean City, yet more lively than Bethany Beach, the boardwalk offers all the action you could want at the beach including terrific views of the ocean, french fries, T-shirt shops, games, candy stores, and entertainment. The

boardwalk is wide and clean and stretches from Penn Street at the south end to Virginia Avenue at the north end. Parking is available on Rehoboth Avenue, and parking meters are enforced during the summer months 10am-midnight. The meters take quarters and credit cards. Change machines are available at the Bandstand on Rehoboth Avenue.

REHOBOTH BEACH MUSEUM

The **Rehoboth Beach Museum** (511 Rehoboth Ave., 302/227-7310, www.rehobothbeachmuseum.org, Labor Day-Memorial Day Mon.-Fri. 10am-4pm, Sat.-Sun. 11am-3pm, free but donations appreciated) is a small museum with displays portraying the history of Rehoboth Beach. Visitors can see vintage bathing suits, postcards, and classic boardwalk rides and games, and learn about the early beach hotels in town.

Entertainment and Events
The **Clear Space Theatre Company**

(www.clearspacetheatre.org) is a year-round professional theatrical company that presents musical and dramatic productions. Performances are held in the **Rehoboth Theatre of the Arts** (20 Baltimore Ave.).

The **Rehoboth Beach Jazz Festival** (www.rehobothjazz.com) is an annual event that takes place for four days in October. There are three stages throughout the town for performances as well as additional venues in local establishments.

Shopping

The first thing shoppers should know is that there is no sales tax in Delaware. The second thing is that every outlet store you can think of may be found in a large shopping area on Route 1 between Rehoboth and Lewes, at **Tanger Outlets** (36470 Seaside Outlet Dr., 302/226-9223, www.tangeroutlet.com, Mon.-Sat. 9am-9pm, Sun. 10am-7pm).

Recreation

Jungle Jim's River Safari Water Park (36944 Country Club Rd., 302/227-8444, www.funatjunglejims.com, daily in summer 10am-8pm, $38) is Delaware's largest water park and also offers go-karts, mini golf, batting cages, and bumper boats. **Funland at**

Rehoboth Beach (6 Delaware Ave., 302/227-1921, www.funlandrehoboth.com, mid-June-mid-Aug. daily, games starting at 10am, rides starting at 1pm, park closes at 11pm, shorter hours on weekends in mid-late May and daily in early-mid-June) is a tradition on the boardwalk dating back to the early 1960s. It offers 19 rides and operates on a ticketed basis ($0.35 per ticket).

Food
AMERICAN
Salt Air (50 Wilmington Ave., 302/227-3744, www.saltairrestaurant.com, Sun., Wed. and Thurs. 5pm-9pm, Fri.-Sat. 5pm-10pm, $16-46) is a busy, upscale farm-to-fork restaurant with a good vibe. Patrons can watch the skilled kitchen at work and get a text message when their table is ready. The cuisine is American, and there are a lot of creative seafood dishes. Start with the crab deviled eggs; a plate of four can be a bite each for a small group. The menu is full of little surprises (but changes often) such as boardwalk fries, oven-roasted honey sriracha wings, and seafood stew. They also serve incredible salads, such as the kale caesar salad. The kids' menu is worth mentioning, because it strays from the usual chicken tenders to provide small portions of real

Rehoboth Beach Boardwalk

food, like filet mignon and grilled fish. This is a wonderful place for dinner and cocktails and their creativity includes a long list of delightful martinis.

a(MUSE.) (44 Baltimore Ave., 302/227-7107, www.amuse-rehoboth.com, Tues.-Sun. 5pm-9pm, Fri.-Sat. 5pm-10pm, small plates $5-18, main $22-31) is a one-of-a-kind restaurant that takes guests through a culinary amusement park of fresh, small plates made of local ingredients. If this doesn't sound like your cup of tea, they also offer full-size entrées that are just as delectable as the small plates. A sample of their menu includes potted chicken, yellow perch, north Atlantic halibut, and strip steak. Their menu changes according to what is available from mid-Atlantic farmers, fisherman, ranchers, and foragers. A five-course tasting menu is available for $69 and a seven-course tasting menu is available for $89.

The original **Dogfish Head Brewery** (320 Rehoboth Ave., 302/226-2739, www.dogfish.com, Sun.-Thurs. noon-11pm, Fri.-Sat. noon-1am, $6-26) is on the main strip of Rehoboth Avenue. They serve a nice variety of fish, burgers, sandwiches, and pizza along with many varieties of their delicious beer. Seasonal beers are always rotating with a few staples available all year. The Indian Brown Ale is a personal favorite, along with the salmon sandwich.

FRENCH

For several decades, the ★ **Back Porch Café** (59 Rehoboth Ave., 302/227-3674, www.backporchcafe.com, June-Sept. daily, May and Oct. weekends, lunch 11am-3pm, après-surf menu 3pm-5:30pm, dinner 6pm-10pm, $34-42) has delighted visitors with upscale creations from its award-winning chef and owner. The cuisine is unmistakably French, with many wonderful sauces, root veggies, and some entrées such as rabbit, but they also look to seasonal ingredients for inspiration. Start with the crab ravioli, a sure crowd-pleaser, and then choose carefully from the interesting array of main courses. If the wild king salmon is on the

menu, it is one good choice; it is served with a savory butternut squash bisque. The interior is cozy with a bar and some outdoor seating. This restaurant is open for lunch, brunch, and dinner in the summer but is closed in the off-season. Reservations are encouraged. There is no kid's menu.

ITALIAN

Lupo Italian Kitchen (247 Rehoboth Ave., 302/226-2240, www.lupodimarerehoboth.com, Sun.-Thurs. 5pm-9pm, Fri.-Sat. 5pm-10pm, $10-29) is a beautiful little restaurant (formerly called Lupo di Mare) on the first floor of the Hotel Rehoboth on Rehoboth Avenue. It is light and airy inside and offers a menu of flatbread, salad, homemade pasta, and other delightful Italian choices. Their fried calamari is perhaps the best in the area. Their salads offer delicious combinations such as roasted beet and citrus with goat gouda, pickled shallot, beet chips, and candied pistachios. Entrees include lobster bucatini, crab and casarecce, and classics such as chicken parmesan and lasagna. They have shorter hours in the off-season and different off-season specials each night of the week (such as 25 percent off your check on Mondays).

Touch of Italy (19724 Coastal Hwy, 302/227-3900, www.touchofitaly.com, Sun.-Thurs. 10:30am-9pm, Fri.-Sat. 10:30am-10pm, $10-45) is a dine-in and carryout Italian deli focused on specialty meats, cheeses, and Italian pastries. They have a huge menu and all sandwiches are made to order.

It would be almost negligent to not mention the classic Rehoboth Beach pizza joint, **Nicola Pizza** (8 N. 1st St., 302/227-6211, www.nicolapizza.com, daily 11am-midnight, $5-27). This pizzeria has been a staple in town since 1971, and for many it is *the* beachy place to bring the family. The wood floors and booths are a reminder of the restaurant's long history. Wait times in the summer can easily be an hour or more. The most popular dish is the "Nic-o-Boli," which is their name for stromboli (they can sell up to 2,000 in one night). This is worth a try if you've never had one, although the regular pizza is also a good choice. There's a second location at 71 Rehoboth Avenue.

Another classic pizza place in Rehoboth is **Grotto Pizza** (36 Rehoboth Ave., 302/227-3278, www.grottopizza.com, Sun.-Thurs. 11am-10pm, Fri.-Sat. 11am-11pm, under $15). This well-recognized restaurant has been around since 1960 and has three locations in Rehoboth Beach. The other two locations are on the boardwalk at 15 Boardwalk and Baltimore Avenue and 17 Surf Avenue. They offer dine-in, carryout, and walk-up pizza.

SNACKS

Fisher's Popcorn (48 Rehoboth Ave., 302/227-2691, www.fishers-popcorn.com, daily Memorial Day-Labor Day, weekends year-round) is a staple on the Maryland and Delaware beaches. You can buy the addicting little morsels by the bucket (0.5-6.5 gallons). They are known for the caramel popcorn but offer several other flavors. Please note: It is easy to eat this until you feel sick. Stopping is hard to do. You've been warned.

Perhaps no beach trip is complete without at least one stop at **Thrasher's French Fries** (26 Rehoboth Ave., 302/227-7366, daily from 11am). This local icon serves up buckets of fresh boardwalk fries from the walk-up window on the boardwalk. Even die-hard ketchup lovers will want to try them with salt and vinegar.

A fun place to stop is **Kaisy's Delights** (70 Rehoboth Ave., 302/212-5360, www.kaisysdelights.com, Sun.-Thurs. 7:30am-5pm, Fri.-Sat. 7:30am-7pm, under $10) for an Austrian Kaisy (a treat made of sweet custardy dough with your choice of toppings such as ice cream or fruit sauce). Their delicious samples may lure you into a sweet Kaisy or even a breakfast Kaisy (they are available with eggs, sausage, and bacon). The coffee is also good. They're open all year.

Accommodations

The **Avenue Inn & Spa** (33 Wilmington Ave., 800/433-5870, www.avenueinn.com, $269-419) is an independently owned hotel one block from the beach. There are 60 guest rooms with many amenities such as full breakfast, complimentary wine and cheese, evening cookies, a day spa, indoor heated pool, fitness room, sauna, beach chairs, beach shuttle, and free parking.

The **Bellmoor Inn and Spa** (6 Christian St., 302/227-5800, www.thebellmoor.com, $379-639) is a comfortable inn about three blocks from the beach. They offer 22 guest rooms and suites. There are two pools on-site and an enclosed hot tub. Breakfast is served daily (with omelets on the weekends), and the staff is friendly and helpful.

The ★ **Boardwalk Plaza Hotel** (2 Olive Ave., 302/227-7169, www.boardwalkplaza.com, $324-679) is an elegant, Victorian-style oceanfront hotel right on the boardwalk. The hotel is furnished with antiques and antique-style furniture and offers oceanfront rooms with deluxe amenities. The hotel is friendly to children (and even offers special events for them such as craft time) but also has special amenities and areas for adults only (including a rooftop hot tub). The 84 guest rooms are comfortable, clean, and warmly decorated. The staff is friendly and goes out of its way to make visitors feel at home. There's also a restaurant on-site that offers water-view dining, a cozy bar, and a boardwalk patio.

A great choice for a clean, affordable, welcoming stay near the boardwalk is the **Beach View Hotel** (6 Wilmington Ave., 302/227-2999, www.beachviewmotel.com, $234-304). This small hotel offers ocean-view rooms with private balconies and poolside rooms with no balconies. Continental breakfast is included. This hotel is a good value in a convenient location.

Information and Services

For additional information on Rehoboth Beach, visit www.cityofrehoboth.com, www.rehobothboardwalk.com, and www.downtownrehoboth.com or stop by the **Rehoboth Beach-Dewey Beach Chamber**

of Commerce and Visitors Center (501 Rehoboth Ave., 302/227-2233, year-round Mon.-Fri. 9am-5pm, Sat.-Sun. 9am-1pm).

LEWES

Lewes is seven miles north of Rehoboth and can be summed up in one word: charming. This quaint little town near the beach is a relaxing alternative to the busier beaches along the Delaware and Maryland shore. Lewes is also known as the "first town in the first state," since it was the site of the first European settlement in Delaware, founded in 1631. The town has an upscale beach feel to it and draws visitors of many age groups who come to relax, drink wine, eat good food, and shop.

Sights
★ HISTORIC LEWES

The historic downtown area of Lewes is on the harbor, just a short distance from the Atlantic. Second Street is the main street in town and offers wonderful dining and shopping and a cozy, friendly feel. The downtown area is lovely all year round. It truly is one of the prettiest spots on the mid-Atlantic coast with its historic homes (some dating back to

the 17th century), friendly atmosphere, and tidy, well-kept streets. Boutique stores and independently owned restaurants line the sidewalks, and the local residents are friendly and welcoming to tourists.

Shipcarpenter Square (www. shipcarpentersquare.com) is a community of delicately and accurately preserved and restored 18th- and 19th-century homes in the historic district. The homes in Shipcarpenter Square are mostly colonial farmhouses built in the late 1700s-late 1800s in other parts of Sussex County and moved to the site in the early 1980s. Other relocated buildings include three barns, a schoolhouse, an inn, a log home, a lifesaving station, a lighthouse, a market, and two Victorian houses.

The Shipcarpenter Square community stretches from 3rd and 4th Street on the east and west side to Burton Street and Park Streets on the north and south sides. Parking and walking access are provided to homeowners in this area. Pedestrians can enter a foot traffic-only area from Park Street and two areas on the north and south edges of the common greens that are located in the heart of the community.

EASTERN SHORE
DELAWARE BEACHES

harbor in Lewes

ZWAANENDAEL MUSEUM

The **Zwaanendael Museum** (102 Kings Hwy., 302/645-1148, http://history.delaware. gov, Apr.-Oct. Tues.-Sat. 10am-4:30pm, Sun. 1:30pm-4:30pm, Nov.-Mar. Wed.-Sat. 10am-4:30pm, free, donations appreciated) is an interesting-looking building (a replica of the Town Hall of Hoorn in the Netherlands) that features Dutch elements from the 17th century such as terra-cotta roof tiles, decorated shutters, a stepped facade gable, and stonework. The museum takes visitors through the history of Lewes as the state's first European settlement (by the Dutch) in 1631 and offers exhibits on the attack on Lewes by the British during the War of 1812, the Delaware coastline, and the Cape Henlopen Lighthouse. The museum also includes a maritime and military history of the town.

CAPE MAY-LEWES FERRY

The **Cape May-Lewes Ferry** (43 Cape Henlopen Dr., 800/643-3779, www. capemaylewesferry.com, Apr.-Sept. 8am-6pm, Oct.-Mar. 8:30am-4:30pm, car and driver one-way $27-45, extra passenger or pedestrian one-way $10) docks on Cape Henelopen Drive and makes daily 70-minute trips across Delaware Bay to Cape May, New Jersey. Auto and foot passengers are allowed on board, and there is no fee for bicycles. Ferry schedules vary throughout the season. Check the website for current departure times.

Shopping

The primary shopping district in historic Lewes is on 2nd Street, off Savannah Street. Upscale boutiques, houseware shops, and even a wonderful store for dogs line the manicured street. Ice-cream shops and other snack shops offer a nice break from sightseeing or shopping.

Sports and Recreation

Cape Henlopen State Park (15099 Cape Henlopen Dr., 302/645-8983, www. destateparks.com, daily 8am-sunset year-round, $10) covers five miles of shoreline at the mouth of Delaware Bay where it meets the Atlantic. It has a long military and shipping history. A storm in 1920 took out the lighthouse that used to guide ships through the bay, but breakwater barriers still provide a safe harbor during storms and rough water.

A military base was established at the cape in 1941, and bunkers were hidden among the dunes for protection. Observation towers built of cement, which are still standing, were also put in place along the shore to search for enemy ships. The park was created in 1964. Today the park provides many acres of seaside habitat. There's a nature center, hiking, fishing, swimming, a picnic pavilion, fishing pier, and camping in the park. The two swimming beaches are watched over by lifeguards in the summer.

There are several companies offering fishing supplies and charters in Lewes including **Katydid Charters** (Anglers Rd., 302/858-7783 or 302/645-8688, www. katydidsportfishing.com, starting at $375 for 10 people), **Angler's Fishing Center** (213 Anglers Rd., 302/644-4533, www. anglersfishingcenter.com, starting at $50), and **First Light Charters** (907 Pilottown Rd, 302/853-5717, www.firstlightcharters.net, starting at $275).

Sightseeing cruises are also available at the **Fisherman's Wharf** (107 Anglers Rd., 302/645-8862, www.fishlewes.com, $29-35). They offer two- and three-hour dolphin-watching cruises and a sunset cruise that leaves each evening during the summer at 6:30pm from the wharf docks. The trip goes down the canal and out to the ocean and then turns around near the ferry terminal.

Dogfish Head Brewery (302/745-2925, www.dogfish.com, $65) offers a "Pints and Paddles" tour May-October. This kayaking outing for beer enthusiasts is a unique out-and-back paddle on the Broadkill River in the McCabe Nature Preserve (a Nature Conservancy area), followed by a tour of the Dogfish Head Brewery (including samples for those over 21). Trips leave at noon on Wednesday, Friday, and Saturday from the

Beacon Motel parking lot (514 E. Savannah Rd.). A souvenir pint glass is included in the outing.

Golfers can enjoy a round at the **Marsh Island Golf Club** (21383 Camp Arrowhead, 302/945-4653, $55). This 18-hole course has a course rating of 65 and a slope rating of 96. It was designed by Herman John Schneider.

Food

The ★ **Agave Mexican Grill and Tequila Bar** (137 2nd St., 302/645-1232, www.agave-mexicanrestaurant.net, Mon.-Sat. noon-9pm, Sun. 3pm-9pm, $7-24) is a funky, upscale, sought-after Mexican dining spot that Laura Bush even stopped in one evening unannounced to sample the authentic cuisine. All the food is delicious, but they do a particularly good job with their mole, shrimp and garlic guacamole, and fish tacos. For something a little different, try the apple and moon cheese guacamole. Brightly painted glasses adorn patrons' tables and hold three sizes of margaritas (they have more than 70 types of tequila). The atmosphere is great, the service is attentive and friendly, and the clientele is lively. The only downside to this fabulous little gem is the long wait times for a table (sometimes as much as two hours or more). Plan a late lunch or early dinner to get a jump on the competition. Another option is to put your name on the list and stroll around the town while you wait.

The Buttery (102 2nd St., 302/645-7755, www.butteryrestaurant.com, daily lunch and dinner and Sun. brunch, hours vary by season, $26-36) is a local favorite right on 2nd Street. This beautiful Victorian restaurant specializes in upscale seafood entrées and appealing food presentation. The service is professional yet personal, and they can even accommodate diet restrictions. The menu is not large, but everything is done top-notch. They also offer a casual pub menu in the evenings and a daily three course pre fixe menu from 5pm to 6:45pm for $33. There have a lovely year-round veranda and beautiful plantings around the house. Reservations are a must.

For good seafood in a lively pub atmosphere, dine at **Striper Bites** (107 Savannah Rd., 302/645-4657, www.striperbites.com, lunch and dinner daily from 11:30am, $10-28). They offer casual dining indoors or on a patio. The seafood choices are excellent, and the service is friendly and usually prompt. The decor is wood furnishings and things from the sea. This is a go-to place for many locals. They don't take reservations, and on a busy night it can be quite loud indoors, but for the most part it offers a pleasant dining experience and delicious food.

Crooked Hammock Brewery (36707 Crooked Hammock Way, 302/644-7837, www.crookedhammockbrewery.com, daily 11am-1am, $8-22) is a fun brewery that offers an energetic atmosphere and a large outdoor space. They have a good selection of craft beers and a menu of casual appetizers, salads, sandwiches, and main dishes such as chicken fried chicken, beef short rib, clam bake, and salmon.

The Buttery

Accommodations

INNS AND HOTELS

★ **The Inn at Canal Square** (122 Market St., 302/644-3377, www.theinnatcanalsquare. com, $245-625) is a pretty canal-front inn in the heart of Lewes. The inn has 22 rooms and three VIP suites and can accommodate short- or long-term stays. Most of the rooms have water views and balconies, and the suites offer two bedrooms, full kitchens, washers and dryers, fireplaces, screened porches, and decks. The grounds are adorned with lavish plantings, and fresh flowers are brought into the common areas weekly. Special packages such as golf package and a Dogfish Head Brewery package are available. Breakfast is included with your stay, and the friendly staff can assist with recommending the perfect restaurant for lunch and dinner. The inn is convenient to all the shops and dining options on 2nd Street, and it provides free parking and wireless Internet.

The **Hotel Blue** (110 Anglers Rd., 302/645-4880, www.hotelblue.info, $299-349) is a comfortable boutique hotel with some nice little touches such as mirrored televisions and glowing ice buckets. The lobby is inviting, and the 16 guest rooms are modern and spacious. Each room has a fireplace, private balcony, and pillow-top mattresses. There are also a beautiful rooftop pool and lounge area and a fitness room.

BED-AND-BREAKFASTS

There are several wonderful bed-and-breakfasts in Lewes near the historic district. Most have minimum night stays during the season, some do not allow small children, and some do not take credit cards, so be sure to ask about these things when you make your reservation if they are important to you.

The **Savannah Inn** (330 Savannah Rd., 302/645-0330, www.savannahinnlewes.com, $190-295) is a lovely turn-of-the-20th-century brick home that was remodeled and now offers six contemporary guest rooms with modern

bathrooms. The owners are very personable and take pride in their establishment, which goes a long way in making guests feel welcome. The inn is very clean, and the decor is airy and inviting. It is an easy walk to the historic downtown area and the waterfront. The inn is a family-run business, from the reservations to the kitchen. There is an adorable yellow Labrador who lives here, but the owners are careful about not allowing him in guest areas.

The **John Penrose Virden House** (217 2nd St., 302/644-0217, www.virdenhouse.com, $175-245) is a charming green-colored 19th-century Victorian bed-and-breakfast centrally located on 2nd Street. The three guest rooms are well appointed with antiques and offer beach equipment such as towels and chairs. The hosts do a lovely job of making visitors feel welcome and greet guests with fresh fruit and flowers in their rooms. They also serve a scrumptious homemade breakfast to remember and hold a cocktail hour with snacks and beverages. Bicycles are also available for guests. They do not accept credit cards, only cash or checks.

The **Blue Water House** (407 E. Market St., 302/645-7832, www.lewes-beach.com, $200-235) is a bed-and-breakfast a short walk from the beach and geared toward sandy fun. It offers a slightly funky decor with bright colors. There are nine guest rooms, each with private bathrooms. The owner pays attention to every last detail and goes above and beyond to make guests feel welcome and to keep the house immaculate. Guests are offered many beach amenities such as towels, beach chairs, sunscreen, umbrellas, cold water, and bicycles. Children are welcome, and the house is equipped with games and books.

Information and Services

For additional information on Lewes, visit www.lewes.com or stop by the **Lewes Visitors Center** (120 Kings Hwy., 302/645-8073, www.leweschamber.com, Mon.-Fri. 10am-4pm).

Washington DC

Look for ★ to find recommended
sights, activities, dining, and lodging.

Highlights

★ **Washington Monument:** One of the most easily recognized landmarks in the country, this 555-foot-tall monument is a tribute to America's first president and a focal point of the National Mall (page 161).

★ **Lincoln Memorial:** This stunning Doric-style monument sitting on the banks of the Potomac River is a grand memorial to President Abraham Lincoln (page 162).

★ **Vietnam Veterans Memorial:** This moving memorial honors those who fought and died or went missing in action during the Vietnam War (page 163).

★ **National Museum of Natural History:** The most visited natural history museum in the world, this treasure features more than 126 million specimens in 325,000 square feet of exhibit space (page 167).

★ **National Air and Space Museum:** This impressive museum features the largest collection of air- and spacecraft in the world (page 168).

★ **White House:** Tour the home and workplace of the president of the United States (page 170).

★ **Jefferson Memorial:** Sitting on the shore of the famous Tidal Basin is this stunning memorial to the author of the Declaration of Independence (page 171).

★ **U.S. Capitol:** Perhaps the biggest symbol of the free world, the grand neoclassical-style Capitol Building is the official meeting site for the U.S. Congress (page 173).

★ **National Cathedral:** This massive Gothic cathedral in Upper Northwest DC is the sixth-largest cathedral in the world (page 183).

Awe-inspiring Washington DC, nestled between Virginia and Maryland on the banks of the Potomac River, is best known for government, politics, and museums. Stunning marble monuments dominate the landscape and

are a constant reminder of our country's powerful beginnings, while stately government buildings act as the working engine guiding our nation.

One of the largest cities in the nation, Washington is also home to several universities, trendy neighborhoods, professional sports arenas, and attractions like the National Zoo. The city boasts tremendous nightlife, art, theater, and upscale shopping. On average, around 24 million visitors come to DC annually.

Although much of the city is historic and upscale, there are also parts of Washington DC that are impoverished, comprising mostly minority demographics. Many of these residents face homelessness and unemployment. These areas exist side by side with the affluent and wealthy. In a strange way, Washington DC does truly represent the country, even if its residents don't have voting representation in Congress.

ORIENTATION

The city is divided into four quadrants, with the U.S. Capitol sitting in all four. The Capitol Building, however, doesn't sit in the center of the city, which means that the quadrants are not equal in terms of square mileage. The majority of the city, and the lion's share of the attractions, are in the northwest quadrant of Washington. The city is laid out in a grid pattern of lettered and numbered streets, so it is relatively easy to navigate, especially with the help of large landmarks like the Washington Monument and the Capitol Building.

If you asked 10 people how they would divide up the city to explain it to a visitor, you would get 10 different answers. Some would do it simply by quadrants, others by key neighborhoods, and still others by the sights themselves. For the sake of this guide, we are going to divide the city by popular tourist areas so that we can include key areas where many of the popular sights are located, as well as

Previous: architectural detail of the U.S. Capitol; cherry blossoms along the Tidal Basin. **Above:** National World War II Memorial.

Washington DC

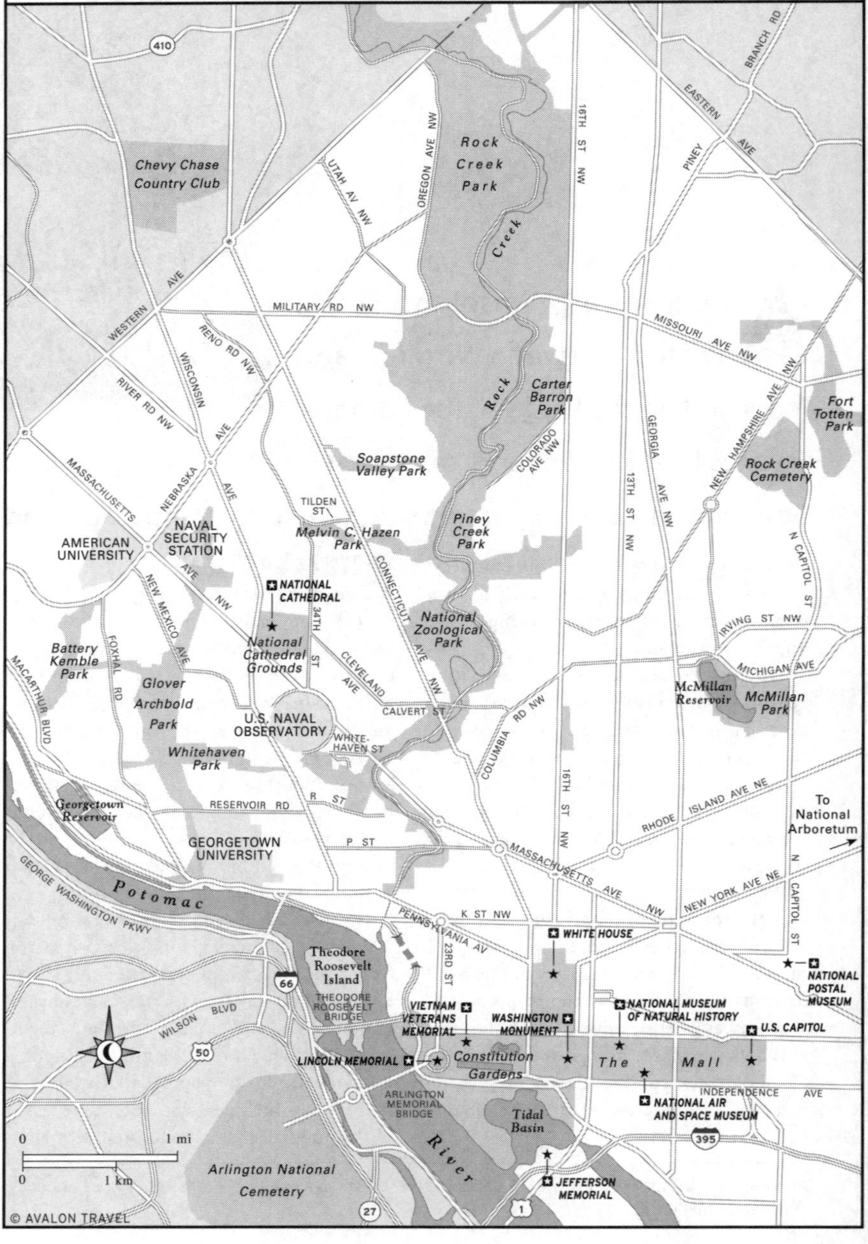

410

Chevy Chase
Country Club

Rock
Creek
Park

16TH ST NW

UTAH AV NW

OREGON AVE NW

Rock Creek

EASTERN AVE

PINEY

BRANCH RD

WESTERN AVE

MILITARY RD NW

MISSOURI AVE NW

RENO RD NW

WISCONSIN AVE

RIVER RD NW

Rock Creek

Carter
Barron
Park

COLORADO AVE NW

GEORGIA AVE NW

13TH ST NW

NEW HAMPSHIRE AVE NW

Fort
Totten
Park

MASSACHUSETTS AVE

NEBRASKA AVE

Soapstone
Valley Park

TILDEN ST

Rock Creek
Cemetery

AMERICAN
UNIVERSITY

NAVAL
SECURITY
STATION

Melvin C. Hazen
Park

Piney
Creek
Park

N CAPITOL ST

NEW MEXICO AVE NW

★ NATIONAL CATHEDRAL

34TH ST

CONNECTICUT AVE

National
Zoological
Park

IRVING ST NW

MICHIGAN AVE

Battery
Kemble
Park

FORDHAM RD

National
Cathedral
Grounds

CLEVELAND AVE

MACARTHUR BLVD

Glover
Archbold
Park

U.S. NAVAL
OBSERVATORY

CALVERT ST

McMillan
Reservoir

McMillan
Park

Whitehaven
Park

WHITE-HAVEN ST

COLUMBIA RD NW

16TH ST NW

Georgetown
Reservoir

RESERVOIR RD

R ST

RHODE ISLAND AVE NE

To
National
Arboretum

P ST

MASSACHUSETTS AVE NW

NEW YORK AVE NE

N CAPITOL ST

GEORGETOWN
UNIVERSITY

GEORGE WASHINGTON PKWY

Potomac

K ST NW

PENNSYLVANIA AV

23RD ST

✪ WHITE HOUSE

✪ NATIONAL
POSTAL
MUSEUM

Theodore
Roosevelt
Island

66

THEODORE
ROOSEVELT
BRIDGE

WILSON BLVD

50

VIETNAM
VETERANS
MEMORIAL

WASHINGTON ✪
MONUMENT

★

✪ NATIONAL MUSEUM
OF NATURAL HISTORY

★

✪ U.S. CAPITOL

LINCOLN MEMORIAL ✪

★ Constitution
Gardens

★

The ★ Mall ★

ARLINGTON
MEMORIAL
BRIDGE

✪ NATIONAL AIR
AND SPACE MUSEUM

INDEPENDENCE AVE

0   1 mi

0   1 km

Arlington National
Cemetery

27

Tidal
Basin

395

✪ JEFFERSON
MEMORIAL

River

1

© AVALON TRAVEL

popular neighborhoods where you can find a tremendous selection of food, nightlife, and festivals.

The National Mall

Many people are surprised to learn that the National Mall is a national park and administered by the National Park Service. It is part of an area known as the National Mall and Memorial Parks unit. The exact boundaries of the mall have always been difficult to define, but according to the National Park Service, it is "the area encompassed by Constitution and Pennsylvania Avenues NW on the north, 1st Street on the east, Independence and Maryland Avenues on the south, and 14th Street on the west." It may be easier to visualize by saying that the Mall is basically the entire three-mile stretch between the Lincoln Memorial at the west end and the U.S. Capitol at the east end. The Washington Monument is a focal point of the Mall and sits just to the west of its center. Often, many areas just outside the Mall's official boundaries are still considered to be "on the Mall."

A plan for the National Mall originally designed in 1791 by Pierre L'Enfant laid out a "Grand Avenue," but it was never carried out. The Mall served several other purposes prior to reaching its current state. During the Civil War, the land was utilized primarily for military purposes—drilling troops, the production of arms, and even slaughtering cattle. Permission was even given to the railroad in the late 1800s to lay tracks across part of the Mall.

The National Mall is the primary tourist area in Washington DC, and visitors should plan on spending a significant amount of time here. Simply put, it is packed with monuments and lined with museums. (Some are even underground.) The Department of Agriculture is also on the Mall. When you set out to explore, wear comfortable walking shoes and bring extra camera batteries.

Capitol Hill

Capitol Hill is the political center of the country. It is home to the U.S. Congress and also the largest historical residential neighborhood in the city. It packs in approximately

U.S. Capitol

35,000 residents in less than two square miles. Geographically, Capitol Hill is literally a hill that rises as you approach the Capitol from the west. The U.S. Capitol is on the crest of the hill.

Capitol Hill sits in both the southeast and northeast quadrants of the city. To the north is the H Street Corridor, to the south is the Washington Navy Yard, to the east is the Anacostia River, and to the west is the National Mall.

Many politicians, their staff, journalists, and lobbyists live on Capitol Hill. Residential streets are lined with homes from different periods, many of which are historic.

Pennsylvania Avenue is the hub of the commercial district on Capitol Hill and offers restaurants, bars, and shops. The oldest continually running fresh food market in the city, called **Eastern Market,** is just east of the Capitol Building. This popular shopping spot is housed in a 19th-century brick building.

Downtown

"Downtown" may sound a bit broad, but the term actually refers to the central business district in northwest Washington DC. Geographically, the area is difficult to clearly define, but it is generally accepted as being bordered by P Street NW to the north, Constitution Avenue NW to the south, 4th Street NW to the east, and 15th Street NW to the west.

Some notable areas included in the downtown district are the **K Street Corridor,** which used to be known as the Power Lobbying Corridor and still houses many law firms and businesses (although most of the lobbying firms have relocated to other parts of the city); **Federal Triangle** (bordered by 15th Street NW, Constitution Avenue NW, Pennsylvania Avenue NW, and E Street NW), a triangular area that is home to 10 large federal and city buildings; and **Judiciary Square** (bounded by H Street NW to the north, Pennsylvania Avenue to the south, the I-395 access tunnel to the east, and 6th Street NW to the west), a small neighborhood

Who was Pierre L'Enfant?

Washington DC owes a great portion of its inspiring design to Pierre Charles L'Enfant (1754-1825), a French-born American architect and civil engineer. L'Enfant came to America to fight in the Revolutionary War and later became George Washington's number one city planner. L'Enfant designed Washington DC from scratch. He dreamed up a city that was to rise out of a mix of hills, forests, marshes, and plantation land into an extravagant capital city with wide avenues, beautiful buildings, and public squares.

L'Enfant's city included a grand "public walk," which is seen today in the National Mall. His city plan was based on European models, but incorporated American ideals. The design was created from the idea that every citizen is equally important. This is shown in the Mall design, since it is open in all corners.

housing federal and municipal courthouses and offices.

The area also includes the **Penn Quarter** neighborhood, which extends roughly between F and H Streets NW and between 5th and 10th Streets. The name "Penn Quarter" is relatively new. This once sketchy area had new life breathed into it with the opening of the **Verizon Center** (7th and F Streets) in 1997, which was originally called the MCI Center and is home to the **Washington Capitals** professional hockey team and the **Washington Wizards** and **Washington Mystics** professional basketball teams. Now the area is a bustling arts and entertainment district with galleries, museums, restaurants, hotels, and shopping.

At its northern boundaries, Penn Quarter overlaps with the small historic neighborhood of **Chinatown.** Chinatown runs along H and I Streets NW between 5th and 8th Streets NW. It has roughly 20 authentic Asian restaurants and small businesses and is known for its annual Chinese New Year celebration as well as its signature Friendship Arch built over H Street at 7th Street.

Dupont Circle

Dupont Circle is a historic district in Northwest Washington DC. It is technically also the traffic circle at the intersection of Massachusetts Avenue NW, Connecticut Avenue NW, New Hampshire Avenue NW, P Street NW, and 19th Street NW, as well as a park and a neighborhood.

The neighborhood of Dupont Circle lies roughly between Florida Avenue NW to the north, M Street NW to the south, 16th Street NW to the east, and 22nd Street NW to the west.

Dupont Circle is often considered the center of Washington DC's nightlife. It is home to many people in their 20s and also a popular neighborhood among the gay and lesbian community. There are many multilevel apartment buildings and row houses that have been split into apartments here.

Northwest of Dupont Circle along Massachusetts Avenue is an area of the city where many foreign embassies are located. This is commonly referred to as **Embassy Row.** Although less than half of the more than 175 embassies in DC are in this area, it has one of the largest concentrations (most are between Scott Circle and Wisconsin Avenue). Many of the embassies were formerly the homes of wealthy families who made their fortunes from the railroad, mining, banking, publishing, and even politics in the late 1800s. You'll recognize the embassies by the country flags flying out front.

Georgetown

Georgetown has long been known as a trendy yet historic neighborhood with excellent shopping, food, and nightlife. It sits on the Potomac River in Northwest DC, west of downtown and upriver from the National Mall. The area can be loosely defined as being bordered by the Potomac River to the south, Glover Park to the north, Rock Creek to the east, and Georgetown University to the west.

The intersection of M Street and Wisconsin Avenue is the hub of the commercial area,

M Street in Georgetown

Choosing the Location of the Nation's Capital

Prior to 1800, the newly formed Congress met in several locations in the mid-Atlantic region. Where to establish the permanent federal government became a highly contested topic that went unresolved for many years. Finally, on July 16, 1790, President George Washington was officially put in charge of selecting a location for the permanent capital and appointing three commissioners to oversee its birth. Washington chose a 10-square-mile piece of land from property in both Virginia and Maryland sitting on both sides of the Potomac River.

The old myth is that DC was built on a swamp. This isn't exactly true. The area was a tidal plain but encompassed tobacco fields, cornfields, woods, waterside bluffs, and wetlands along the river. Washington DC is rich with waterways (the Potomac River, Anacostia River, Rock Creek, and others), but most of the land designated for the city was not marshy.

Congress met in the new location for the first time on November 17, 1800, and the move was completed in 1801. In 1846, land that formerly belonged to Virginia (on what is now the Virginia side of the Potomac River) was returned to Virginia. It is said that George Washington never felt comfortable calling the capital Washington, so instead he referred to it as "The Federal City."

where high-end stores, top-notch restaurants, bars, and The Shops at Georgetown Park are located. Washington Harbor is also a popular area of Georgetown and offers waterfront dining on K Street, between 30th and 31st Streets. The historic Chesapeake & Ohio Canal (C&O Canal) runs between M and K Streets.

Georgetown is home to many politicians and lobbyists and traditionally one of the most affluent neighborhoods in Washington. Famous people who have lived here include Thomas Jefferson, Francis Scott Key, Alexander Graham Bell, John F. Kennedy, John Kerry, Bob Woodward, and Madeleine Albright.

Many movies have also been filmed in the neighborhood. One of the most notable was the 1973 horror flick *The Exorcist,* which was set here and filmed here in part. Other films include *St. Elmo's Fire* (1985), *No Way Out* (1987), *True Lies* (1994), *Enemy of the State* (1998), *Minority Report* (2002), *The Girl Next Door* (2004), *Wedding Crashers* (2005), and *Transformers* (2007).

Georgetown is not directly accessible by the Metrorail, Washington DC's subway system, but the local DC Circulator bus runs from 19th Street and N Street at the Dupont Metrorail station (on the Dupont-Georgetown-Rosslyn route) to the Rosslyn Metrorail station in Arlington, and it stops along M Street in Georgetown. The Union Station-Georgetown route also stops in Georgetown as it runs from Union Station to Georgetown along K Street. It also has stops on M Street.

Adams Morgan

Adams Morgan is a lively neighborhood in Northwest DC centered on the intersection of 18th Street and Columbia Road. This culturally diverse neighborhood is north of Dupont Circle, south of Mt. Pleasant, east of Kalorama, and west of Columbia Heights. It is considered to be the center of the city's Hispanic community.

Adams Morgan is known for its thriving nightlife. It has more than 40 bars, a great selection of restaurants, nightclubs, coffeehouses, galleries, and shops (most are located along 18th Street). Cuisine from all parts of the globe can be found, from Ethiopian to Caribbean.

Adams Morgan is a popular neighborhood for young professionals and has many 19th- and early 20th-century apartment buildings and row houses.

Upper Northwest

Some of the country's wealthiest people live in the Upper Northwest section of Washington DC. It is a very pretty part of the city that is largely residential with many suburban-looking tree-lined streets. Although the sights are somewhat spread out, many are accessible from the Metrorail.

Just a half mile north of Georgetown is **Glover Park,** a neighborhood of apartment buildings and row houses that were built in the 1920s and '30s. Much of the area's nightlife is found in Glover Park, although compared to neighboring Georgetown, it caters to a slightly older clientele and is less crowded. Glover Park is also slightly west of the **U.S. Naval Observatory** (home to the nation's **Master Clock**) and the vice president's mansion (Number One Observatory Circle).

Northeast of Glover Park is **Woodley Park,** which has some key attractions such as the **National Cathedral** and the **National Zoo.** Farther north are **Cleveland Park, Van Ness,** and **Tenleytown,** along Wisconsin and Connecticut Avenues. Each has their own local restaurants, bars, and shopping. To the west is **American University.**

Southwest of American University is a lesser-known neighborhood called the **Palisades** on the western border of the city along the Potomac River and C&O Canal. This is an elite neighborhood with a few good, high-end restaurants.

Farther north and right on the Maryland state line is **Friendship Heights,** which is technically part of **Chevy Chase.** Friendship Heights has notable wealth and is known for its upscale stores along Wisconsin Avenue and a mall called the **Chevy Chase Pavilion.**

Metrorail's Red Line operates throughout Upper Northwest. The stops are easy to navigate because the stations are named after neighborhoods and sights. The National Cathedral, Glover Park, and the Palisades do not have Metrorail service.

U Street Corridor

The U Street Corridor is a residential and commercial neighborhood in Northwest Washington DC that extends for nine blocks along U Street between 9th and 18th Streets. In the 1920s, this part of the city was known as "Black Broadway," and was one of the largest African American communities in

the Adams Morgan neighborhood

the National Museum of the American Indian on the National Mall

the country. Several famous jazz musicians lived in the neighborhood, including Duke Ellington and Jelly Roll Morton. Others frequented the area's jazz clubs.

Today the U Street Corridor is home to restaurants, nightclubs, music venues, and shops. The intersection of 9th and U Streets is known as "Little Ethiopia" for its concentration of Ethiopian businesses and restaurants.

PLANNING YOUR TIME

Washington DC encompasses approximately 68 square miles, so it is easy to get from one attraction to the next. The truth is, Washington DC has so much to offer, it could take weeks to feel that you've exhausted your opportunities for exploration. That's why it is best to focus on a few key areas when familiarizing yourself with the city and to come prepared with a plan of action or at least a list of the top sights you'd like to see.

The National Mall and Memorial Parks are where most of the key monuments and

museums are located. This is an area most first-time visitors focus on to see known landmarks such as the Washington Monument, Lincoln and Jefferson Memorials, and several Smithsonian museums. This area can be explored in a long weekend, but allow more time if you want to visit each of the museums.

Most people spend their first trip to Washington DC exploring the National Mall and visiting the government buildings on Capitol Hill. Repeat visitors, or those with ample time, then branch out to explore some of the wonderful neighborhoods in Northwest DC, spending time in Georgetown, Dupont Circle, Adams Morgan, and other key locations to get more of the flavor of the city and to take in the zoo or National Cathedral.

Above all, be realistic about what you and any travel companions can take in during a day. Three or four top sights a day can be more than enough if they include walking through museums and taking tours.

If you are planning to stay in Washington

DC and not stray far from the city limits, there is no need to have a car during your visit. Many of the sights, restaurants, and hotels are accessible by public transportation or a short cab ride, and parking can be expensive and sometimes difficult to find.

Sights

THE NATIONAL MALL

The National Mall (www.nps.gov/nacc) is open 24 hours a day. National Park Service rangers are available to answer questions at most of the sights daily 9am-10pm.

★ Washington Monument

The Washington Monument (2 15th St. NW, 202/426-6841, www.nps.gov/wamo, daily except July 4 and Dec. 25, 9am-5pm with longer summer hours, free but ticket required) is one of the most easily recognized landmarks in the country. This slender, 555-foot-tall stone structure is centrally located on the Mall (east of the Reflecting Pool and the Lincoln Memorial) and is a great landmark

Washington Monument

with which to orient yourself when touring the Mall.

The Washington Monument is a tribute to the first U.S. president and also the world's tallest true obelisk. Made of marble, granite, and bluestone gneiss, its construction spanned 36 years. Work started in 1848 but was interrupted by several events between 1854 and 1877, including the Civil War. If you look closely at the monument, you can tell that about 150 feet up (a little more than a quarter of the way) the shading of the marble differs slightly. This was due to the long break in construction. The capstone was finally set in 1884, and the monument was dedicated in early 1885. It opened to the public in 1888.

The Washington Monument, upon its completion, was the world's tallest structure. It only held this distinction for one year, however: The Eiffel Tower took over the honor after it was completed in Paris, France.

Visitors can take an elevator to the top of the monument to enjoy stunning views of the city. From the viewing windows, the White House can be seen to the north, the Jefferson Memorial to the south, the Capitol Building to the east, and the Lincoln Memorial to the west.

Although admission is free, tickets must be obtained either in person at the Washington Monument Lodge or over the phone. Located along 15th Street, the Lodge opens at 8:30am and distributes same-day tickets on a first-come, first-served basis. Up to six tickets can be obtained per person. Tickets have specific times, but it is possible to request a preferred ticket time. Be aware that lines form long before the ticket window opens. To order tickets in advance by phone, call 877/444-6777 for individual tickets and 877/559-6777 for

The National Mall

© AVALON TRAVEL

group tickets. Although tickets are free, there is a $1.50 service charge per ticket. Tickets can be ordered up to three months in advance and picked up at the will-call window of the Washington Monument Lodge.

★ Lincoln Memorial

A stunning tribute to America's 16th president is the **Lincoln Memorial** (off 23rd Street NW, 202/426-6841, www.nps.gov/linc, 24 hours, free). This grand limestone and marble monument was built in the Greek Doric style on the western end of the National Mall across

from the Washington Monument. It has 36 exterior columns, which represent the number of states that existed at the time of Lincoln's death. The monument was dedicated in 1922.

Inside the memorial is a huge sculpture of Abraham Lincoln and inscriptions from two of his best-known speeches (the Gettysburg Address and his second inaugural address). The sculpture was created by Daniel Chester French, an acclaimed American sculptor of the late 19th and early 20th centuries, and carved by the Piccirilli brothers, who were well-known marble carvers at the time. The

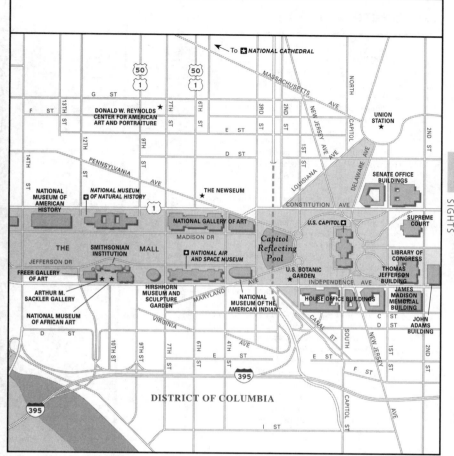

memorial is one of the most recognized landmarks in Washington DC and has been the site of many famous speeches, including Martin Luther King Jr.'s "I Have a Dream" speech.

Albert Einstein Memorial

Where else but on the National Mall can you sit with one of the greatest scientific minds of all time? Just north of the Lincoln Memorial is the bronze **Albert Einstein Memorial** statue sculpted by Robert Berks. It is set in a group of trees on the southwest side of the grounds of the **National Academy of Sciences** (2101 Constitution Ave. NW). Einstein is seated and has papers with mathematical equations in his lap symbolizing his scientific achievements.

War Memorials
★ VIETNAM VETERANS MEMORIAL

One of the most visited war memorials is the **Vietnam Veterans Memorial** (Constitution Avenue between 21st and 23rd Streets, 202/426-6841, www.nps.gov/vive, www.thewall-usa.com, 24 hours, free). This moving memorial

Secrets of the Lincoln Memorial

Many myths surround the Lincoln Memorial. Some say Abraham Lincoln is buried under the monument or entombed inside it, but this is false (Lincoln is buried in Springfield, Illinois). Others think the 57 steps leading up to the statue chamber represent Lincoln's age when he died, but in reality, he was only 56.

One question that is repeatedly asked throughout the local community is what, if anything, lies underneath the memorial? Given that the structure was built on tidal marsh from the Potomac River that was once actually under water, it might make sense that nothing could be under it, but the rumor that something exists there is actually true.

Underneath the Lincoln Memorial is a cavernous area with dirt floors and concrete walls. Hanging from the ceiling beneath where Lincoln sits are hundreds of stalactite formations. The stalactites are long, slender, and pale in color, and they are growing in this artificial cave as the result of water slowly dripping through the monument, which started when it was built.

Other interesting features in the underbelly of the monument are cartoon drawings that were sketched on several support columns by the workers who built the monument. One of the drawings depicts characters from the old *Mutt and Jeff* cartoon, which started running in 1907 and was the first daily newspaper comic strip.

Tours of the cavernous area ceased after 9/11, but this author can vouch for its existence, since in the 1970s and '80s, local children were treated to a tour on elementary school field trips.

the sculpture of Abraham Lincoln in the Lincoln Memorial

honors U.S. service members who fought and died in the Vietnam War and also those who are missing in action. There are three parts to the memorial: the **Three Soldiers Statue,** the **Vietnam Women's Memorial,** and the **Vietnam Veterans Memorial Wall.**

The focal point of the memorial is the Vietnam Veterans Memorial Wall. Completed in 1982, it is actually two 246-foot walls that are sunken into the ground and have the names of more than 58,000 service members who died in the war etched into them in chronological order. (The exact number

changes each year as names are added.) When visitors look at the wall, they can see their reflections next to the etched names, symbolically linking the past and present. There is a path along the base of the wall so visitors can walk along it, read names, and if desired, make pencil rubbings of a particular name.

The memorial is at the west end of the National Mall, adjacent to the Lincoln Memorial in West Potomac Park. It is open to the public 24 hours a day, and park staff conduct free daily interpretive tours on the hour 10am-11pm.

NATIONAL WORLD WAR II MEMORIAL

The **National World War II Memorial** (17th Street between Constitution and Independence Avenues, 202/426-6841, www.wwiimemorial.com, www.nps.gov/nwwm, 24 hours, free) honors the more than 400,000 people who died in World War II, the 16 million people who served the United States during the war in the armed forces, and the millions of people who provided support from home. The memorial contains 56 pillars and two triumphal arches arranged in a semicircle around a fountain and plaza. A Freedom Wall sits on the west side of the memorial bearing more than 4,000 gold stars on it, each representing 100 Americans who lost their lives in the war. An inscription in front of the wall reads, "Here we mark the price of freedom." The memorial opened to the public in 2004 and is administered by the National Park Service. It is on the east end of the Reflecting Pool, between the Washington Monument and the Lincoln Memorial.

KOREAN WAR VETERANS MEMORIAL

The beautiful and haunting **Korean War Veterans Memorial** (17th Street SW, 202/426-6841, www.nps.gov/kwvm, 24 hours, free) is also in West Potomac Park, southeast of the Lincoln Memorial. Erected in 1995, it is dedicated to service members who served in the Korean War. The memorial was designed in the shape of a triangle intersecting a circle with walls depicting images of land, sea, and air troops who supported the war. The focal point, however, is 19 larger than life-size stainless steel statues designed by Frank Gaylord within the walled triangle. The seven-foot-tall figures represent a patrol squad with members from each branch of the armed forces making their way through the harsh Korean terrain, represented by strips of granite and bushes. The figures are dressed in full combat gear and look incredibly lifelike. The memorial is lit up at night, and when the figures are reflected on the surrounding wall, there appear to be 38 soldiers, which represents the 38th parallel dividing the two Koreas.

National Gallery of Art

The **National Gallery of Art** (4th St. and Constitution Ave. NW, 202/737-4215, www.nga.gov, Mon.-Sat. 10am-5pm, Sun. 11am-6pm, free), opened in 1937, was conceived by Andrew W. Mellon, who donated funding and a large art collection. The gallery traces the development of Western art from the Middle Ages to current times through paintings,

the National World War II Memorial

the Korean War Veterans Memorial

prints, drawings, sculpture, photographs, and other media. The only portrait in the Western Hemisphere painted by Leonardo da Vinci is housed in this museum. The gallery is a campus that includes the original museum building (the West Building), which features sculpture galleries with over 900 works or art; the newer East Building, which contains a collection of modern paintings, drawings, prints, offices, and research centers; and a 6.1-acre outdoor sculpture garden (open year-round) that offers an ice-skating rink from mid-November through mid-March.

Smithsonian Institution Museums

The **Smithsonian Institution** (www.si.edu) is the largest museum and research complex in the world. It was founded in 1846 and is administered by the U.S. government.

Oddly, the founding donor of the institution was British chemist and mineralogist James Smithson, who had never even been to the United States. Smithson inherited a large estate but had no heirs to leave it to. His will stipulated that his estate would be donated to the founding of an educational institute in Washington DC.

The Smithsonian Institution was established as a trust and functions as a body of the U.S. government, separate from the legislative, executive, and judicial branches. Funding for the museums comes from contributions, the institution's own endowment, memberships, government support, and retail and concession revenues. The Smithsonian employs approximately 6,300 people.

The majority of the Smithsonian museums, 19 in fact, are in DC, and many of them are architectural and historical landmarks. Nine research centers and the National Zoological Park are also part of the Smithsonian collection in DC.

First-timers to Washington DC will want to visit at least one of the major Smithsonian museums. Most of the Smithsonian facilities are open to the public daily except for December 25, with free admission. Visitors should be aware that most of the museums on the National Mall do not offer dedicated parking facilities and require visitors to pass through security screenings upon entry.

SMITHSONIAN CASTLE

Information on the Smithsonian can be found on the south side of the Mall at its headquarters, called the **Smithsonian Castle** (1000 Jefferson Dr. SW, 202/633-1000, daily 8:30am-5:30pm, free). This sandstone building, which opened in 1855, looks like something out of a fairy tale and houses an exhibit hall, administration offices, and Smithson's remains (which were laid to rest in a crypt under the castle).

NATIONAL MUSEUM OF AFRICAN AMERICAN HISTORY & CULTURE

The **National Museum of African American History & Culture** (1400 Constitution Ave. NW, 202/633-1000, www.nmaahc.si.edu, daily 10am-5:30pm, free), which opened in September 2016, is the only national museum devoted exclusively to the documentation of African American life, history, and culture. The museum owns close to 37,000 artifacts and its collections explore topics such as the American South, civil rights, and literature.

You must have a timed entry pass to enter the museum. At the time of publication, passes were sold out several months in advance, but a limited number of same day passes were available daily at 9:15am. Passes can be reserved on the website or by calling 866/297-4020.

NATIONAL MUSEUM OF AMERICAN HISTORY

The **National Museum of American History** (1400 Constitution Ave. NW, 202/633-1000, www.americanhistory.si.edu,

daily 10am-5:30pm, free) is devoted to exhibits explaining the cultural, social, scientific, technological, military, and political development of the United States. The museum has three floors housing more than three million artifacts. Wings on each floor represent a different theme, each of which is represented by a large, landmark object. For example, the 1865 Vassar Telescope is in the west wing of the first floor, which is focused on science and innovation.

Some museum highlights include the Star-Spangled Banner, George Washington's uniform, Dorothy's ruby slippers from the *Wizard of Oz,* and the inaugural dresses worn by all the first ladies.

The one-hour guided tours offered are a good way to see the highlights quickly if you have a full docket of sights to get to on the same day. There is no public parking at the museum. Visitors riding Metrorail can use either the Smithsonian Mall stop or Federal Triangle.

★ NATIONAL MUSEUM OF NATURAL HISTORY

Another favorite Smithsonian creation is the **National Museum of Natural History** (10th St. and Constitution Ave. NW, 202/633-1000,

WASHINGTON DC
SIGHTS

"Henry" at the National Museum of Natural History

www.mnh.si.edu, daily 10am-5:30pm, free). It first opened its doors in 1910 and is said to be the most visited natural history museum worldwide. The main building encloses 325,000 square feet of exhibit space and is overall the size of 18 football fields. The museum collections include more than 126 million specimens.

Visitors can expect to see plants, animals, fossils, rocks, meteorites, and cultural artifacts including "Henry," the iconic 13-plus-foot-tall African elephant (the largest ever killed by humans), the jaws of a giant prehistoric shark, and the stunning Hope Diamond (which is 45.52 carats). There's also a live butterfly pavilion ($6) and an IMAX theater ($7.50-12.50). The museum is also home to the largest group of scientists (approximately 185) dedicated to studying the history of the world. Visitor concierges are available to answer questions throughout the museum and can be identified by their green vests. There is no public parking at the museum. Visitors riding Metrorail should exit at the Smithsonian station (Mall exit) on the Blue and Orange Lines.

NATIONAL MUSEUM OF THE AMERICAN INDIAN

The **National Museum of the American Indian** (4th St. and Independence Ave. SW, 202/633-1000, www.nmai.si.edu, daily 10am-5:30pm, free) opened in 2004 and is the first national museum focused exclusively on Native Americans. The five-story, 250,000-square-foot limestone building sits on more than four acres of what is made to look like wetlands. The museum features approximately 825,000 items that represent more than 12,000 years of history and 1,200 indigenous American cultures. It also offers exhibits, film screenings, public programs, cultural presentations, and school programs.

★ NATIONAL AIR AND SPACE MUSEUM

An overwhelming favorite in the Smithsonian family of museums is the **National Air and Space Museum** (Independence Ave. at 6th St. SW, 202/633-2214, IMAX 866/868-7774, www.airandspace.si.edu, daily 10am-5:30pm, free, IMAX and planetarium entry extra). This incredible museum features the largest collection of air- and spacecraft in the world and is also a center for research on historic aviation, spaceflight, planetary science, geophysics, and terrestrial geology. The current exhibit space of 21 galleries and more than 160,000 square feet of floor space opened in 1976. Most of the hundreds of aircraft,

National Air and Space Museum

spacecraft, rockets, missiles, and other aviation artifacts on display are originals.

Some highlights you can expect to see include the *Spirit of St. Louis,* the Apollo Lunar Module, a DC-3 airplane, a real lunar rock, and the *Star Trek* starship *Enterprise* studio model.

Another great attraction located inside the National Air and Space Museum is the **Albert Einstein Planetarium** ($9). Several shows are offered daily and take visitors through the night sky with a first-of-its-kind SkyVision dual digital projection system and digital surround sound.

Other favorite attractions in the museum include the **Lockheed Martin IMAX Theater** (IMAX shows $9, feature films $15) and flight simulators. One of the best museum shops is also here, and dining facilities are offered on-site.

Museum tours are offered daily at 10:30am and 1pm. There is no public parking at the museum, but several public pay lots are nearby. Metrorail riders should use the L'Enfant Plaza stop and exit at Maryland Avenue.

HIRSHHORN MUSEUM

Many people think the **Hirshhorn Museum and Sculpture Garden** (700 Independence Ave. SW, 202/633-4674, www.hirshhorn. si.edu, daily 10am-5:30pm, free) looks like a giant spaceship parked near the Mall. The design is an open concrete cylinder (231 feet in diameter) standing on four large supports. The idea behind this structure was for it to provide a sharp contrast to everything else around it. It succeeded. This modern art museum, which opened in the 1960s, houses one of the premier collections of contemporary paintings and sculptures in the country focusing on the post-World War II era. A sculpture garden is located outside the museum.

NATIONAL MUSEUM OF AFRICAN ART

The **National Museum of African Art** (950 Independence Ave. SW, 202/633-4600, www.africa.si.edu, daily 10am-5:30pm, free) is part of a quadrangle complex behind the

Smithsonian Castle. The building is mostly underground and contains the largest public collection of African art in the nation with approximately 9,000 artifacts. Pieces include sculpture, jewelry, musical instruments, maps, films, and photographs.

FREER GALLERY OF ART AND ARTHUR M. SACKLER GALLERY

The **Freer Gallery of Art** and the subterranean **Arthur M. Sackler Gallery** (1050 Independence Ave. SW, 202/633-1000, www.asia.si.edu, daily 10am-5:30pm, free) together form the national collections of Asian art. They contain the largest Asian art research library in the country (inside the Sackler Gallery) as well as art from all parts of Asia. Their collection of American art includes pieces by well-known artists such as Winslow Homer, Augustus Saint-Gaudens, and John Singer Sargent.

The Freer Gallery features Asian collections spanning 6,000 years that date back to the Neolithic era. Specific collections include stone sculptures from ancient Egypt, Chinese paintings, Persian manuscripts, and Korean pottery.

The Freer's most famous exhibit is the **Peacock Room** painted by American artist James McNeill Whistler. The room has been restored to how it appeared in 1908 when the founder of the museum, Charles Lan Freer, used it to display over 250 ceramic art pieces he had collected from Asia. Freer was a railroad car manufacturer in Detroit who was a self-taught connoisseur.

The Sackler Gallery contains a founding collection of approximately 1,000 items that were donated by American psychiatrist, entrepreneur, and philanthropist Arthur M. Sackler. The collection has both ancient and contemporary items including South and Southeast Asian sculpture, Chinese jade, and Middle Eastern ceramics. The museums are on the south side of the Mall.

MALL CAROUSEL

It may come as a surprise that the Smithsonian operates the **Mall Carousel** (12th St. and

Jefferson Dr. SW, 202/633-1000, www.national-carousel.com, daily 10am-5:30pm, $3.50). This favorite children's thrill ride with the blue and yellow awning is in front of the Smithsonian Castle. It offers three minutes of fun on faded painted ponies that were built in the 1940s. The carousel was originally at the Gwynn Oak Amusement Park in Maryland prior to coming to the Mall.

WHITE HOUSE AREA
★ White House

Not technically part of the National Mall, the **White House** (1600 Pennsylvania Ave., 202/456-1111, www.whitehouse.gov, free) sits nearby on Pennsylvania Avenue and can be seen from Constitution Avenue. The White House is easily the most recognized residence in the country as the home and workplace of the president of the United States.

The site for the White House was chosen by George Washington in 1791, but John Adams was the first president to live there in 1800. (Mrs. Adams is said to have hung their wash in the East Room.) The house suffered a fire set by the British during the War of 1812, but it was rebuilt and has undergone several renovations since then. The White House currently has 6 levels, 132 rooms, and 35 bathrooms.

It is possible to take a self-guided tour of the White House (the only presidential home in the world that is open to the public), but requests must be made through your member of Congress. Tours are available Tuesday-Thursday 7:30am-11am and Friday-Saturday 7:30am-1:30pm. Requests can be made up to six months in advance but must be made at least three weeks in advance. There is no charge for the tour, but it is advised to make a reservation early since space is limited. Citizens of a foreign country may request a tour through their individual embassies in Washington DC. All visitors are required to present current government-issued photo identification or a passport.

The **White House Visitor Center** (1450 Pennsylvania Ave. NW, daily 7:30am-4pm, free) is in the Commerce Building. It offers an information booth, exhibits, restrooms, telephones, drinking fountains, and a first-aid area.

Lafayette Square

Lafayette Square (H St. between 15th and 17th Sts. NW, www.nps.gov/nr, 24 hours, free) is a seven-acre park across Pennsylvania Avenue from the White House (it is also known as **Lafayette Park**). The park was designed as part of the White House grounds—and was originally named President's Park—

Presidential Firsts

- Andrew Jackson was the first president to ride in a train.

- James Polk was the first president to have his photograph taken.

- Millard Fillmore was the first president to have a bathtub with running water.

- Rutherford B. Hayes was the first president to have a telephone in the White House.

- Benjamin Harrison was the first president to have a Christmas tree in the White House.

- Theodore Roosevelt was the first president to ride in a car. He was also the first to travel outside the country while in office.

- Calvin Coolidge was the first president to be heard over radio.

- Franklin D. Roosevelt was the first president to fly in an airplane and the first to appear on television.

the White House

but was separated when Pennsylvania Avenue was built in 1804. Lafayette Square has a checkered past. It has been home to a racetrack, a slave market, a graveyard, and a soldier encampment during the War of 1812. It's no wonder the park is said to be the most haunted location in the city. Today, the park offers green grass and five large statues: an equestrian statue of President Andrew Jackson and four of Revolutionary War heroes. The closest Metrorail stop is McPherson Square. The park is maintained by the National Park Service.

President's Park South

President's Park South, which is more commonly referred to as **The Ellipse,** is a 52-acre park that sits just south of the White House. Technically, the Ellipse is the name of the street that runs the circumference of the park. The park is a large grassy circle that is open to the public and is the site of various events. If you hear locals say they are at or on the Ellipse, they mean they are in the park bordered by Ellipse Road.

TIDAL BASIN AREA
The Tidal Basin

The Tidal Basin is a 107-acre reservoir in **West Potomac Park** that sits between the Potomac River and the Washington Channel (a two-mile-long channel that empties into the Anacostia River). Several major memorials are adjacent to the Tidal Basin, including the Jefferson Memorial, the Martin Luther King, Jr. Memorial, and the Franklin Delano Roosevelt Memorial. The Tidal Basin is best known as the center of the National Cherry Blossom Festival; it is lined with many Japanese cherry trees.

★ Jefferson Memorial

Although it was only built in 1942, the **Jefferson Memorial** (701 W. Basin Dr., 202/426-6841, www.nps.gov/thje, 24 hours, free), which sits on the south shore of the Tidal Basin in West Potomac Park, is one of the most recognized memorials in DC. This neoclassical building dedicated to our third president is built on land that once served as a popular bathing beach along the Potomac River.

The memorial building is made up of circular marble steps, a portico, a circular colonnade, and a shallow dome open to the elements. Inside stands a 19-foot-high bronze statue of Thomas Jefferson designed by Rudulph Evans, looking north toward his former residence, the White House. The statue was added to the memorial four years after its

Jefferson Memorial

dedication. Many of Jefferson's writings are inscribed on the memorial.

The site of the Jefferson Memorial is adorned with many Japanese cherry trees, which were a gift from Japan in 1912. The trees are world famous for their beautiful spring blossoms and are the centerpiece for the annual Cherry Blossom Festival.

Martin Luther King, Jr. Memorial

One of the newest memorials is the **Martin Luther King, Jr. Memorial** (1964 Independence Ave. SW, 202/426-6841, www.nps.gov/mlkm, 24 hours, free) in West Potomac Park southwest of the National Mall. The memorial sits on four acres and was unveiled in 2011.

The design of the memorial is based on a line from King's "I Have a Dream" speech: "Out of a mountain of despair, a stone of hope." A 30-foot-high relief of the civil rights leader is called the *Stone of Hope,* sculpted by Lei Yixin, and stands just past two pieces of granite symbolizing the "mountain of despair." Additionally, a 450-foot-long wall includes inscriptions of excerpts from many of King's speeches. Martin Luther King Jr. is the first African American to be honored with a memorial near the National Mall. He is also

only the fourth person to be memorialized who was not a U.S. president.

Franklin Delano Roosevelt Memorial

The **Franklin Delano Roosevelt Memorial** (near the intersection of Independence Ave., W. Basin Dr., and Ohio Dr. SW, 202/485-9880, www.nps.gov/frde, 24 hours, free) sits on more than seven acres and consists of four outdoor rooms, one for each of FDR's office terms. Running water is an important component of the memorial, as are sculptures depicting scenes with FDR. Each of the rooms contains a waterfall, and the sculptures become larger and more detailed in consecutive rooms. The intention was to show the increasing complexities faced by FDR during his presidency as related to the depression and war. This is the only memorial to include a depiction of a first lady: Eleanor Roosevelt is depicted in a bronze statue standing before the United Nations emblem.

There is, in fact, another FDR Memorial. FDR was said to have told his trusted friend and Supreme Court justice Felix Frankfurter, "If they are to put up any memorial to me, I should like it to be placed in the center of that green plot in front of the Archives Building. I should like it to consist of a block about the

Who is Featured on U.S. Paper Currency?

- $1 Bill: George Washington (1st U.S. president)

- $2 Bill: Thomas Jefferson (3rd U.S. president)

- $5 Bill: Abraham Lincoln (16th U.S. president)

- $10 Bill: Alexander Hamilton (1st secretary of the treasury)

- $20 Bill: Currently Andrew Jackson (7th U.S. president), but he will eventually be replaced by Harriet Tubman (abolitionist and civil rights activist)

- $50 Bill: Ulysses S. Grant (18th U.S. president)

- $100 Bill: Ben Franklin (statesman)

size [of this desk]." Because of this, the first FDR memorial was erected in the 1960s on the corner of 9th Street and Pennsylvania Avenue. It is a simple memorial that met his wishes and consists of a small block of stone that reads, "In Memory of Franklin Delano Roosevelt 1882-1945."

U.S. Holocaust Memorial Museum

The **U.S. Holocaust Memorial Museum** (100 Raoul Wallenberg Pl. SW, 202/488-0400, www.ushmm.org, daily 10am-5:20pm, free) is dedicated to the interpretation of Holocaust history. Its goal is to help leaders and citizens "confront hatred, prevent genocide, and promote human dignity." This museum, perhaps more than most, is of international interest: Visitors from more than 132 countries have walked through its doors since it first opened in 1993. The museum houses more than 12,750 artifacts including prisoner uniforms, a casting of a gas chamber door, and religious

articles. Its collections include 1,000 hours of archival footage and 80,000 photographs. It also has information on 200,000 registered survivors, a library, and archives.

Permanent exhibits that show a chronological history of the Holocaust can be accessed on the first floor. A free pass must be obtained for the permanent exhibits March-August but not during the rest of the year. The passes are available at the museum on the day of your visit or can be reserved online. Entrance to other exhibits and memorial spaces is from the first, second, and concourse levels. There is a café on the 15th Street side of the building. This museum can be overwhelming for young children and is best for teenagers and adults.

Bureau of Engraving and Printing

As its web address indicates, the **Bureau of Engraving and Printing** (14th and C Sts. SW, 202/874-4000, www.moneyfactory. gov, Mon.-Fri. 8:30am-3pm, free) is a huge money factory. It produces U.S. currency notes and literally prints billions of dollars each year. Fresh money is delivered to the Federal Reserve System (the nation's central bank). Visitors can take guided tours or walk along the gallery to view the production floor where millions of dollars are being printed. The free 40-minute tour includes a film and explanation of the production process. No ticket is required for tours September-February. Tours run every 15 minutes between 9am and 10:45am and between 12:30pm and 2pm. During peak season (Mar.-Aug., 8:30am-6pm), free tickets are required for tours. Tickets can be obtained at the ticket booth on-site (which opens at 8am) and are for the same day only. Plan to be in line between 6:30am and 7am for the best chance of getting tickets. One person may get up to four tickets.

CAPITOL HILL
★ U.S. Capitol

The centerpiece of Capitol Hill is none other than the grand neoclassical-style **U.S.**

Capitol Hill

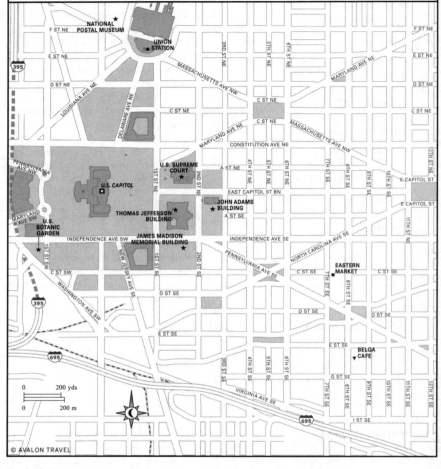

Capitol (1st St. and E. Capitol St., 202/226-8000, www.visitthecapitol.gov, free) itself, which sits on 274 acres at the east end of the National Mall. The Capitol Building is the official meeting location of the U.S. Congress. First-time visitors to the city should take the time to tour this national icon and view our elected officials hard at work.

The Capitol Building comprises a central dome towering above a rotunda, flanked by two wings. The building technically has two fronts, one on the east side and one on the west side. The north wing houses the U.S. Senate chamber and the south wing is for the U.S. House of Representatives chamber. Public galleries sit above each so visitors can watch the proceedings. Each of the many rooms in the Capitol are designated with either an "S" for those on the Senate side of the rotunda or "H" for those on the House side.

George Washington laid the cornerstone of the Capitol in 1793. The Senate wing was

the U.S. Capitol

which opened in 2008. This entry had been planned for many years but wasn't constructed until after two U.S. Capitol Police officers were killed by a visitor in 1998. The center is a security checkpoint, and visitors should be prepared to wait in line for screening before entering. The center also offers educational exhibits, restrooms, and a food court. The visitors center is open Monday-Saturday 8:30am-4:30pm but the Capitol Building itself can only be visited on an official tour. Tours are free but must be arranged in advance through the Advance Reservation System (www.visitthecapitol.gov) or through the office of a senator or representative. Tours are given Monday-Saturday 8:50am-10:50am and last one hour. Those wishing to watch the House or Senate in session must obtain a pass from their senator or representative's office. International visitors can obtain a ticket at the Capitol with valid photo identification. Plan to arrive 45 minutes before a scheduled tour to allow enough time to get through security.

completed in 1800 (Congress held its first session there in 1800) and the House wing was completed in 1811. Since its original construction, the building has undergone many expansions, renovations, and even a rebuilding after it was partially burned by the British during the War of 1812. The Capitol, in its early days, was used for other purposes in addition to government functions. In fact, church services were held there on Sundays until after the Civil War.

Underground tunnels and a private subway connect the Capitol Building with the Congressional office buildings. The Senate office buildings are located to the north on Constitution Avenue, and the House office buildings are located to the south on Independence Avenue. The public may only ride the subway when escorted by a staff member with appropriate identification.

Visitors to the Capitol enter through the three-level underground **U.S. Capitol Visitor Center** (beneath the east front plaza at 1st St. and E. Capitol St., 202/226-8000),

Summerhouse

The **Summerhouse** (on the west front lawn of the U.S. Capitol Building on the Senate side, www.aoc.gov, 24 hours, free), is a little oasis hidden in a group of trees. This small, decorative, hexagonal brick building offers a cool place for visitors to rest. It was constructed around 1880 and is anchored by a fountain that once offered springwater. There are nice benches here with seating for 22 that are covered by a tile roof.

U.S. Supreme Court

Behind the U.S. Capitol Building on 1st Street (between E. Capitol St. and Maryland Ave.) is the **Supreme Court of the United States** (1 First St. NE, 202/479-3000, www.supremecourt.gov, Mon.-Fri. 9am-4:30pm, free). The Supreme Court is the highest court in the nation, and the current building was completed in 1935 (court was previously held in the Capitol Building). The main entrance faces the Capitol Building and welcomes visitors with a 252-foot-wide oval plaza. Fountains,

the U.S. Supreme Court

benches, and flagpoles are on either side of the plaza. Marble columns support the pediment on the Corinthian-style building.

The court building is open to the public during the week, and visitors are encouraged to listen to a variety of courtroom lectures when the Supreme Court is not sitting. Lectures are scheduled every hour on the half hour and begin at 9:30am. The final lecture of the day starts at 3:30pm. A calendar is online with the daily lecture schedule. Visitors can also take in exhibits focused on the work of the Supreme Court, the justices' lives, and the architecture of the Supreme Court building. When the court is sitting, visitors are welcome to see our justice system in action by attending oral arguments. Seating is limited and granted on a first-come, first-served basis and is available for an entire argument or for a three-minute viewing. Prior to the beginning of a session, two lines form in front of the courthouse outside on the plaza. One line is for those wishing to sit in on the entire argument, and the other is for those wishing to witness a three-minute sample.

All visitors are required to pass through a security screening that includes X-raying personal items and walking through metal detectors.

Library of Congress

It's hard to imagine that the original collection of books held by the **Library of Congress** (www.loc.gov) went up in flames during the War of 1812 when the British set fire to the Capitol Building where the collection was kept. Fortunately, Thomas Jefferson had a rather substantial collection of personal books with more than 6,500 volumes that he agreed to sell to Congress to rebuild the collection.

Today the Library of Congress, which is a research library and the country's oldest federal cultural institution, is contained in three government buildings on Capitol Hill and one building in Virginia. It is also the largest library in the world. Its collections include upward of 32 million cataloged books, 61 million manuscripts, more than one million U.S. government publications, one million newspapers from all over the world, and more than 120,000 comic books. Its publications are printed in 470 languages.

The main library building is the beautiful **Thomas Jefferson Building** (1st St. SE between Independence Ave. and E. Capitol St., 202/707-9779). This is the oldest building in the complex, having opened in 1897. This building is a feast for the eyes with its

DC's Skyline: Onward and Upward?

Unlike most large cities in the country, Washington DC has a low skyline. When the first skyscrapers were going up in the late 1800s elsewhere in the world, DC residents became concerned that if tall buildings were constructed in the city, Washington would lose its European feel. So in 1899, Congress passed the Heights of Buildings Act, which limited the vertical reach of buildings in the nation's capital to no more than 130 feet. This act was later amended (in 1910) to allow buildings to be 20 feet higher than the width of the adjacent street. The only exception is on Pennsylvania Avenue between 1st and 15th Streets. More than 100 years later, the act is now being reviewed for possible revision because the inability to expand the skyline upward has limited the city's tax base and potential for growth.

WASHINGTON DC
SIGHTS

murals, mosaics, sculptures, and impressive main reading room containing 236 desks sitting under a 160-foot dome. A visitors center is located at the west front entrance (Mon.-Sat. 8:30am-4:30pm). Free one-hour guided tours are available, during which visitors can learn about the building's architecture and symbolic art. Tours are given Monday-Friday 10:30am-3:30pm and Saturday 10:30am-2:30pm.

The other two library buildings on Capitol Hill are the nearby **John Adams Building** (2nd St. SE between Independence Ave. and E. Capitol St.) and the **James Madison Memorial Building** (between 1st and 2nd Sts. on Independence Ave. SE). The latter is home to the **Mary Pickford Theater,** which is the "motion picture and television reading room" of the library.

The library primarily exists as a research tool for answering inquiries from members of Congress through the Congressional Research Service. The library is open to the public, but only library employees, members of Congress, and other top-level government officials can actually check books out.

U.S. Botanic Garden

A lovely contrast to memorials, office buildings, and monuments, the **U.S. Botanic Garden** (100 Maryland Ave. SW, 202/225-8333, www.usbg.gov, daily 10am-5pm, free) is the oldest continually operating garden of its type in the country. Just southwest of the Capitol, this national greenhouse opened in 1850 and has been in its current location since

1933. Major attractions at the garden include a rose garden, butterfly garden, the First Ladies' Water Garden, the Lawn Terrace, and an outdoor amphitheater. The garden houses nearly 10,000 living specimens; the oldest are more than 165 years old.

Smithsonian National Postal Museum

A lesser-known Smithsonian Institution museum is the **National Postal Museum** (2 Massachusetts Ave. NE, 202/633-5555, daily 10am-5:30pm, free). Located near Union Station, the museum contains exhibits of stamps and philatelic items, mail delivery vehicles, and historical artifacts from America's postal system.

DOWNTOWN
National Archives

Only in Washington DC can you see the original Declaration of Independence, the Constitution, and the Bill of Rights. These powerful documents live in the Rotunda for the Charters of Freedom at the **National Archives Building** (700 Pennsylvania Ave. NW, visitors entrance on Constitution Ave. between 7th and 9th Sts. NW, 866/272-6272, www.archives.gov, daily 10am-5:30pm, extended summer hours, free). They can be viewed by the public daily, but are then lowered into the vault for safekeeping after hours.

Also known as Archives I, the National Archives Building is the headquarters for the National Archives and Records

Downtown DC

© AVALON TRAVEL

Administration, an independent agency of the U.S. government that is responsible for preserving historical records. Countless additional documents are on permanent exhibit in the public vaults, including treaties, photographs, telegrams, maps, and films. Interactive exhibits allow visitors to get close to some of the most interesting documents.

The Newseum

The Newseum (555 Pennsylvania Ave. NW, 202/292-6100, www.newseum.org, daily 9am-5pm, $22.95 plus tax) is a 250,000-square-foot museum dedicated to 500 years of news history. It stands at Pennsylvania Avenue and 6th Street NW, adjacent to the Smithsonian museums. The exterior is easy to identify: It features a wall of glass and a 74-foot-tall marble engraving of the First Amendment.

The Newseum has seven levels and includes 15 galleries, theaters, visitor services, and retail space. Topics such as news history, photojournalism, news coverage related to historical events, and electronic news are explored in the galleries. The largest features a collection of more than 30,000 historic newspapers. Some exhibits in the museum contain strong images involving topics such as death and hate and can therefore be upsetting to children.

Reynolds Center

The revitalized Penn Quarter area of downtown gets more and more hip each year as space is renovated and new attractions move in. A prime example is the Smithsonian's **Reynolds Center** (8th and F Sts. NW, 202/633-1000, www.americanart.si.edu, daily 11:30am-7pm, free) that covers an entire block in the Chinatown neighborhood in what was one of the first patent office buildings. The Reynolds Center is officially named the **Donald W. Reynolds Center for American Art and Portraiture,** and it consists of two recently renovated Smithsonian museums, the **Smithsonian American Art Museum** and the **National Portrait Gallery.** The massive Greek Revival building dates back to 1836 and originally took 31 years to construct. The Smithsonian American Art Museum features a wide variety of American art and houses works by significant artists such Georgia O'Keeffe, Albert Bierstadt, and Nam June Paik. The National Portrait Gallery contains images of many famous Americans. The museums are above the Gallery Place-Chinatown Metrorail station on the Red, Yellow, and Green Lines.

International Spy Museum

Enter the world of espionage at the only public museum in the country dedicated to professional spies. The **International Spy Museum** (800 F St. NW, 202/393-7798, www.spymuseum.org, hours vary by season but open most days 10am-6pm, $21.95) is another great museum in Penn Quarter. Privately owned, this interesting museum houses the largest collection of international artifacts geared toward the secret world of spies. Exhibits focus on some of the most secretive missions across the globe and strive to educate the public about their role in historic events.

The museum features artifacts created specifically for intelligence services (think lipstick pistols, disguises, and Enigma cipher machines) and brings them to life in state-of-the-art exhibits, interactive computer programs, audiovisual programs, and hands-on learning. Their ever-evolving collections keep this an exciting place to visit and include everything from an Exquisitely Evil exhibit on James Bond villains to an Argo Exposed exhibit with details about the real man behind the true story of *Argo*. Plan on spending a minimum of two hours here.

National Building Museum

If architecture, building, and design intrigue you, the **National Building Museum** (401 F St. NW, 202/272-2448, www.nbm.org, Mon.-Sat. 10am-5pm, Sun. 11am-5pm, $10) is a must see. As the country's leading cultural institution committed to interpreting the impact and history of the "built environment," this family-friendly museum

the Newseum

offers exhibits, public programs, and festivals. The museum itself is a spectacular building with an impressive Great Hall that contains 75-foot Corinthian columns, and a 1,200-foot terra-cotta frieze. Exhibits include *House & Home*, which provides a tour of familiar and surprising homes and *Play Work Build,* an exploration exhibit that allows children and adults to fill an exhibition wall with virtual blocks and then knock them down.

Ford's Theatre National Historic Site and Center for Education and Leadership

Still a thriving theatrical venue, the famous **Ford's Theatre** (511 10th St. NW, 202/347-4833, www.fordstheatre.org, daily 9am-4pm, $3) is the site where President Lincoln was assassinated on April 14, 1865. It also houses a museum focusing on Abraham Lincoln's presidency, assassination, and legacy as well as an education center. Artifacts featured in the museum include the contents of Lincoln's pockets on the day he died, the single-shot .44-caliber derringer that John Wilkes Booth used to kill Lincoln, and two life masks. The education center has a 34-foot tower full of books on Lincoln, accessible by a winding staircase. The books in the tower are made from aluminum and represent 205 real titles on Lincoln. This unusual work of art symbolizes that the last word about Lincoln will never be written.

There are two suggested itineraries for visiting the theater. If you have limited time, the Museum and Ranger Talk, lasting approximately one hour and 15 minutes, includes a self-guided tour of the museum and a 30-minute presentation, given by a National Park Service ranger, inside the theater itself. The presentation covers key facts regarding President Lincoln's assassination. If you have two hours and 15 minutes to devote to the theater, you can take in the Full Ford's Theatre Experience. This includes a theatrical audio tour of the theater (for an additional $5), a self-guided museum tour, a 30-minute presentation by a ranger, a self-guided tour of the Petersen House across the street (15 minutes),

I Got You Babe

Just southwest of Dupont Circle on New Hampshire Avenue is a small, triangular wedge of land that memorializes pop star and politician **Sonny Bono.** Officially called Sonny Bono Park, the patch of grass has benches and a plaque (that draws a striking resemblance to a manhole cover) honoring the late statesman who died in a ski accident in 1998.

where Lincoln was tended to after the shooting and died, and exploration of the **Center for Education and Leadership** (514 10th St., adjacent to the Petersen House, allow 45 minutes), where exhibits explain the aftermath of the assassination including the hunt for John Wilkes Booth and the funeral route. Ford's Theatre is located in the Penn Quarter area.

DUPONT CIRCLE
Dupont Circle Park

Maintained by the National Park Service, the **Dupont Circle Park** has been the location of many political rallies, and it is also a gathering place for chess players to challenge one another on permanent stone chessboards (one of the top players there is a formerly homeless man who became a renowned national chess player). The central double-tiered white marble fountain, installed in 1920, offers seating; it replaced a memorial statue of Samuel Francis Du Pont, a rear admiral during the Civil War that was placed there in 1884. The fountain was designed by the cocreators of the Lincoln Memorial and represents the sea, stars, and wind.

The Phillips Collection

The Dupont Circle neighborhood is home to the original late 19th-century Renoir painting *Luncheon of the Boating Party*. It lives at **The Phillips Collection** (1600 21st St. NW, 202/387-2151, www.phillipscollection.org, Tues.-Sat. 10am-5pm, Sun. 12pm-7pm, $12), an intimate impressionist and modern art

Dupont Circle

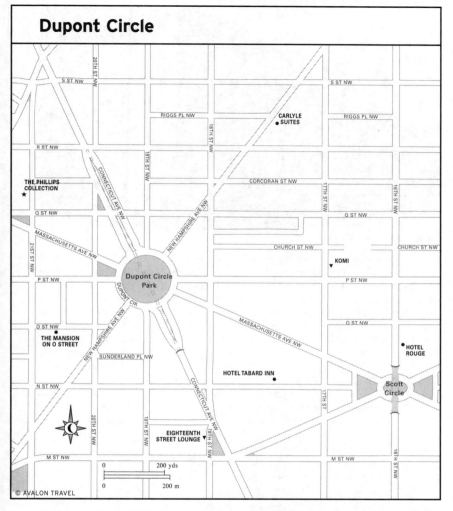

© AVALON TRAVEL

museum founded in 1921 by Duncan Phillips. The museum includes the founder's former home and extensive new galleries. Other featured works (there are more than 3,000) include pieces by Vincent Van Gogh, Claude Monet, Pablo Picasso, Georgia O'Keeffe, and Winslow Homer.

GEORGETOWN
Dumbarton Oaks
The **Dumbarton Oaks Research Library**

and Collection (1703 32nd St. NW, 202/339-6401, www.doaks.org, museum Tues.-Sun. 11:30am-5:30pm, free, gardens Tues.-Sun. Nov. 1-Mar. 14 2pm-5pm, free, Mar. 15-Oct. 31 2pm-6pm, $10) is a gorgeous, historic, and romantic estate museum and garden. It was a private estate for many years before being donated to Harvard University in 1940. The estate was the site of a series of important diplomatic meetings in 1944 that laid the foundation for the development of the United

Dupont Circle neighborhood

Nations. Today the museum offers exhibitions of Byzantine and pre-Columbian art (including more than 12,000 Byzantine coins); Asian, European, and American art; and European furnishings. The 10-acre park boasts a fine example of a European-style formal garden, with more than 1,000 rosebushes, an herb garden, and stone fountains.

Georgetown University

Georgetown is anchored by the 104-acre campus of **Georgetown University** (37th and O Sts. NW, 202/687-0100, www.georgetown. edu). Noted for its law school in particular, this private research university offers eight graduate and undergraduate schools with a total enrollment of around 15,000 students. Georgetown was established in 1789 and is the oldest Catholic and Jesuit university in the country. Notable alumni include President Bill Clinton and the late U.S. Supreme Court justice Antonin Scalia.

Old Stone House

The oldest standing building in DC, and also the city's last pre-Revolutionary colonial building still on its original foundation, was built in 1765 and is simply called the **Old Stone House** (3051 M St. NW, 202/426-6851, www.nps.gov/olst, Wed.-Sun. noon-5pm,

free). This excellent example of vernacular architecture was constructed in three phases and served many purposes throughout the years including being a hat shop, tailor, locksmith, and even a used car dealership. The house was renovated in the 1950s and turned into a museum by the National Park Service. Today, visitors can learn the history of the house from park rangers and view the home's kitchen, bedrooms, and parlor, all authentically furnished to reflect the daily lives of average Americans in the 18th century. The Old Stone House is said to be haunted by countless spirits.

Exorcist Stairs

One of the most notable movie scenes filmed in Georgetown was the climactic scene in *The Exorcist,* where the priest hurls himself out the window of a house and down a steep staircase to his death to rid himself of the devil. The famed staircase is still part of the Georgetown landscape and has 75 steps that connect Prospect Street with M Street. There are three landings on the staircase and the entire length of the stairs is equal to the height of a five-story building. For filming purposes, a fake front was constructed on the house located at the top of the steps to make it appear that the bedroom in the movie overlooked the

Georgetown

staircase. In real life, the home is set back a healthy distance from the top of the stairs. It is not uncommon to see Georgetown students running the stairs. Hoya athletes are known to run it 10 or more times. The steps are located at the end of 36th Street.

ADAMS MORGAN
Meridian Hill Park

Meridian Hill Park (15th, 16th, W, and Euclid Sts. NW, free) is a 12-acre urban park maintained by the National Park Service. It is near Adams Morgan in the Columbia Heights neighborhood. The park was built in the early 1900s and sits on a hillside. It is well landscaped and includes dramatic staircases, benches, and concrete walkways. The focal point of the park is a 13-basin cascading waterfall fountain in a formal garden. There are also a number of statues in the park. This is a popular place to steal some relaxation in the summer, and many people take advantage of this secret little garden in the city. Drummers form circles on Sunday afternoons in the summertime, but people come to spread a blanket and play catch nearly all year.

UPPER NORTHWEST
★ National Cathedral

Many visitors are filled with awe when they see the beautiful gothic **National Cathedral** (3101 Wisconsin Ave. NW, 202/537-6200, www.nationalcathedral.org, Mon.-Fri. 10am-5:30pm, Sat. 10am-4:30pm, Sun. 1pm-4pm,

Adams Morgan and Upper Northwest

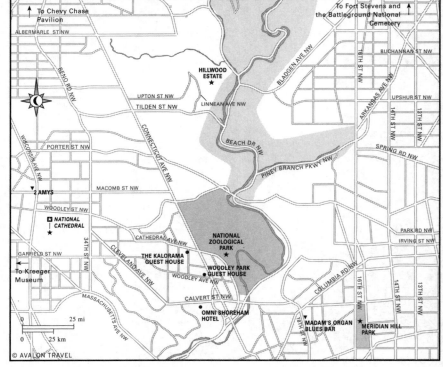

$11). This imposing edifice, which is the sixth-largest cathedral in the world, is hard to miss. It took 83 years (1907 to 1990) to carve the 150,000 tons of stone, and this impressive building has a few tricks up its sleeve. A tour is a must (they offer 16 different ones), since the great docents will provide you access to the towers and crypt that are off limits should you try to go there on your own. Although the regular tours are impressive, the behind-the-scenes tour ($26) is the best. You'll walk through hidden hallways, get a close look at the stunning stained glass windows, and learn the cathedral's secrets (like how Darth Vader lives high on the northwest tower in the form of a grotesque that was sculpted after a public competition was held to suggest designs for grotesques and gargoyles). You'll also get a grand view from the cathedral's roof. Be ready for stair climbing, heights, and close quarters. Participants must be at least 11 years old. Reservations can be made online.

Organ demonstrations are given on most Mondays and Wednesdays at 12:30pm. They are impressive and loud. Regular Episcopal worship services are held at the cathedral; a schedule is posted on the website. A café (Mon.-Fri. 7am-6pm, Sat.-Sun. 8am-6pm) is located in the Old Baptistry building next to the cathedral where the public can purchase light fare such as sandwiches, coffee, and pastries. Parking is available under the cathedral.

Rock Creek Park

It's hard to believe that with all DC has to offer in such a small area, there's room for a

the National Cathedral

1,754-acre park. **Rock Creek Park** (202/895-6070, www.nps.gov/rocr, open during daylight hours, free) is a prime recreation area in the city that offers running, walking, equestrian, and cycling trails, a golf course, a professional tennis stadium, a nature center and planetarium, an outdoor concert venue, playground facilities, wildlife, and cultural exhibits. The park is administered by the National Park Service.

Visitors can enjoy a real sense of outdoors in this urban park, which consists of woods, fields, and creeks and is home to wildflowers and wildlife such as coyotes, beavers, and fox. The park borders Upper Northwest DC to the east and has long stretches of roads (including Rock Creek Parkway and Beach Drive) that are closed to cars on weekends. Fifteen miles of hiking trails, a bike path that runs the entire length of the park and connects the Lincoln Memorial to the Maryland border, and horseback riding from **Rock Creek Park Horse Center** (5100 Glover Rd., 202/362-0117, www.rockcreekhorsecenter.com, Mon.-Fri. 10am-6pm, Sat.-Sun. 9am-5pm, lessons $50-90 per hour, one-hour trail rides $40) are just some of the activities available to visitors. The park's **Nature Center** (5200 Glover Rd., 202/895-6070, Wed.-Sun. 9am-5pm) is a good place to start your exploration. Another attraction is the **Peirce Mill** (2401 Tilden St.

NW at Beach Dr., 202/895-6070, Apr.-Oct. Wed.-Sun. 10am-4pm, Nov.-Mar. Sat.-Sun. 12pm-4pm). It is the only existing water-powered gristmill in DC.

The park is relatively safe for a city park, but it is still advisable to enjoy it with a friend. Leashed dogs are allowed in the park. It is good to keep in mind that on weekdays Rock Creek Parkway is one-way going south between 6:45am and 9:30am and one-way going north 3:45pm-6:30pm.

National Zoological Park

The Smithsonian's **National Zoological Park** (3001 Connecticut Ave., 202/633-2614, www.nationalzoo.si.edu, daily Oct. 1-Mar. 14, grounds 8am-5pm, visitor center and exhibit buildings 9am-4pm, Mar. 15-Sept. 30 grounds 8am-7pm, visitor center and exhibit buildings 9am-6pm, free), commonly called the National Zoo, is one of the oldest zoos in the country. The 163-acre park is near the Woodley Park Metrorail station on the edge of Rock Creek Park. The zoo, founded in 1889, is constantly undergoing updates and renovations. Hundreds of animals are tucked into habitats along hillsides, in the woods, and in specially built temperature-controlled animal houses. Since entrance to the park is free, many local residents use the several miles of nicely paved pathways on their regular walking or running routes.

Well-known residents include giant pandas from China, great apes, elephants, Komodo dragons, and much more. Many of the species at the zoo are endangered. Unique exhibits include the Elephant Walk, where Asian elephants can take daily treks for exercise, and a skywalk for orangutans where a series of high cables and towers allow them to move between two buildings and over spectators below. Another favorite is the newly completed American Trail, which features sea lions, wolves, eagles, and other animals native to North America. The zoo also features a Think Tank, where visitors can learn how animals think through a series of interactive displays that are available to the zoo's orangutans at their leisure. The best time to visit the zoo is on weekday mornings when there are fewer crowds and the animals are more active. Although it is free to enter the zoo, there is a parking fee.

Hillwood Estate, Museum & Gardens

Those in the know are fans of the wonderful **Hillwood Estate, Museum & Gardens** (4155 Linnean Ave. NW, 202/686-5807, www.hillwoodmuseum.org, Tues.-Sun. 10am-5pm, $18), the former home of prominent businesswoman, philanthropist, and heiress to the Post Cereal fortune, Marjorie Merriweather Post. This stately and luxurious home with a Georgian-style facade was purchased by Post in 1955 and used for entertaining and to house her abundant collections of French and Russian art, including an extraordinary collection of Fabergé eggs. The artwork is rivaled by the exquisite French and Japanese-style gardens where visitors can relax after taking a tour. One-hour guided tours (11:30am and 1:30pm) and self-guided tours are available with the price of admission. A café and gift shop are on-site.

Kreeger Museum

The **Kreeger Museum** (2401 Foxhall Rd.

NW, 202/338-3552, www.kreegermuseum.org, Fri. and Sat. 10am-4pm, Tues. and Thurs. tours by reservation, $10, sculpture garden Tues.-Sat. 10am-4pm, free) is a private museum that often passes under the radar of tourists due to its Foxhall neighborhood location and small size. This little gem of an attraction features 19th- and 20th-century sculptures and paintings by many world-renowned artists such as Monet, Picasso, Rodin, and Van Gogh. It also offers works by local artists and traditional African art. The building is the former home of David and Carmen Kreeger and sits on more than five acres of sculpture gardens and woods.

Battleground National Cemetery

One of the smallest national cemeteries in the nation is the **Battleground National Cemetery** (6600 block of Georgia Ave., 202/895-6000, www.nps.gov, daily dawn-dusk, free). It is the burial ground for 41 Union soldiers who died in the 1864 Battle of Fort Stevens, the sole Civil War battle to take place in DC. The engagement marked the end of a Confederate effort to act offensively against the national capital. The battle is the only one in Civil War history during which the U.S. president (Abraham Lincoln) came under direct fire. Lincoln rode out to observe the fight and was fired on briefly by sharpshooters (he was then ordered to take cover). After the battle, a one-acre plot of farmland was seized and used to bury the dead. That night, Lincoln came to the site and dedicated it as a national cemetery. Visitors can see grave markers, four monuments to the units that fought in the battle, and a marble rostrum that has eight Doric columns. The rostrum is the site of the annual Memorial Day services at the cemetery. The National Park Service manages the cemetery.

Nearby **Fort Stevens** (1339 Fort Stevens Dr., 202/290-1048, www.nps.gov, daily dawn-dusk, free), the actual site of the battle, is partially restored and is also maintained by the National Park Service. It was part of a series of fortifications constructed around Washington

DC during the Civil War. Visitors can see much of the fort still intact, including the cannons (now facing urban streets). You can even stand in the spot where then future Supreme Court justice Oliver Wendell Holmes is said to have shouted at President Lincoln, "Get down, you fool!" when he was shot at.

NORTHEAST DC
National Arboretum

Northeast of Capitol Hill (2.2 miles from the Capitol Building) is a little-recognized attraction that first opened in 1927: the **National Arboretum** (3501 New York Ave. NE, 202/245-2726, www.usna.usda.gov, daily 8am-5pm, free). This lovely 446-acre campus has more than nine miles of roads that connect many gardens and plant collections where there is always something in bloom. Seventy-six staff members and more than 140 volunteers oversee the arboretum, which was created to "serve the public need for scientific research, education, and gardens that conserve and showcase plants to enhance the environment." Parking areas are available near many of the major collections and bike racks are also on hand. The original 22 columns from the east side of the Capitol Building found a home here when the Capitol was enlarged in the 1950s; they now sit on display in a field. The **National Bonsai & Penjing Museum** (daily 10am-4pm, free) is also located on the arboretum grounds, as is a gift shop. Leashed pets are welcome, and there are public restrooms in the administrative building.

TOURS

A great way to see the city is to take an organized tour. There are a wide variety available to choose from including trolley tours, boat tours, and walking tours.

Trolley, Bus, and Boat Tours

One of the most popular motorized tours in the city is given by **Old Town Trolley** (202/832-9800, www.trolleytours.com, daily 9am-5pm, $39). This lively narrated tour covers more than 100 points of interest and offers a "hop on-hop off" format where guests can get off at 20 stops and pick up another trolley (which stops at each location every 30 minutes) at their leisure. Sights include the Lincoln Memorial, Georgetown, the White House, Smithsonian Institution museums, and many more. No reservations are required, and visitors can board and re-board all day. Tickets can be purchased online or at the sales desk in **Union Station** (50 Massachusetts Ave. NE, stop #4) and at the **Washington Welcome Center** (1005 E St. NW, stop #1).

Old Town Trolley also offers a 2.5-hour **Monuments by Moonlight** ($39) tour that allows visitors to see the illuminated monuments and memorials. Stops include the FDR Memorial, Iwo Jima Memorial (in Arlington, Virginia), the Lincoln Memorial, and Vietnam Veterans Memorial. This narrated tour includes some fun ghost stories as well. The tour leaves nightly from Union Station.

Old Town Trolley tours cover more than 100 points of interest.

WASHINGTON DC SIGHTS

A third tour through Old Town Trolley that is also popular is their **DC Ducks Tour** (daily 10am-4pm, $39). Guests explore the city on both land and water in a fully restored 1942 "Duck," a unique vehicle that is part bus, part boat. Ninety-minute trips start at Union Station (50 Massachusetts Ave. NE), drive to the National Mall, and end with a cruise along the Potomac River. The tours are narrated by "wise-quacking" captains who offer a wealth of historical facts and corny jokes.

Another "hop on-hop off" tour is the **Open Top Big Bus Tour** (877/332-8689, www.big-bustours.com, daily 9am-4pm, 24 hours $36, 48 hours $44). Guests can take in four routes around the city from a double-decker bus with an open-air top deck. Tickets are available for 24 and 48 hours. Tickets can be purchased online and on any of their buses.

For a view from the water, take an hour-long **DC Cruise** (301/765-0750, www.dc-cruises.com, $22-25) along the Potomac River. Riders will see the Kennedy Center and many monuments along the way. Cruises leave from Washington Harbor at the foot of 31st Street.

Walking Tours

Free guided walking tours of DC's monuments are available through **DC By Foot** (202/370-1830, www.freetoursbyfoot.com/dc, free but tips appreciated). These unique tours feature animated, energetic tour guides who work purely on tips. Because of this, they do their best to entertain you while providing unique stories about Washington's most famous residents. Private tours are also available.

Ghost tours are a good way to get in touch with the spirits of the city. Several tour operators offer walking tours around some of the most haunted sites in the city. **Washington Walks** (1799 New York Ave. NW, 202/484-1565, www.washingtonwalks.com, $20) offers **Most Haunted Houses** tours (Apr.-Oct. Thurs.-Sat. at 7:30pm). Two-hour walking tours begin at the corner of New York Avenue and 18th Street NW. No reservations are necessary.

Entertainment and Events

THEATER

The premier theater in Washington DC is the **John F. Kennedy Center for the Performing Arts** (2700 F St. NW, 202/467-4600, www.kennedy-center.org). This incredible venue is a landmark on the banks of the Potomac River and first opened in 1971. It hosts more annual performances than any other facility in the country, with approximately 2,000 theater, dance, musical, and multimedia performances each year. There are three primary theaters within the center. The **Concert Hall** seats approximately 2,400 guests and is the largest performance space in the center. It features seven Hadeland crystal chandeliers (courtesy of Norway) and a 4,144-pipe organ (a gift from the Filene Foundation of Boston). The Concert Hall is also home to the **National Symphony Orchestra** (202/467-4600, www.kennedy-center.org). The **Opera House,** with its unique red and gold silk curtain (a gift from Japan), seats approximately 2,300 guests and features a Lobmeyr crystal chandelier (courtesy of Austria). It is the primary venue for opera, ballet, and large-scale musical performances and home to the **Washington National Opera** (202/467-4600, www.kennedy-center.org), the **Suzanne Farrell Ballet** (202/467-4600, www.kennedy-center.org), and the yearly **Kennedy Center Honors.** The **Eisenhower Theater** seats approximately 1,163 guests and hosts smaller-scale operas, plays, and musicals. Public parking is available under the center.

The historic **National Theatre** (1321 Pennsylvania Ave. NW, 202/628-6161, www.nationaltheatre.org) playhouse is the oldest

the National Theatre

Nearby, **Ford's Theatre** (511 10th St. NW, 202/347-4833, www.fordstheatre.org) is most famous as the location of the assassination of President Lincoln in 1865. Following his death, the theater closed. After a long stint as a warehouse and an office building, it finally reopened more than 100 years later in 1968 and again began to host performances. Today it is an active venue with a full schedule of plays and musicals.

A well-known regional theater company in DC is the **Shakespeare Theatre Company** (202/547-1122, www.shakespearetheatre.org). This highly regarded company presents primarily Shakespearian productions but also offers works by other classic playwrights. The company manages the **Harman Center for the Arts,** which consists of two venues in Penn Quarter, the **Landsburgh Theatre** (450 7th St. NW) and **Sidney Harman Hall** (610 F St. NW).

For more experimental, cutting-edge performances, catch a production by the **Woolly Mammoth Theatre Company** (641 D St. NW, 202/393-3939, www.woollymammoth. net). They develop and produce new plays and pride themselves on being "Washington's most daring theatre company."

In Southwest DC, **Arena Stage at the Mead Center for American Theater** (1101 6th St. SW, 202/488-3300, www.arenastage. org) takes the title of being the largest not-for-profit theater in the city. It features a broad range of performances including the classics and new play premiers as well as educational programs.

A unique performance venue is the **Carter Barron Amphitheatre** (4850 Colorado Ave. NW, 202/426-0486, www.nps.gov/rocr) in Rock Creek Park. The beautiful 4,200-seat outdoor amphitheater is operated by the National Park Service and offers a range of performances including concerts, theater, and dance. Many are provided at no charge.

The historic **Uptown Theatre** (3426 Connecticut Ave. NW, 202/966-8805, www. amctheatres.com) is a single-screen movie theater in the Cleveland Park neighborhood

theater venue in DC. It is three blocks from the White House and has entertained many presidents since its founding in 1835. In fact, Abraham Lincoln's son Tad was attending a production of *Aladdin and the Wonderful Lamp* at the National Theatre at the time his father was assassinated in Ford's Theatre. Today the theater is known for hosting mostly Broadway musicals.

Originally built as a movie palace in 1924, the **Warner Theatre** (513 13th St. NW, 202/783-4000, www.warnertheatredc.com) was then called the Earle Theatre and hosted live vaudeville and silent movies. During the 1940s the theater showed movies exclusively and was renamed for its owner, Harry Warner of Warner Brothers fame. The theater suffered in the 1970s, but was revived shortly after as a concert venue. After major renovations between 1989 and 1992, the theater reopened with theatrical, dance, and musical productions and has since hosted great performers such as Frank Sinatra. It is a landmark in the Penn Quarter neighborhood.

run by AMC Loews. The theater first opened in 1936 and has been the site for many Hollywood movie premieres. The curved, 70-foot-long and 40-foot-high screen is considered to be the best in the DC area, and the theater can seat 850 people.

ARENAS AND HALLS

There are several large performance arenas in the city. The **Verizon Center** (601 F St. NW, 202/628-3200, www.verizoncenter.com), which anchors the Penn Quarter neighborhood, is home to several professional sports teams (Washington Capitals, Washington Wizards, and Washington Mystics), but also hosts numerous concerts and other large-scale performances. The **Robert F. Kennedy Memorial Stadium (RFK)** (2400 E. Capitol St. SE, 202/587-5000, www.dcunited.com) is the former home of the Washington Redskins and now hosts rock concerts, conventions, and other events. It is also the home field for the D.C. United professional soccer team. RFK Stadium is just east of Capitol Hill.

The historic **DAR Constitution Hall** (1776 D St. NW, 202/628-1776, www.dar.org), near the White House, was built in 1929 by the Daughters of the American Revolution as a venue for their annual convention. This 3,200-seat hall, which formerly only hosted classical shows and opera, is now a concert venue for rock, pop, hip-hop, and soul.

The 2.3 million-square-foot **Walter E. Washington Convention Center** (801 Mt. Vernon Place NW, 202/249-3000, www.dcconvention.com) offers 703,000 square feet of event space, 77 meeting rooms, and the largest ballroom in the city. It hosts countless events throughout the year in the Downtown area.

MUSIC VENUES

The **U Street Corridor** can be called the center of the music scene in Washington DC. Once the haunt of legends such as Duke Ellington, the area carries on his legacy through venues such as **Bohemian Caverns** (2001 11th St. NW, 202/299-0800, www.bohemiancaverns.com), which is known as DC's premier jazz club and one of the oldest jazz clubs in the nation, having opened in 1926. It is at the same address today as it was back then, but was originally in the basement under a pharmacy (it is still downstairs but there's a traditional club upstairs). Although the club has not operated continuously over its long history, it has seen many notable performers including Miles Davis and Bill Evans. Today the club anchors Washington's jazz community. It hosts many headline national performers and local performers, and it has its own jazz orchestra. It is also an integral part of the city's annual jazz festival.

Twins Jazz (1344 U St. NW, top floor, 202/234-0072, www.twinsjazz.com) is another good choice for live jazz, which is offered 5-6 nights a week. This unassuming club with red interior walls looks like someone's home on the outside. It also features Ethiopian, Caribbean, and American food.

For a broader range of music options, the popular **9:30 Club** (815 V St. NW, 202/265-0930, www.930.com) hosts everyone from Echo and the Bunnymen to Corey Smith. This unassuming-looking venue is on the corner of 9th and V Streets. Shows are general admission and standing room only. They have four full bars and a coffee bar, and also serve food.

The **Black Cat** (1811 14th St. NW, 202/667-4490, www.blackcatdc.com) hosts a variety of local, national, and international independent and alternative bands. They offer two stages and are a cash-only establishment.

Two small venues that highlight primarily local bands are the **Velvet Lounge** (915 U St. NW, 202/462-3213, www.velvetloungedc.com) and **DC9** (1940 9th St. NW, 202/483-5000, www.dcnine.com).

Other areas of the city entertain great musical artists as well. An intimate venue for hearing live jazz is **Blues Alley** (1073 Wisconsin Ave. NW, 202/337-4141, www.bluesalley.com) in Georgetown. This local landmark consistently delivers quality jazz and a fun atmosphere. They serve food, but the main attraction is the music.

U Street Corridor

W ST NW

12TH ST NW

11TH ST NW

10TH ST NW

9TH ST NW

NW FLORIDA AVE

V ST NW

▼ BUSBOYS
AND POETS

13TH ST NW

NW 14TH ST

9:30 CLUB

V ST NW

8TH ST NW

BEN'S CHILI
BOWL
▼

BOHEMIAN
CAVERNS
▼

VERMONT AVE NW

FLORIDA AVE NW

U ST NW

▼ TWINS JAZZ

0   200 yds

0   200 m

WALLACH PL NW

© AVALON TRAVEL

Two blocks from the White House, **The Hamilton** (600 14th St. NW, 202/787-1000, www.thehamiltondc.com) hosts visionary musical performers in an intimate setting.

NIGHTLIFE
Downtown

For the chance to rub elbows with celebrities, professional athletes, and young, hip Washingtonians, grab a drink at the downtown **P.O.V. Roof Terrace and Lounge** at the **W Washington D.C. Hotel** (515 15th

St. NW, 202/661-2400, www.starwoodhotels.com, Sun.-Thurs. 11am-midnight, Fri.-Sat. 11am-2am). This rooftop bar and terrace is one of the top hot spots in DC and has phenomenal views of the city through 12-foot-tall windows. They serve premium-brand liquor and a tapas menu. No sneakers or athletic wear are permitted; collared shirts are preferred. Expect a wait to get in on weekends.

Perfect martinis and a more relaxed atmosphere can be found across from the White House at the **Off the Record Bar** (800 16th

W Washington D.C. Hotel

Best Rooftop Bars

There may be no better way to soak up the vibe of the city than by grabbing a cool drink on a summer evening at a rooftop bar. Following are some of the most popular DC bars and lounges with a bird's-eye view:

- The **DNV Rooftop Bar** (1155 14th St. NW, 202/379-4366, www.zentanrestaurant.com) is in The Donovan hotel in Thomas Circle at the intersection of Massachusetts Avenue, Vermont Avenue, 14th Street, and M Street NW. This lively poolside lounge offers chaise lounges, a full-service bar, Asian food, panoramic views, and great martinis.

- Take in views of Embassy Row and the Dupont Circle neighborhood from the **Sky Bar** at the **Beacon Bar and Grill** (1615 Rhode Island Ave. NW, 202/872-1126, www.bbgwdc.com). They offer full bar service and light fare.

- A lively rooftop bar located in a Mexican restaurant in the U Street Corridor is **El Centro D.F.** (1819 14th St., 202/328-3131, www.richardsandoval.com). Their two-level rooftop has two bars and 200 types of tequila.

- Another U Street neighborhood favorite is **Marvin** (2007 14th St. NW, 202/797-7171, www.marvindc.com). Their rooftop beer garden offers more than 30 Belgian ales and blondes.

- The largest open-air seating area in Adams Morgan is at **Perry's Restaurant** (1811 Columbia Rd. NW, 202/234-6218, www.perrysadamsmorgan.com). They have good happy hour specials, views of the city, and a fun rooftop atmosphere.

- One of "the" places to go in DC is the **P.O.V. Roof Terrace and Lounge** at the **W Washington D.C. Hotel** (515 15th St. NW, 202/661-2400, www.povrooftop.com). This rooftop bar and terrace is one of the top hot spots in DC and has phenomenal views of the city through 12-foot-tall windows.

St. NW, 202/695-1761, www.hayadams.com, Sun.-Thurs. 11:30am-midnight, Fri.-Sat. 11:30am-12:30am) at the Hay-Adams Hotel.

Just a little west of Downtown and a little south of Dupont Circle on M Street is **Ozio Restaurant and Lounge** (1813 M St. NW, 202/822-6000, www.oziodc.com, Tues.-Thurs. 5pm-2am, Fri. 5pm-3am, Sat. 6pm-3am, Sun. 12pm-2am). This huge, multilevel club is somewhat upscale and often has a business crowd. They have great martinis, cigars, and a lively rooftop lounge.

Dupont Circle

One of the most exclusive nightlife spots in the city is the **Eighteenth Street Lounge** (1212 18th St. NW, 202/696-0210, www.eighteenthstreetlounge.com, Tues.-Thurs. 5:30pm-2am, Fri. 5:30pm-3am, Sat. 9:30pm-3am, Sun. 9pm-2am) in the former home of Teddy Roosevelt. This restored row house mansion is classy, and you must be dressed appropriately to enter. There are high ceilings, a dance floor, retro decor, and multiple rooms, each with its own theme and bar.

The **Bar Rouge** (1315 16th St. NW, 202/232-8000, www.rougehotel.com, daily 5pm-10:30pm) in the Hotel Rouge is a popular choice for happy hour and evening cocktails. This sleek, modern lounge has good happy hour specials on weekdays. They also serve food.

A lively Latin American scene can be found at **Café Citron** (1343 Connecticut Ave. NW, 202/530-8844, www.cafecitrondc.com, Mon.-Thurs. 4pm-2am, Fri.-Sat. 4pm-3am), a two-level lounge that features salsa and other international music. This place can get rowdy on weekends, and they are known for having outstanding mojitos.

Georgetown

A sophisticated place to grab a drink at pretty much any time is the **Degrees Bar and Lounge** (3100 S St. NW, 202/912-4100, www.ritzcarlton.com, Sun.-Thurs. 2:30pm-11:30pm, Fri.-Sat. 2:30pm-1am) in the Ritz-Carlton Georgetown. This relaxing lounge brings a bit of New York City to the nation's capital with its chic decor, dependable drinks, and great potential for people watching. They have a bar and a few small tables for groups.

A Georgetown favorite since 1962, **The Tombs** (1226 36th Street. NW, 202/337-6668, www.tombs.com, Mon.-Thurs. 11:30am-1:30am, Fri. 11:30am-2:30am, Sat. 11am-2:30am, Sun. 9:30am-1:30am) is a casual bar and local hangout for students at Georgetown University. This place served as the inspiration for the setting of *St. Elmo's Fire.* Owned by the Clyde's family of restaurants, it is located in the basement of upscale restaurant 1789. If you're in the mood for good burgers, beer, and a college crowd, or if you're just a fan of *St. Elmo's Fire,* this is the place for you.

If you're looking for live music and an inviting bar scene, check out **Gypsy Sally's** (3401 K St. NW, 202/333-7700, Vinyl Lounge, Tues. 6pm-12am, Wed.-Sat. 6pm-2am., Sun.-Mon. if there is a show in the Music Room; Music Room is open on show nights only). Not quite your typical nightlife spot, it's located in a renovated old building below the Whitehurst Freeway where K Street gives way to a recreation trail. Folk bands draw a casual, down-to-earth crowd that isn't afraid to have a few drinks and dance. When a show is going on, you must have tickets to visit the Music Room, but the Vinyl Lounge upstairs (with views of the Potomac River) is open for dinner and drinks.

A trendy, upscale bar with expert mixologists and a view of the C&O Canal, **Rye Bar** (1050 31st St. NW, 202/617-2400, www.capellahotels.com, daily 11am-2am) is located in the Capella Hotel. This is a quiet, tasteful spot to bring a date and enjoy serious (translation: expensive) drinks. They specialize in fine American rye whiskeys. Leather armchairs, marble tables, dark wood, and large windows accent a sophisticated yet modern ambience.

Adams Morgan

Adams Morgan is known as one of the city's top nightlife area. It has the largest concentration of bars, restaurants, and nightclubs of any neighborhood in the city. Be aware that on weekend nights the streets can be so packed with people that it is hard to move around.

One of the best-known bars is **Madam's Organ Blues Bar** (2461 18th St. NW, 202/667-5370, www.madamsorgan.com, Sun.-Thurs. 5pm-2am, Fri.-Sat. 5pm-3am), which offers a diverse crowd, nightly live music, and dancing. This is a dive-type bar with a slightly older crowd than the frequent college or just-out-of-college patrons that inhabit many of the establishments in Adams Morgan.

Club Heaven and Hell (2327 18th St., 202/667-4355, www.clubheavenandhelldc.com, Wed.-Sun 3pm-2am, closed Mon.-Tues.) has the largest dance floor in Adams Morgan. They have three floors—Heaven, Purgatory, and Hell—with DJs spinning top 40, hip-hop, and retro music.

Bossa Bistro and Lounge (2463 18th St. NW, 202/667-0088, www.bossaproject.com, Tues.-Thurs. 5:30pm-2am, Fri.-Sat. 5:30pm-3am, Sun. 5:30pm-2am, closed Monday) is a cozy neighborhood restaurant that serves Brazilian food and offers live music (such as jazz and international) four nights a week and DJs on other nights. In contrast to many options in Adams Morgan, this is an intimate place to relax in a low-key, dimly lit interior with food and atmosphere.

Habana Village (1834 Columbia Rd. NW, 202/462-6310, www.habanavillage.com, Sun. 5pm-9pm, Mon. 6pm-10pm, Wed. 5:30pm-11pm, Thurs. 5:30pm-2am, Fri.-Sat. 5:30pm-3pm, closed Tues.) is a Cuban restaurant and dance club offering live music and dance lessons.

Bourbon (2321 18th St. NW, 202/332-0800, www.bourbondc.com, Tues.-Fri. 5pm-11pm, Sat. 2pm-11pm, Sun. 4pm-9pm) serves bourbon—several hundred types to be exact. This comfy bar has a neighborhood feel but draws patrons from all over the city because of its unique specialty.

Upper Northwest

Although Upper Northwest is not the most happening nightlife spot in the city, it does offer some friendly, comfortable options for those not looking to see or be seen.

Atomic Billiards (3427 Connecticut Ave. NW, 202/363-7665, www.atomicbilliards.com, Sun.-Thurs. 4pm-2am, Fri.-Sat. 4pm-3am), in the Cleveland Park neighborhood, is a funky, futuristic-looking pool hall. They also have shuffleboard and darts. They serve good beer on tap but don't have a kitchen.

If a basement dive bar with pool, table tennis, shuffleboard, beer, and sandwiches is more your style, try **Breadsoda** (2233 Wisconsin Ave. NW 202/333-7445, www.breadsoda.com, Sun.-Thurs. noon-2am, Fri.-Sat. noon-3am). Tuesdays are tacos-and-table tennis night in this cozy 1970s-style subterranean bar.

For live blues Thursday-Saturday and live jazz on Sunday, grab a beer in the neighborhoody **Zoo Bar** (3000 Connecticut Ave. NW, 202/232-4225, www.zoobardc.com, Sun.-Thurs. 11am-2am, Fri.-Sat. 11am-3am). Across the street from the National Zoo, this is an authentic dive bar surrounded by a touristy neighborhood.

U Street Corridor

Made-to-order drinks are created at **The Gibson** (2009 14th St. NW, 202/232-2156, www.thegibsondc.com, daily from 6pm), just off U Street. This interesting establishment could be called a modern-day speakeasy. Call ahead and make a reservation at the bar or at one of their booths or tables, then ring the bell when you arrive at the nondescript tenement-style building. A professional mixologist will concoct something special for you, or you can order a drink off the small menu. Don't expect to eat (they don't serve food), and above all, don't stay longer than your allotted two hours; there's sure to be someone waiting to take your spot.

EVENTS

The nation's capital hosts countless events year-round. Whether it's a festival, athletic event, or holiday celebration, there is something going on nearly every day of the year.

Restaurant Week (www.ramw.org/restaurantweek, lunch $22, dinner $35) happens twice a year in January and August. Two hundred of the most popular restaurants in DC offer prix fixe lunch and dinner menus. The event is sponsored by the Restaurant Association of Metropolitan Washington. Reservations are recommended.

Chinese dragon dances, live music, and a parade are just some of the festivities during the 15-day annual **Chinese New Year Celebration** (H St. NW between 5th and 9th Sts.) in the Chinatown area of Downtown DC. Beginning with the new moon on the first day of the Chinese New Year and ending with the full moon, this late January or early February celebration brings the area's culture to life with a bang of fireworks. The Gallery Place-Chinatown Metrorail stop will put you in the right place for this free event.

The yearly **Washington Auto Show** (www.washingtonautoshow.com, $12) is a large event that brings more than 700 new vehicles from both domestic and overseas automakers to the Washington Convention Center. The show is held for 10 days at the end of January or beginning of February and draws hundreds of thousands of visitors.

The coming of the Easter Bunny brings the annual **White House Easter Egg Roll** (www.whitehouse.gov), a tradition that started back in 1878 when President Rutherford B. Hayes opened the White House grounds to local children for egg rolling on the Monday after Easter. Successive presidents have continued this long-standing event, which takes place on the South Lawn.

Washington's signature event is the annual **National Cherry Blossom Festival** (www.nationalcherryblossomfestival.org). This three-week event coincides (ideally) with the blooming of the hundreds of Japanese cherry trees that were given to the United States in 1912 by Japan. The trees are planted all around the Tidal Basin and, when blooming, are a spectacular sight to see. Unfortunately, this huge event means gridlock on the highways and congestion on the sidewalks, but it is a great time to photograph the city. There's a parade, a kite festival, concerts, a 10-mile footrace, and much more. The festival is held late March-mid-April.

Memorial Day is big in Washington DC as thousands descend on the city for a day of remembrance. Many family-friendly events are held throughout the city and the free **National Memorial Day Concert** (www.pbs.org) is held on the West Lawn of the U.S. Capitol. The concert features patriotic themes to honor Americans who have served our country during times of conflict. Other events include the **National Memorial Day Parade** (www.americanveteranscenter.org/avc-events/parade) and the **Rolling Thunder Motorcycle Rally** (www.rollingthunderrun.com).

June brings the annual **Capital Pride** (www.capitalpride.org) event celebrating the gay, lesbian, bisexual, and transgender communities. There are more than 50 educational and entertainment events including a street festival and parade.

The **DC Jazz Festival** (www.dcjazzfest.org) is also held in June and features more than 100 jazz performances throughout the city. Major jazz artists from around the globe participate in this 12-day celebration. Venues include clubs, museums, hotels, and restaurants.

The **Smithsonian Folklife Festival** (www.festival.si.edu) takes place annually during the last week in June and the first week in July. It is held outdoors on the National Mall. The festival is a living heritage exposition with music, crafts, and artistry. The festival is free to attend.

There's no better place to celebrate the Fourth of July than the National Mall. **America's Independence Day Celebrations** include a parade along Constitution Avenue (www.july4thparade.com), concerts, and a spectacular fireworks display over the Washington Monument.

The premier running event in DC is the annual **Marine Corps Marathon** (www.marinemarathon.com). Known as "The People's Marathon," this 26.2-mile race was first held in 1975 and now has 30,000 participants each October.

Another completely different type of race is the annual **High Heel Race** in Dupont Circle. Each Tuesday before Halloween at 9pm, dozens of drag queens sporting elaborate outfits sprint down 17th Street NW over the three blocks between R Street and Church Street. The event has been held for more than 25 years and draws thousands of spectators.

During the first week in December, the **National Christmas Tree Lighting** (www.thenationaltree.org) is a special event that takes place on the Ellipse. The president attends the lighting, which is surrounded by additional highlights such as military band concerts and performances by celebrities. A separate event is held annually for the lighting of the national menorah (www.afldc.org).

Shopping

Washington DC has great neighborhood shopping with unique stores and boutiques. Some of the stores are geared toward high-end consumers, but there are also many "finds" if you know where to look.

CAPITOL HILL

Traditional retail shopping can be found on Capitol Hill at **Union Station** (50 Massachusetts Ave. NE, 202/289-1908, www. unionstationdc.com), which has more than 65 stores including national retailers such as Ann Taylor, The Body Shop, Jos. A. Bank Clothiers, and Victoria's Secret. A handful of specialty boutiques are also represented, such as **Lost City Art** (202/289-6977), which offers Indonesian statues, masks, murals, jewelry, and household items; and **Appalachian Spring** (202/682-0505), which offers jewelry, handbags, pottery, and household items.

Eastern Market (225 7th St. SE, 202/698-5253, www.easternmarket-dc.org) is a prime destination in DC for fresh food and handmade arts and crafts. For more than 135 years, the market has been a community hub on Capitol Hill. It offers several shopping spaces: The **South Hall Market** (Tues.-Fri. 7am-7pm, Sat. 7am-6pm, Sun. 9am-5pm) is an indoor space featuring 13 merchants offering a large variety of food such as produce, baked goods, meat, and dairy products. The **Weekend Farmers' Line** is an open-air space that is open on weekends and offers fresh local produce and snacks. Those searching for local crafts and antiques can find them at the **Weekend Outdoor Market.** Vendors in this area carry ethno-specific handcrafts, vintage goods, and arts and crafts.

DOWNTOWN

The revitalized Penn Quarter area features more than just museums, the Verizon Center, and cool new restaurants. The neighborhood has plenty of shopping and features some of the best-known national retailers such as Pottery Barn and Urban Outfitters. A selection of trendy individual shops is also here, such as **Fahrney's Pens** (1317 F St. NW, 202/628-9525, www. fahrneyspens.com), a pen store with a long DC tradition, and **Pua Naturally** (701 Pennsylvania Ave. NW, 202/347-4543), a retail studio that works with a cooperative of master tailors, block printers, and seamstresses in Nepal and India.

DUPONT CIRCLE

Lively Dupont Circle features an eclectic choice of gift shops, clothing stores, bookstores, and art galleries. If you're looking for a quirky gift, one-of-a-kind handcrafts, greeting cards, or chocolate, stop in **The Chocolate Moose** (1743 L St. NW, 202/463-0992, www.chocolatemoosedc.com). Serious antiques lovers will be intrigued by the offerings at **Geoffrey Diner Gallery** (1730 21st St. NW, 202/904-5005, www.dinergallery.com). They have items from the 19th and 20th centuries, contemporary fine art, European and American crafts, and Tiffany lamps.

GEORGETOWN

Everyone from first ladies to celebrities have made their way down M Street looking for a special find. Georgetown offers great antiques, cool clothing, and one-of-a-kind local boutiques. Most of the stores can be found along M Street and Wisconsin Avenues. The famous mall, **The Shops at Georgetown Park** (3222 M St., 202/342-8190, www.shopsatgeorgetownpark.com, Mon.-Sat. 10am-9pm, Sun. noon-6pm) underwent major renovations and was sold to new owners in 2014. Since then it's been steadily adding a mix of major bargain and luxury brands as well as restaurants.

UPPER NORTHWEST

The best shopping in Upper Northwest is in the Friendship Heights neighborhood, along the Maryland state border. The **Chevy Chase Pavilion** (5335 Wisconsin Ave., 202/686-5335, www.ccpavilion.com, Mon.-Sat. 7am-11pm, Sun. 7am-9pm) is an upscale shopping mall that underwent a $32 million renovation in 2012. It features national chains such as J. Crew, World Market, and Old Navy. It is across Wisconsin Avenue from another small, upscale mall, **Mazza Gallerie** (5300 Wisconsin Ave., 202/966-6114, www.mazzagallerie.com, Mon.-Fri. 10am-8pm, Sat. 10am-7pm, Sun. noon-6pm). Mazza Gallerie features stores such as Neiman Marcus, Heritage, and TW Luggage and Leather. There is also a movie theater at the mall and a parking garage. The shopping district is accessible by Metrorail on the Red Line at the Friendship Heights stop.

Sports and Recreation

SPECTATOR SPORTS

The nation's capital is home to many professional sports teams and hosts countless sporting events throughout the year.

The city is in a frenzy over the **Washington Nationals** baseball team, which came to DC in 2005 and moved into their current home, **Nationals Park** (1500 S. Capitol St. SE, 202/675-6287, www.washington.nationals.mlb.com), in 2008. The stadium sits on the banks of the Anacostia River in the Navy Yard neighborhood and seats approximately 41,500 people. The Washington Monument and Capitol Building can be seen from the upper stands.

The **Verizon Center** (601 F St. NW, 202/628-3200, www.verizoncenter.com) in Penn Quarter is home to the city's professional hockey team (the NHL's **Washington Capitals**), two pro basketball teams: (the NBA's **Washington Wizards** and the WNBA's **Washington Mystics**) and Georgetown University's men's basketball team (the Georgetown Hoyas).

Making good use of the former Washington Redskins stadium, DC's professional soccer team, **D.C. United,** plays at **Robert F. Kennedy Memorial Stadium (RFK)** (2400 E. Capitol St. SE, 202/587-5000, www.dcunited.com). At the time of publication, the team was scheduled to move to a brand-new stadium in 2018 at Buzzard Point, two miles south of the U.S. Capitol. The **Washington Redskins** (www.redskins.com) now play at **FedEx Field** in Landover, Maryland.

Other professional sporting events make their way annually to DC. The **Citi Open** (www.citiopentennis.com), formerly the Legg Mason Tennis Classic, is part of the U.S. Open Series. Professional tennis players from around the globe compete for more than $1.8 million in this world-class tennis event. The nine-day tournament is held at the tennis center in Rock Creek Park at the end of July and beginning of August.

The **Washington International Horse Show** (www.wihs.org) is a yearly championship event held at the Verizon Center at the end of October. Approximately 600 horses and riders compete for more than $400,000 in prize money and titles. The event includes show jumping, dressage, equitation, hunters, barrel racing, and terrier races.

CANOEING AND KAYAKING

Those interested in paddling a canoe or kayak on the Potomac River are in for a treat. Viewing the city from the calm of the river puts it in a whole new perspective. Rent a kayak from **Key Bridge Boathouse** (3500 Water St. NW, 202/337-9642, www.boatingindc.com, $15 per hour for a single, $20 for a tandem) in Georgetown and paddle under the Key Bridge and within easy sight of the Washington Monument and Lincoln

Run DC

Runners and triathletes make their way to Washington DC regularly to partake in many annual races. These are just a few of the numerous events scheduled throughout the year.

- **Rock 'n' Roll DC Marathon & Half Marathon** (Mar., www.runrocknroll.competitor.com)
- **Credit Union Cherry Blossom Ten Mile Run** (Apr., www.cherryblossom.org)
- **Capitol Hill Classic 10K** (May, www.capitolhillclassic.com)
- **Komen Global Race for the Cure 5K** (June, www.komendcrace.info-komen.org)
- **Nation's Triathlon** (Sept., www.nationstri.com)
- **Army 10-Miler** (Oct., www.armytenmiler.com)
- **Marine Corps Marathon** (Oct., www.marinemarathon.com)

Memorial. **Thompson Boat Center** (2900 Virginia Ave. NW, 202/333-9543, www.thompsonboatcenter.com, $16.50-55) is another good option for rentals.

BIKING

Those who prefer pedals over paddles can take a relaxing ride along the **C&O Canal Towpath** (a scenic 184.5-mile-long trail connecting Georgetown with Cumberland, Maryland) on the north bank of the Potomac River; rent a bike in Georgetown from **Big Wheel Bikes** (202/337-0254, www.bigwheelbikes.com, $7 per hour or $35 per day). **Bike and Roll Washington DC** (202/842-2453, www.bikeandrolldc.com, $40 per day) offers bike rentals for touring the city's sights from a convenient National Mall location. Their helpful staff can share tips on where to ride.

Another great option for getting around the city on two wheels is joining **Capital Bikeshare** (www.capitalbikeshare.com) for a day, three days, a month, or a year. Members gain access to more than 1,800 bikes in 350 locations throughout the city (including Arlington and Alexandria in Virginia). Twenty-four-hour memberships are $8 and include the first half hour of each ride. Additional time is then charged by the half hour. Passes can be purchased at kiosks at each bike station.

An 11-mile Rail-to-Trail route called the **Capital Crescent Trail** starts in Georgetown on K Street. The trail runs parallel to the C&O Canal Towpath for the first three miles but then goes through upscale neighborhoods in Northwest DC. The initial seven miles between Georgetown and Bethesda, Maryland, are paved, but an additional four miles of unpaved trail (mostly crushed stone) can be ridden to Silver Spring, Maryland. The two trails are connected by a tunnel under downtown Bethesda.

Bike Tours

Year-round daily bike tours around Washington DC are offered by **Capital City Bike Tours** (502 23rd St. NW, 202/626-0017, www.dc.capitalcitybiketours.com, $39). Comfortable beach cruisers are used in the tours and riders can expect to see sights such as the Lincoln Memorial, White House, Vietnam Veterans Memorial, and the Capitol Building. Tours are three hours and leave from the Capital City Bike Tours office.

Another popular bike tour company is **Bike and Roll Washington DC** (202/842-2453, www.bikethesites.com). They offer seasonal guided bike (three hours, $40) and

Segway (2.5 hours, $64) tours from their National Mall location (955 L'Enfant Plaza SW) and year-round tours from their Union Station location (50 Massachusetts Ave., 202/962-0206).

GOLF

Golfers might be surprised to learn that there are three golf courses right in the city (www.golfdc.com). **Langston Golf Course** (2600 Benning Rd. NE, 202/397-8638, $18-32), an 18-hole course, is five minutes from Capitol Hill. **East Potomac Golf Course** (972 Ohio Dr. SW, 202/554-7660, $10-28), which has one 18-hole course and two 9-hole courses, is at Haines Point near the National Mall. **Rock Creek Golf Course** (16th and Rittenhouse Streets NW, 202/882-7332, $15-25) is an 18-hole course at the northern end of Rock Creek Park.

HORSEBACK RIDING

Horse enthusiasts don't need to leave the city to find great riding. **Rock Creek Park Horse Center** (5100 Glover Rd. NW, 202/362-0117) in Rock Creek Park offers trail rides and lessons.

ICE-SKATING

A great way to impress a date on a cold winter night is by going ice-skating at the **National Gallery of Art Sculpture Garden and Ice Skating Rink** (700 Constitution Ave. NW, 202/216-9397). Skate in the shadows of some of the city's most well-known buildings and in view of many of the garden's wonderful sculptures. This enchanting rink is especially romantic at night.

PLAYGROUND

For the coolest playground in town, visit **Turtle Park** (Friendship Park, 4500 Van Ness St. NW, 202/282-2198) in Upper Northwest. The focal point is a huge sandbox with turtle sculptures for climbing on and a "sprayground" for cleaning off the sand and cooling off. There are also ball fields in the park and a recreation center.

Food

THE NATIONAL MALL
Asian Fusion

For a trendy night out, dine at **The Source** (575 Pennsylvania Ave. NW, 202/637-6100, www.wolfgangpuck.com, brunch Sat. 11:30am-3pm, lunch Mon.-Fri. 11:30am-2pm, dinner Mon.-Thurs. 5:30pm-10pm and Fri.-Sat. 5:30pm-11pm, $31-50). This popular Wolfgang Puck restaurant is adjacent to the Newseum and was a date night choice for Michelle and Barack Obama. The Source offers a three-course prix fixe lunch for $45 (and a discount on Newseum admission), and the lower-level lounge offers small plates and a Dim Sum Brunch on Saturday. The modern dining room on the second floor offers a contemporary Asian menu. Floor-to-ceiling windows and a polished tile floor give the space an inviting atmosphere, and there is plush leather seating. There is also a four-person hot pot table and a two-person chef's tasting menu counter. A beautiful wine wall with more than 2,000 bottles is a focal point. A seasonal patio is available for outdoor dining.

CAPITOL HILL
American

On the north side of Capitol Hill in the Atlas District is an authentic cheesesteak place owned by two Philadelphia natives. **Taylor Charles Steak & Ice** (1320 H St. NE, 202/388-6880, www.steakandice.com, Sun.-Thurs. 11am-9pm, Fri.-Sat. 11am-3:30am, under $10) offers flavorful made-to-order cheesesteak sandwiches (they also offer chicken and portobello sandwiches). There are several options for toppings and, of course, house-made cheese whiz. A nice treat is their soda fountain, stocked with birch beer, creamy sodas, and Kool-Aid.

A Capitol Hill classic is the **Tune Inn** (331 Pennsylvania Ave. SE, 202/543-2725, Sun.-Thur. 8am-2am, Fri.-Sat 8am-3am, $5-17). This historic burger-and-beer bar suffered a fire in 2011 but bounced right back to its quirky self (the regulars are even still sitting at the bar). The decor is a symphony in taxidermy (complete with a deer rump and a beer-drinking black bear), but the beer is cheap (by DC standards) and the burgers are tasty. They are open daily for breakfast, lunch, and dinner.

Bakery

A charming little bakery in Northeast, and a relative newcomer to the restaurant scene is the **Batter Bowl Bakery** (403 H St. NE, 202/675-2011, www.the-bbb.com, daily 8am-8pm, under $10). They serve delicious boules, baguettes, and bakery items, plus a scant selection of breakfast and lunch sandwiches (each named after local streets) served on their homemade bread. All sandwiches are made to order, so be prepared to wait a few minutes. They will be packed in a hefty takeout container with a small side salad. The bakery also offers wonderful cookies, macaroons, and Danishes.

Belgian

The intimate **Belga Café** (514 8th St. SE, 202/544-0100, www.belgacafe.com, lunch Mon.-Fri. 11am-4pm, brunch Sat.-Sun. 9am-4pm, dinner Mon.-Thurs. 4pm-10pm, Fri.-Sat. 4pm-11pm, and Sun.4pm-9:30pm, $15-30) serves weekend brunch, weekday lunch, and dinner daily. Their waffles are knee weakening (with savory or sweet toppings), and their dinner entrées are delicious renditions of items such as mussels (flecked with bacon and steamed in red ale), truffle macaroni and cheese, and grilled sea bass. They also have a nice beer list. The place is small (the first floor of a row house), and there is exposed brick inside with an open kitchen (read: the noise level is high). There is usually a wait, but the staff

is friendly (even to children) and on nice days there is added seating outside.

DOWNTOWN
American

It's hard to pass on an opportunity to dine at **Old Ebbitt Grill** (675 15th St., 202/347-4800, www.ebbitt.com, Mon.-Fri. 7:30am-1am, Sat.-Sun. 8:30am-1am, $14-28). This historic restaurant is near the White House and was frequented by presidents such as Grant, Cleveland, and Theodore Roosevelt. Currently part of the Clyde's restaurant group, this old favorite is always bustling with political personalities, journalists, and theater patrons. It's a casual, fun place but shows its long history through marble bars and mahogany booths outfitted in velvet. They have an oyster bar and a menu of burgers, pasta, steak, and seafood. They also serve breakfast during the week and brunch on weekends.

Wine lovers will feel at home eating at ★ **Proof** (775 G St. NW, 202/737-7663, www.proofdc.com, lunch Tues.-Fri. 11:30am-2pm, dinner Mon.-Thurs. 5:30pm-10pm, Fri.-Sat. 5:30pm-11pm, and Sun. 5pm-9:30pm, $25-35, four-course tasting menu $75) in Penn Quarter. This "wine-centric" Wolfgang Puck restaurant offers a well-designed modern American menu topped off with friendly, knowledgeable service. There is a tasting menu with wine pairings, first course (small plates), and second course (entrée) selections. The restaurant focuses on local, organic, sustainable ingredients and does so in an elegant yet casual environment with leather seating, European lighting, and wine on the wall. Although the restaurant is known for its international cheese and charcuterie, many of the menu items are worth noting, such as the pillowy gnocchi and the duck breast. End the meal with sticky toffee pudding. This is a great place for a date or to bring out-of-town guests. It is also a convenient choice after visiting the Reynolds Center next door.

Indian

Upscale Indian cuisine can be found at

Food Truck Culture

Food trucks line up to serve lunch.

Food trucks have always been part of the lunch scene in Washington DC, but in the past several years their quality and diversity have elevated them to noteworthy status.

Dangerously Delicious Pies (www.dangerouspiesdc.com) was the first truck to spawn off a brick-and-mortar eatery (at 1339 H St.), although the majority of the trucks are stand-alone businesses. Dangerously Delicious Pies serves both sweet and savory pie slices out of its bright red truck. **Tokyo in the City** rolls fresh sushi with nontraditional names like "Gangnam Style" and "Las Vegas," while the **BBQ Bus** (www.bbqbusdc.com) serves up tender ribs and pulled pork. Even more specialized is **Ball or Nothing,** which serves meatballs. This local favorite offers traditional meatballs, veggie meatballs, wild boar meatballs, and interesting sides such as mascarpone polenta and roasted peach and spinach salad.

So how do you find these rolling treasures? These meals on wheels can be found on many major roads in the business and tourist areas of the city. Some have their own websites that give their location schedule and others use Twitter to provide their up-to-the-minute whereabouts. Many can also be found on **Food Truck Fiesta** (www.foodtruckfiesta.com), a website geared toward tracking the trucks. When in doubt, try the truck with the longest line. It doesn't take long for word to spread about a great food truck find.

★ **Rasika** (633 D St. NW, 202/637-1222, www.rasikarestaurant.com, lunch Mon.-Fri. 11:30am-2:30pm, dinner Mon.-Thurs. 5:30pm-10:30pm and Fri.-Sat. 5pm-11pm, $17-36) in Penn Quarter. This fabulous restaurant is one of the best in the area for modern Indian cuisine. The Palak Chaat or Shrimp Uttapam is a must for an appetizer, and a personal favorite for an entrée is the lamb Roganjosh (although the black cod is also spectacular). The butternut squash makes a good side dish, and what Indian meal is complete without naan? They also offer a pre-theater three-course menu before 6:30pm for $35. This restaurant is red-hot on the popularity list, and a reservation is highly recommended. They have a second location at 1190 New Hampshire Avenue NW.

Italian

The vintage-style pizzeria bistro **Matchbox** (713 H St. NW, 202/289-4441, www.

matchboxchinatown.com, Mon.-Thurs. 11am-10:30pm, Fri. 11am-11:30pm, Sat. 10am-11:30pm, Sun. 10am-10:30pm, $10-31) is a favorite in the Chinatown neighborhood for pregaming before an event at the Verizon Center. They are known for their incredible pizza and also for their mini-burger appetizers topped with onion straws, but they also offer a full menu of sandwiches and entrées. The atmosphere in this multilevel hot spot is fun, lively, and slightly funky. There are also locations on Capitol Hill (521 8th St. SE) and in the U Street Corridor (1901 14th St. NW).

Spanish/Portuguese

The toughest reservation in town and one that will blow you away (first when you taste the food and again when you see the bill) is ★ **Minibar by José Andrés** (855 E St. NW, 202/393-0812, www.minibarbyjoseandres. com, Tues.-Sat., seatings at 6pm, 6:30pm, 8:30pm, and 9pm, $275 per person). This "culinary journey" of molecular gastronomy comprises a preset 25-plus-course tasting menu (1-2 bites each) that is a combination of art and science. There is no menu; you simply eat what is served that evening (examples include beech mushroom risotto with truffle, pillow of PB&J, grilled lobster with peanut butter and honey, and apple meringue shaped pigs with bacon ice cream).

Seatings are small, just six guests at each of four seatings a night. Guests move through different rooms during the meal. The serving team walks guests through each course (plan on staying about 2-3 hours) and shares the beauty of the ingredients that were selected for each and the technique behind their creation. The $275 price tag does not include drinks, tax, or gratuity. Optional drink pairings are available for an additional $85, $115, and $200. Reservations are taken in three-month periods (starting one month prior), but it can take several months to actually get one. This is truly a unique, once-in-a-lifetime dining experience. Reservations are by email only (reserve@minibarbyjoseandres.com).

Turkish/Greek

Another creation of chef José Andrés is the very popular **Zaytinya** (701 9th St. NW, 202/638-0800, www.zaytinya.com, Sun.-Mon. 11am-10pm, Tues.-Thurs. 11am-11pm, Fri.-Sat. 11am-midnight, small plates $7-20). They serve a large and delicious menu of tapas in a casual setting. This is a good choice for both vegetarians and meat eaters. Menu examples include pan-roasted dorado, Turkish-style pastirma, and knisa lamb chops. They also offer a chef's experience for $55. There is a bar overlooking the dining room for people-watching. This is a good place to try some of the creations of one of DC's most famous chefs.

DUPONT CIRCLE

American

Nage (1600 Rhode Island Ave. NW, 202/448-8005, www.nagedc.com, breakfast daily 7am-10:30am, brunch Sat.-Sun. 11am-2:30pm, lunch Mon.-Fri. 11:30am-2:30pm, dinner Mon.-Thurs. 5pm-10pm, Fri.-Sat. 5pm-10:30pm, Sun. 5pm-9pm, $18-31) has undergone many changes in recent years. The result is a fresh-feeling place overseen by a popular local chef. Located in the Courtyard Washington Embassy Row hotel, the restaurant provides an American menu full of favorites such as crab cakes, lobster macaroni and cheese, rockfish, lamb shank, and delightful "bottomless" Bloody Marys and mimosas during weekend brunch ($15).

Just south of the Dupont Circle neighborhood is the famed **Vidalia** (1990 M St. NW, 202/659-1990, www.vidaliadc. com, dinner Mon-Sat starting at 5pm, closed Sunday, $30-40). As the Georgian onion name implies, they serve American food inspired by the South, but with a Chesapeake Bay regional influence. The menu revolves around terrific seasonal vegetables, fruit, and local seafood. The result is selections such as mouthwatering shrimp and grits, tenderloin with corn pudding and broccoli, and duck breast. They also have a five-course tasting menu for $78. Vidalia is below ground, but the sleek modern decor is so nice you won't miss the windows. They also have a well-selected wine bar with more than 30 wines by the glass.

If you're looking for a casual, contemporary little bistro, **CIRCA at Dupont** (1601 Connecticut Ave. NW, 202/667-1601, www. circaatdupont.com, Mon.-Fri. 11am-close, Sat.-Sun. 10am-close, $8-26) is a friendly choice. They have communal tables indoors for those who like to make new friends, along with some regular tables and bar high-tops. They offer a large wine list, good bartenders, a heated patio, and a variety of menu options including small plates, salads, flatbread, sandwiches, steak, and seafood. They are known for their chicken lettuce wraps.

Greek

Tucked inside a seemingly normal-looking row house (next door to a CVS) is one of the best culinary outposts in the city. ★ **Komi** (1509 17th St. NW, 202/332-9200, www.komirestaurant.com, Tues.-Sat. 5:30pm-9:30pm, $150) serves a preset multicourse dinner for $150 per person. The experience starts with several light dishes and progresses to hearty fare and finally dessert. Wine pairing is offered as an option for an additional $75. They do not even have a printed menu. This intimate eatery is steered by a young chef named Johnny Monis, who prepares incredible Greek dishes inspired by family recipes. The menu is different every night, making this the perfect find for foodies—foodies with deep pockets, that is.

Thai

Authentic Thai food can be found at **Little Serow** (1511 17th St. NW, www.littleserow. com, Tues.-Thurs. 5:30pm-10pm, Fri.-Sat. 5:30pm-10:30pm, $49). The food is primarily inspired by northern Thailand, so many of the dishes are not typical of the Thai food at other area restaurants; this is definitely part of the appeal. They do not take reservations. They open at 5:30pm, and people line up at the door as early as 4:30pm. If you don't make it inside for the first seating, they will text you

with a time to come back. It's a little hard to find because there is no sign outside (if you see their sister restaurant, Komi, you're close). There is very limited seating, and they cannot accommodate parties larger than four. They offer one fixed-price family-style menu for $49; everyone there eats the same thing (so no ogling the meal next to you). The menu changes weekly and is posted on their website each Tuesday. The dining room is very dark, but the food is absolutely delicious and worth the quirkiness of getting a table. Another plus is the great staff. They're very friendly and attentive.

GEORGETOWN
American

Timeless quality can be found at **1789** (1226 36th St. NW, 202/965-1789, www.1789restaurant.com, Mon.-Thurs. 6pm-10pm, Fri. 6pm-11pm, Sat. 5:30pm-11pm, Sun. 5:30pm-10pm, $28-46), which has been around more than 50 years. Part of the Clyde's family of restaurants, 1789 is tried-and-true with starched linen tablecloths and candlelight. The restaurant has three floors and six rooms for dining, each with a unique name, ambience, and a common theme of antiques and equestrian decor. Jackets used to be required but are now preferred. The restaurant serves a diverse menu broken down into "Sustainable Seafood," "Humanely Farmed Animals," and "Eggs and Flour" (French-inspired crepes, and pasta). The food is high quality and consistent, and the service is impeccable. This is a lovely spot for a date or a business dinner.

Just east of Georgetown on M Street is a traditional American restaurant that is known for hosting power players from DC's political scene. It also prides itself in using simple flavor-enhancing cooking methods like smoking, braising, and roasting. The **Blue Duck Tavern** (24th and M Sts. NW, 202/419-6755, www.blueducktavern.com, breakfast daily 6:30am-10:30am, lunch Mon.-Fri. 11:30am-2:30pm, dinner Sun.-Thurs. 5:30pm-10:30pm, Fri.-Sat. 5:30pm-11pm, brunch Sat.-Sun.

11am-2:30pm, $15-38) is known for both its food and its lovely atmosphere. Handmade wood furnishings and an open kitchen help give it a warm, gathering place-type feel, although with a contemporary flair. The food sounds simple, with selections such as beef ribs, organic chicken, and halibut, but the dishes are elegantly prepared and beautifully served.

Farmers Fishers Bakers (3000 K St. NW, Washington Harbor, 202/298-8783, www.farmersfishersbakers.com, breakfast Mon.-Fri- 7:30am-10am, brunch Sat.-Sun. 9am-2pm, lunch/dinner Mon.-Wed. 11am-10pm, Thurs. 11am-11pm, Fri. 11am-midnight, Sat. 2pm-midnight, Sun. 2pm-10pm, $10-28) is part of the Farmers Restaurant Group and is a modern, upscale, casual option in Washington Harbor. The restaurant group supports American family farmers and sources regionally and seasonally when possible. Farmers Fishers Bakers offer an in-house bakery, full bar with 24 beer taps, a sushi counter, and a patio with views of the water. Guests are greeted outside in winter with a fire pit and the inside decor features several different themes for varying dining experiences. The menu is large and includes pizza, sandwiches, salads, and seafood. Their burger with blue cheese and a side of potato salad is a good choice on any day.

Bakery

The cupcake fad has taken DC by storm. Many people have heard of **Georgetown Cupcake** (3301 M St. NW, 202/333-8448, www.georgetowncupcake.com, Mon.-Sat. 10am-9pm, Sun. 10am-8pm), made famous by the reality television series *DC Cupcakes*, but they may not know about a nearby gem called **Baked & Wired** (1052 Thomas Jefferson St. NW, 703/663-8727, www.bakedandwired.com, Mon.-Thurs. 7am-8pm, Fri. 7am-9pm, Sat. 8am-9pm, Sun. 9am-8pm, under $10), south of the C&O Canal between 30th and 31st Streets. This little independent bakery sells great coffee and a large variety of freshly made bakery items including more

than 20 types of cupcakes with names like Chocolate Cupcake of Doom and Pretty Bitchin'. They turn out amazing baked goods amid a fun, inviting atmosphere. Look for the pink bicycle outside and don't forget to take home some Hippie Crack (homemade granola) for later.

Italian

The place to celebrity-spot in Georgetown is **Café Milano** (3251 Prospect St. NW, 202/333-6183, www.cafemilano.com, Wed.-Sat. 11:30am-midnight, Sun.-Tues. 11:30am-11pm, $17-65). Political VIPs and visiting Hollywood stars frequent this upscale Italian restaurant, as do local Georgetown socialites. The southern coastal Italian cuisine is consistently good, but diners come more to people-watch and enjoy the pleasant atmosphere afforded by the floor-to-ceiling windows and open sidewalk patio. There is normally a sophisticated crowd, and good wine is flowing.

Another great choice for Italian is **Filomena Ristorante** (1063 Wisconsin Ave. NW, 202/338-8800, www.filomena.com, daily 11:30am-11pm, $13-46). This well-known restaurant opened in 1983 and serves authentic, delicious Italian cuisine. You can even see the pasta being made on the way in. Many celebrities and dignitaries have dined here, including Bono from U2 and President Clinton. Seating is a little close together but the excellent food will make you overlook this. Portions are large and the service is friendly and attentive. Personal favorites include the Linguini Cardinale and Gnocchi Della Mamma.

ADAMS MORGAN
American

If you're up for pushing your comfort zone on trying new food, consider going to **Mintwood Place** (1813 Columbia Rd. NW, 202/234-6732, www.mintwoodplace.com, brunch Sat.-Sun. 10:30am-2:30pm, dinner Tues.-Thurs. 5:30pm-10pm, Fri.-Sat. 5:30pm-10:30pm, Sun. 5:30pm-9pm, $18-29). They have a truly unique menu with interesting combinations like duck breast with sauerkraut and wood-grilled shrimp and mackerel with goat and espelette curd. This is a great place to try something new and maybe impress a date. The restaurant is small and some of the tables are close together, but it has a casual neighborhood feel despite its chunky price tag.

Good burgers and an excellent beer selection help make the **Black Squirrel** (2427 18th St. NW, 202/232-1011, www.blacksquirreldc.com, Mon.-Fri. 5pm-close, Sat.-Sun. 11am-close, $10-15) a popular choice in Adams Morgan. With nearly 20 burger toppings and more than 50 draft beers (they also do 4-ounce pours), this is a relaxing place with a serious crowd of well-informed beer fanatics and those looking to explore new brew styles.

Cashion's Eat Place (1819 Columbia Rd. NW, 202/797-1819, www.cashionseatplace.com, Sat.-Sun. brunch 10:30am-2:30pm, dinner Tues. and Sun. 5:30pm-10pm, Wed.-Sat. 5:30pm-11pm, $13-26) has been described as "funky elegant," and this seems like an accurate analysis of this low-key Adams Morgan restaurant. They serve American food with a Mediterranean influence. The menu changes daily, making this a wonderful place to return to again and again. They also have a terrific wine list. The interior is spacious and airy and offers sidewalk seating when it is nice outside.

Vegetarian

A vegetarian hot spot that the rest of us can also enjoy, the **Amsterdam Falafelshop** (2425 18th St. NW, 202/234-1969, www.falafelshop.com, Sun.-Mon. 11am-midnight, Tues.-Wed. 11am-2:30am, Thurs. 11am-3am, Fri.-Sat. 11am-4am, under $10) is known for its perfectly crisp, yet soft, balls of fried chickpeas placed inside pita bread or in a bowl. The concept is simple: You order your falafel, they make it for you in under five minutes, and then you decide which of the 21 toppings and sauces you want from the garnish bar. The shop is open late and also offers sides and desserts.

American

One of the sister restaurants to the popular Volt in Frederick, Maryland, is ★ **Range** (5335 Wisconsin Ave. NW, 202/803-8020, www.voltrange.com, lunch and dinner, $5-120). At first glance, the price range may seem like a misprint, but the latest creation by revered chef Bryan Voltaggio is what he terms a shared-plate environment of main courses and side dishes, each ordered separately. The restaurant, located in the Chevy Chase Pavilion, seats 300 patrons. Food is prepared at numerous food stations, where more than two dozen chefs are hard at work. Dishes are served as they are ready and consist of a large variety of choices such as oysters from the raw bar, beef, grilled pork loin, lamb breast, and even pizza. The sides are culinary delights, beginning with the famed bread basket, which offers a cornucopia of fresh-baked delights. The restaurant itself has floor-to-ceiling windows and a curved design. The focus is the food, which is presented beautifully and tastes equally as delightful. Save room for dessert: a tantalizing cart of sinfully delicious options will appear at your table when your main courses are cleared.

In the Palisades neighborhood is **BlackSalt** (4883 MacArthur Blvd. NW, 202/342-9101, www.blacksaltrestaurant.com, lunch Mon.-Sat. 11:30am-2:30pm, brunch Sun. 11am-2pm, dinner Mon.-Thurs. 5:30pm-9:30pm, Fri. 5:30pm-11pm, Sat. 5pm-11pm, Sun. 5pm-9pm, $15-38), a well-known spot serving New American seafood. The seafood is extremely fresh, and they offer innovative combinations like jumbo prawn in pepper stew and Atlantic bigeye tuna with caramelized pork belly. They also offer a five-course tasting menu for $80 and a seven-course tasting menu for $98. Wine pairings are $46 and $60. There's an adjoining seafood market that sells some of the best fish in the city.

A traditional greasy-spoon breakfast joint is **Osman & Joe's Steak 'n Egg Kitchen** (4700 Wisconsin Ave. NW, 202/686-1201, www.osmanandjoes.com, 24 hours, $3-18). It offers all the wonderful eggs, sausages, hash browns, and biscuits you could ask for, with ultracasual 24-hour diner charm. As the name implies, they also have steak, as well as burgers, sandwiches, shakes, and good coffee.

German

Take it from a German girl who has eaten her way through the Old Country: Some of the best traditional German fare in the entire DC area is served at **Old Europe** (2434 Wisconsin Ave. NW, 202/333-7600, www.old-europe. com, lunch Wed.-Sat. 11:30am-2:30pm, Sun. 12pm-3:30pm, dinner Sun. 4pm-9pm, Wed.-Thurs. 5pm-9pm, Fri.-Sat. 5pm-10pm, $8-25). They have all the favorites including schnitzel, sauerbraten, and brats, all served in a lively homeland atmosphere. The menu is wide ranging and includes a good selection of traditional side dishes (potato pancakes, red cabbage, potato dumplings). They also have German wine, beer, and spirits (have you ever seen Jägermeister on a printed menu?).

Greek

A Mediterranean gem that serves wonderful tapas is **Café Olé** (4000 Wisconsin Ave. NW, 202/244-1330, www.cafeoledc.com, brunch Sat.-Sun. 11am-3:30pm, dinner Mon.-Thurs. 11am-9pm, Fri.-Sat. 11am-10pm, Sun. 11am-9pm, $8-16). This popular lunch, brunch, and dinner spot puts a refreshing spin on Greek fare. Their large-size tapas menu (with more than 30 choices) allows diners to taste multiple creations without the usual heaviness of some Greek food. The fare here is flavorful and interesting. This is a good place for vegetarians, meat lovers, and seafood enthusiasts. If you like lamb, they have a special hummus with lamb in it; the spices in the lamb make this a wonderful choice. They also have more than 25 wines by the glass, microbrews, and a martini happy hour on weekdays. The decor is modern, and they have an attractive bar. There is a lot of seating, but the tables are close together. They also have a nice patio. Another plus to this restaurant is that they have validated underground parking. They also do takeout.

Italian

DC's most popular pizzeria is easily ★ 2 **Amys** (3715 Macomb St. NW, 202/885-5700, www.2amysdc.com, Mon. 5pm-10pm, Tues.-Thurs. 11am-10pm, Fri.-Sat. 11am-11pm, Sun. noon-10pm, $7-14). This gourmet Italian restaurant specializes in authentic Neapolitan pizza. The incredible smell alone will make your mouth water when you walk into this hopping, noisy establishment. The cute bar area is a great place to wait for your table. You can even make good use of the time by studying the menu. Although they make other menu items just as well, the focus here is really on the pizza, which lives up to the hype. It is actually one of the few restaurants in the country certified by the D.O.C. (Denominazione di Origine Controllata), an Italian entity that specifies the legally permitted ingredients and preparation methods required to make authentic Neapolitan pizza.

Japanese

It's hard to imagine that good sushi can be found in DC at a decent price, but **Kotobuki** (4822 MacArthur Blvd. NW, 202/625-9080, www.kotobukidc.com, lunch Mon.-Sat. noon-2:30pm, dinner Mon.-Thurs. 5pm-9:30pm, Fri.-Sat. 5pm-10:30pm, Sun. 5pm-9:30pm, $8-28) is that needle in a haystack. It is a tiny restaurant (above another one owned by the same people), and there is usually a line for a table, but the prices are good, the fish is fresh, and the sushi is authentic.

U STREET CORRIDOR
American

A long-standing tradition on U Street is ★ **Ben's Chili Bowl** (1213 U St. NW, 202/667-0909, www.benschilibowl.com, breakfast Mon.-Fri. 6am-10:45am, Sat. 7am-10:45am, main menu Mon.-Thurs. 10:45am-2am, Fri.-Sat. 10:45am-4am, Sun. 11am-12am, under $10). This historic eatery opened in 1958 and has seen a lot of history. It has weathered the rise, fall, and rebirth of the U Street Corridor and could well be the only business on this stretch of street that survived both the

Ben's Chili Bowl, in operation since 1958

smiling and friendly, and celebrities and regular folks are all treated equally.

Busboys and Poets (2021 14th St. NW, 202/387-7638, www.busboysandpoets.com, Mon.-Thurs. 8am-midnight, Fri. 8am-1am, Sat. 9am-1am, Sun. 9am-midnight, $9-24) is a local gathering place and restaurant that opened in the DC area more than a decade ago and quickly gained a loyal following. It now has six locations. It is known as a progressive establishment and also as a community resource for artists, activists, and writers. The 14th Street location is large and serves breakfast daily until 11am. The rest of the day they offer soup, sandwiches, panini, pizza, and entrées (after 5pm) with a Southern flair (think catfish, shrimp and grits, and pasta). They offer vegetarian, vegan, and gluten-free selections as well, and there is a progressive bookstore on-site.

Greek

Fantastic gyros are what all the hype is about at **The Greek Spot** (2017 11th St. NW, 202/265-3118, www.greekspotdc.com, Mon.-Fri. 11am-10:30pm, Sat. noon-10:30pm, $4-14). This is a very casual "fast-food" restaurant that makes tasty Greek meals in a hurry. They serve lamb gyros, vegetarian gyros (made with soy steak strips), chicken souvlaki, and other sandwiches and burgers. The food is tender and inexpensive and has developed quite the local following. They also prepare and deliver takeout orders.

riots of 1968 following the assassination of Martin Luther King Jr. and the construction of the Metrorail Green Line. Ben's is "Home of the Famous Chili Dog," which is what has drawn people (including Barack Obama and the Travel Channel's Anthony Bourdain) through its doors and to its red barstools for decades. They serve breakfast and a "main menu" the rest of the day, but chili dogs are available anytime they're open. The staff is

Accommodations

Accommodations in Washington DC run the gamut in price range. However, choice hotels near the popular attractions are pricey year-round and some are downright outrageous. An alternative choice for booking a room is to stay across the Potomac River in nearby Arlington or Alexandria, Virginia. It can be less expensive, yet still convenient to the city's major attractions by car, bus, or Metrorail.

UNDER $100

Reservations for a hostel stay can be made months in advance with **Hostelling International-Washington DC** (1009 11th St. NW, 202/737-2333, www.hiwashingtondc.org, $29-119). Accommodations are close to the National Mall, Metrorail, and many of the popular DC attractions. This former hotel has 250 beds and offers shared dorm-style lodging and some semiprivate rooms. Bathrooms are shared, and there is a kitchen and laundry facility on-site. There is also high-speed Internet.

$100-200

One of the best values in the city is the ★ **Hotel Tabard Inn** (1739 N St. NW, 202/785-1277, www.tabardinn.com, $155-250), five blocks from the White House on a pretty, tree-lined street. The hotel has 40 uniquely designed rooms in three town houses. The houses were built between 1880 and 1890. Rates vary depending on the size of the room and whether they have a shared or private bathroom. Reservations are taken for specific price categories, not for specific rooms.

All rates include a guest pass to the local YMCA, and an included continental breakfast is served in the restaurant. Free wireless Internet is also available throughout the inn. The inn is known for having live jazz.

The **Kalorama Guest House** (2700 Cathedral Ave. NW, 202/588-8188, www.kaloramaguesthouse.com, $89-249) is actually two Victorian town houses—the main house and a nice brick town house—in Upper Northwest with 10 guest rooms total. Located in a cute neighborhood less than a block from the National Zoo, it is a good bargain for the area. Don't expect many amenities in the rooms (no telephone and no television). Some of the rooms have shared bathrooms, but you can fall asleep listening to the sound of monkeys howling in the distance at the zoo and wake to a freshly made continental breakfast in the main house.

The **Days Inn Connecticut Avenue** (4400 Connecticut Ave. NW, 202/244-5600, www.daysinn.com, $120-160) is a standard chain hotel in the Forest Hills area of Upper Northwest DC. The hotel is about three miles from the National Mall. It offers free wireless Internet and 37-inch HD TVs. Parking is available for an additional fee.

★ **Woodley Park Guest House** (2647 Woodley Rd. NW, 202/667-0218, www.dcinns.com, $140-240) is one of the nicest bed-and-breakfasts in DC. In a historic neighborhood in Upper Northwest, they offer 15 comfortable and quiet guest rooms and exceptional service. The owners are truly service-oriented, and they help make the city feel personal and accessible. This is a wonderful choice in a quiet location for both business and leisure travel. The rooms have free wireless Internet and a delicious, fresh continental breakfast is served daily.

$200-300

A wonderful Kimpton hotel in the Dupont Circle neighborhood is the ★ **Carlyle Suites Hotel** (1731 New Hampshire Ave. NW, 202/234-3200, www.carlylesuites.com, $139-339). This art deco hotel has 170 rooms with ample space, sitting areas, fully equipped kitchens, and Tempur-Pedic beds. The eight-story offering is on a residential street, three blocks from the Dupont Circle fountain. There is a restaurant on-site, a fitness center, free bike use, and valet parking ($42). The hotel is pet friendly.

The **Embassy Suites Washington, D.C. at the Chevy Chase Pavilion** (4300 Military Rd. NW, 202/362-9300, www.embassysuites-dcmetro.com, $209-538) has an upscale feel and is located in a high-end shopping area in Upper Northwest. The hotel is conveniently right off the Metrorail at the Friendship Heights stop and caters to business travelers. They offer 198 suites, each with a separate bedroom and sitting room. This is a nice option if you like your space. They also have large bathrooms. The hotel is good for extended stays.

The **Omni Shoreham Hotel** (2500 Calvert St. NW, 202/234-0700, www.omnihotels.com, $245-389) is a luxurious landmark built in 1930 in Upper Northwest DC. It has 836 guest rooms, some of which have wonderful views of Rock Creek Park. This historic hotel hosted its first inaugural ball in 1933 (for Franklin D. Roosevelt) and has hosted inaugural balls for each president that followed during the 20th century (Bill Clinton even played his saxophone there during his ball in 1993). At

The Ghost Suite

It's no secret that the **Omni Shoreham Hotel** (2500 Calvert St. NW, 202/234-0700, www. omnihotels.com, $245-389) in Upper Northwest DC has some pretty peculiar things going on in Suite 870. The grand and historic hotel, which was built in 1930, originally had an extravagant apartment on the eighth floor where a minor shareholder in the property lived with his family and housekeeper. Shortly after they moved into the apartment, the housekeeper was found dead in her bed in the apartment. Not long after, the family's adopted daughter (the only child in the family) also died mysteriously in the apartment amid rumors of suicide or a possible drug overdose.

The family remained in the apartment for 40 years and finally moved out in 1973. The once extravagant apartment was in shambles when they left and was closed off to the rest of the hotel and abandoned. Once the apartment was empty, guests in neighboring rooms began reporting disturbances. Televisions and lights would go on and off, doors would slam shut, people would feel breezes as if someone had walked by, and many reports of loud noises (including someone playing the piano) were reported coming from the apartment. Many of the strange sounds were reported to be coming from Room 864, which was the housekeeper's bedroom.

In 1997 the hotel decided to renovate the apartment and turn it into a presidential suite. During construction, a worker fell from the balcony to his death. Upon completion of the suite's restoration, the hotel appropriately named it "The Ghost Suite."

It is reported that to this day many guests claim seeing a little girl running through the halls and an older woman in a long dress roaming around alone.

one time, it was the number one choice for accommodations for dignitaries and the rich and famous and has housed such notables as the Beatles and emperors. The hotel offers rooms and suites of varying sizes and prices, with the lower-end rooms being quite affordable and the upper-end suites being very expensive. An elegant restaurant is located in the hotel. The rooms have free wireless Internet, and there is an outdoor heated pool, a fitness center, and more than 100,000 square feet of meeting space.

OVER $300

For a presidential stay in DC, book a room at the ★ **Hay-Adams Hotel** (800 16th St. NW, 202/638-6600, www.hayadams.com, $379-1,879) at 16th and H Streets NW. This beautiful Downtown hotel has 145 guest rooms and 21 luxury suites. Some of the rooms offer stunning views of local landmarks such as the White House and Lafayette Square. The Hay-Adams was built in 1928 in the Italian Renaissance style and has the appearance of a large private

mansion. It sits on the land where the homes of Secretary of State John Hay and historian Henry Adams (author and relative of John Adams and John Quincy Adams) once stood.

The hotel has hosted many important political figures and was the choice for President Obama and his family in the weeks leading up to his first inauguration in 2008.

Visitors taking in the National Mall sights will enjoy the convenient location of this hotel, situated near the White House, Downtown attractions, and the Metrorail. The hotel features beautiful, traditionally decorated rooms with molded ceilings, quality furnishings, ample space, comfortable beds, and wonderful amenities such as fluffy bathrobes. The food at the hotel is also excellent.

The service at the Hay-Adams is outstanding, and from the moment you walk through the front door, it is obvious you will be well taken care of. The hotel's slogan is, "Where nothing is overlooked but the White House," and they mean it.

If you're traveling to DC for the full historical experience and you'd like to indulge in famous accommodations, then the ★ **Willard InterContinental Hotel** (1401 Pennsylvania Ave. NW, 202/628-9100, www.washington.intercontinental.com, $249-3,500) is a good choice. The Willard is more than 150 years old and is considered to be one of the most prestigious hotels in the city. It is one block from the White House and has been called the "Residence of Presidents" because it has hosted nearly every U.S. president since Franklin Pierce stayed there in 1853. Other famous guests include Martin Luther King Jr. (who stayed there during the time he delivered his famous "I Have a Dream" speech), Charles Dickens, Mark Twain, and Buffalo Bill. The hotel even has its own little museum.

The Willard is beautifully restored and has a grand lobby, comfortable rooms, and outstanding service. The hotel has 12 floors, 335 guest rooms, and 41 suites. It also has a wonderful on-site restaurant.

Another beautifully restored historic hotel is **The Jefferson** (1200 16th St. NW, 202/448-2300, www.jeffersondc.com, $375-675), located roughly halfway between the White House and Dupont Circle. Built as a luxury apartment building in 1923, the beaux arts building was converted to a hotel in 1955 and underwent major renovations in 2009, which included incorporating modern-day features (such as a chef's kitchen and spa) into the original framework. The hotel maintains a large collection of antiques, artwork, and original signed documents. It has 95 guest rooms and suites and three on-site restaurants. They also have an Executive Canine Officer (ECO) named Lord Monticello (Monti)—a rescue dog that lives at the hotel. The hotel is dog friendly ($50 fee) and provides dog beds, bowls, treats, and a map of nearby dog-friendly establishments and walking routes.

Off Lafayette Park near the White House is the lovely **Sofitel Washington DC Lafayette Square** (806 15th St. NW, 202/730-8800, www.sofitel.com, $220-600). This sophisticated hotel is art deco with a modern flair. The rooms are beautifully appointed and feature soft lighting and fluffy linens. There is also a comfortable lounge area for guests and an on-site restaurant. The location is perfect for touring the city since it is near the National Mall, Downtown attractions, and the Metrorail. Ask for a room facing south or east (or simply ask to face the White House).

For a five-star stay in Georgetown, make a reservation at the **Four Seasons Washington, DC** (2800 Pennsylvania Ave., 202/342-0444, www.fourseasons.com, $575-2,025). This high-end hotel is known for its spacious rooms and suites. It is also the only five-star, five-diamond luxury hotel in the city. The Four Seasons is a contemporary hotel with a warm and welcoming ambience. The professional staff is truly exceptional and tends to every guest personally. There is a fitness center, a pool, steam rooms, a sauna, and an aerobics studio on-site. Babysitting is also available. This is a very busy hotel when special events are going on in the city, yet even when the hotel is full, it never feels crowded and the service is spot on. The hotel is in a romantic Georgetown neighborhood, yet is convenient to the National Mall and all the city attractions.

A trendy boutique hotel in the Dupont Circle neighborhood is the 137-room **Hotel Rouge** (1315 16th St. NW, 202/232-8000, www.rougehotel.com, $159-599). This popular Kimpton hotel has a modern design, a fitness room, good amenities, and is pet friendly. Red is their signature color, which seems to be worked in everywhere. Their rooms are well outfitted with stocked minibars, high-speed Internet, 37-inch plasma televisions, Aveda bath products, and voice mail. Ten rooms feature kitchenettes and entertainment areas. There is a great bar on-site, and approximately 75 restaurants are within walking distance. They also have a state-of-the-art fitness center. The staff is exceptional. Pets are welcome.

The most imaginative hotel in the city is **The Mansion on O Street** (2020 O St. NW, 202/496-2000, www.omansion.com, $350-25,000), just southwest of Dupont Circle. This one-of-a-kind boutique hotel consists of four

1892 townhomes linked to form a luxury inn complex containing guest rooms, a ballroom, multiple dining rooms, conference rooms, and many surprises. Each accommodation has its specialty: It could be a rainforest shower, pirate's tub, tanning room, a shower made from an English telephone booth, extensive gardens with fountains and a barbecue, an aquarium, or a bathroom that's so incredible that legendary jazz musician Miles Davis decided to have dinner in it. That's just the tip of the iceberg at this ultracreative mansion. There's a museum on-site that is equally creative and changes displays daily; there are also 32 secret doors to explore, and hidden passageways. Everything in the mansion is for sale, so if you really like something, for a price, it can be yours. Many famous people have stayed in this eclectic world of fantasy, including Kim Basinger, Hillary Clinton, and Sylvester Stallone. Reservations are only taken online.

Information and Services

VISITORS INFORMATION

Additional information on Washington DC can be found at www.washington.org and www.visitingdc.com or by stopping by the **Washington Welcome Center** (1005 E St. NW, 202/347-6609, Mon.-Sat. 8am-5pm).

MEDIA

The most widely circulated daily newspaper in Washington DC is the *Washington Post* (www.washingtonpost.com), featuring world and local news and with an emphasis on national politics. The *Washington Times* (www.washingtontimes.com) is another daily newspaper that has a wide following.

Weekly and specialty newspapers include the *Washington City Paper* (www.washingtoncitypaper.com), an alternative weekly newspaper, and the *Washington Informer* (www.washingtoninformer.com), a weekly newspaper serving the DC area's African American population.

EMERGENCY SERVICES

In the event of an emergency, call 911.

The **Metropolitan Police Department of the District of Columbia** (202/727-9099, anonymous tip line 202/727-9099, www.mpdc.dc.gov) is the municipal law-enforcement agency in Washington DC. It is one of the 10 largest police forces in the country.

There are no fewer than 10 hospitals in the city. Some of the ones ranked highest nationally include **MedStar Washington Hospital Center** (110 Irving St. NW, 202/877-7000, www.whcenter.org), **MedStar Georgetown University Hospital** (3800 Reservoir Rd. NW, 202/444-2000, www.medstargeorgetown.org), and **George Washington University Hospital** (900 23rd St. NW, 202/715-4000, www.gwhospital.com).

Getting There

AIR

Three major airports serve Washington DC. **Ronald Reagan Washington National Airport (DCA)** (703/417-8000, www.metwashairports.com), just outside the city in Arlington, Virginia, is serviced by the Blue and Yellow Lines of the Metrorail. Taxi service is available at the arrivals curb outside the baggage claim area of each terminal. Rental cars are also available on the first floor in parking garage A. A shuttle operates outside each baggage claim area to the rental car counter. It is a 15-minute drive to downtown Washington DC from the airport.

Washington Dulles International Airport (IAD) (703/572-2700, www.metwashairports.com), 27 miles west of the city in Dulles, Virginia, is a 35-minute drive from downtown Washington DC. Bus service between Dulles Airport and the Metrorail at the Wiehle Avenue Station in Reston (Silver Line) is available through **Washington Flyer** (888/927-4359, www.washfly.com/coach.html, $10 one-way, $18 round-trip). Tickets can be purchased at the ticket counter in the main terminal at arrivals door #4 or at the Metrorail station at Wiehle Avenue. Buses depart approximately every 30 minutes. Passengers going from the Wiehle Avenue Metrorail station should follow signs for the Washington Flyer bus stop. Tickets can be purchased from the bus driver. **Metrobus** (202/637-7000, www.wmata.com) operates an express bus (Route 5A) between Dulles Airport and the L'Enfant Plaza Metrorail station in Washington DC. Passengers can board the bus at the airport at the Ground Transportation Curb (on the Arrivals level) at curb location 2E. An extension of Metrorail's Silver Line is planned and will provide a one-seat ride to downtown Washington DC from Dulles Airport in 2018.

Baltimore/Washington International Thurgood Marshall Airport (BWI) (410/859-7040, www.bwiairport.com), 32 miles from Washington DC near Baltimore, Maryland, is approximately 50 minutes by car to Washington DC. It is serviced on weekdays by MARC commuter trains at the BWI Marshall rail station. Free shuttles are available from the station to the airport terminal. Shuttle stops can be found on the lower level terminal road. Metrobus service is available between BWI and the Greenbelt Metrorail station (Green Line) on the **BWI Express Metro.** Bus service is available

seven days a week with buses running every 40 minutes.

Washington Dulles Transportation (703/729-4977, www.sedan4dulles.com) provides chauffeur service for passengers at all three airports. Shuttle service is also available from all three airports by **Super Shuttle** (800/258-3826, www.supershuttle.com).

CAR

Arriving in Washington DC by car is fairly common. Several major highways lead into the city such as I-395 from the south in Virginia, I-66 from the southwest in Virginia, and I-295 from the northeast in Maryland. U.S. 50 is the only primary road that runs through the city (on the eastern side) and connects Virginia and Maryland. Most hotels have some provision for parking although it may come at a significant cost. There is also public parking on some streets and many public garages throughout the city.

TRAIN

Amtrak (800/872-7245, www.amtrak.com) provides service to Washington DC through beautiful **Union Station** (40 Massachusetts Ave., www.unionstationdc.com) on Capitol Hill. Amtrak connects with the **Maryland Area Rail Commuter (MARC)** system (410/539-5000, http://mta.maryland.gov), a service that runs Monday-Friday and connects Union Station with the Baltimore area, southern Maryland, and northeastern West Virginia; and with **Virginia Railway Express** (703/684-1001, www.vre.org), a service that runs weekdays only between Fredericksburg, Virginia, and Union Station and Manassas, Virginia, and Union Station.

BUS

The **Greyhound** (1005 1st St. NE, www.greyhound.com) bus station in Washington DC is about a 10-minute walk (north) from Union Station; however, it is a good idea to take a taxi to and from the bus station, as the area can be a little rough, especially at night.

Getting Around

METRORAIL

Washington DC and the surrounding area has a clean, reliable, and generally safe subway system called the **Metrorail** (202/637-7000, www.wmata.com) that is run by the **Washington Metropolitan Area Transit Authority (WMATA).** The Metrorail system is commonly known as "The Metro" and provides service to more than 700,000 customers a day. The system is number two in the country in terms of ticket sales and serves more than 80 stations throughout DC, Virginia, and Maryland. Visit the WMATA website for current delays and alerts.

There are six color-coded rail lines: Red, Orange, Blue, Yellow, Green, and Silver. The system layout is easy to understand (most stations are named for the neighborhood they serve) and getting from one station to another normally requires no more than a single transfer. Metrorail stations are marked with large "M" signs at the entrance that have colored stripes around them to show which line they serve. A complete list of fares and a map of each train line can be found on the website (fares range $3.15-6.90 during peak hours). Metrorail opens at 5am on weekdays and 7am on weekends. It closes at midnight every day. Bicycles are permitted during non-peak hours. It is important to note that doors on each train do not operate like an elevator door and will not reopen if you stick your arm or hand in them as they close. Never stand in the way of a closing door.

Permanent, rechargeable farecards called **SmarTrip** cards can be purchased online and at Metrorail stations. Riders can recharge their cards online. SmarTrip holders receive a discount on Metrorail and Metrobus service (the cards can be used for both).

METROBUS

WMATA also runs **Metrobus** (202/637-7000, www.wmata.com, $1.75-4) service from Metrorail stops and throughout the city. They operate 325 routes to 11,500 bus stops in Washington DC, Virginia, and Maryland. For a complete listing, visit the website. Bicycle racks are provided on Metrobuses and can accommodate two bikes. Permanent, rechargeable farecards called **SmarTrip** cards can be purchased online and at Metrorail stations. Riders can recharge their cards online. Metrobus accepts SmarTrip or cash.

The **DC Circulator** (202/567-3040, www.dccirculator.com, hours vary by route, $1) is another local bus service with six bus routes to key areas in the city. Some of the areas it serves include Georgetown, Dupont Circle, Rosslyn (in Arlington, Virginia), Union Station, the Navy Yard Metrorail stop, Adams Morgan, and the Potomac Avenue Metrorail stop. SmarTrip cards are accepted.

TAXIS AND PRIVATE TRANSPORT

Some neighborhoods in the city, such as Georgetown and Adams Morgan, are not serviced by Metrorail, so traveling by taxi can be an easy way to reach these areas and is also a good alternative for direct transport between two locations. Fares are charged on a meter on a distance-traveled basis. There are many taxi services throughout the city. Sixteen companies can be booked through **DC Taxi Online** (www.dctaxionline.com). Standard taxi fares in Washington DC are $3.25 for the first eighth of a mile, with each additional eighth of a mile costing $0.27. Hourly wait rates are $25.

Uber (www.uber.com) quickly gained popularity throughout Washington DC. The rideshare service provides on-demand taxi, "black car," and SUV service and can be hailed over the Internet. Charges for the services are made directly to your credit card and a 20 percent driver tip is included. This is a fast, easy way to travel around the city and doesn't require the added time of paying your driver. Rates are quoted on the website.

The Capital Region

Bordering Washington DC to the north, Montgomery County is trendy and urban, with cultural and historical sights and attractions. To the east of DC is Prince George's County, more suburban and rich in natural beauty.

Montgomery County has easy access to Washington DC via road and the Metrorail service. It is one of the most affluent counties in the country, with trendy city centers and a variety of restaurants, shopping areas, and hotels.

Prince George's County is a hub for federal government agencies. It includes the National Harbor, an area along the Potomac River that has become a hot spot for tourism, dining, and nightlife. It's also home to the stadium for the Washington Redskins and one of the best fossil parks in the eastern United States.

PLANNING YOUR TIME

Cities in Maryland's Capital Region are relatively close together, so it is advantageous to select the sights you are most interested in seeing to determine where and how long you will stay. Many sites can be visited as a half- or full-day trip when staying in Washington DC, or the Capital Region can be your home base while exploring DC. Accommodations in Montgomery and Prince George's Counties are generally less expensive than those in DC, yet are still convenient to the major downtown sites.

Commercial air service to Maryland's Capital Region is provided at **Ronald Reagan Washington National Airport (DCA)** (703/417-8000, www.mwaa.com) in Arlington, Virginia; **Washington Dulles International Airport (IAD)** (703/572-2700, www.mwaa.com) in Dulles, Virginia; and **Baltimore Washington International Thurgood Marshall Airport (BWI)** (410/859-7111, www.bwiairport.com) near Baltimore, Maryland.

Train service is available on **Amtrak** (www.amtrak.com) to Rockville in Montgomery County and to Landover in Prince George's County.

The **Washington Metropolitan Area Transit Authority (WMATA)** (www.wmata.com) provides **Metrorail** and **Metrobus** service to both counties. Montgomery County is serviced by Metrorail's Red Line, while Prince

---

Previous: rural area near Sugarloaf Mountain; Montpelier Mansion. **Above:** National Harbor.

Look for ★ to find recommended sights, activities, dining, and lodging.

Highlights

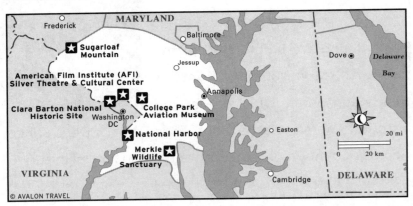
© AVALON TRAVEL

★ **Clara Barton National Historic Site:** This beautiful home was the residence of the pioneering woman who founded the American Red Cross (page 220).

★ **American Film Institute (AFI) Silver Theatre & Cultural Center:** This state-of-the-art film center grew out of the restored art deco Silver Theatre, built in 1938 (page 231).

★ **Sugarloaf Mountain:** This popular recreation area offers hiking, picnicking, and rock climbing (page 235).

★ **National Harbor:** Built right on the Potomac River, this harbor hosts a range of restaurants, shops, and entertainment options for both adults and kids (page 236).

★ **Merkle Wildlife Sanctuary:** This wildlife sanctuary is the wintering ground for thousands of Canada geese (page 239).

★ **College Park Aviation Museum:** This great little museum set in a historic airport focuses on the earliest days of mechanical flight (page 244).

The Capital Region

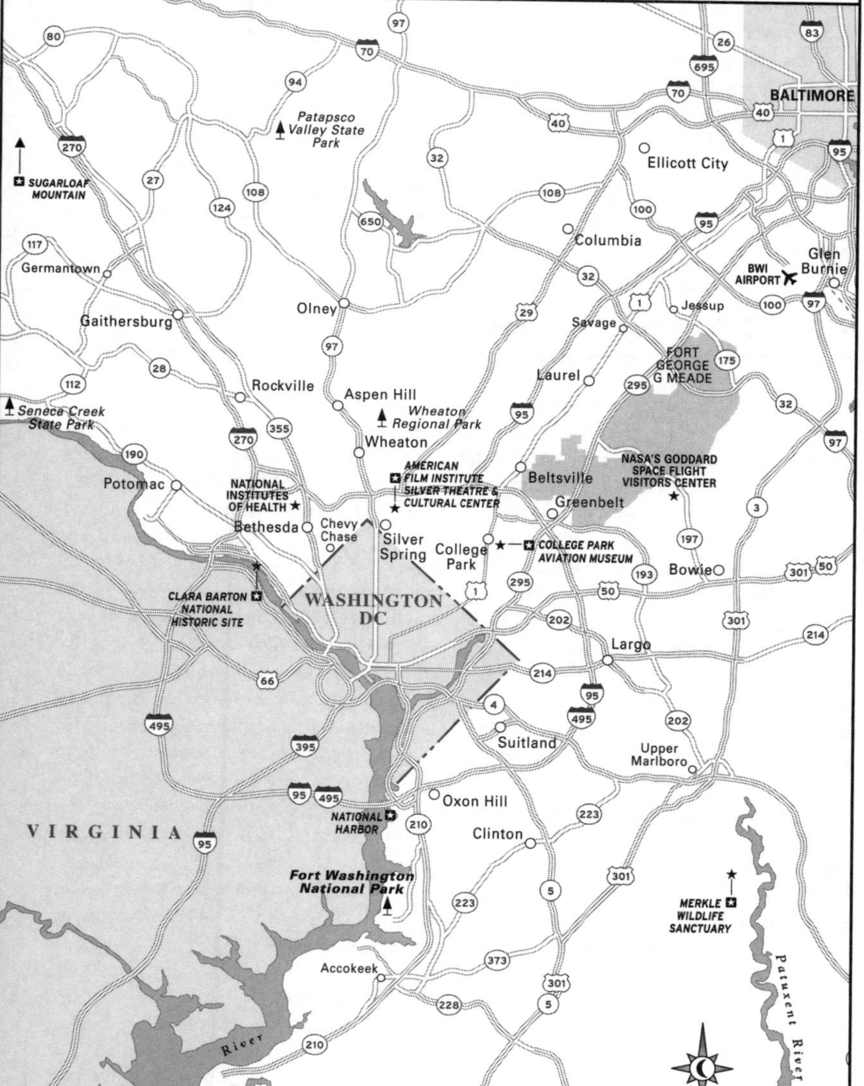

BALTIMORE

Ellicott City

Columbia

BWI AIRPORT

Glen Burnie

Germantown

Jessup

Savage

FORT GEORGE G MEADE

Gaithersburg

Olney

Laurel

Rockville

Aspen Hill

Wheaton Regional Park

Wheaton

Beltsville

NASA'S GODDARD SPACE FLIGHT VISITORS CENTER

Potomac

Seneca Creek State Park

NATIONAL INSTITUTES OF HEALTH ★

AMERICAN FILM INSTITUTE SILVER THEATRE & CULTURAL CENTER ★

Greenbelt

Bethesda

Chevy Chase

Silver Spring

College Park

COLLEGE PARK AVIATION MUSEUM ★

Bowie

CLARA BARTON NATIONAL HISTORIC SITE

WASHINGTON DC

Largo

SUGARLOAF MOUNTAIN

Patapsco Valley State Park

VIRGINIA

Suitland

Upper Marlboro

NATIONAL HARBOR

Oxon Hill

Clinton

Fort Washington National Park

MERKLE ★ WILDLIFE SANCTUARY

Accokeek

Potomac River

Patuxent River

MARYLAND

0   5 mi

0   5 km

George's County is serviced by the Green, Blue, and Orange Lines.

Montgomery County has a public bus transit system called **Ride On** (www.montgomerycountymd.gov/dot-transit/) and Prince George's County has a public bus system called **TheBus** (www.princegeorgescountymd.gov).

The Maryland Transit Administration's **Maryland Area Rail Commuter (MARC)** (http://mta.maryland.gov) rail runs train service to both Montgomery County and Prince George's County.

Travel by car around the Capital Region is easy if you are prepared to deal with traffic. I-270 is a primary northwest-southeast roadway that connects to the Capital Beltway (I-495). Montgomery County, in particular, is known for its use of automated speed cameras and red-light cameras, especially on secondary roads, so keep this in mind when traveling by car. Rush hour throughout the Capital Region is spread out over many hours. For the best chance of missing traffic during the week, travel between the hours of 10am and 2pm.

Montgomery County

Montgomery County is named after Revolutionary War general Richard Montgomery and was the first county in Maryland not named after royalty. As a densely populated metropolitan area, the boundaries between cities and towns in Montgomery County are blurred at best. There are a few clearly defined city centers, such as in Bethesda and Rockville, but in many other parts of the county one neighborhood runs into the next.

Just north of Washington DC is the bustling business hub of Silver Spring. Its once-tired downtown area recently realized a grand rebirth and now offers a vibrant city center for entertainment and shopping.

The I-270 Technology Corridor runs through Rockville, Bethesda, and Gaithersburg and is home to many biotechnology and software companies. Northwest of Gaithersburg is the fast-growing suburb of Germantown, which encompasses many neighborhoods and suburban communities.

In the farther western reaches of the county, along the Potomac River, rural routes are still detectable, and towns are loosely connected by private farmland.

GETTING THERE AND AROUND

Montgomery County is serviced by several public transportation systems. **Amtrak** (307 S. Stonestreet Ave., 800/872-7245, www.amtrak.com) provides train service to Rockville, and the **Maryland Transit Administration** MARC train (410/539-5000, http://mta.maryland.gov) has three Montgomery County stations on the Brunswick Line in Gaithersburg, Rockville, and Silver Spring. **Metrorail** and **Metrobus** service, operated by the **Washington Metropolitan Area Transit Authority (WMATA)** (202/637-7000, www.wmata.com), is available throughout much of the county. Metrorail's Red Line enters the county at Friendship Heights and continues through Bethesda past Rockville to Shady Grove. The Red Line also serves Silver Spring through Wheaton to Glenmont. The Amtrak station is also housed at the Rockville Metro station.

The county has a public bus transit system called **Ride On** (240/777-0311, www.montgomerycountymd.gov, $1.75).

BETHESDA

Bethesda is a busy metropolitan area about seven miles north of Washington DC. With a local population of more than 60,000, it offers a bustling downtown shopping and business district and dozens of restaurant choices. It is also home to the **National Institutes of Health (NIH)** (www.nih.gov) headquarters.

The Bethesda Metrorail station (in the

A Golf-Crazy County

Montgomery County is known for its golf. As host to the annual **Quicken Loans National** (www.tigerwoodsfoundation.org), held at the Congressional Country Club in Bethesda in June, the area draws national attention from the golfing community.

Visitors can enjoy many public golf courses in Montgomery County, including the following:

- **Blue Mash Golf Course** (5821 Olney-Laytonsville Rd., Laytonsville, 301/670-1966)—18 holes/driving range
- **Falls Road** (10800 Falls Rd., Potomac, 301/299-5156)—18 holes/driving range
- **Hampshire Greens** (616 Firestone Dr., Silver Spring, 301/476-7999)—18 holes
- **Laytonsville Golf Course** (7130 Dorsey Rd., Gaithersburg, 301/948-5288)—18 holes
- **Little Bennett Golf Course** (25900 Prescott Rd., Clarksburg, 301/253-1515)—18 holes
- **Needwood Golf Course** (6724 Needwood Rd., Derwood, 301/948-1075)—18 holes
- **Northwest Golf Course** (15711 Layhill Rd., Silver Spring, 301/598-6100)—27 holes
- **Poolesville Golf Course** (16601 W. Willard Rd., Poolesville, 301/428-8143)—18 holes
- **Rattlewood Golf Course** (13501 Penn Shop Rd., Mt. Airy, 301/607-9000)—18 holes/driving range
- **Sligo Creek Golf Course** (9701 Sligo Creek Pkwy., Silver Spring, 301/585-6006)—9 holes

For additional information on golfing in Montgomery County, visit www.mcggolf.com.

center of the downtown area) moves more than 15,000 passengers on a normal weekday.

Sights
RATNER MUSEUM

The **Dennis & Phillip Ratner Museum** (10001 Old Georgetown Rd., 301/897-1518, www.ratnermuseum.org, Sun. 10am-4:30pm, Mon.-Thurs. noon-4pm, closed Aug., free) is a lovely and unique art museum with both permanent and traveling exhibits. The upper level of the museum features a permanent collection of artwork by contemporary artist Phillip Ratner that depicts stories from the Bible through sculpture, drawings, paintings, and other graphics. Visitors can literally take a walk through the Bible by looking at the displays. The lower level, where exhibits change monthly, features work from both established and upcoming local artists. Mediums include painting, photography, glass, wood, and silk panels. Other traveling exhibits are also featured. A children's art and literature museum is housed in another building called the Resource Center. Additional activities held at the museum complex include lectures, concerts, and readings. Phillip Ratner is perhaps best known for being the artist of five sculptures at the Statue of Liberty and 40 sculptures at Ellis Island. Dennis Ratner is Phillip's second cousin and owner of the nation's largest privately owned salon chain, the Hair Cuttery. The two established the museum together.

BE WITH ME CHILDREN'S PLAYSEUM

The **Be With Me Children's Playseum** (7000 Wisconsin Ave., 301/807-8028, www.playseum.com, Mon.-Fri. 10am-5pm, Sat. 9am-7pm, $9) is a great play space for young kids offering many rooms with individual themes such as a grocery store, kitchen, and princess dress-up, all of which kids can enjoy at their leisure. There is also an arts and crafts room (some projects cost extra) and an open play area with a stage and musical instruments. This is a fun and entertaining place to spend an afternoon.

MCCRILLIS GARDENS

A little-known treasure in a quiet residential neighborhood near downtown Bethesda is **McCrillis Gardens** (6910 Greentree Rd., 301/962-1455, daily 10am-sunset, free). This lovely garden and the home that sits on the grounds were donated to the Maryland National Capital Park and Planning Commission in 1978 by its former owners. The gardens are considered a premier shade garden and offer beautiful ornamental trees, shrubs (including many azalea bushes), annuals, ground covers, perennials, and other flowers. There is a pavilion and benches on the grounds. There is also no parking on the grounds, but some street parking is available during the week. On weekends (and after 4pm on weekdays), parking is available across the street at the Woods Academy.

AUDUBON NATURALIST SOCIETY

The **Audubon Naturalist Society's Woodend Sanctuary** (8940 Jones Mill Rd., Chevy Chase, 301/652-9188, www.audubonnaturalist.org, trails open daily dawn to dusk, free) in nearby Chevy Chase is the headquarters for the Audubon Naturalist Society. The sanctuary is one of the few grand old estates remaining in the area and sits on 40 acres. The Woodend Mansion, which was designed in the 1920s and bequeathed to the Audubon Naturalist Society in 1968, is a beautiful example of Georgian revival architecture. Visitors can enjoy self-guided nature trails, a wildflower meadow, and a pond on the grounds. No pets are allowed in the sanctuary. Free beginner bird walks are offered at 8am on Saturday mornings September-November and March-June. They are offered monthly in December-February. A bookshop sells nature and birding books and gifts.

★ CLARA BARTON NATIONAL HISTORIC SITE

Just southwest of Bethesda in Glen Echo is the **Clara Barton National Historic Site** (5801 Oxford Rd., Glen Echo, 301/320-1410, www.nps.gov/clba, open daily with guided home tours on the hour between 10am and 4pm, free). Clara Barton was a pioneer among American women who is credited with founding the American Red Cross. The historical site was established at the home where Barton spent the last 15 years of her life (1897-1912). This National Park

Audubon Naturalist Society's Woodend Sanctuary

Clara Barton: Angel of the Battlefield

Clara Barton National Historic Site

Clara Barton was born on Christmas Day in 1821 in Massachusetts. She is known as a pioneer for her work as a teacher, patent clerk, nurse, and humanitarian, all during a time when very few women held jobs outside the home.

Barton was dedicated to helping others and always held a passion for nursing. At a young age she nursed her injured dog back to health when he hurt his leg, and later saved her brother's life by nursing him back to health after he fell off their family's barn roof.

Barton first became a schoolteacher and later opened a free school in New Jersey. Although attendance at her school rapidly grew to more than 600 students, the school's board hired a man to head the operation instead of Barton. After this insult, Barton moved to Washington DC and became a clerk at the U.S. Patent Office. She was the first woman to receive a salary equal to a man in a substantial clerkship position in the federal government.

During the Civil War, Barton was put in charge of the hospitals at the front of the Army of the James (a Union army that included units from Virginia and North Carolina). She soon became known as the "Angel of the Battlefield."

After the war, Barton lead the Office of the Missing Soldiers in Washington DC and gained wide recognition for giving lectures across the country on her experiences during the war. During this time, she began a long association with the women's suffrage movement and also became an activist for African American civil rights.

During a trip to Geneva, Switzerland, Barton became acquainted with the Red Cross and provided the society assistance during the Franco-Prussian War. Barton also engaged in additional humanitarian work throughout Europe for a couple of years. Upon returning to the United States, Barton started a movement for recognition by the U.S. government of the International Committee of the Red Cross. After much effort, Barton succeeded by arguing that the American Red Cross could assist with crisis situations other than just war. She became the president of the American branch of the Red Cross and held the first branch meeting in her home in Washington DC in 1881.

Clara Barton died at her home in Maryland on April 12, 1912. She was buried in Massachusetts.

Service site is a tribute to her accomplishments and one of the first National Historic Sites dedicated to a woman. The home also shares the early history of the American Red Cross, and was the first headquarters for the organization. The restored home can be visited by guided tour only and offers visitors the chance to see 11 of the original 30 rooms including Barton's bedroom, the parlors, and the Red Cross offices. Tours last approximately one hour. The site is seven miles northwest of Washington DC sitting on a bluff looking over the Potomac River.

At the time of publication, this site was closed to the public for a rehabilitation project. It is expected to reopen in late 2016.

Entertainment and Events

The **Strathmore** (5301 Tuckerman Ln., North Bethesda, 301/581-5100, www.strathmore.org) is a beautiful concert venue in North Bethesda. The hall itself is a work of art, with contemporary styling, light woodwork, wonderful acoustics, and comfortable seats. World-class performers and international artists make up a full schedule of offerings including folk, rock, blues, pop, R&B, jazz, and classical music. Friendly and professional staff and volunteers make the experience at the Strathmore even better, and parking is free.

The **Imagination Stage** (4908 Auburn Ave., 301/961-6060, www.imaginationstage.org) is a theater arts center for young people in downtown Bethesda and known as the "largest multidisciplinary theater arts organization for young people" in the mid-Atlantic. its shows are professionally prepared, entertaining, and offer a nice break for kids from museums and playgrounds. The theater is open year-round. Pay attention to the target age for each performance.

Live stand-up comedy can be found at the **Laugh Riot at the Hyatt** (7400 Wisconsin Ave., http://standupcomedytogo.com, Sat. 8pm-10pm, $10) on Saturday nights. The shows are R rated, and seating is on a first-come first-served basis. A full bar service is available during the show. Admission is cash only.

The **Round House Theatre** (4545 East-West Hwy., 240/644-1100, www.roundhousetheatre.org) is a professional theater company that produces just under 200 performances a year.

The annual **Bethesda Literary Festival** (www.bethesda.org, free) is held for three days in April throughout downtown Bethesda. It hosts many local and national authors, poets, and journalists during more than 20 events. Authors discuss the craft and their work with other writers and attendees. Writing contests are also held during this free event.

A great weekend-long event held annually in mid-May is the **Bethesda Fine Arts Festival** (www.bethesda.org, free). Visitors can enjoy artwork created by more than 125 national artists, entertainment, and local food in the Woodmont Triangle neighborhood, along Norfolk, Auburn, and Del Ray Avenues.

Shopping

Downtown Bethesda is home to almost 700 retail stores and businesses. Most any shopping need or desire can be met in this destination. Fashion boutiques, art galleries, home furnishings stores, and salons are just a few examples of the types of retailers available. For a searchable list of stores visit www.bethesda.org/shopping-guide.

Sports and Recreation

A great place to bring the little ones (including the four-footed kind) is **Cabin John Regional Park** (7400 Tuckerman Ln., 301/765-8702, daily sunrise to sunset, free). This great park has just about everything, including playgrounds, trails, a little train (spring-fall), picnic tables, an amphitheater, and a dog park. The dog park is split into two areas: one for dogs 20 pounds and over and one for dogs less than 20 pounds. The park is very popular but also has plenty of room.

Just west of Bethesda on the Potomac

Billy Goat Trail

Hikers of all abilities can enjoy the popular Billy Goat Trail, running between the C&O Canal and the Potomac River in Montgomery County near Great Falls. The trail is 4.7 miles long and has three sections.

The northern section (Section A) is 1.7 miles long and the most heavily traveled. It runs through rocky terrain on Bear Island. There is a steep climb along a cliff face bordering the Potomac River in Mather Gorge that requires scrambling in parts. Pets are not allowed on Bear Island. Section A is accessible from the **Great Falls Tavern Visitor Center** (11710 MacArthur Blvd., Potomac, 301/767-3714).

Section B is less strenuous and has only one short segment where scrambling is required. It is 1.4 miles long. Section C is the easiest, with no scrambling. It is 1.6 miles long. Sections B and C can be accessed from **Carderock Recreation Area.** Leashed dogs are allowed on these two sections.

The three sections of the trail are not continuous but are connected by the C&O Canal Towpath. The Billy Goat Trail is marked with light blue blazes. Access to the trail is free, although a small parking fee is charged by the visitors center. There is no fee at Carderock.

River is **Carderock Recreation Area** (off Clara Barton Pkwy., Carderock, daily dawn to dusk, free), a 100-acre park that is part of the **Chesapeake & Ohio Canal National Historical Park** and one of the premier rock-climbing destinations in the Washington DC area with more than 100 established climbing routes and plentiful bouldering. Climbers can enjoy friction slabs, cracks, and overhangs.

Most routes are best with a toprope. Climbs range 30-50 feet and have seen such notable climbers as Chris Sharma.

Carderock also offers hiking, biking, and picnicking. A section of the Billy Goat Trail passes through the park, and the C&O Canal Towpath can be accessed via a short wooded trail across the parking lot from the restrooms in the northernmost parking lot. The park is

Carderock Recreation Area

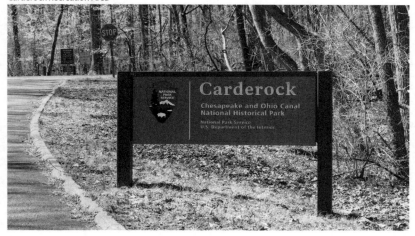

near the Carderock Division of the Naval Surface Warfare Center. Access to the park is free.

Food

There is no shortage of wonderful restaurant choices in Bethesda. In fact, this area is known for its great variety of international cuisine. A stroll through the eight-block "restaurant row" between Rockville Pike/Wisconsin Avenue and Old Georgetown Road will give you a taste of what is available. If you're in the mood for something different, you won't be disappointed.

AMERICAN

Upscale American cuisine that includes burgers, seafood, and steak can be found at **Woodmont Grill** (7715 Woodmont Ave., 301/656-9755, www.hillstone.com/woodmontgrill, Mon.-Sat. 11:30am-10pm, Sun. 11:30am-9pm, $14-52). Their prices may seem high for what sounds like casual fare ($18 for a cheeseburger, $33 for barbecue ribs, etc.) but the quality of the food is excellent, the atmosphere is relaxing, and their bread is made fresh in house. This is a great choice for business, family, and romantic occasions. There is live jazz nightly and free parking on-site. Be sure to make a reservation; the restaurant is very popular.

ASIAN

A good consistent "go-to" restaurant for sushi is **Raku Asian Dining, Sushi and Sake** (7240 Woodmont Ave., 301/718-8680, www.rakuasiandining.com, lunch Mon.-Fri. 11:30am-2:30pm, Sat.-Sun. noon-3pm, dinner Sun.-Thurs. 5pm-10pm, Fri.-Sat. 5pm-10:30pm, $8-40). This is a favorite lunch restaurant among the local business crowd, and that is no accident. They serve great sashimi, sushi, and rolls for all tastes, along with scrumptious soup and bento boxes. They offer a modern, Asian decor and friendly service. The food is freshly prepared and nicely presented. They have been in business

for more than a dozen years have quite a following.

ITALIAN

For good, reasonably priced Italian food, dine at **Olazzo** (7921 Norfolk Ave., 301/654-9496, www.olazzo.com, Mon.-Thurs. 11:30am-10pm, Fri. 11:30am-11pm, Sat. 11:30-11pm, Sun. 11:30-10pm, $9-24). This is a very popular restaurant that doesn't take reservations, so plan on a wait during prime time. The food is delicious and consistent, with warm, fresh bread, wonderful martinis, and scrumptious entrées. The rose sauce is delectable. The atmosphere is cozy and rustic with dim lighting and candles on the tables. This is a good value for the quality of the food.

MEDITERRANEAN

Seafood lovers will go wild for the Mediterranean dishes at the family-owned and operated ★ **Chef Tony's** (4926 St. Elmo Ave., 301/654-3737, www.cheftonysbethesda.com, lunch Wed.-Fri. 11:30am-2:30pm, dinner Mon.-Sat. 5pm-10pm, Sun. 11am-8pm, $5-46). The ambience is simple and the food is simply excellent. Sample menu items include pan-roasted PEI mussels, Turkish bronzino, lobster pasta, and grilled surf and turf. Save room for dessert—they have a sizable selection of delicious sweets, including cheesecake, tiramisu, and caramelized sweet potato pie. They also offer a seven-course tasting menu for $65 (advance reservations only). Chef Tony partners with local farmers whenever possible.

PERSIAN

Great Persian food is served at **Kabob Bazaar** (7710 Wisconsin Ave., 301/652-5814, www.kabobbazaar.com, lunch and dinner, $9-19). This authentic restaurant has delicious, flavorful soup, kabobs (prepared on an open-fire grill), and platters, all served with a smile. The rice is perfectly light and fluffy, and the atmosphere is warm with soft, instrumental, traditional Iranian music playing in the background and soft lighting. This restaurant is suited for both business and a romantic evening.

Accommodations
$100-200

The **Golden Tulip Bethesda Court Hotel** (7740 Wisconsin Ave., 301/656-2100, www.bethesdacourtwashdc.com, $159-309) is a European-style hotel in a nice Bethesda neighborhood just eight miles from Washington DC. It offers 74 guest rooms, an English garden, free wireless Internet, a fitness room, and complimentary continental breakfast. The rooms are clean, and the staff is very helpful. Guests can walk to downtown Bethesda, and there are more than 100 restaurants within a two-block radius of the hotel. Parking is available on-site.

$200-300

A good extended-stay hotel is the **Bethesda Marriott Suites** (6711 Democracy Blvd., 301/897-5600, www.marriott.com, $239-279), which is 30 minutes from downtown Washington DC by car and popular for business travel. It offers 272 suites on 11 floors and has 10 meeting rooms. The facility includes a fitness center, an indoor heated pool, and a seasonal outdoor pool.

The **Residence Inn Bethesda Downtown** (7335 Wisconsin Ave., 301/718-0200, www.marriott.com, $189-319) is a modern, friendly facility in a central location near the Metrorail and dining. They offer 187 suites on 13 floors with well-equipped kitchens, wireless Internet, and free breakfast. A seasonal, outdoor, rooftop pool and year-round fitness center are also available to guests. There is a $25 valet parking fee (no self-parking) and a $175 fee for pets.

A short walk from the Bethesda Metro Station (7450 Wisconsin Ave.) is the **Hilton Garden Inn Washington DC/Bethesda** (7301 Waverly St., 301/654-8111, www.hiltongardeninn3.hilton.com, $159-299). They offer 216 large, comfortable rooms with high-speed Internet and good beds. A fitness center and pool are on-site. Self-parking is $16.50 (no valet).

Information and Services

For additional information on Bethesda, visit www.bethesda.org.

Getting Around

There is garage parking in many parts of Bethesda, and it is mostly free on the weekends. Taxi service is also readily available on most streets.

ROCKVILLE

Rockville is the third-largest city in Maryland and encompasses a little more than 13 square miles in central Montgomery County. It is approximately 12 miles north of Washington DC and has always had close connections to the nation's capital. In 1873, the first public transportation between Rockville and Washington was established with the arrival of the Baltimore & Ohio Railroad. Not too long after, trolley service began between Georgetown and Rockville, which continued until the automobile became the preferred mode of transportation.

During the Cold War, Rockville was considered a safe place for evacuation during a nuclear attack, and as such, many bomb shelters were built and I-270 was designated as an emergency landing runway for aircraft. Two Nike missile sites were also located in Rockville until the mid-1970s. The Nuclear Regulatory Commission headquarters is just south of Rockville's corporate limits.

Rockville's downtown area has had ups and downs since the 1960s but in recent years has enjoyed a rebirth with boutique stores, trendy restaurants, and upscale condominiums. It was even featured in REM's popular song released in 1984 titled "(Don't Go Back To) Rockville," written by Mike Mills.

Sights
BEALL-DAWSON HISTORIC HOUSE

The **Beall-Dawson Historic House** (103 W. Montgomery Ave., 301/762-1492, www.montgomeryhistory.org, Wed.-Sun. noon-4pm, $5) was built in 1815 for the county's clerk of the court, Upton Beall. The large, federal-style brick house is impressive both inside and out and remained a private home until the 1960s. At that time, it was purchased by the city as the headquarters for the Montgomery County Historical Society. The home is now a furnished museum that depicts life in the early 19th century, reflecting the lifestyle of both the upper-class homeowners and the enslaved African Americans who lived there with them.

Rotating gallery exhibits are displayed in two rooms and feature collections owned by the historical society. Tours of the home also include a tour of the **Stonestreet Museum of 19th Century Medicine,** a historic one-room doctor's office located on the property. Tours last between 45 minutes and an hour.

GLENVIEW MANSION

Glenview Mansion (603 Edmonston Dr., 240/314-8660, www.rockvillemd.gov, Mon.-Fri. 8:30am-5pm, free) is a beautiful 19th-century home that sits on the grounds of the 153-acre Rockville Civic Center Park. Visitors can take a guided tour (docents are available during business hours) or walk through the pillared, neoclassical mansion that dates back to 1836 on their own. The home can be rented for private events and also features an art gallery on the second floor that showcases local artwork. The mansion grounds offer walking trails and a formal garden.

F. SCOTT AND ZELDA FITZGERALD GRAVE

It may seem odd that F. Scott Fitzgerald and his wife, Zelda, are buried near a busy thoroughfare in Rockville, but Fitzgerald's father's family was from the area, and he visited here many times. Many members of his family are buried in **St. Mary's Catholic Cemetery** (500 Viers Mill Rd.), the oldest cemetery in Rockville. After attending his father's funeral in 1931, Fitzgerald decided that he and his wife would also be buried there. The quote on their joint tombstone is the final line of *The Great Gatsby,* "So we beat on, boats against the current, borne back ceaselessly into the past."

ASPIN HILL PET CEMETERY

One of the oldest pet cemeteries in the country is the **Aspin Hill Pet Cemetery,** also known as the **Aspen Hill Memorial Park & Animal Sanctuary** (13630 Georgia Ave., 240/252-2555, www.ahmemorialpark.org). The cemetery was established in 1921 and is owned by the Montgomery County Humane

Glenview Mansion

Society. The memorial park is the final resting place of General Grant or Jiggs, whom you might know better as Petey from the *Little Rascals*. This cute dog with the circle around one eye lived from 1928 to 1938. He is kept company by J. Edgar Hoover's dogs, and a few dozen humans who are buried with their pets. The cemetery is also the site of a memorial to medical rats. It was originally named after a kennel in England, which explains why the name is sometimes spelled with an "i" rather than an "e" in Aspen.

Entertainment and Events

The **F. Scott Fitzgerald Theatre** (603 Edmonston Dr., 240/314-8690, www.rockvillemd.gov) is a 446-seat performing arts venue in the Rockville Civic Center Park. Both local and professional touring companies offer stage performances at the theater.

One of the most popular annual events in Rockville is the **Rockville Antique and Classic Car Show** (603 Edmonston Dr., www.rockvillemd.gov) at the end of October. It features more than 500 classic automobiles from 25 local car clubs. Live music, food, and a flea market are also part of the festivities.

Shopping

Rockville Town Center (200 E. Middle Ln.) is a pedestrian-friendly town square with locally owned and operated shops and restaurants. It is also a thriving neighborhood with ice-skating in the winter and year-round programs. Shopping is a favorite pastime in the square, with more than 20 stores to choose from. Clothing boutiques, jewelry stores, home furnishing shops, and specialty athletic stores can all be found here, as well as salon and spa services.

There are also plenty of neighborhood shopping areas in Rockville. **Congressional Plaza** (1626 E. Jefferson St., 301/998-8176, www.congressionalplaza.com) has more than 50 stores and restaurants, including national chains, local boutiques, and a gourmet grocery store. **Falls Grove Village Center**

(14919-14943 Shady Grove Rd., 301/294-9304, www.fallsgrovevillagectr.com) offers retail, restaurants, and a grocery store. The **King Farm Village Center** (403 Redland Blvd., www.kingfarmvillagecenter.com) is a charming local shopping area with retail stores, a grocery store, and restaurants. **Montrose Crossing** (Montrose Rd. and Rockville Pike, 301/341-8433) is home to mostly chain retail stores that specialize in home furnishings, sports, and clothing. The **Traville Village Center** (9700 Traville Gateway Dr., 703/821-0500, www.travillecenter.com), which is accessible from Darnestown Road and Shady Grove Road, is a neighborhood shopping area that offers a mix of boutique stores, a grocery store, and restaurants. **Wintergreen Plaza** (815-895 Rockville Pike, 301/718-4220, www.wintergreenplaza.com), on Rockville Pike, is home to many specialty stores, restaurants, food providers, and services.

Two popular seasonal **farmers markets** are held in Rockville. The first is at the Rockville Town Center on the corner of Route 28 and Monroe Street on Saturday mid-May to mid-November (9am-1pm). The second is on Wednesday at the Rockville Town Square (200 East Middle Lane) in front of Dawson's Market from the beginning of June through October (11am to 2pm).

Sports and Recreation

Rock Creek Regional Park (6700 Needwood Rd., Derwood, 301/948-5053, www.montgomeryparks.org, daily sunrise to sunset, free) is an 1,800-acre park with two lakes (Lake Needwood and Lake Frank), 13 miles of wooded trails, picnic facilities, a playground, archery range, and nature center. Boat rentals are available on-site ($10 per hour and $35 per day for kayaks, canoes, and rowboats, $8 per half hour for pedal boats), and 30-minute pontoon boat tours are offered on weekends for $2.

The **Chesapeake & Ohio Canal National Historical Park** (301/739-4200, www.nps.gov/choh), a 184.5-mile path that stretches from Georgetown in Washington DC to Cumberland, Maryland, runs along the Potomac River near Rockville. A lovely stretch in Montgomery County is located between Rileys Lock (0.2 miles before milepost 23) and Swains Lock (0.4 miles before milepost 17). The terrain is mostly hard-packed dirt or pebble dirt and the scenery is woodlands with river and canal views. The path is ideal for mountain biking, horseback riding, walking, and running.

Wanna feel like Tarzan? Then an afternoon at **Go Ape** (6129 Needwood Lake Dr., 800/971-8271, www.goape.com, $58) is a must. This incredible treetop adventure is a big obstacle course in the trees that is designed for most age groups. Test your climbing skills and fear of heights on ladders, bridges, walkways, ropes, zip lines, and even tunnels. Safety instruction and all equipment are included.

For something a little different, catch a **Free State Roller Derby** (www. freestaterollerderby.com) competition. This flat-track roller derby league is based in Rockville.

Food

When it comes to food, neighborhood gems are scattered throughout Rockville, mostly camouflaged in drab-looking strip malls. International cuisine is some of the best in the region, if you know where to look.

ECLECTIC

Have you ever tried a waffle sandwich? If not, the place to have your first is ★ **Mosaic** (186 Halpine Rd., 301/468-0682, www. mosaiccuisine.com, Sun.-Thurs. 8am-9pm, Fri.-Sat. 8am-10pm, $7-21), near the Twinbrook Metro station. Mosaic is an eclectic internationally inspired restaurant with a passion for waffles. Their food is loosely based on French cuisine with influences from all over the globe. You'll find pesto soup from Italy, Asian duck rolls, French brie—you get the picture. Now back to the waffles. The chefs at Mosaic searched for a good alternative to using bread or tortillas for their sandwiches.

Out of this creative desire to differentiate themselves with a healthy alternative, the waffle sandwich was born. They then spent time perfecting a unique light and crispy waffle recipe suitable for sandwiches, with fewer carbs and more protein. The result is a menu of waffles served all day (breakfast, lunch, and dinner). Breakfast is by far their most popular meal. They offer traditional favorites like eggs Benedict and French toast, but also have an entire menu section devoted to their beloved waffles. With lunch comes salads and a variety of hot and cold sandwiches, available on a choice of breads including their waffles. Dinner is an unusual mix of steak, seafood, pasta, and again, a menu of waffle sandwiches.

GREEK

Scrumptious Greek food can be found at **Cava Mezze** (9713 Traville Gateway Dr., 301/309-9090, www.cavamezze.com, lunch Mon.-Fri. 11:30am-2pm, dinner Mon.-Thurs. 5pm-10pm, Fri.-Sat. 5pm-11pm, Sun. 5pm-9:30pm, $8-15). They serve traditional Greek food in a small-plates format. The restaurant was started by two energetic friends and a chef on a shoestring budget, and their endeavor has blossomed into a five-restaurant success story. The saganaki (flamed cheese) is delightful, as are the scallop risotto, lamb meatballs, and grilled octopus. The atmosphere is energetic yet with a cozy, inviting ambience. Although the service isn't overly friendly, it is prompt. If you're in the mood for very flavorful Greek food, this is a good choice.

LATIN

A plain exterior and average interior atmosphere don't detract from the draw of **La Brasa** (12401 Parklawn Dr., 301/468-8850, www.labrasarockville.com, Mon.-Thurs. 11am-9pm, Fri.-Sat. 11am-10pm, $9-21), which serves great Latin food in an out-of-the-way location. Customers are greeted with warm smiles and fantastic South American dishes. Try the carne asada and the pupusas. They also have great plantains. The dining room is small, but there are a few additional patio seats during the warmer months. This restaurant is family-owned and operated, and they offer takeout service.

MEXICAN

Villa Maya (5532 Norbeck Rd., 301/460-1247, www.villamayarestaurant.com, Mon.-Fri. 11am-midnight, Sat.-Sun. 10am-midnight, $9-18) is a great Mexican restaurant hidden behind a plain exterior in a local strip mall. The food is a step above traditional Mexican, the service is good, and the drinks will make you not care about either. This is a fun place with a large menu of both zesty Mexican fare and mild dishes. The seafood burritos are a favorite, as is the fresh guacamole made at your table. If you're looking for a different appetizer to share, try the yucca con chicharron (tender pork in a savory juice). The place is packed on weekends, so be prepared for a wait. The staff does an excellent job of taking care of the patrons and is particularly accommodating to seniors.

PERUVIAN

★ **La Limena** (765-B Rockville Pike, 301/424-8066, www.lalimenarestaurant. com, Sun.-Thurs. 11am-9pm, Fri.-Sat. 11am-10pm, $8-20) is one of a growing number of Peruvian restaurants that are sprouting up throughout the Washington DC suburbs. As the Peruvian culture spreads, wonderful, soul-soothing Peruvian food is making its way into many people's "go-to" restaurant rotation. At first glance, La Limena appears to be a hole-in-the-wall eatery in a strip mall. Once you step inside, it's clear this little bistro is a blend of sophisticated cuisine in a casual, family atmosphere. The food is simply delicious and features dishes such as ceviche with soft sweet potatoes, fried trout with sliced garlic, and a strip steak topped with a fried egg. They also serve Cuban dishes.

Accommodations

Accommodations in Rockville are primarily chain hotels. There is a big variety, so it is best to select a hotel based on location. If you do not need to be near the Metrorail or the center of town, cheaper rates can be found on the outskirts of the city.

$100-200

The **Sheraton Rockville Hotel** (920 King Farm Blvd., 240/912-8200, www. starwoodhotels.com, $94-199) is in the King Farm development near I-270. It has 152 guest rooms with comfortable beds, 32-inch flat-screen televisions, high-speed Internet, and work desks. Amenities include a fitness center, indoor lap pool, whirlpool, on-site restaurant, and gift shop. The hotel is about eight miles north of downtown Rockville, but it is reasonably priced for the quality of the facility.

Another solid choice in this price range is the **Best Western Plus Rockville Hotel and Suites** (1251 W. Montgomery Ave., 301/424-4940, www.bestwestern.com, $159-189). They have 164 guest rooms and are close to I-270. They offer a complimentary breakfast, a fitness center, a seasonal outdoor pool, free high-speed Internet, and free shuttle to the Metro.

$200-300

The **Homewood Suites by Hilton Rockville-Gaithersburg** (14975 Shady Grove Rd., 240/507-1900, www.homewood-suites3.hilton.com, $199-269) is a good choice for extended stays or those who want a fully equipped kitchen. Located in the business district, this is a popular hotel for business travel. Complimentary shuttle service to the Shady Grove Metrorail station and other locations within a three-mile radius of the hotel is offered. Each of the 87 suites has a full kitchen, large living area, and free wireless Internet. A full complimentary breakfast is also included. Hotel amenities such as an indoor heated pool, 24-hour fitness center, whirlpool, and kids' entertainment room with books, DVDs, foosball, and air hockey allow guests several options for relaxation outside their studio, one-bedroom, or two-bedroom suites.

The Homewood Suites is joined at the lobby to the **Hilton Garden Inn Rockville Gaithersburg** (14975 Shady Grove Rd., 240/507-1800, www.hiltongardeninn3.hilton. com, $189-229). Both hotels are relatively new and have excellent staff. They also share some amenities.

Information and Services

For additional information on Rockville, visit www.rockvillemd.gov.

SILVER SPRING

Silver Spring is just north of Washington DC and is a prime business hub with numerous office buildings and a dense population. The city is said to be named after a spring that was discovered by Francis Preston Blair, an American journalist and politician, in 1840 when he was thrown from his horse while riding through the countryside looking for an area to build his personal retreat from Washington. As legend goes, the mica and sand around the spring glimmered like silver, and thus the name.

In recent years, the original downtown area, which had paled compared to some of the region's trendy city centers, began a rebirth of sorts. New businesses moved in to stake their claim, including major retail outlets, restaurants, and residential and office developments. Downtown Silver Spring is now a vibrant city center with entertainment, shopping, and other conveniences. One of its most prominent business residents is Discovery Communications, the parent company of Discovery Channel and a dozen other television networks.

Sights
NATIONAL MUSEUM OF HEALTH AND MEDICINE

The **National Museum of Health and Medicine** (2500 Linden Ln., 301/319-3300, www.medicalmuseum.mil, daily 10am-5:30pm, free) is one of the few museums where visitors can see the impact of disease on the human body. The museum is a National Historic Landmark that was established during the Civil War and dates back to 1862. It offers unique exhibits and educational programs, and engages in ongoing medical research.

Instruments used to diagnose and treat disease can be seen as well as the case histories of patients with the diseases (some exhibits may be a bit graphic for young children). The goal of the museum is to promote the understanding of both historic and modern-day medicine.

Children play around the fountain in downtown Silver Spring.

Special attention is given to military medicine. Fascinating artifacts on display include the bullet that killed Abraham Lincoln and bone fragments from Lincoln's skull.

In the museum's initial years, the first curator collected artifacts from doctors treating soldiers in the Union army. Photos of wounded soldiers were also collected that showed the impact of gunshot wounds and the resulting amputations and surgical procedures. Since then much research has been conducted at the museum and a sophisticated method of cataloging was established, which formed the framework for the National Library of Medicine.

At the onset of World War II, the museum began to focus primarily on pathology and became a division of the new Army Institute of Pathology. After several name changes, the museum became known under its current title in 1989.

Adult visitors should be prepared to present photo identification at the entrance and personal belongings may be subject to search for security purposes.

NATIONAL CAPITAL TROLLEY MUSEUM

In the northern reaches of the Silver Spring area is the popular **National Capital Trolley Museum** (1313 Bonifant Rd., Colesville, 301/384-6088, www.dctrolley.org, Sat.-Sun. noon-5pm, $7). This unusual museum strives to preserve artifacts from electric street railways and to help understand their effect on community development in the Washington DC area. There is a visitors center and several exhibit halls, and guests can enjoy authentic streetcar rides through Northwest Branch Park. Many historic trolleys are on display, and educational programs are also offered.

THE *HAND OF NOAA* SCULPTURE

An interesting piece of public art is located outside the National Oceanic and Atmospheric Administration (NOAA) headquarters. Known as the *Hand of NOAA* (1325 East-West Hwy.), the sculpture depicts a large bronze hand releasing seagulls to the ocean. The seagulls are part of the agency's logo, and the sculpture symbolizes NOAA's commitment to protecting the environment.

★ AMERICAN FILM INSTITUTE (AFI) SILVER THEATRE & CULTURAL CENTER

The **American Film Institute (AFI) Silver Theatre & Cultural Center** (8633 Colesville Rd., 301/495-6700, www.afi.com) is a state-of-the-art exhibition, education, and cultural center that grew out of the restored 1938 art deco Silver Theatre. It offers multiple stadium-seating theaters in 32,000 square feet of space, along with a reception area, exhibit space, offices, and meeting space. They feature retrospectives, new releases, and tribute shows. A full schedule of films is shown there, and memberships are available. Each June, the center hosts the premier seven-day documentary film festival called **AFI DOCS.** It is considered one of the world's best documentary festivals.

AFI Silver Theatre

Entertainment and Events

The historic **Fillmore Theater** (8656 Colesville Rd., 301/960-9999, www.fillmoresilverspring.com) has brought entertainment to Silver Spring for more than 40 years. With a capacity of 2,000, it offers first-class music and entertainment in the center of the downtown area. A schedule of events can be found on the website.

Shopping

The center of activity in Silver Spring is the **Silver Spring Town Center** (www.silverspringtowncenter.com). Located on Georgia Avenue, it comprises retailers, restaurants, a movie theater, and a Whole Foods grocery store. The town center is the anchor to the newly revitalized downtown area. Year-round activities are held at the center including craft fairs, festivals, and concerts. There is also a seasonal farmers market. A splash fountain is open May-September.

Recreation

The **Capital Crescent Trail** (www.cctrail.org) is an 11-mile off-road rail trail that is designated for shared use by walkers, runners, bikers, and inline skaters. The trail was created in an old railbed of the Georgetown Branch of the B&O Railroad. It runs from Georgetown in Washington DC through Bethesda and ends in west Silver Spring (in Lyttonsville). The trail is heavily used by commuters and recreational users and passes through wooded areas and parks, over four historic bridges, and through two tunnels. Parts of the trail have scenic views of the Potomac River.

Food

The **Sergio Ristorante Italiano** (8727 Colesville Road, 301/585-1040, Mon.-Fri. 11:30am-9:30pm, Sat. 5pm-9:30pm, $13-22) is underappreciated. This cozy little establishment serves authentic Italian fare with a personal touch. The food is consistently delicious and the owner is very involved in making sure each guest has a good experience.

For a classic diner experience, the **Tastee Diner** (8601 Cameron St., 301/589-8171, www.tasteediner.com, open 24/7, under $10) is hard to beat. This landmark diner originally opened in 1946 on Georgia Avenue and was moved to its current location in 1999 when Discovery Communications was built. It remains one of two original diners with a vintage railroad car design in Montgomery County. They are known for their BLTs, but have a wide variety of breakfast, lunch, and dinner menu items.

The historic **Mrs. K's Toll House** (9201 Colesville Rd., 301/589-3500, www.mrsks.com, brunch Sun. 10:30am-3pm, lunch Tues.-Sat. 11:30am-2:30pm, dinner Tues.-Thurs. 5pm-9pm, Fri.-Sat. 4:30pm-9:30pm, Sun. 5pm-8pm, $16-38) offers a quaint country-house atmosphere in one of the last existing tollhouses in the county. Built in the early 1900s, the home was a working tollhouse with living quarters for the keeper and his family. The home was turned into a restaurant in 1930 offering a charming ambience, beautiful gardens, and a variety of interior antiques. The menu offers filet, seafood, venison, lamb, and vegetarian dishes. The menu is not oriented towards children. There is a lovely wine bar in the basement.

A good seafood house that takes pride in its food is **Crisfield Seafood Restaurant** (8012 Georgia Ave., 301/589-1306, www.crisfieldseafood.com, Tues.-Thurs. 11am-9pm, Fri.-Sat. 11am-10pm, Sun. noon-9pm, $15-28). This traditional restaurant has an old-time counter, tiled walls, and a truly retro feel (not a trendy, hip feel—this is the real deal). They serve delicious seafood and some of the best crab cakes in the county. The decor isn't fancy, but the food is simple and fresh.

Accommodations

Silver Spring offers mostly chain hotel accommodations such as the **Hilton Garden Inn Silver Spring North** (2200 Broadbirch Dr., 301/622-3333, www.hiltongardeninn3.hilton.com, $189-199) and the **Courtyard by Marriott Silver Spring Downtown** (8506

Fenton St., 301/589-4899, www.marriott.com, $269-319) in downtown Silver Spring.

A nice bed-and-breakfast alternative is the **Bed & Breakfast at Lansdowne Way** (2009 Lansdowne Way, 301/960-3331, www. bblansdowneway.com, $165-300), on a quiet, tree-lined, neighborhood street. It offers four comfortable guest rooms and suites. A healthy continental breakfast is served to guests.

Getting There and Around

Downtown Silver Spring can be reached from Washington DC by car in less than 20 minutes (using Georgia Avenue or 16th Street). Metrobus service is available in Silver Spring as are Montgomery County's Ride On buses.

GAITHERSBURG

Gaithersburg is in central Montgomery County, five miles north of Rockville, and was incorporated in 1878. It has a population of around 60,000 and is the fourth-largest incorporated city in Maryland. I-270 runs through Gaithersburg, dividing it into east and west sections of the city.

Eastern Gaithersburg is home to a historic business district that is sometimes referred to as "Olde Town" Gaithersburg. The Montgomery County Fair Grounds are also on the eastern side of the city.

The west side of Gaithersburg is primarily neighborhoods, although several major employers are located there such as the National Institute of Standards and Technology (NIST) and several information systems and global services corporations.

Sights
RIO WASHINGTONIAN CENTER

The main center of activity in Gaithersburg is the **Rio Washingtonian Center** (9811 Washingtonian Blvd., 301/921-4686, www. riowashingtonian.com). This premier shopping area is in the heart of the city in combination with the **Waterfront and Rio Entertainment Center.** Together they offer 760,000 square feet of retail space, restaurants, and entertainment venues. The center is set on a lake, and there is a walkway around the lake and paddleboats for rent on the water. Outdoor dining is plentiful, and the area is generally safe and clean. Parking can be a little tough on the weekends.

INTERNATIONAL LATITUDE OBSERVATORY

The only National Historic Landmark in Gaithersburg is the **International Latitude Observatory** (100 DeSellum Ave., 301/258-6350, www.gaithersburgmd.gov, call ahead for tours). This small, 13-square-foot building was constructed in 1899 as part of an international effort to record the earth's wobble on its polar axis. The observatory is one of six in the world (in the United States, Japan, Russia, and Italy) that gathered information still used by today's scientists. The station was in operation until 1982, when its functions were replaced by computers. The original Zenith telescope that was used in the observatory is now on display at the **Gaithersburg Community Museum** (9 S. Summit Ave., 301/258-6160, www.gaithersburgmd.gov, Thurs.-Sat. 10am-3pm, free), which is in the historic 1884 B&O Railroad Station complex and offers exhibits on the city's history.

Recreation

East of Gaithersburg, on the border with neighboring Howard County, are two wonderful recreational lakes: the **Triadelphia Reservoir** and the **Rocky Gorge Reservoir.** They share an information center (2 Brighton Dam Rd., Brookeville, 301/206-7485, www. wsscwater.com) where boat launch permits ($6) and maps can be obtained. The lakes are both dammed portions of the Patuxent River and provide water to Montgomery and Prince George's Counties. There are no natural lakes in Maryland, so without the creation of reservoirs, it would have been difficult to provide water to the many homes and businesses in the state. The Washington Suburban Sanitary Commission, which is more than 85 years old, created both Triadelphia Reservoir and Rocky

Gorge Reservoir and is still responsible for maintaining them. Both are wonderful locations for kayaking and fishing. No gasoline-powered engines are allowed on either lake.

The **Metropolitan Ballet Theatre and Academy** (220 Perry Pkwy, #8, 301/762-1757, www.mbtdance.org) provides training in ballet, jazz, tap, hip-hop, and modern dance. Students perform with the company in professional performances (sometimes with professional artists).

Food

Il Porto (245 Muddy Branch Rd., 301/590-0735, www.ilportorestaurant.com, Mon.-Sat. 11:30am-10pm, Sun. 11:30am-9pm, $10-20) is a delicious, reasonably priced Italian restaurant. They feature traditional Italian dishes and fresh seafood. All food is made to order. The service is outstanding, and this popular restaurant doesn't seem to rest on its laurels despite its excellent reputation. Expect a crowd on weekend evenings.

Good Mediterranean food can be found in the Kentlands area at **Vasilis** (705 Center Point Way, 301/977-1011, www.vasilisgrill.com, Mon.-Thurs. 11am-9pm, Fri.-Sat. 11am-10pm, $8-27). They serve a traditional Greek menu with succulent fresh vegetable side dishes. The lamb is especially savory, meaty, and cooked to perfection. This is a popular restaurant, but they do not take reservations so plan accordingly.

Great beer and upscale pub food can be found at **Dogfish Head Alehouse** (800 W. Diamond Ave., 301/963-4847, www.dogfishalehouse.com, Mon.-Thurs. 11am-11pm, Fri.-Sat. 11am-midnight, Sun. 11am-10pm, $10-20). The restaurant is a little off the beaten path (west of downtown), but is still convenient to many businesses and neighborhoods. They serve sandwiches, pizza, fish, and other pub food, plus a great selection of standard and seasonal beers.

Accommodations

Accommodations in Gaithersburg include many popular chain hotels. The **Comfort Inn Shady Grove** (16216 S. Frederick Rd., 301/330-0023, www.choicehotels.com, $119-129) is one of the nicest Comfort Inns in the area and offers 127 comfortable rooms, good service, and reasonable rates. The **Hyatt House Gaithersburg** (200 Skidmore Blvd., 301/527-6000, www.gaithersburg.house.hyatt.com, $144-175) is a suite hotel in a residential area of Gaithersburg, approximately one mile from the Shady Grove Metro station. It is a good option for extended stays. The hotel is pet friendly.

The **Courtyard by Marriott Gaithersburg Washingtonian Center** (204 Boardwalk Pl., 301/527-9000, www.marriott.com, $159-219) is a lovely hotel on the lake at the Washingtonian Center. It is very convenient to shopping and restaurants and has 203 rooms and seven suites.

GERMANTOWN

Germantown sits 6.5 miles northwest of Gaithersburg along I-270 and is the third-most populous place in Maryland with more than 86,000 people. It is one of Montgomery County's fastest-growing areas and has seen a large increase in the number of neighborhoods, communities, and schools in recent years. Germantown is approximately 25 miles from Washington DC.

Sights and Entertainment
BLACK ROCK CENTER FOR THE ARTS

The center of Germantown is along Middlebrook Road. This is where the **Black Rock Center for the Arts** (12901 Town Commons Dr., 301/528-2260, www.blackrockcenter.org), a cultural center offering shows, classes, camps, and an art gallery, is located, as well as the **Germantown Commons** (13060 Middlebrook Rd.) shopping area.

BLACK HILL REGIONAL PARK

Just north of Germantown and west of I-270 is **Black Hill Regional Park** (20930 Lake Ridge Dr., Boyds, 301/528-3490, www.

montgomeryparks.org, daily sunrise-sunset, free). This lovely 1,843-acre park is home to a scenic recreational lake called **Little Seneca Lake,** a great place to kayak and fish with 505 acres of water and 15 miles of shoreline. The park also features hiking trails and the **Black Hill Visitors Center** (20926 Lake Ridge Dr., 301/528-3488, daily 11am-6pm). Kayak, canoe, and rowboat rentals are available May-September for $8 per hour or $27.50 per day.

★ SUGARLOAF MOUNTAIN

North of Germantown in nearby Frederick County is **Sugarloaf Mountain** (Comus Road, Dickerson, 301/874-2024, www.sugarloafmd.com, daily 8am-one hour prior to sunset, free). Sugarloaf Mountain is a popular recreational area for people in Maryland's Capital Region. It is a small mountain (1,282 feet) that is a designated National Natural Landmark.

Sugarloaf Mountain is a monadnock, which is an isolated mountain that rises sharply from the surrounding ground. Because of this, the mountain can be seen for miles away and is an easily recognizable landmark.

The mountain is a public park that is accessible for recreation at no charge. Activities in the park include hiking, picnicking, and rock climbing. It is also known for its scenic views of the Monocacy Valley.

Sugarloaf Mountain is 15 miles northwest of Germantown and 10 miles south of Frederick. From I-270 take the Hyattstown exit to Route 109 to Comus. Turn right on Comus Road. This will lead to the Sugarloaf Mountain entrance.

WHITE'S FERRY

Sixteen miles west of Germantown on the Potomac River in Dickerson is **White's Ferry** (24801 Whites Ferry Rd., Dickerson, 301/349-5200, $5 one-way or $8 round-trip), the only one of about 100 ferries that used to be in business on the Potomac River that is still in operation. It is the only crossing on the river between the American Legion Bridge on I-495 and the bridge at Point of Rocks in Frederick County, Maryland. Commuters rely on the small ferry for daily transportation, and the ferry is heavily used by recreational travelers on weekends. The ferry runs on a wire cable every 20 minutes year-round 5am-11pm daily unless the river is flooded or there is bad weather. Bicycles ($2) and pedestrians ($1) are welcome aboard.

Prince George's County

Prince George's County was named after Prince George of Denmark (1653-1708), who was married to Queen Anne of Great Britain. Today the county is a hub for federal government agencies.

Part of the Atlantic coastal plain, Prince George's County has a combination of gently rolling hills and valleys. The county borders the Patuxent River on its east side and has some lovely wildlife habitat.

Prince George's County is more city suburb than tourist destination and faces more crime issues and economic challenges than neighboring Montgomery County. However, there are some gems worth visiting while in the area, including the newly established National Harbor, the home stadium for the Washington Redskins, and a well-known site for dinosaur fossils.

GETTING THERE AND AROUND

Amtrak (4300 Garden City Dr., 800/872-7245, www.amtrak.com) provides train service to Landover at the New Carrollton station. The **Maryland Transit Administration** MARC train (410/539-5000, http://mta.maryland.gov) provides weekday-only service to five stations in Prince George's County on the Camden Line (College Park, Greenbelt, Muirkirk,

Laurel, and Riverdale) and three stations on the Penn Line (New Carrollton, Seabrook, and Bowie).

The **Washington Metropolitan Area Transit Authority (WMATA)** (202/637-7000, www.wmata.com) provides **Metrorail** and **Metrobus** service to Prince George's County. The county is serviced by Metrorail's Green Line in College Park and Greenbelt, the Blue Line to Largo, and the Orange Line to New Carrollton.

A local bus system in Prince George's County is **TheBus** (301/324-2877, www.princegeorgescountymd.gov, $1.25), which operates on weekdays only.

★ NATIONAL HARBOR

Twelve miles south of downtown Washington DC, National Harbor sits across the Potomac River from Old Town Alexandria. This trendy addition to the Washington DC metro area is a little oasis in Prince George's County, offering world-class dining, accommodations, and activities. The area was previously a forgotten 350-acre parcel of land on the Potomac River banks that was the site of an abandoned plantation. Then a large local development firm embarked on a seven-year project to create a new hot spot of local and tourist activity.

The first phase of the project opened in 2008, and since then, the site has become the location of a convention center, multiple hotels, restaurants, retail space, and condominiums. The area continues to undergo development. Festivals and other outdoor events are also held at National Harbor.

Sights
CAPITAL WHEEL

The **Capital Wheel** (116 Waterfront St., 301/842-8650, www.thecapitalwheel.com, hours vary daily, $15) is a prime attraction at National Harbor. This 180-foot-tall modern Ferris wheel sits on a pier on the Potomac River. The ride offers terrific views of the river and harbor. Each climate-controlled gondola seats up to eight people, with the exception of the VIP gondola, which holds four. The VIP gondola has leather bucket seats and a glass floor ($50). All rides are 12-15 minutes.

CAROUSEL AT NATIONAL HARBOR

The **Carousel at National Harbor** (137 National Plaza, 301/842-8650, www.nationalharbor.com, mid-May-day before Memorial Day Fri.-Sun. noon-8pm, Memorial Day-Labor Day Mon.-Thurs. noon-8pm, Fri.-Sat. noon-10pm, Sun. noon-8pm, $7) is an

National Harbor

Americana-themed carousel, located at the north end of National Harbor on the waterfront. Kids of all ages can enjoy its whimsical animals. There is a playground near the carousel.

THE *AWAKENING* SCULPTURE

The *Awakening* is a five-part, 70-foot, cast-iron sculpture that depicts a bearded giant waking up and rising out of the earth. The pieces include the giant's head, hand, outstretched arm, knee, and foot. This impressive artwork by J. Seward Johnson was originally part of a public art exhibition in Washington DC in 1980, when it was installed at Hains Point near the Jefferson Memorial. After the exhibition, the sculpture remained on loan to the National Park Service. The *Awakening* was purchased by the Peterson Companies (which developed National Harbor) in 2008 and moved to the beach at the harbor.

Entertainment and Events

Dinner cruises of 2-4 hours aboard the glass-enclosed *Odyssey Washington DC* (866/306-2469, www.odysseycruises.com) leave from National Harbor and provide great views of Washington DC, entertainment, and a full dinner. Reservations can be made for individual seating or the boat can be booked for large functions. Dining cruises can also be booked on the *Spirit of Washington* (866/302-2469, www.spiritcruises.com).

If a dueling piano bar sounds like fun, make a reservation at **Bobby McKey's** (172 Fleet St., 301/602-2209, www.bobbymckeys.com, $7-20). This is a two-story venue that holds up to 450 people and hosts regular shows and private parties. Reservations can be made online for standing room or a reserved seat. Due to the popularity of this place as the only live music venue in National Harbor and the only dueling piano bar in the Washington DC area, it's best to reserve a seat. This is a loud but unique show and can be a lot of fun if you're in the mood for it. Tips are expected for requests.

ICE! (www.gaylordhotels.com) is an annual ice sculpture event held at the Gaylord National Resort & Convention Center. Visitors walk through a huge winter wonderland carved from 5,000 blocks of ice shipped in from a factory in Ohio. More than 40 international sculptors work for 30 days prior to the event to produce a themed ice "land" where people can see, touch, and walk inside the amazing works of art. The event has a different theme each year and runs mid-November through early January. Tickets are around $30.

Shopping

The **American Market** (www.americanmarketnh.com, Sat. 10am-4pm) is an upscale farmers market that is held in National Harbor May-October. The market is on American Way, between Waterfront and Fleet Street. The market features locally grown produce and handmade crafts.

Sports and Recreation

National Harbor offers a first-class marina with large floating docks and easy water access to many attractions in the Washington DC area via the Potomac River. Kayak and pedal boat rentals are available right at the dock, and electric boat rentals are available through **Duffy Electric Boat Rentals** (www.experiencetheduffyboat.com, $200 for the first hour, $150 for the second hour, and $100 for each additional hour). Sightseeing cruises are also a popular activity at the harbor and can be booked with **Potomac River Boat Company** (www.potomacriverboatco.com, $32 for 90 minutes). Guided bass fishing is also available through **National Bass Guide Service** (www.nationalbass.com, starting at $295 for four hours).

The harbor is also the site of many annual athletic events. Whether you are looking to do a short fun run, a half marathon, a triathlon, a competitive open-water swimming event, or you simply want to do yoga on the beach, National Harbor is the place. A list of events is available on the website (www.nationalharbor.com).

A nice beachfront walking path along the Potomac connects the National Harbor to a bike trail on the Woodrow Wilson Bridge. This allows walking and cycling into Alexandria across the river.

Food

Upscale dining at the **Old Hickory Steakhouse Restaurant** (201 Waterfront St., 301/965-4000, www.gaylordhotels.com, daily 5:30pm-10:30pm, $28-52) in the Gaylord Hotel is hard to beat. The atmosphere is first-rate, with views of the harbor, and the food is dependable and delicious. This sophisticated restaurant serves 100 percent antibiotic- and hormone-free steak and delicious seafood. They also have an award-winning wine list. Three hours of complimentary parking is available at the Gaylord for dinner guests.

Upscale Mexican food can be found at **Rosa Mexicano** (153 Waterfront St., 301/567-1005, www.rosamexicano.com, Sun.-Thurs. 11:30am-10pm, Fri.-Sat. 11:30am-11pm, $9-27) on the waterfront. They offer indoor and outdoor seating (weather permitting) and a lively decor. The menu consists of fresh Mexican dishes featuring seafood, steak, and other delicious ingredients. The signature Guacamole en Mocajete is made tableside and a great choice for a starter. They have an extensive bar menu (not cheap, but good), and the service is wonderful.

For a quick burger, stop in **Elevation Burger** (108 Waterfront St., 301/749-4014, www.elevationburger.com, Sun.-Thurs. 11am-9pm, Fri.-Sat. 11am-midnight, under $10). This inexpensive dining option offers good gourmet burgers with many choices for patty combinations and toppings. This is one of the few casually priced eateries in National Harbor.

Accommodations

The ★ **Gaylord National Resort and Convention Center** (201 Waterfront St., 301/965-4000, www.marriott.com, $249-399 plus $18 resort fee) is a Marriott-owned hotel that anchors the National Harbor. This massive 18-floor hotel has 1,890 guest rooms, an impressive 18-story glass atrium, indoor gardens, and panoramic views of the Potomac River. A conference center with 89 meeting

Gaylord National Resort and Convention Center

rooms, the hotel is always bustling, but the staff is friendly and the rooms are very comfortable. There are a fitness center, indoor pool, and spa on-site. Self-parking is available for $26 a day and valet for $39.

The **Residence Inn National Harbor** (192 Waterfront St., 301/749-4755, www. marriott.com, $229-309) is a less expensive alternative to the Gaylord and has 162 suites on seven floors, some with great views of the water. This Marriott hotel offers roomy suites with full kitchens and separate sitting areas. There is a small pool, a small fitness room, a complimentary breakfast buffet, and a manager's reception Monday-Thursday. The hotel is within walking distance of attractions and restaurants in National Harbor, and there is a parking lot near the rear hotel entrance (a discount on parking is offered to hotel guests).

Another good option for accommodations in National Harbor is the **Hampton Inn & Suites National Harbor** (250 Waterfront St., 301/567-3531, www.hamptoninn3.hilton.com, $259-289). This 151-room hotel is welcoming and convenient to the National Harbor attractions. Guests can enjoy a complimentary breakfast buffet, wireless Internet, a pool, and a fitness center. Self-parking is available for $16.

Information and Services
For additional information on National Harbor, visit www.nationalharbor.com or stop by the **National Harbor Visitor's Center** (168 National Plaza, Oxen Hill, 877/628-5427).

Getting There
National Harbor is a 20-minute drive south of Washington DC. The closest major highway is the Beltway (I-495), but from DC, I-295 is the primary route. **Water taxi** service is also available from Old Town Alexandria in Virginia (www.potomacriverboatco.com, $8 each way).

GREATER UPPER MARLBORO
Greater Upper Marlboro is a suburb of Washington DC with approximately 22,000

residents. It is 18 miles west of DC in south-central Prince George's County off Routes 301 and 4. The area encompasses approximately 77 square miles and is primarily residential with many neighborhoods and housing developments. The Patuxent River runs near Upper Marlboro and with it brings protected land for wildlife and recreation near the city.

Sights
★ MERKLE WILDLIFE SANCTUARY
The **Merkle Wildlife Sanctuary** (11704 Fenno Rd., 301/888-1377, www.dnr.state.md.us, daily sunrise to sunset, free) is the only wildlife sanctuary run by the Maryland Department of Natural Resources. It is best known as the wintering ground for the largest concentration of Canada geese on the western shore of the Chesapeake Bay. The sanctuary offers visitors a one-way, self-guided 4.3-mile Critical Area Driving Tour (CADT), open to cars on Sunday 10am-3pm year-round. The CADT is available to hikers, bikers, and horseback riders daily January 1 through September 30, but closed to these users the rest of the year in order to provide a peaceful area for the migrating geese and other waterfowl.

The **Frank Oslislo Visitors Center** (weekends 10am-4pm) sits on a hill overlooking several ponds. This beautiful building has a two-story wall of windows, balconies for viewing the surrounding area, and a large bird feeder viewing area. The center features exhibits on Canada geese and other wildlife and environmental topics. A live animal exhibit with turtles, snakes, and toads is also offered for children.

Four hiking trails at the sanctuary provide access to upland forests and marsh areas. The trails are only open to hikers, and weekly nature hikes are available.

Five fishing ponds are open to the public between April 1 and October 1 for largemouth bass, bluegill, and other types of fishing. Those planning to fish should sign in outside the visitors center.

Merkle Wildlife Sanctuary

PATUXENT RURAL LIFE MUSEUMS

The **Patuxent Rural Life Museums** (16000 Croom Airport Rd., 301/627-6074, http://history.pgparks.com, Apr.-Oct. Sat.-Sun. 1pm-4pm, free) comprises several museums and farm buildings that preserve the heritage of southern Prince George's County. The buildings are in the 7,000-acre **Patuxent River Park** and include a tool museum, a blacksmith shop, a tobacco farming museum, a log cabin (with a smokehouse), a 1923 Sears catalog house, and a hunting, fishing, and trapping museum. Exhibits are on display in the museums, and living-history demonstrations are featured. Guided tours of the museums are available all year by appointment (301/627-6074, $2). Guided nature tours ($2), river ecology boat tours (free), and archaeology presentations (free) are also available and take 45-60 minutes. All-day kayaking/canoeing tours can be scheduled for small groups (8:30am-3:30pm, $20 per person).

DARNALL'S CHANCE HOUSE MUSEUM

Darnall's Chance House Museum (14800 Governor Oden Bowie Dr., 301/952-8010, www.pgparks.com, guided house tours by appointment Tues.-Thurs. 10am-4pm, tours by walk-in Fri. and Sun. noon-4pm, $5) interprets the history and culture of Prince George's County women in the 18th century. The focus is on a longtime resident of the house, Lettice Lee, who lived there prior to the American Revolution. The home is listed in the National Register of Historic Places, the National Underground Railroad: Network to Freedom Trail, and the Star-Spangled Banner National Historic Trail. The home and grounds are portrayed as they were in 1760 when Lee's first husband passed away and the contents of the house were documented room by room. The museum also portrays the lives of the enslaved African American women who worked in the home, and tours address the similarities and differences between their lives and that of Lee.

A rare 17-foot-long burial vault was discovered at the museum in 1987. It contained household garbage from the 18th and 19th century as well as the remains of nine people (three adults and six children).

Recreation and Events

The **Prince George's Equestrian Center** (14900 Pennsylvania Ave., 301/952-7900) is the primary event venue in Upper Marlboro and includes numerous tracks, a schooling ring, and stables for more than 200 horses. The center hosts the annual **Prince George's County Fair** (www.countyfair.org) each September. The fair began in 1842 and is the longest-running fair in Maryland. Other popular events that take place at the center include antique shows and concerts. The center is also the site of the **Show Place Arena** (www.showplacearena.com), which hosts circuses, rodeos, hockey games, conventions, and trade shows.

Six Flags America (13710 Central Ave., 301/249-1500, www.sixflags.com, mid-May-Aug. daily, early May and Sept.-Oct. select weekends, $53 online and $63 at gate) is located between Upper Marlboro and Bowie (near Largo). This large theme park is the only one of its kind in Maryland and features more than 100 rides, a water park (Hurricane Harbor), shows, and other attractions. This is a fun place to bring the kids, but the park is a bit aged and it is not uncommon for some of the rides to be closed due to malfunctions. The park has eight roller coasters and new rides open seemingly every season. They also have specific rides for small kids. The park opens at 10:30am but closing times vary a lot throughout the season; check the website or call ahead for more information.

Watkins Regional Park (301 Watkins Park Dr., 301/218-6700, www.pgparks.com, daily dawn-dusk, free) is a great regional park with an antique carousel, train, nature center, tennis, camping, and miniature golf. The **Old Maryland Farm** (Tues.-Fri. 9am-4pm, Sat. 9am-4:30pm, Sun. 11:30am-4:30pm) is within the park (a short walk from the train station) and features agricultural exhibits, gardens, and live animals.

Food

Jasper's (9640 Lottsford Ct., Largo, 301/883-9500, www.jaspersrestaurants.com, Sun. 10am-midnight, Mon.-Thurs. 11:30am-1am, Fri.-Sat. 11:30am-2am, Sun. 10am-midnight, $7-24) offers seafood, steak, burgers, and sandwiches in an upscale and casual environment. This is a popular restaurant with good food. They are open late and are often very busy on weekends. The entire menu is available to go.

If you're in the mood for a neighborhood dive bar with good pizza, burgers, wings, and a friendly atmosphere, visit **Grizzly's** (9544 Crain Hwy., 301/599-0505, daily 11am-10pm, under $15) off Route 301 in the Marlton Shopping Center.

Accommodations

Upper Marlboro isn't known for its selection of good accommodations. Visitors may prefer to spend the night in neighboring Largo, northwest of Upper Marlboro, where there are a few choices such as the **Holiday Inn Express I-95 Beltway Largo** (9101 Basil Ct., 301/636-6090, www.hiexpress.com, $153-227), which has 89 rooms, an indoor pool, and a fitness center; or the **Hampton Inn Washington I-95, Largo** (9421 W. Largo Dr., 301/499-4600, www.hamptoninn3.hilton.com, $149-159), with 127 guest rooms, free breakfast, a fitness room, and free wireless Internet.

LANDOVER

Landover is a suburban area northwest of Upper Marlboro and Largo. It is 11 miles northeast of Washington DC and is best known as the home of the **Washington Redskins** professional football team. Their home field, **FedEx Field** (1600 FedEx Way, 301/276-6000, www.redskins.com) was built in 1994 and originally called Jack Kent Cooke Stadium after the former owner of the team. When the team was purchased by Daniel Snyder, FedEx Corporation purchased the naming rights. Although FedEx Field is the largest football stadium in terms of seating capacity in the NFL (with seating for 85,000), it sells out all non-premium tickets every year and has a season ticket waiting list of more than 30 years.

FedEx Field has its own exit from I-495 (the Beltway): 16 (Arena Drive).

GREENBELT

Greenbelt, seven miles north of Landover and 30 minutes from Washington DC, is home to **NASA's Goddard Space Flight Visitors Center** (8800 Greenbelt Rd., 301/286-8981, www.nasa.gov, Sept.-June Tues.-Fri. 10am-3pm, Sat.-Sun. noon-4pm, July-Aug. Tues.-Fri. 10am-5pm, Sat.-Sun. noon-4pm, free). The center is a wonderful place to learn about NASA's work in earth science, astrophysics, planetary science, technology development, and other projects. Unique interactive exhibits teach people of all ages about topics such as climate change and space exploration. Exhibits include *Frozen: Cold Matters,* where places on earth are featured where temperatures are generally below freezing all year; *Goddard Rocket Garden,* a collection of artifacts from space; and *Largest,* an exhibit on the planet Jupiter. Visitors can also experience monthly model rocket launches. This is a fun place for kids who are interested in space travel.

BOWIE

Ten miles northeast of Landover is the city of Bowie. With a population of nearly 55,000, the city has blossomed from its beginnings as a small rail stop on the Baltimore & Potomac Railroad to the biggest municipality in the county.

Bowie was originally called Huntington City when it was founded in 1870. The original downtown area is now referred to as "Old Bowie," but some landmarks still bear the Huntington name.

Sights

BELAIR MANSION

The **Belair Mansion** (12207 Tulip Grove Dr., 301/809-3089, www.cityofbowie.org, Tues.-Sun. noon-4pm, free) is a Georgian plantation home that was built in 1745 for the provincial governor of Maryland, Samuel Ogle. In the early 1900s, the mansion became the residence of a noted Thoroughbred horse breeder named William Woodward. The home is listed in the National Register of Historic

Greenbelt: A Planned City

Greenbelt was conceived as a New Deal housing project and will be forever known as the first planned community in the country to be built by the federal government. It was designed in 1935 as a complete city, including housing, businesses, schools, roads, government facilities, and recreational facilities. The city was an experiment in social and physical planning modeled after 19th-century English garden cities. It included one of the first mall shopping centers.

The name came from the area of green forests that surround the city and from the "belts" of natural areas between its neighborhoods that keep residents in contact with nature. Greenbelt is a National Historic Landmark.

Places, and the museum interprets the lives of the people who lived there between 1747 and 1950. Visitors can see items such as family silver, a stunning colonial revival card table, paintings, and other artwork. The mansion's stables now operate as the **Belair Stable Museum** (2835 Belair Dr., 301/809-3089, www.cityofbowie.org, Tues.-Sun. noon-4pm, free). Although horse breeding began on the property in the 1740s, the current barn that houses the museum was built in 1907 as part of the Belair Stud Stable, one of the top breeding stables in the country from the 1920s to 1960. The only father/son horses to win the Triple Crown race series (Gallant Fox in 1930 and Omaha in 1935) were raised in the stable. The museum highlights the 200-year Thoroughbred-racing legacy of the Belair's bloodstock and explains other agricultural uses of the property. Both museums are operated by the city of Bowie.

BOWIE RAILROAD MUSEUM

The **Bowie Railroad Museum** (8614 Chestnut Ave., 301/809-3089, www.cityofbowie.org, Tues.-Sun. 10am-4pm, free) sits next to active train tracks at the no-longer-in-service Bowie Railroad Station. The museum features displays on the history of the railroad in Bowie and includes photographs and artifacts in three structures: a switch tower, a passenger waiting shed, and a freight depot. A caboose that dates back to 1922 and was part of the Norfolk and Western Railroad is on the museum grounds.

NATIONAL CAPITAL RADIO AND TELEVISION MUSEUM

Radio and television buffs will enjoy the **National Capital Radio and Television Museum** (2608 Mitchellville Rd., 301/390-1020, www.ncrtv.org, Fri. 10am-5pm, Sat.-Sun. 1pm-5pm, free). This small, two-story museum offers a tour back in time through the evolution of radio and television. There are displays of memorabilia and a large collection of antique receivers. Visitors can hear authentic radio broadcasts and view early television shows on vintage televisions.

Sports and Recreation

A great minor league baseball park (home of the Class AA Bowie Baysox) is **Prince George's Stadium** (4101 Crain Hwy., 301/805-6000, http://bowie.baysox.milb.

com). This clean, friendly ballpark offers reasonably priced seats, free parking, and the opportunity to see up-and-coming Baltimore Orioles players.

A pleasant 85-acre, family-oriented park is **Allen Pond Park** (3330 Northview Dr., 301/809-3011, www.cityofbowie.org, daily sunrise to sunset). It has a pond, walking path, playground, skateboard ramp, indoor ice rink (Bowie Ice Arena), amphitheater, basketball courts, fields for baseball, lacrosse, and soccer, and more. The park hosts a great fireworks display each July Fourth.

Food

"Fresh, Casual, and Friendly," is the slogan of the **Chesapeake Grille & Deli** (6786 Race Track Rd., 301/262-4441, www.chesapeakegrille.com, breakfast Sat.-Sun. 8am-11am, lunch and dinner Sun.-Thurs. 11am-9pm, Fri.-Sat. 11am-10pm, $6-17), and they deliver with flavorful sandwiches, seafood, skewers, and steak. This is not a fancy place, but the family-owned restaurant offers good food and dependable service. They are open daily for lunch and dinner.

The only place to find the original "Crab Bomb" is **Jerry's Seafood** (15211 Major Lansdale Blvd., 301/805-2284, www.

the Belair Mansion

jerrysseafood.com, Mon.-Sat. 11:30am-10pm, Sun. noon-8pm, $27-40). This family-owned seafood house is known for its crab dishes (the trademarked Crab Bomb includes 10 ounces of jumbo lump crabmeat), but they also offer other types of seafood and several non-seafood dishes. This restaurant is also known for good service.

Accommodations

For short and extended stays, the **Towne Place Suites Bowie Town Center** (3700 Town Center Blvd., 301/262-8045, www.marriott.com, $154-164) is hard to beat. This Marriott hotel offers 119 suites on four floors, a fitness center, pool, and free on-site parking. The rooms are amply sized and clean. Pets are allowed for an additional fee. It is near shopping and restaurants.

The **Comfort Inn Conference Center** (4500 Crain Hwy., 301/464-0089, www.bowiemdhotel.com, $135-165) offers mini fridges, microwaves, and coffeemakers in each room, complimentary breakfast, and wireless Internet. On-site parking is available, and there is a restaurant and bar at the hotel. This is a good hotel for business travelers. The wireless connection is strong and stable, and the breakfast food is above average for a chain hotel.

Information and Services

For additional information on Bowie, visit www.cityofbowie.org or stop by the **Old Town Bowie Welcome Center** (8606 Chestnut Ave., 301/575-2488, Tues.-Sun. 10am-4pm).

COLLEGE PARK

College Park is 13 miles west of Bowie in the northwestern part of Prince George's County. The city has a population of around 30,000 and is best known as the location of the **University of Maryland, College Park.** The U.S. National Archives and Records Administration also has a facility in College Park known as Archives II.

Sights

UNIVERSITY OF MARYLAND, COLLEGE PARK

The **University of Maryland, College Park** (301/405-1000, www.umd.edu) was founded in 1856 as a public research university. It is the largest university in Maryland, with more than 37,000 students, and it offers more than 120 undergraduate majors and 110 graduate programs. On campus is a 150-acre research park that was honored as an Outstanding Research Park in 2015. The campus also features the Physical Science Complex, which is still in the process of being completed. The building encompasses more than 160,000 square feet and will be a space for collaborative efforts with nearby federal agencies, like NASA.

★ COLLEGE PARK AVIATION MUSEUM

The **College Park Aviation Museum** (1985 Corporal Frank Scott Dr., 301/864-6029, www.collegeparkaviationmuseum.com, daily 10am-5pm, $5) is a nice little museum that is affiliated with the Smithsonian Institution and focuses on the earliest days of mechanical flight. Many of the exhibits in the 27,000-square-foot space are geared toward children and offer a hands-on experience with coloring, video games, puzzles, a flight simulator, and a plane to climb on. There is also information on the Wright Brothers, who made a flight attempt nearby.

The museum is in an open 1.5-story exhibit space on the site of the world's oldest continuously operating airport. The airport opened in 1909 when Wilbur Wright gave flight instruction there to the inaugural group of military aviators in the first army aviation school. The airport has numerous other notable "firsts" in the aviation field, such as the first mile-high flight, the first bomb-dropping test, the first female passenger in the United States, and many more. Visitors can watch planes on the runway from the glass windows inside the museum.

This is a nice family museum, and the volunteers are friendly and informative. There are no food services at the museum, but visitors can picnic outside in nice weather.

Entertainment and Events

The **Clarice Smith Performing Arts Center** (3800 Clarice Smith Performing Arts Center at University Blvd. and Stadium Dr., 301/405-2787, www.theclarice.umd.edu) is part of the University of Maryland, College Park, and offers many free and reasonably priced events such as musical and theatrical performances, lectures, and workshops.

Food

Get the traditional diner experience at the **College Park Diner** (9206 Baltimore Ave., 301/441-8888, open 24/7, under $10). This great little place runs like a well-oiled machine. The breakfast food is the best choice (served all day), but the country-fried steak is also a winner. Patrons can watch their meal being cooked since the kitchen is at the front of the building. This is a good place to come when looking for a local establishment or a late-night eatery. The tables turn over quickly, the servers are friendly and helpful, and you may even be called "Hon."

Good, inexpensive pho can be found at **Pho D'Lite** (8147 Baltimore Ave., 301/982-5599, www.phodlite.com, daily 10:30am-9:30pm, $4-20). They offer good specials on weekday afternoons. Try their Thai iced tea.

Accommodations

There are a handful of national hotels in College Park. For the most part, they are fairly comparable with standard accommodations and conveniences. Three hotels that are convenient to the University of Maryland campus are the **Holiday Inn Washington College Park** (10000 Baltimore Ave., 301/345-6700, www.holidayinn.com, $106-130), which has 220 guest rooms on five floors and free wireless Internet; the **Hampton Inn College Park** (9670 Baltimore Ave., 301/345-2200,

www.hamptoninn3.hilton.com, $159-179) with 80 guest rooms, free breakfast, free high-speed Internet, and a fitness room; and the **Best Western Plus College Park** (8419 Baltimore Ave., 301/220-0505, www.bestwestern.com, $130-145), with 40 guest rooms, complimentary full breakfast, a fitness center, and free Wi-Fi.

Information and Services

Additional information on College Park can be found at www.collegeparkmd.gov.

LAUREL

Laurel is 10 miles north of College Park in northern Prince George's County and also spills into Anne Arundel and Howard Counties. It was originally developed as a mill town, its cotton mills utilizing the power of the Patuxent River. It has a population of around 25,000.

Sights
DINOSAUR PARK

You may be surprised to learn that one of the most important dinosaur sites east of the Mississippi River is in Laurel. Most people rush past the site on Route 1 and never have a clue of what lies nearby. At **Dinosaur Park** (13201 Mid-Atlantic Blvd., 301/627-7755, http://history.pgparks.com, daily dawn-dusk, free), rare fossil deposits from the Early Cretaceous period include those from several types of dinosaurs (including *Astrodon johnstoni*), early mammals, and early plants and trees. What makes this location special is that it is part of an exposed layer of the Muirkirk Deposit, a rare fossil-bearing clay found on the East Coast. The park was created to preserve and protect the rare fossil deposits, to provide a natural laboratory for scientists to discover new fossils, and to allow the public the opportunity to work with paleontologists to uncover new findings. The public is welcome to explore an interpretive garden that is open daily and features descriptions of the prehistoric landscape in Maryland and

Maryland's State Dinosaur

Dinosaur bones were found in Maryland as early as the late 1800s. The first dinosaur remains discovered in Maryland were that of a long-necked plant-eater named *Astrodon johnstoni* (think "vegiesaur" from the movie *Jurassic Park*). Astrodon was gigantic (at least 60 feet long) and weighed several tons. One femur was found in the 1990s that weighed 220 pounds and was six feet long. The name Astrodon came from a starburst pattern found in a cross section of the dinosaur's teeth. The species name *johnstoni*, was added later in honor of a Maryland Academy of Sciences dentist, Christopher Johnson, who played a significant role in its identification.

In 1998, the Maryland State Assembly officially designated *Astrodon johnstoni* the official state dinosaur. Only six states (Maryland, Colorado, Wyoming, Missouri, New Jersey, and Texas) and the District of Columbia have official dinosaurs.

the dinosaurs that lived there. A fenced-in fossil area is only accessible during featured programs and during open houses held on the first and third Saturday of each month noon-4pm.

NATIONAL WILDLIFE VISITOR CENTER

The **National Wildlife Visitor Center** (10901 Scarlet Tanager Loop, 301/497-5770, www.fws.gov, daily 9am-4:30pm, free) is a U.S. Fish and Wildlife Service facility that sits on more than 12,000 acres in the **Patuxent Research Refuge.** The center is the largest science and environmental education center within the U.S. Department of the Interior. The center features interactive exhibits that teach the value of wildlife research and also focus on worldwide environmental issues. They also explore migratory bird routes, wildlife habitat, and recovery efforts for endangered species. There are countless opportunities for recreation in the surrounding forests, lakes, and trails.

MONTPELIER MANSION

The **Montpelier Mansion** (9650 Muirkirk Rd., 301/377-7817, www.pgparks.com/parks_and_rec_home.htm, Thurs.-Tues. 11am-3pm, $5) is a Georgian-style mansion that was built in the 1780s for Major Thomas Snowden and his wife. Many noteworthy guests were entertained in the home, including George Washington. The home sits on 70 acres and is

a National Historic Landmark. Several rooms in the mansion were refurbished to appear as they did at the close of the 18th century. Both guided and self-guided tours of the home are available. Montpelier Mansion hosts many concerts, festivals, and seminars.

Entertainment and Events

The **Venus Theatre** (21 C St., 202/236-4078, venustheatre.org) is a regional theater with the largest production company in Maryland. Their focus is on the adaptation of classics.

The **Laurel Mill Playhouse** (508 Main St., 301/617-9906, www.laurelmillplayhouse. org) is a local playhouse that is home to the Burtonsville Players, a community theater group that has been around for more than 35 years.

Sports and Recreation

The **Laurel Park Racecourse** (Route 198 and Racetrack Rd., 301/725-0400, www.laurelpark.com) is a Thoroughbred racetrack that opened in 1911. The track has hosted legendary horses such as War Admiral and Secretariat. Races are still held there regularly and a schedule can be found on the website.

The **Fairland Sports and Aquatics Complex** (13820 and 13950 Old Gunpowder Rd., 301/362-6060, www. Rosa Mexicanoparks.com) is part of the **Fairland Regional Park.** The complex includes facilities for swimming, tennis, racquetball, gymnastics, weightlifting, and massage therapy.

The **Gardens Ice House** also within the park offers three ice rinks for skating, hockey, curling, and speed skating.

Food

The **Dutch Country Farmers Market** (9701 Fort Meade Rd., 301/421-1454, www.burtonsvilledutchmarket.com, Thurs. 9am-6pm, Fri. 9am-8pm, Sat. 8am-3pm) is a wonderful market that's open three days a week. Stop in and enjoy the smell of fresh-baked pies and other delectables. There is a good variety of food to purchase including meat, fresh produce, homemade soup, smoothies, and bread. There is also a nice restaurant on-site that serves simple but tasty food and has good service.

Accommodations

Like much of Prince George's County, Laurel primarily offers national chain hotel accommodations. One worth considering is the **Hampton Inn Laurel** (7900 Braygreen Rd., 240/456-0234, www.hamptoninn3.hilton.com, $154-169). It provides 80 guest rooms with strong, free wireless Internet service and complimentary breakfast.

The **Double Tree by Hilton Laurel** (15101 Sweitzer Ln., 301/776-5300, www.doubletreelaurel.com, $159-179) has 208 guest rooms on six floors, a fitness center, and wireless Internet. There's a restaurant on-site.

The **Holiday Inn Express Laurel** (14402 Laurel Pl., 301/206-2600, www.ihg.com, $122-149) has 117 suites, offers complimentary breakfast, is pet friendly, and has free high-speed Internet access, an indoor pool, and a fitness center. Guest laundry services are also available.

Information and Services

For additional information on Laurel, visit www.cityoflaurel.org.

Frederick and Western Maryland

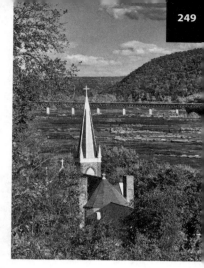

S ettled by German immigrants in 1745, Frederick was founded as a trading outpost and a crossroads for goods making their way to outlying settlements and farms. Today, the city's wonderful boutiques, antiques shops, and

nearby Civil War attractions provide plenty of options for visitors to explore. Although the surrounding area has seen an explosion of suburban housing, the historic city center has maintained its colonial-era charm.

Beyond Frederick is Western Maryland, the "mountain side" of the state, where the biggest decision of the day can be whether to go fishing or hiking. Deep Creek Lake in Garrett County offers beautiful private homes, inns, restaurants, and parks providing year-round recreation.

Western Maryland also hosted several well-known Civil War battles, including the Battle of Antietam, and the Battle of Gettysburg was just over the Pennsylvania state line. Even just one day spent exploring these sites will give you a sense of the depth of history throughout this region. The historic town of Harpers Ferry, just over the West Virginia state line, is also included with this region. It was the location of abolitionist John

Brown's 1859 raid on a national arsenal, an event that helped trigger the Civil War.

PLANNING YOUR TIME

How big a history buff you are will dictate how long it will take to explore Frederick and Western Maryland. Geographically, the area can be explored in 2-3 days, but the battlefields themselves can warrant a half day or even a full day of exploration for those with a keen interest in Civil War history. Major travel routes in the region include I-70 and I-68.

If your time is limited, select a couple of key towns to explore, such as Frederick, Gettysburg, or Harpers Ferry. Gettysburg is a must-see from a historical perspective; Harpers Ferry is both historic and an outdoor recreation haven; and Frederick offers a wonderful downtown and dining experience. All can be visited as day trips from Baltimore and Washington DC, although to thoroughly

Previous: Carroll Creek flows through downtown Frederick; Antietam. **Above:** St. Peter's Church in Harpers Ferry.

Look for ★ to find recommended sights, activities, dining, and lodging.

Highlights

★ **National Museum of Civil War Medicine:** Learn little-known facts about medical practices during the Civil War (page 252).

★ **Gettysburg National Military Park:** Commemorate the historic three-day Battle of Gettysburg that took place on July 1-3, 1863 (page 260).

★ **Harpers Ferry National Historical Park:** This well-preserved area at the confluence of the Shenandoah and Potomac Rivers includes more than 25 historic buildings and 3,700 acres of protected land (page 266).

★ **Antietam National Battlefield:** The Battle of Antietam was the bloodiest single-day confrontation in American history. The battlefield serves as a reminder of the 23,000 casualties suffered there (page 271).

★ **The Western Maryland Scenic Railroad:** This fun 32-mile excursion offers passengers a tour of the beautiful countryside between Cumberland and Frostburg (page 274).

★ **Thrasher Carriage Museum:** This great little museum houses one of the country's best collections of horse-powered carriages (page 278).

★ **Spruce Forest Artisan Village:** A dozen cabins house working art studios where visitors can watch fine craftsmanship in progress (page 280).

★ **Savage River State Forest:** This 54,000-acre forest offers a wealth of outdoor recreation year-round (page 280).

★ **Deep Creek Lake State Park:** This beautiful park boasts one mile of shoreline and endless recreation (page 282).

Gettysburg National Military Park in Pennsylvania

explore Gettysburg an overnight trip is recommended unless you have a lot of energy.

The far western reaches of the state are best traveled by car and can be explored in a long weekend. Many people make the popular Deep Creek Lake area their destination for a longer vacation, which allows time to enjoy lake activities and visit the many parks along and near its shores. Those traveling in winter can enjoy skiing and other cold-weather activities but should be advised to check weather conditions prior to their trip. Driving through the mountains can offer challenges in inclement weather.

Harpers Ferry National Historical Park

Frederick and Western Maryland

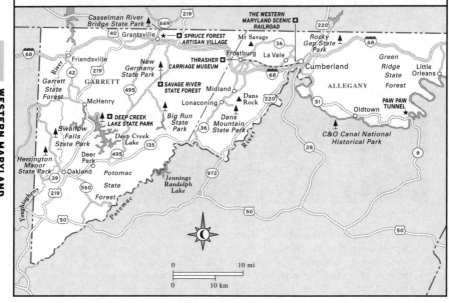

Frederick

The city of Frederick was founded by German settlers in 1745. It was an important crossroads during the Civil War, and several major battles, including those at Antietam and Gettysburg, were fought in the region. Frederick was spared from burning during the Civil War when a hefty ransom ($200,000) was paid by the townspeople to the Confederates. It served as a hospital town for those wounded in the battles fought around the region.

By the turn of the 20th century, Frederick had begun making its living off of canning, knitting, and tanning and utilizing the railroad to deliver its goods to Baltimore.

Today, downtown Frederick is a lovely collection of shops, galleries, restaurants, and antiques stores. It is less than an hour's drive from Washington DC and is a popular spot for a day trip of antiques hunting. There is a 40-block historic district, and the town is the hub of arts, culture, and commerce in Frederick County.

Many of Frederick's attractions and restaurants are near the center of town. Park your car on one of the side streets and make your way around on foot. The layout of the town is a simple grid, so it's hard to get lost. The central intersection is Market Street and Patrick Street.

SIGHTS
★ National Museum of Civil War Medicine

The **National Museum of Civil War Medicine** (48 E. Patrick St., 301/695-1864, www.civilwarmed.org, Mon.-Sat. 10am-5pm, Sun. 11am-5pm, $9.50) is tucked away on Patrick Street in the historic area of Frederick. This interesting little museum

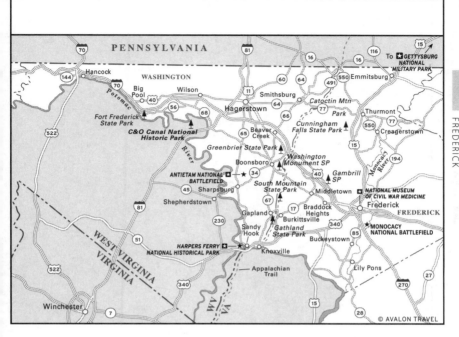

the National Museum of Civil War Medicine

started as a private collection. Exhibits cover many little-known facts about medicine and disease during the war (such as two-thirds of the 620,000 soldiers who died during the war succumbed to disease, not wounds, and doctors at the time had no knowledge of antiseptic practices or germ theory). It even explains the process used to embalm dead soldiers on the battlefield so they could be transported home. In fact, the historic building that the museum is housed in served as an embalming station following the Battle of Antietam in 1862. Information on veterinary medicine during the war and the development of large-animal infirmaries is also featured, as the armies were dependent on horses and mules. There are also many original artifacts such as medical tools and even an operating table. The museum is not appropriate for small children, and kids under age 16 must be accompanied by an adult. Allow 1-2 hours to see the museum on the self-guided tour.

Frederick

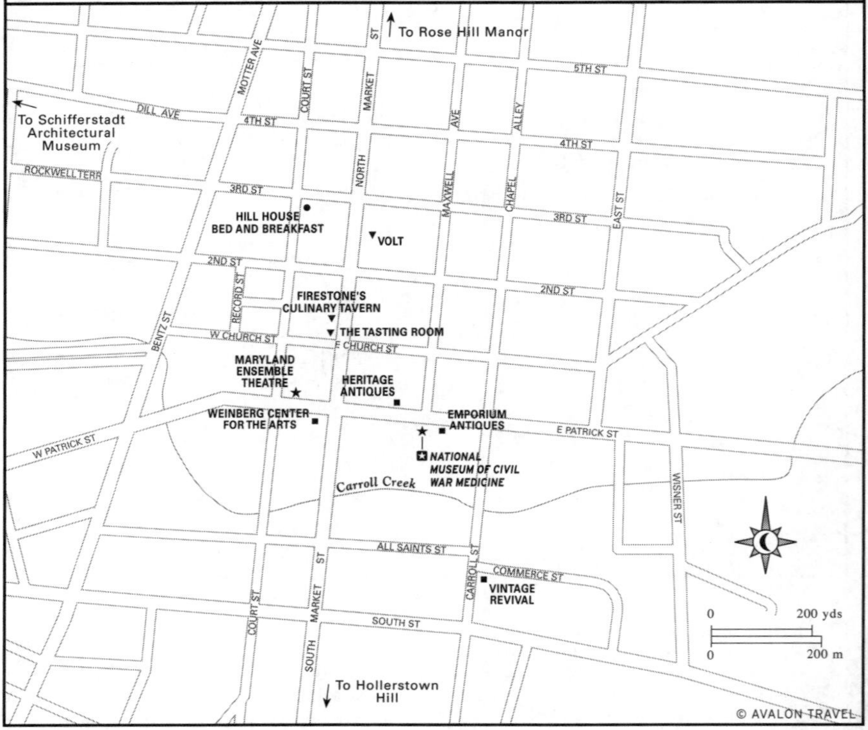

To Rose Hill Manor
5TH ST
To Schifferstadt Architectural Museum
DILL AVE
4TH ST
MOTTER AVE
COURT ST
NORTH MARKET ST
MAXWELL AVE
CHAPEL ALLEY
EAST ST
ROCKWELL TERR
3RD ST
HILL HOUSE BED AND BREAKFAST
VOLT
2ND ST
RECORD ST
FIRESTONE'S CULINARY TAVERN
THE TASTING ROOM
BENTZ ST
W CHURCH ST
E CHURCH ST
MARYLAND ENSEMBLE THEATRE
HERITAGE ANTIQUES
WEINBERG CENTER FOR THE ARTS
EMPORIUM ANTIQUES
E PATRICK ST
W PATRICK ST
NATIONAL MUSEUM OF CIVIL WAR MEDICINE
Carroll Creek
WISNER ST
ALL SAINTS ST
CARROLL ST
COMMERCE ST
VINTAGE REVIVAL
SOUTH MARKET ST
SOUTH ST
0
200 yds
0
200 m
To Hollerstown Hill
© AVALON TRAVEL

Schifferstadt Architectural Museum

The **Schifferstadt Architectural Museum** (1110 Rosemont Ave., 301/663-3885, www.frederickcountylandmarksfoundation.org, Apr.-early Dec. Sat.-Sun. 1pm-4pm, $5) is in one of the oldest homes in Frederick, dating back to 1758 and one of the best examples of early colonial German architecture in the nation. The simple stone home was built during the French and Indian War at a time when many settlers were forced to leave their farms due to raids. It is thought that Schifferstadt may have provided a safe refuge for entire families. The museum provides wonderful insight into the French and Indian War era and also shares information on early German settlers.

Monocacy National Battlefield

Southwest of the city is the **Monocacy National Battlefield** (5201 Urbana Pike, 301/662-3515, www.nps.gov/mono, daily sunrise-sunset, free), site of the "Battle That Saved Washington." The Civil War conflict that took place here in July 1864 is formally known as the **Battle of the Monocacy Junction,** so named since the fighting occurred on the banks of Monocacy River. It is often credited with saving the Federal capital because it was one of the last battles fought in Union territory as a Confederate army approached Washington DC and threatened to capture it.

Visitors should begin their exploration at the visitors center, which features interactive multimedia exhibits and maps of the

Schifferstadt Architectural Museum

battle. There is also a bookstore at the center. Information on driving and walking tours to five monuments located on the grounds can be picked up at the center.

ENTERTAINMENT
Theater

Two downtown theaters may be found on Patrick Street. The **Maryland Ensemble Theatre (MET)** (31 W. Patrick St., 301/694-4744, www.marylandensemble.org) is a 100-seat black box theater that puts on an eclectic schedule of thought-provoking plays. The **Weinberg Center for the Arts** (20 W. Patrick St., 301/600-2828, www.weinberg-center.org) is a historic performing arts venue with a full schedule of performances throughout the year including music, theater, dance, film, a speakers series, and other visual arts.

Brewery Tours

The **Flying Dog Brewery** (4607 Wedgewood Blvd., 301/694-7899, www.flyingdogbrewery.com, tours Fri. 3:30pm, 4:30pm, and 5:30pm, Sat. 12:30pm, 1:30pm, 2:30pm, 3:30pm, and 4:30pm, tasting room Thurs.-Fri. 3pm-8pm, Sat. noon-8pm, Sun. noon-6pm) is a great local brewery that produces terrific beer and offers one of the best brewery tours around. Tour leaders are humorous, informative, and present a good mix of interesting information and beer samples. This is a fun time for beer lovers. Tours are two hours and include five tastings and a souvenir glass. Tour participants must be 21 or older.

SHOPPING

Shopping is what brings many visitors to the historic district in Frederick. Many antiques shops line the streets, making the town a popular destination for treasure hunters. Some shops are even dog friendly, including **Emporium Antiques** (112 E. Patrick St., 301/662-7099, www.emporiumantiques.com), which offers more than 100 dealers and is known for vintage furnishings and home decor items; **Vintage Revival** (124 Carroll St., 301/624-4032), offering arts and crafts; and **Heritage Interiors** (39 E. Patrick St., 301/668-0299, www.heritagein-frederick.com), a consignment store carrying antique, traditional, and modern furniture. Art galleries and studios are also plentiful in Frederick as are home furnishings stores, clothing boutiques, and jewelry stores.

SPORTS AND RECREATION

A 15-minute drive north of Frederick on U.S. 15 will take you to **Cunningham Falls State Park** (Rte. 15, Thurmont, 301/271-7574, www.dnr2.maryland.gov, Apr.-Oct. daily 8am-sunset, Nov.-Mar. daily 10am-sunset, $5). This wonderful 5,000-acre park sits on Catoctin Mountain and offers swimming, hiking, a 43-acre lake, fishing, a boat launch ($5), canoeing, and a remarkable 78-foot waterfall. The park is made up of two primary areas. The Manor Area off U.S. 15 (three miles south of Thurmont) includes an aviary, camping, and the historic Catoctin Iron Furnace, where iron was made for more than 100 years. The second section, the William Houck Area, is three miles west of Thurmont on Route 77 and encompasses the lake, falls, and a camping area.

Adjacent to Cunningham Falls State Park is a unit of the National Park Service called **Catoctin Mountain Park** (6602 Foxville Road, Thurmont). The park has 25 miles of hiking trails, rental cabins, camping, and live demonstrations. The park is best known as the site of Camp David.

Northwest of Frederick is **Gambrill State Park** (8602 Gambrill Park Rd., 301/271-7574, www.dnr2.maryland.gov, Apr.-Oct. 8am-sunset, Nov.-Mar. 10am-sunset, $5). This beautiful park off Route 40 in the Catoctin Mountains in Frederick County is known for its 16 miles of trails suitable for hiking, mountain biking, and horseback riding. There are two primary areas in the park: Rock Run and High Knob, the latter with several stunning overlooks from its namesake 1,600-foot knob. The park offers camping, picnic areas, and a small fishing pond.

Frederick is home to the **Frederick Keys** minor league baseball team. This Class A affiliate of the Baltimore Orioles plays at **Harry Grove Stadium** (21 Stadium Dr., 301/662-0018, www.milb.com), which is a great family venue. Ticket prices are reasonable, and there's not a bad seat in the house. There are also many nice choices for food vendors.

FOOD

American

The **Firestone's Culinary Tavern** (105 N. Market St., 301/663-0330, www.firestones-restaurant.com, Tues.-Sat. 11am-1:30pm, Sun. 10am-1am, $10-44) is a fun place to meet friends or have a romantic dinner. The mix of wood, white tablecloths, and delicious gourmet menu items makes this a comfortable restaurant with an upscale feel. The dinner entrées include many steak and seafood choices such as pan-seared scallops, hanger steak, cowboy steak, and salmon. Their tavern menu offers pizza, sandwiches, and salad. Sunday brunch is lovely and includes traditional favorites such as eggs Benedict, as well as a great list of appetizers that can be combined into a meal.

★ **Volt** (228 N. Market St., 301/696-8658, www.voltrestaurant.com, brunch Sat.-Sun. 11:30am-2pm, dinner Tues.-Sun. 5:30pm-9:30pm, $80-150) may be in a league of its own for Frederick dining. This creative, upscale, American-style restaurant is perhaps the crown jewel of town. Executive chef Bryan Voltaggio (who was a contestant on Bravo's *Top Chef*) showcases his delicious creations in his hometown restaurant using fresh local ingredients. The menu changes frequently and includes seafood, pasta, meat, and game. The restaurant itself is a masterpiece, housed in a 19th-century brownstone mansion. The elegant yet contemporary dining room reflects the original Gilded Era building construction, while a glass-enclosed conservatory shows off the walled garden outside. There is also a chef's dining room.

The food at Volt is simply outstanding and very pricey. They offer a six-course tasting menu for $95 per person, with a $65 beverage pairing option. There is also a special seating at "Table 21" (a 21-course meal prepared and eaten right in the kitchen) for $150 per person. It is available Tues.-Thurs. at 7pm and Fri.-Sun. at 5:30pm and 8:30pm. It is not uncommon for the reservations for Table 21 to be booked weeks in advance, as there are only eight seats. Their dress code is business casual.

The Frederick Wine Trail

Travel historic roads around Frederick County to sample wine, tour vineyards, and enjoy many events.

- **Black Ankle Vineyards** (14463 Black Ankle Rd., Mount Airy, 301/829-3338, www.blackankle.com)

- **Elk Run Vineyards** (15113 Liberty Rd., Mount Airy, 410/775-2513, www.elkrun.com)

- **Linganore Winecellars** (13601 Glissans Mill Rd., Mount Airy, 301/831-5889, www.linganorewines.com)

- **Loew Vineyards** (14001 Liberty Rd., Mount Airy, 301/831-5464, www.loewvineyards.net)

- **Sugarloaf Mountain Vineyard** (18125 Comus Rd., Dickerson, 301/605-0130, www.smvwinery.com)

A popular modern American restaurant and wine bar is **The Tasting Room** (101 N. Market St., 240/379-7772, www.trrestaurant.com, Mon.-Thurs. 11am-10pm, Fri.-Sat. 11am-11pm, Sun. 11am-8pm, $30-50). This upscale establishment offers, as they say, a "cosmopolitan atmosphere" in the heart of downtown Frederick. The interior is nicely done with floor-to-ceiling windows that provide a view of the historic district. The food is consistently good, and the dishes are prepared with many local ingredients. Whether you have one of several delicious seafood selections, the rack of lamb, or a center cut of beef tenderloin, each is presented well and tastes equally remarkable. The service is highly professional, and the specialty drinks are imaginative. They also have a great wine list.

Scrumptious handcrafted sandwiches are the sought-after items at **a.k.a. Friscos** (4632 Wedgewood Blvd., 301/698-0018, www.akafriscos.com, Mon.-Thurs. 11am-7pm, Fri.-Sat. 11am-9pm, Sun. 11am-4pm, under $10). This lively, friendly place is a little hard to find (it's located in an industrial park), but it's still the best place in town for a sandwich. Try the "exploded" potatoes, a house special. Portions are generous, so arrive hungry.

Irish

The **Shamrock** (7701 Fitzgerald Rd., Thurmont, 301/271-2912, www.shamrockrestaurant.com, Mon.-Thurs. 11am-9pm, Fri.-Sat. 11am-10pm, Sun. noon-9pm, $8-26), in nearby Thurmont, is one of those places you pass by again and again (it's right next to U.S. 15) and think, "why is it always so crowded, even in the middle of the day?" This local landmark offers casual dining and a friendly atmosphere. They are known for their excellent fried shad roe, but also offer other traditional Irish fare. The restaurant is 15 miles north of Frederick and 15 miles south of Gettysburg, but is convenient if you're spending the afternoon at **Cunningham Falls State Park.**

ACCOMMODATIONS

$100-200

The **Fairfield Inn & Suites by Marriott** (5220 Westview Dr., 301/631-2000, www.marriott.com, $132-165) is a modern hotel with three floors and 105 guest rooms. The rooms are clean, the beds are comfortable, and a hot breakfast is included with your stay. They have a swimming pool and fitness center on-site as well as free wireless Internet. Ask for a room on one of the upper floors.

Hollerstown Hill (4 Clarke Pl., 301/228-3630, www.hollerstownhill.com, $129-149) is a quaint bed-and-breakfast with four cozy guest rooms. This late Victorian home was built around 1900. The house is amply decorated and showcases the owners' collectibles and antiques. It is located in a quiet neighborhood outside of the downtown area. Wireless Internet access is included.

Hill House Bed and Breakfast (12 W. 3rd St., 301/682-4111, www.hillhousefrederick.com, $145-195) is in a three-story Victorian town house in downtown Frederick. The location is perfect for easy access to shopping and restaurants (it is around the corner from Volt). The house was built in 1870 and offers four pleasant guest rooms. This is not a luxurious bed-and-breakfast, but if you are looking for convenience while visiting Frederick, the address is ideal.

$200-300

The perfect location for a relaxing weekend or romantic getaway is **Stone Manor Estate / The Inn at Stone Manor** (5820 Carroll Boyer Rd., Middletown, 301/371-0099, www. stonemanorcountryclub.com, $200-225). The inn is on a 100-acre estate eight miles from downtown Frederick in Middletown, Maryland. The manor house is a beautifully maintained 18th-century stone mansion with a sprawling stone terrace and manicured grounds. The house was built in three sections, the oldest dating to 1750. Each of the six guest suites is unique and individually appointed with appropriate period antiques. The innkeepers are well known for being warm, helpful, and making each guest feel welcome and comfortable. Since each suite is different, guests can select the specific amenities they want including a private porch, fireplace, whirlpool tub, or a separate sitting room. All suites have private, modern bathrooms, and your stay includes a hearty, homemade breakfast served with fresh fruit.

CAMPING

Camping is available in **Cunningham Falls State Park** (Rte. 15, Thurmont, 301/271-7574, www.dnr.state.md.us) from April through October in the William Houck Area (three miles west of Thurmont on Route 77) and Manor Area (off U.S. 15). They offer standard tent sites, campsites with electricity, camper cabins, 4-person cabins, and 6-person cabins. Reservations start at $21.49 per night plus reservation ($4.51-4.61) and daily use fees ($5). There are 180 sites total.

Camping is also available at **Gambrill State Park** (off Rte. 40 in the Catoctin Mountains in Frederick County, 301/293-4170, www.dnr.state.md.us) from June through August. They offer standard campsites, campsites with electricity, and camper cabins. Reservations start at $18.49 per night plus reservation ($4.51-4.61) and daily use fees ($5). There are 31 sites.

INFORMATION AND SERVICES

For additional information on Frederick, visit www.visitfrederick.org or stop by the **Frederick Visitor Center** (151 S. East St., 301/600-4047, daily 9am-5:30pm).

GETTING THERE

Most people travel to Frederick by car. Frederick is about an hour's drive northwest of Washington DC (49 miles) via I-270 and an hour's drive west of Baltimore (49 miles) via I-70. Bus service is available on **Greyhound** (100 East St. South, 301/663-3311, www.greyhound.com).

The **Frederick Municipal Airport (FDK)** is just east of the city. It is a general aviation airport with two runways.

Gettysburg, Pennsylvania

Gettysburg (10 miles from the Maryland state line) was the site of the famous Battle of Gettysburg. The town was founded in 1761 with a single tavern, but by 1860 it was home to 2,400 people and had a thriving community of tanneries, carriage manufacturing, shoemaking and other industries.

The town was etched into American history in July 1863, when the Confederate Army of Northern Virginia (consisting of 75,000 men led by General Robert E. Lee) and the Union's Army of the Potomac (consisting of 95,000 men led by Major General George G. Meade) converged here for a bloody three-day battle.

Gettysburg

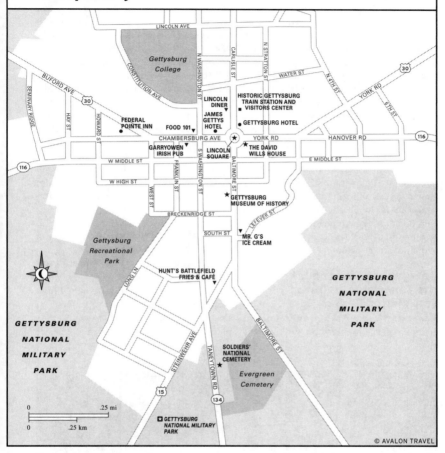

The Battle of Gettysburg is considered the great conflict of the Civil War. With 51,000 casualties, more men fought, died, and were wounded in this battle than in any other land engagement in American history. The battle also signaled a turning point in the war when the North's eventual victory became clear.

Several months after the battle, on November 19 of the same year, President Abraham Lincoln gave his famous Gettysburg Address here at the dedication ceremony of the Soldiers' National Cemetery, established as a final resting place for Union soldiers killed in the battle.

SIGHTS

When visiting Gettysburg, you feel the history all around. Since the town itself was part of the battlefield, many homes and businesses standing during the battle still bear the scars of bullet holes and other artillery fire, such as the famous **Jennie Wade House** (548 Baltimore St.), which was the site of the only civilian death during the Battle of Gettysburg (the house is now a museum and gift shop). **Lincoln Square** is a focal point of the town, where several primary roads come together at a traffic circle. Buildings here have a Lincoln Square street address, and there is a life-size statue of Lincoln next to a statue of a man dressed in modern-day clothing (so it looks as if Lincoln is talking to a tourist) in a prominent location in front of the David Wills House, where Lincoln slept the night before giving the Gettysburg Address.

The citizens of Gettysburg embrace their historical past and are eager to share it with visitors. Many historical tours and ghost tours are available throughout the town, and actors in period clothing are a common sight in the streets and establishments. By far the biggest attraction is Gettysburg National Military Park (the battlefield), which visitors can tour by car or foot, guided or unguided, to see the battlefield and cemetery.

Gettysburg Museum of the American Civil War and Visitor Center

The best place to begin your tour of Gettysburg is at the **Park Service Visitor**

Center (1195 Baltimore Pike, www.nps.gov, Nov.-Mar. daily 8am-5pm, Apr.-Oct. daily 8am-6pm). Visitors can obtain information on the park and Gettysburg area in general at the visitors center, and can then take in the 22,000-square-foot **Gettysburg Museum of the American Civil War** (admission $12.50). This wonderfully detailed museum offers exhibits, Civil War relics, multimedia presentations, and interactive programs on Gettysburg. The museum covers the battle from start to finish and even provides details on the horrifying aftermath experienced by the town. Be sure to catch the film *A New Birth of Freedom,* narrated by actor Morgan Freeman. Outdoor ranger programs are also offered during the summer months, and lectures are held in the winter.

★ Gettysburg National Military Park

The **Gettysburg National Military Park** (1195 Baltimore Pike, 717/334-1124, www. nps.gov/gett, Apr.-Oct. daily 6am-10pm, Nov.-Mar. daily 6am-7pm, free) is the site of the three-day Battle of Gettysburg that took place July 1-3, 1863. Visitors can see nearly

Gettysburg National Military Park

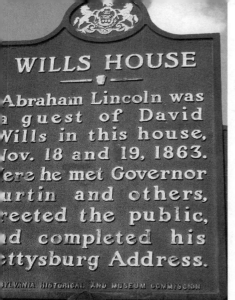

WILLS HOUSE

Abraham Lincoln was a guest of David Wills in this house, Nov. 18 and 19, 1863. Here he met Governor Curtin and others, greeted the public, and completed his Gettysburg Address.

PENNSYLVANIA HISTORICAL AND MUSEUM COMMISSION

the David Wills House

$30). Reservations can be made ahead of time by calling 877/874-2478.

A unique way to see the park is on horseback. Tours are offered through **Hickory Hollow Farm** (717/334-0349, www.hickory-hollowfarm.com, $40) in groups of up to 10 riders. Tours last a minimum of two hours.

The **Gettysburg Heritage Center** (297 Steinwehr Ave., 717/334-6245) also offers iPad rentals containing a fully interactive Gettysburg battlefield tour app called **InSite Gettysburg.**

Soldiers' National Cemetery

The historic **Soldiers' National Cemetery** (97 Taneytown Rd., 717/334-1124, www.nps. gov, Apr.-Oct. daily 6am-10pm, Nov.-Mar. daily 6am-7pm, free) is a popular stop in Gettysburg. It is the burial site for thousands of Union soldiers who lost their lives here. The cemetery was dedicated when President Lincoln gave his famous Gettysburg Address on November 19, 1863. Graves marked by plain rectangular slabs of gray granite are arranged by state. Each marker extends nine inches above the lawn. Officers and enlisted men are buried next to each other in an effort to reinforce the egalitarian practices of the Union army. Additional war veterans have been buried here since the late 1880s. Visitors can park in a lot across Taneytown Road from the cemetery. A walking tour brochure is available at the visitors center (within walking distance to the cemetery).

David Wills House

The **David Wills House** (8 Lincoln Sq., 717/334-2499, www.nps.gov, May-Aug. 10am-5pm., reduced schedule rest of the year, $6.50) sits on the corner in Lincoln Square in downtown Gettysburg. The home weathered the famous battle in Gettysburg and soon after became the center of recovery efforts for the town. It is best known as the home where President Abraham Lincoln stayed the night before delivering the Gettysburg Address and the location where he finished writing

1,400 monuments and historic markers on the 6,000-acre battlefield. Allow a minimum of four hours to explore the park. A self-guided auto tour (by map, no cost) and a self-guided audio tour (available for purchase at the visitors center bookstore, 717/334-2288) are great ways to tour the park. Field exhibits also help interpret significant sights throughout the battlefield.

Visitors are welcome to hike or bike through the park, and designated trails are marked for this purpose. Park brochures are available at the visitors center with trail maps. Biking is allowed on paved paths only.

For those wanting a more personal tour experience, licensed tour guides are available to drive you in your car as you explore the battlefield. Tours are about two hours in duration. Reservations are required at least three days in advance. Personal tour fees start at $65 and go up depending on the number of people in your group. Bus tours are available during peak summer months (two hours, the famous speech. The house is open to the public as a museum and contains exhibits on Gettysburg, the battle, and the creation of the Soldiers' National Cemetery. A life-size statue of Lincoln stands on the street just in front of the house.

Engraved bricks are fixed in the historic pathway in front of the house as a way for people to honor veterans, family, and friends. The bricks cost $150 each and become the property of the Borough of Gettysburg.

Gettysburg Lincoln Railroad Station

The **Gettysburg Lincoln Railroad Station** (35 Carlisle St., 717/334-6274, http://www.destinationgettysburg.com, Memorial Day-Labor Day daily 10am-5pm, shorter hours rest of year, free) was built in 1859 and was the western terminus of the Gettysburg Railroad line. It also served as a field hospital after the Battle of Gettysburg, processing some 15,000 wounded soldiers. During that time the station served as a symbol of hope, as it was the exit point for escaping the horror of the battle. President Lincoln arrived at the station on November 18, 1863, prior to delivering the Gettysburg Address. Visitors can see special exhibits throughout the year at this historic station, which is also available for event rentals. The station is listed in the National Register of Historic Places.

Gettysburg Museum of History

The **Gettysburg Museum of History** (219 Baltimore St., 717/337-2035, www.gettysburgmuseumofhistory.com, Sun. and Tues.-Wed. 11am-5pm, Thurs.-Sat. 11am-8pm, shorter hours in off-season, free, donations appreciated) is a great little museum stuffed full of interesting artifacts (4,000 of them). Easy to understand, easy to view, and covering history beyond the Civil War, this is a great gem of a museum right on Baltimore Street. Exhibits include artifacts from the Civil War, World War I, World War II, presidencies, and pop culture (including Elvis Presley's X-rays, books, and personal toiletries).

Lincoln Train Museum

Near the site of Lincoln's Gettysburg Address is the **Lincoln Train Museum** (425 Steinwehr Ave., 717/334-5678, www.lincolntrain.com, June-July daily 9am-9pm, shorter hours the rest of the year, $7.70). This museum offers a simulated interactive journey through American history with Abraham Lincoln. It also welcomes visitors aboard the full-size Lincoln Funeral Train Car. The museum also offers displays of working model trains.

Walking Tours

One of the most popular visitor activities in Gettysburg is taking a walking ghost tour. Several tour operators offer guided tours led by costumed interpreters/storytellers including **Gettysburg Ghost Tours** (47 Steinwehr Ave., 717/338-1818, www.gettysburgghosttours.com, starting at $9), **Sleepy Hollow of Gettysburg** (717/337-9322, www.sleepyhollowofgettysburg.com, starting at $8), and **Miss Betty's Ghosts** (443/789-9602, www.missbettysghostsingettysburg.com, $20).

Historical walking tours (not ghost related) are another great way to see the town. The **Gettysburg Convention and Visitors Bureau** (717/334-6274, www.destinationgettysburg.com) offers a free, self-guided walking tour that can be mailed out on request, downloaded from the website, and or downloaded as a free app. The tour helps visitors understand life in the town prior to the Civil War, as well as during and after the war.

Gettysburg Wine & Fruit Trail

Wine and food enthusiasts may enjoy the **Gettysburg Wine & Fruit Trail** (www.gettysburgwineandfruittrail.com). This agritourism trail showcases farms, orchards, vineyards, cafes, and accommodations in the South Mountain region of Pennsylvania. Information on the trail and each location featured can be found on the trail website.

ENTERTAINMENT AND EVENTS

Ten miles northwest of Gettysburg is the South Mountain Fairgrounds and the site of the annual **National Apple Harvest Festival** (Rte. 234 near Arendtsville, PA, www.appleharvest.com, $10). This annual event features more than 300 arts and crafts vendors and is held over the first two weekends in October. There is also live entertainment, food, hayrides, and other activities. If the weather is nice, the crowds can be large, so expect to be sitting in traffic on your way in.

Civil War buffs won't want to miss the annual **Gettysburg National Civil War Battle Reenactment** that is held in July in Gettysburg near the Gettysburg National Military Park. This three-day event includes three exciting battles, field demonstrations, live mortar fire demonstrations, and living history programs (www.gettysburgreenactment.com, $29 for one day, $49 for two days, and $69 for three days).

FOOD

American

The **Lincoln Diner** (32 Carlisle St., 717/334-3900, open 24 hours, under $10) is everything you'd expect from a small-town diner. The breakfast is all-American with eggs, pancakes, omelets, and french toast (okay, almost all American). The food is homemade (even the pies), dependable, and fresh, and they accommodate special orders. They somehow manage to cook eggs perfectly every time. Their milk shakes are a favorite also. If you're lucky, you'll witness the exchange of a few friendly insults between the regulars and waitstaff.

A "must" for cheesesteak lovers is ★ **Hunt's Battlefield Fries & Café** (61 Steinwehr Ave., 717/334-4787, daily 8am-8pm, under $10). This family-owned café is a true diamond in the rough. Walking in, you'd never expect to eat one of the best cheesesteaks of your life. Seat yourself, order a cheesesteak, and them amuse yourself by reading the vintage posters tacked on every wall. The friendly owners may come chat with you (they are longtime residents of the area). Be careful when ordering the fries, as a large bucket will feed a town. This restaurant is small, so expect a wait in peak tourist season or opt for takeout.

Another good option for outstanding casual fare is **Food 101** (101 Chambersburg St., 717/334-6080, www.food101gettysburg.com, Sun.-Thurs. 11am-8pm, Fri.-Sat. 11am-9pm, $7-16). They serve a little of everything, including pizza, salads, sandwiches, and entrees such as pasta, chicken, salmon, and steak. Their fried brussels sprouts are a winner, as is their mac and cheese.

Irish

Guinness and a Reuben. That's all you need to know about the **Garryowen Irish Pub** (126 Chambersburg St., 717/337-2719, www.garryowenirishpub.net, daily 11am-2am, $9-25). The most authentic Irish pub in town, Garryowen (aka "The GO") serves up great traditional Irish fare and equally impressive beer and whiskey selections. The prices are reasonable too. The staff and Irish owners are friendly, and the ambience is authentic and cozy. It's a great choice for celebrating St. Patrick's Day, but get there early! Beware if you order the fish-and-chips—the fish is bigger than your head.

Italian

Deliso Pizza (829 Biglerville Rd., 717/337-9500, under $15) is a wonderful casual Italian restaurant with great pizza. The homemade sauce and bread are worth the short drive just north of town. The atmosphere inside is very casual, but they offer pizza by the slice and takeout. Place your order at the counter and find a table if you're eating in. Their pastas and subs are good too. Entrées come with a fresh salad and bread.

Snacks

Curb your sweet tooth at **Mr. G's Ice Cream** (404 Baltimore St., 717/334-7600, under $5). They serve yummy homemade ice cream and also soft serve. There are many interesting flavors to choose from, and the building has a lot of character.

ACCOMMODATIONS

There are charming and historic hotels in Gettysburg that complement the historical nature of the town.

The **Gettysburg Hotel** (1 Lincoln Sq., 717/337-2000, www.hotelgettysburg.com, $234-294) is a charming historic property dating back to 1797. The hotel is a public landmark in Lincoln Square in downtown Gettysburg. It withstood the battle at Gettysburg and, nearly a century later, became the site of President Dwight D. Eisenhower's national operations center while he recovered from a heart attack suffered at his nearby farm. The hotel has undergone extensive renovations and currently offers 119 guest rooms and suites. It is also a popular choice for wedding receptions and offers a banquet room, fitness room, restaurant, pub, rooftop swimming pool, business center, and high-speed Internet. The rooms are comfortable and charming, but not extravagant. Parking is available in a public garage just behind the hotel. The hotel is centrally located within walking distance to the battlefield, museums, shops, and restaurants. Make your last stop before bedtime the bar at One Lincoln, just off the reception area. They offer a large variety of pints and have a friendly staff, and a quick drink will help make the beds a little more comfortable.

The **James Gettys Hotel** (27 Chambersburg St., 717/337-1334, www.jamesgettyshotel.com, $170-270) offers 12 guest suites in a historic downtown hotel. This glorified bed-and-breakfast has individually decorated rooms with a sitting room, kitchenette, and private bathroom. A continental breakfast basket is provided daily. Each suite has free wireless Internet. The interior is comfortable but a bit dated, and is decorated with European touches. The staff is friendly and helpful, and the hotel is within walking

the Gettysburg Hotel

distance to many attractions. There is free parking, and no extra charge for the "ghosts" that may live there.

A beautiful and interesting hotel is the **Federal Pointe Inn** (75 Springs Ave., 717/334-7800, www.federalpointeinn.com, $180-200). This elegant boutique hotel is in a historic 1897 schoolhouse in downtown Gettysburg. It has 18 guest rooms and suites with modern amenities. The rooms are tasteful yet not overstuffed and have high ceilings and granite bathrooms. The innkeepers are professional and friendly.

GETTING THERE AND AROUND

Gettysburg is about 10 miles from the Pennsylvania-Maryland border off U.S. 15. It is a 45-minute drive (35 miles) north of Frederick. Most people arrive by car, but the **Gettysburg Regional Airport (GTY),** two miles west of Gettysburg, is a general aviation airport with one runway.

Harpers Ferry, West Virginia

Harpers Ferry is a beautiful historic town at the confluence of the Shenandoah and Potomac Rivers in West Virginia. It is well known as the location of **John Brown's Raid,** when in 1859, famous abolitionist John Brown led 20 men in a raid on a national arsenal. His plan was to use the weapons in the arsenal to start a slave uprising in the South. Five of the men in the raid were African Americans (three free African Americans, one freed slave, and one fugitive). At the time, it was illegal to assist a fugitive slave, which further compounded the severity of the raid. The raid resulted in a force of 86 marines coming to the town, led by Robert E. Lee. The raiders were captured but not without casualties.

Harpers Ferry is also known for its hard times during the Civil War, when the town changed hands eight times. It also was the site of the largest surrender of Federal troops during the war when, in 1862, General Stonewall Jackson captured a 12,500-soldier Union garrison.

Harpers Ferry is also the site of **Storer College,** one of the first integrated schools in the United States. It operated from 1865 to

Harpers Ferry

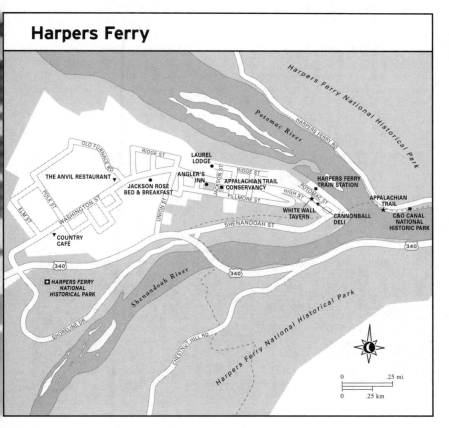

1955. The school's former campus is now part of Harpers Ferry National Historical Park.

Harpers Ferry is about a 1.5-hour drive from both Washington DC and Baltimore, Maryland. The town is known as an outdoor recreation destination and offers adventures in hiking, white-water rafting, tubing, canoeing and kayaking, mountain biking, and fishing.

Parking in the lower part of town is difficult. Strict parking restrictions were put in place to maintain the historic appearance of the town.

SIGHTS
★ Harpers Ferry National Historical Park

Harpers Ferry National Historical Park (304/535-6029, www.nps.gov/hafe, daily 9am-5pm, $10 by car, $5 on foot) is made up of 3,700 acres of parkland and the lower portion of the town of Harpers Ferry. It features more than 25 historic buildings in the Shenandoah Street, High Street, and the Potomac Street areas. The town sits at the confluence of the Potomac and Shenandoah Rivers (which makes it prone to flooding during high water).

The best way to begin exploration is to park at the **Visitors Center** (171 Shoreline Dr.), tour the center, pick up a map of the town, and then hop on a bus to the historic downtown area. It is possible to drive into the historic downtown area, but there is very limited parking since the Park Service does not allow street parking in an effort to preserve the original look of the town. There is a small parking lot at the **Harpers Ferry Train Station** on Potomac Street.

The park includes many 19th-century homes that were erected by the federal government for people working for the **Harpers Ferry National Armory.** The armory mass-produced military arms for the United States and was one of two such arsenals in the country (the other was located in Massachusetts). The armory was the site of the famous raid by abolitionist John Brown in 1859, part of an unsuccessful attempt to start a slave revolt. After the Civil War started in 1861, the armory became an important point of control for both armies since it was near the Mason-Dixon line.

John Brown's Fort in Harpers Ferry National Historical Park

Its strategic location resulted in much turmoil for Harpers Ferry, as the town changed hands numerous times during the war.

The armory site became the location of the **Harpers Ferry Train Station** in 1889 and remains as such today. **John Brown's Fort** (which was the armory's guardhouse) is the only surviving building from the Civil War. It was moved several times and now sits approximately 150 feet east of its original location (the original site is now covered by the railroad).

Victorian and federal-style homes in the town entertained well-known guests such as Woodrow Wilson, Mark Twain, and Alexander Graham Bell. General Stonewall Jackson also spent time in Harpers Ferry during the Civil War when he used the town as a command base.

There are many museums and historic landmarks in town, including a museum on **Meriwether Lewis,** who came to Harpers Ferry in 1803 to purchase weapons from the U.S. National Arsenal for his transcontinental expedition. Among the items he bought were 15 rifles, 15 powder horns, 30 bullet molds, knives, tomahawks, and repair tools. Another landmark is **White Hall Tavern** on Potomac Street. The tavern was owned by Frederick Roeder, the first civilian casualty of the Civil War in Harpers Ferry. The tavern was a drinking house for armory employees but was taken over by Northern forces after Roeder's death and used as a site for strategic planning. It was located on the south side of Potomac Street across from the original armory (now the train station).

Another historic building in the park is the **Stipes' Boarding House** (Shenandoah Street) where Cornelia Stipes took in visitors during the Civil War. Among others, she hosted military officers and one of the first war correspondents, James Taylor, who captured pieces of the war in his military sketches. Other buildings include a mill, blacksmith shop, dry goods store, and bookshop. Just outside the historic park area but still within the town of Harpers Ferry are shops and restaurants that are easily reached on foot.

The park is technically located in three states—West Virginia, Virginia, and Maryland—and is managed by the National Park Service. Harpers Ferry National Historical Park offers many opportunities for outdoor adventure including trail hiking, boating, biking, and guided ranger tours. Visitors can get a lovely view of the water gap where the Potomac and Shenandoah Rivers meet by hiking up to the spot visited by Thomas Jefferson on October 25, 1783, now called **Jefferson Rock.** From the lower part of town, make your way to High Street and the stone steps that lead up to St. Peter's Church. The steps continue past the church and turn into a steep 5-minute climb. The view is spectacular, and you will find out why Jefferson said it was "worth a voyage across the Atlantic." Much of the area is tree covered, and more than 170 bird species and 30 mammal species are found in the park.

Appalachian Trail Conservancy Headquarters and Visitors Center

Harpers Ferry is one of the few towns that the **Appalachian Trail (AT)** passes directly through. The **Appalachian Trail Conservancy Headquarters** (799 Washington St., 304/535-6331, www.appalachiantrail.org, daily 9am-5pm) is just a quarter of a mile off the trail. They offer maps, membership services, books, and other merchandise for sale. They can also answer all types of questions regarding the AT. The center is home to an enormous raised-relief map of the entire Appalachian Trail. It is one-of-a-kind and more than 10 feet long. Pictures of more than 15,000 Appalachian Trail thru-hikers and section-hikers who have passed through the town since 1979 are kept in photo albums in the headquarters building.

The **Harpers Ferry AT Visitor Center** is in the same building as the Appalachian

Following the Appalachian Trail

The Appalachian Trail passes through 14 states on the East Coast and is approximately 2,180 miles long. It is the longest continuously marked trail in the world. The trail's northern terminus is in Katahdin, Maine, and the southern terminus is at Springer Mountain in Georgia.

Each year, between 2 and 3 million people hike on the Appalachian Trail and more than 2,500 people attempt to hike the entire trail in one season. These people are called "thru-hikers." About 25 percent who start hiking with the intent of completing the trail in one season finish each year. For those who hike it end to end, it normally takes between five and seven months. Thru-hikers normally adopt a "trail name" or are given one by other hikers they meet along the way. The names are often funny or descriptive such as "Iron Toothpick," "Thunder Chicken," or "Mr. Optimist."

The Appalachian Trail was completed in 1937 and is part of the national park system, although it is managed by a combination of public and private entities. Although Harpers Ferry is home to the trail headquarters, only about four miles of the trail pass through West Virginia. Virginia claims the most miles along the trail at approximately 550.

There are literally hundreds of entrances to the Appalachian Trail, making it accessible to millions of people. Some people called "section-hikers" also hike the entire length of the trail, but do so in segments over several years. The total elevation gain on the Appalachian Trail equals the elevation gain of climbing Mt. Everest 16 times.

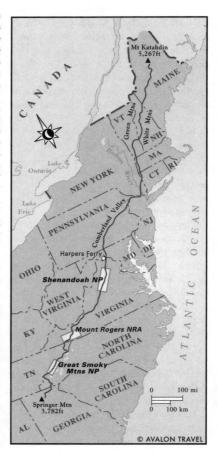

Additional information can be found on the Appalachian Trail Conservancy website at www.appalachiantrail.org.

Appalachian Trail Conservancy Headquarters and Visitor Center

Trail Conservancy headquarters and shares the same address, phone number, and hours. It offers great information on the town and is a starting point for many beautiful day hikes.

ENTERTAINMENT

For a great history lesson and a pleasant hour-long walk, join historian Rick Garland and his **Ghost Tours of Harpers Ferry** (304/725-8019, www.harpersferryghost.20m.com, $14). This is a wonderful and entertaining way to learn about the buildings in town and the stories behind them. The tour is family and dog friendly and sometimes draws a large crowd. Tours are given year-round and meet at the Piazza (front patio) of St. Peter's Catholic Church (100 Church Street).

SPORTS AND RECREATION

The **C&O Canal National Historical Park** (www.nps.gov/choh) is a great place to ride a mountain bike or hybrid bike just across the Potomac River from Harpers Ferry. Access to

the park's towpath is from a walkway along the railroad bridge that crosses the Potomac River at the end of Shenandoah and Potomac Streets. Access to the **Appalachian Trail** is from the same footbridge and offers great hiking along the famous 2,180-mile trail.

If you're feeling adventurous, take a **Harpers Ferry Zip Line Canopy Tour** (408 Alstadts Hill Rd., 304/535-2663, www.harpersferryzipline.com, $99). A guide will take you high above the ground through the trees on seven zip lines ranging from 200 to 800 feet long. There are also ladders to climb and bridges to cross. Tours last three hours.

River Riders (800/326-7238, www.river-riders.com) offers white-water rafting trips on the Shenandoah and Potomac Rivers. Trips are 2-3 hours and available guided (Mar.-Nov., $79 includes picnic) or self-guided (Memorial Day-Labor Day, $54). River Riders also offers 1.5-to 2-hour flat-water tubing trips on the Shenandoah (May-Sept., $45), 1- to 3.5-hour white-water tubing trips on the Potomac River

(May-Sept., $44), full-day guided fishing trips (by boat) on the Shenandoah and Potomac Rivers (Apr.-Oct., $500 up to two people), and a "Potomac Play Pass" that allows you to canoe, kayak, stand-up paddleboard, and/or bike for 2-4 hours (Mar.-Nov., $29-39).

The **Harpers Ferry Adventure Center** (540/668-9007, www.harpersferryadventurecenter.com) is another outdoor outfitter in Harpers Ferry that offers guided white-water rafting on the Shenandoah and Potomac Rivers (Apr.-Aug., $72), flat-water tubing on the Shenandoah River (mid-April-Oct., all day $36), white-water tubing trips on the Potomac River (mid-April-Oct., $36), ropes courses, and zip line adventures.

Bike rentals are also available through **River & Trail Outfitters** (301/834-9950, www.rivertrail.com, $21 for a half day).

FOOD

A good place to grab a sandwich is the **Cannonball Deli** (148 High St., 304/535-1762, weekdays 10am-6pm, weekends 10am-8pm, under $10). They offer quick service, a pleasant staff, good food, and a nice patio. The menu has a variety of casual items such as sandwiches, gyros, and hot dogs. This is a popular stop with Appalachian Trail hikers.

If you're yearning for a mom-and-pop restaurant with a friendly atmosphere and good food, stop in the **Country Café** (1723 W. Washington St., 304/535-2327, www.country-cafe.com, Tues.-Sun. 7:30am-3pm, under $10). They serve breakfast and lunch in a cozy atmosphere and have been doing so since 1989.

The Anvil Restaurant (1290 W. Washington St., 304/535-2582, www.anvil-restaurant.com, Wed.-Sun. 11am-9pm, $7-28) is a lovely restaurant specializing in seafood with entrees such as fresh Maryland oysters, shrimp scampi, and their signature crab cakes, but they also offer sandwiches, chicken, pasta, and beef. This is a good choice for a relaxing lunch or dinner after a day outdoors. They have a beer, wine, and children's menu (not together).

ACCOMMODATIONS

An authentic experience in Harpers Ferry can be highlighted with a stay in a lovely historic inn or bed-and-breakfast.

The ★ **Laurel Lodge** (844 E. Ridge St., 304/535-2886, www.laurellodge.com, $165-195) is a charming bed-and-breakfast with a lot of character. It offers gorgeous views of the Potomac River and makes a great home base for exploring the area. There are four guest rooms (three with queen beds and one with two twins). Two have private en suite bathrooms, and the other two have private hall bathrooms. A delicious locally sourced breakfast is served each morning with a hot entrée. Little extras throughout the lodge make for an extra-comfortable stay such as locally made soap, plentiful board games, Civil War-era artifacts, and an overall tasteful décor.

The Jackson Rose Bed and Breakfast (1167 W. Washington St., 304/535-1528, www.thejacksonrose.com, $140-160) is known to have served as Stonewall Jackson's headquarters for a short time near the start of the Civil War. This beautiful bed-and-breakfast offers four nicely appointed guest rooms and welcoming innkeepers. They are also known for serving scrumptious breakfasts.

The Angler's Inn (867 W. Washington St., 304/535-1239, www.theanglersinn.com, $155-185) is another nice option in a good location on Washington Street. They offer four comfortable guest rooms with private bathrooms. Professional fishing guide services are available through the inn.

GETTING THERE

Harpers Ferry is 21 miles southwest of Frederick via U.S. Route 340 west. It is serviced by **Amtrak** (112 Potomac St., 800/872-7245, www.amtrak.com) and **Maryland Area Rail Commuter (MARC)** (410/539-5000, http://mta.maryland.gov, weekdays only). Both offer trains to the historic **Harpers Ferry Train Station** (Potomac and Shenandoah Sts.) that was originally built by the Baltimore and Ohio Railroad and dates back to 1889.

Western Maryland

Western Maryland is made up of a narrow strip of land that is sandwiched between Virginia, West Virginia and Pennsylvania. The area is rural, mountainous, and scenic. I-70 and, farther west, I-68 are the main travel routes through the region. I-68 ebbs and rolls just under the Pennsylvania border. Winter can come early in this part of the state due to its high elevation, and windy conditions often prevail. On average, the region receives about 200 inches of snow per year. Key towns to visit in Western Maryland are Sharpsburg, famous for Antietam National Battlefield; Cumberland, a historic railroad town; Frostburg, a small university town tucked in the mountains; Grantsville, originally founded as a small Amish and Mennonite settlement; and the popular vacation area of Deep Creek Lake.

SHARPSBURG

Sharpsburg is a small town about 70 miles northwest of Washington DC. It has a population of around 700 people and was founded circa 1740. It is best known as the location of the Battle of Antietam, the bloodiest single-day confrontation to ever take place on U.S. soil. Sharpsburg is the ending point on the 126-mile **Antietam Campaign Scenic Byway,** which begins in White's Ferry, Maryland. This byway follows the events of Robert E. Lee's army as they crossed the Potomac River into Maryland and then retreated back into West Virginia after the Battle of Antietam.

Sights
★ ANTIETAM NATIONAL BATTLEFIELD

The **Battle of Antietam** was the first Civil War battle held on Union ground. It was also the bloodiest battle to ever take place in a single day in U.S. history, with approximately 23,000 casualties (from both the North and the South). During the battle on September 17, 1862, the Union Army of the Potomac launched several assaults against the Confederates, who, for the first time, had invaded the North. Vicious counterattacks went back and forth between both armies in areas near Sharpsburg known as **Miller's Cornfield** and the **West Woods.** The day ended in a draw, but the Confederates were checked of any advancement into Northern territory. This tactical victory spurred Abraham Lincoln to issue the Emancipation Proclamation.

Antietam National Battlefield is a National Park Service unit that encompasses more than 3,200 acres in the foothills of the Appalachian Mountains. This park is a small treasure for historians and anyone wishing to visit a non-commercialized yet very relevant battlefield. Visitors should begin at the **Visitor Center** (5831 Dunker Church Rd., 301-432-5124, www.nps.gov/anti, daily 9am-5pm, three-day pass $5 per person and $10 per vehicle)

Antietam National Battlefield

Antietam and the Evolution of Photography

In the spring of 1861, thousands of young soldiers came to Washington DC to defend the capital. In their wake were many photographers, eager to capture camp scenes and confident young greenhorns wearing uniforms for the first time.

Photographer Alexander Gardner, who owned a studio in DC, was eager to increase his business and take advantage of the happenings around him. To that point, nobody had taken photographs on the battlefield as photography was still new, having originated in 1839. In September 1862, Gardner ventured to Antietam two times, once just two days after the battle, and the second time two weeks later when President Lincoln visited the battlefield. Gardner was the first to capture the horror of the battlefield before the dead were buried. This was merely a novelty at first, but ultimately transformed photography into an incredible medium for communication and signaled the true beginning of photojournalism.

to learn about that fated day in 1862 before heading out to the battlefield. The all-inclusive park entrance fee can also be paid there.

The visitors center offers exhibits on the battle and the Civil War, an observation room, ranger-led interpretive talks, and a museum store. A 26-minute orientation film narrated by James Earl Jones is shown every half hour.

The battlefield itself has an 8.5-mile paved road that visitors are welcome to drive, bike, or walk (a tour map can be downloaded from the park website or picked up at the visitors center). It is designed as a self-guided tour that takes approximately 1.5 hours. The route is well marked with informative signs and designated areas where you can get out of the car and tour on foot. Sights along the route include the famous Miller's Cornfield, where much of the early fighting took place; the West Woods, where 2,200 men were killed in under a half hour; and "Bloody Lane," a sunken road where 5,000 casualties occurred. A self-guided audio driving tour with 11 stops can be purchased at the Visitor Center museum shop. Private tours of the battlefield are also available through **R.C.M. History Tours** (301/491-0002, www.rcmhistorytours.com, starting at $62.50 for 2.5 hours), during which expert guides ride along with you in your car.

The battlefield features 96 monuments. Most are dedicated to Union forces since the former Confederacy was not able to pay for monuments after the war. The monuments were erected mostly by veterans of the battle to commemorate the sacrifices made by their fellow soldiers. Six generals fell during the Battle of Antietam, and each is honored at the spot where he was killed or mortally wounded by a mortuary cannon (a cannon barrel that is inverted inside a block of stone).

The battlefield park grounds are beautifully maintained and noncommercialized. It is easy to envision what happened during the battle since the site looks much the same as it did in 1862. The battlefield is open daily during daylight hours. During the summer months, frequent ranger talks are offered. A schedule is available daily in the visitors center. Allow a minimum of three hours for your visit.

ANTIETAM NATIONAL CEMETERY

A key attraction near the battlefield is the **Antietam National Cemetery** (E. Main Street, www.nps.gov, daily dawn-dusk, free). The site is maintained by Antietam National Battlefield and is part of the National Cemetery System.

After the Battle of Antietam, Sharpsburg became a sprawling hospital and burial ground. Soldiers who died during the fight were buried by the hundreds in shallow graves on property extending miles in all directions. After the end of the war, an effort was made to relocate the bodies to proper cemeteries, and the Antietam National Cemetery was formed. Due to a lack of funds from the South and hard feelings over the war in general, the cemetery became a Union cemetery and only contains the remains of Union soldiers from the Civil War (the remains of Confederate soldiers were moved to three other cemeteries in other towns). In later years the cemetery also became a site for graves of veterans and family from the Spanish-American War, World War I, World War II, and the Korean War. Like the battlefield, the cemetery is run by the National Park Service. It is 11 acres and contains more than 5,000 graves.

TOLSON'S CHAPEL

Tolson's Chapel (111 E. High St., www.tolsonschapel.org, tours available by appointment) is a historic African American church in downtown Sharpsburg. The small 1866 wooden church was a key spiritual and educational center for African Americans after the Civil War. The church no longer holds services, but local residents are working to preserve the building and its cemetery. The chapel is listed in the National Register of Historic Places. Tours can be scheduled by emailing tolsons.chapel@gmail.com.

Food

There aren't many choices for food in Sharpsburg, but **Captain Benders Tavern** (111 E. Main St., 301/432-5813, www.captainbenders.com, Mon. 4pm-midnight, Tues.-Thurs. 11am-midnight, Fri.-Sat. 11am-2am, Sun. noon-midnight, $9-29) offers a good selection of sandwiches, wraps, salads, and casual entrées. If you're up for the challenge, their "Monument Tower of Death," which includes three 8-ounce Black Angus burger patties with all the fixings (including cheese fries), is free if you eat it in 30 minutes. They also have a good bar and live music some nights. The tavern has been serving food since 1936 and is named after a C&O Canal boatman.

For a great scoop of ice cream, visit **Nutter's Ice Cream** (100 E. Main St., 301/432-5809, daily 1pm-9pm, under $5). They serve generous portions of delicious ice cream at a great price. The line can be out the door and they only take cash, but you won't be disappointed. Order a "lollipop"—it is the specialty.

Accommodations

The **Jacob Rohrbach Inn** (138 W. Main St., 301/432-5079, www.jacob-rohrbach-inn.com, $165-225) offers five beautiful guest rooms with private bathrooms. Guests are treated to a lovely multicourse breakfast, fresh-baked cookies, coffee, and beverages. The inn's garden provides many herbs, fruits, and flowers. The home was built in 1804 and is conveniently located in town near the battlefield. Gracious hosts add to the charm of this historic bed-and-breakfast.

Another choice is the **Inn at Antietam** (220 E. Main St., 301/432-6601, www.innatantietam.com, $135-195). This charming inn is next to the Antietam National Cemetery and offers five guest rooms. The rooms are comfortable but do not have televisions or Internet access. The inn serves a delightful breakfast and afternoon refreshments.

Captain Benders Tavern

the Inn at Antietam

Getting There

Sharpsburg is near the West Virginia border along Route 34. It is approximately 70 miles northwest of Washington DC and 22 miles west of Frederick.

CUMBERLAND

Cumberland is the largest city in Allegany County, with nearly 21,000 people. It was founded in 1787. Although it is the regional center for business, it is also one of the more economically challenged areas in the country based on per capita income.

Cumberland is going through a renaissance of sorts, with a focus on the revitalization of the downtown area with new stores, restaurants, and galleries. Downtown Cumberland is quaint and charming, with its trademark church steeples, pleasant cobblestoned pedestrian area on Baltimore Street, and extensive railway history. Outdoor enthusiasts will enjoy the Great Allegheny Passage trail and the C&O Canal trail and the sights at Canal Place.

Sights
CANAL PLACE

Canal Place (13 Canal St., 301/724-3655, www.canalplace.org) is a 58-acre park off Canal Street by the Western Maryland Railway Station. The park is home to the **Cumberland Visitor Center** (301/722-8226) for the **Chesapeake & Ohio Canal National Historical Park,** and marks the end of the C&O Canal Towpath. It also offers a picnic area, a replica of a canal boat, shops, and the jumping-off point to the Western Maryland Scenic Railroad. Exhibits at the visitors center explain how the canal was constructed and how cargo was transported on the canal, and also provide information on the locks and crew that kept the canal in operation.

The canal boat replica (called *The Cumberland*) is located in the Trestle Walk at Canal Place, a brick promenade that connects the train station and canal. Visitors can view the captain's cabin, the mule shed, and the hay house.

★ THE WESTERN MARYLAND SCENIC RAILROAD

Western Maryland is railroad country. Many historic railroad milestones occurred in the Cumberland area, including the use of the first iron rail made in the United States and the production of unique steam engines by the Cumberland & Pennsylvania Railroad. **The Western Maryland Scenic Railroad** (13 Canal St., 301/759-4400, www.wmsr.

The Chesapeake & Ohio Canal National Historical Park

The **Chesapeake & Ohio Canal National Historical Park** (301/722-8226, www.nps.gov/choh) is a 184.5-mile-long park covering 12,000 acres that runs parallel to the Potomac River. The park is a linear towpath (7-12 feet wide) along the old canal that extends from Cumberland, Maryland, to Georgetown in Washington DC.

The original canal was in operation between 1831 and 1924 and served many communities along the Potomac River by providing a transport system for coal, lumber, and agricultural products. The canal boats were pulled by mules that walked alongside the canal on the towpath. At one time there could be as many as 2,000 mules working on the canal (operating in six-hour shifts).

The 605-foot elevation change and many stream crossings along the canal were accommodated by 74 locks, more than 150 culverts, and 11 aqueducts. There is also a 3,118-foot tunnel—the Paw Paw Tunnel—that the canal went through.

Cumberland was not planned as the western terminus of the canal, but when the canal reached Cumberland, the project ran out of money. The end of the C&O Canal is marked in Cumberland and a statue of a mule stands nearby at the Chesapeake & Ohio Canal National Historical Park.

The park is a beautiful and popular multistate trail for biking, running, walking, and boating. It passes near several popular towns such as Harpers Ferry, West Virginia, and Sharpsburg, Maryland. Two reproduced canal boats (pulled by mules) offer historical rides in the park (301/739-4200, June-Aug. Fri.-Sun. 11am, 1:30pm, and 3pm, shorter hours rest of the year, $8).

Bike and boat rentals are available through two National Park Service partners at the downstream portion of the canal in Washington DC: **The Boathouse at Fletchers Cove** (milepost 3.2, 4940 Canal Rd. NW, Washington DC, 202/244-0461, www.fletcherscove.com, kayak $13 per hour, canoe $15 per hour, rowboat $15 per hour, bike $9 per hour) and **Thompson Boat Center** (milepost 0, 2900 Virginia Ave. NW, Washington DC, 202/333-9543, www.thompsonboat-center.com, kayak $16.50 per hour, canoe $16.50 per hour, bike $10 per hour).

com, 11:30am departure, days vary by season, coach $40, lounge $65, first class $100) provides fun round-trip excursions from downtown Cumberland to nearby Frostburg on tracks that used to belong to the Western Maryland Railway. The trip is made by diesel locomotive and is 32 miles round-trip. The excursion takes 3.5 hours. There is a 1.5-hour stop in Frostburg where passengers can have lunch, sightsee, and watch the train rotate on a giant turntable to position itself for the return trip. This is an entertaining and educational ride through a scenic Appalachian landscape. The train even passes through the Narrows, a cut in the mountains that was considered at one time to be the gateway to the West. October is the busiest month, so make a reservation early. Dinner trips are also available (lounge $65, first class $125).

EMMANUEL PARISH OF THE EPISCOPAL CHURCH

The **Emmanuel Parish of the Episcopal Church** (16 Washington St., 301/777-3364, www.emmanuelparishofmd.org, free) is on the former site of Fort Cumberland, the place where George Washington started his military career. Earthwork tunnels built in 1755 from the original fort remain under the church and can be visited. The tunnels were created for several purposes: to keep perishable food fresh, to store gunpowder, and to provide British soldiers a safe route to reach their defenses during the French and Indian War. A hundred years later, the same tunnels were used by the Underground Railroad to harbor escaping slaves seeking safety. The gothic revival-style church was originally built in 1803, and the current structure was completed in 1851. It contains beautiful

Western Maryland Scenic Railroad

stained glass windows from three distinct periods. Services are still held regularly, and the public is welcome, as the church makes clear: "We extend a special welcome to those who are single, married, divorced, gay, filthy rich, dirt poor, yo no habla Ingles...those who are crying new-borns, skinny as a rail or could afford to lose a few pounds."

GORDON-ROBERTS HOUSE

The **Gordon-Roberts House** (218 Washington St., 301/777-8678, www.gordon-robertshouse.com, Wed.-Sat. 10am-4pm, guided tours on the hour, $7) is a three-story home offering visitors the chance to learn about life in Cumberland in the late 1800s. The second empire-style home is one of a handful in that style located in the historic district of Washington Street. The home is constructed from handmade bricks. It was owned by an upper-middle-class family and displays furnishings, textiles, art, toys, clothing, and other artifacts. The home is owned and run by the Allegany Historical Society.

Sports and Recreation

Two highly regarded trails meet in Cumberland: the **Chesapeake & Ohio Canal National Historical Park** and the

Great Allegheny Passage. The Chesapeake & Ohio Canal National Historical Park runs 184.5 miles between Cumberland and Georgetown in Washington DC, and the Great Allegheny Passage runs 141 miles between Cumberland and Pittsburgh, Pennsylvania.

Rocky Gap State Park (12500 Pleasant Valley Rd., Flintstone, 301/722-1480, www.dnr2.maryland.gov, daily 7am- sunset, free) is seven miles northeast of Cumberland in

Great Allegheny Passage

Where the C&O Canal Towpath ends, the Great Allegheny Passage (GAP) begins. This 141-mile rail trail connects Cumberland with Pittsburgh, Pennsylvania, and is known as a great biking trail (although it is a multiuse trail and excellent for hiking also). Travelers can enjoy a fairly flat trail that meanders along rivers, through valleys, and through scenic small towns.

The Great Allegheny Passage is part of the Potomac Heritage National Scenic Trail, which is one of only eight scenic trails that is nationally designated. For additional information on the GAP, call 888/282-2453 or visit www.atatrail.org.

Allegany County. This picturesque 3,400-acre park is surrounded by mountains and has a beautiful 243-acre lake, Lake Habeeb, with white-sand beaches. The complex includes a snack bar, a ranger station, bathhouse, and a nature center. There are forested trails for hiking, mountain biking, and trail running, and the park is home to the **Rocky Gap Lodge and Golf Resort,** which features an 18-hole golf course.

Food

Ristorante Ottaviani (25 N. Centre St., 301/722-0052, www.ottavianis.com, Mon.-Sat. 5pm-10pm, Sun. 4pm-8pm, $13-38) offers top-notch Italian food in a romantic atmosphere (white tablecloths, dim lighting). This family-owned restaurant is a favorite in downtown Cumberland, despite its somewhat bland exterior. The menu is imaginative and contains recipes passed down for generations. The staff is extremely accommodating and goes out of its way on special occasions. The wine list is well planned and reasonably priced.

The **Baltimore Street Grill** (82 Baltimore St., 301/724-1711, Mon.-Sat. 11am-10pm, $11-30) is a great local place with lively conversation, friendly patrons (and staff), and good food. This is the "happening spot" in Cumberland, and in the summer the outdoor seating makes it even better. They have good pub food—think crab cakes, Cajun food, spicy wings, salads, and more.

The **M and M Bake Shop** (80 Baltimore St., 301/722-2660, Mon.-Sat. 5:30am-2pm) is an old-style bakery in downtown Cumberland. They sell all sorts of sweet delights, such as cookies, brownies, doughnuts, pies, and cakes, as well as bread. All items are made on-site.

For a good quick lunch and some local flair, stop by **Curtis Famous Weiners** (35 N. Liberty St., 301/759-9707, Mon.-Sat. 9am-9pm, under $10). This old-time hot dog shop has been a Cumberland fixture since the early 1900s. Generations of local families have memories of eating yummy hot dogs and fries and drinking root beer here. These are hands down the best hot dogs in town, and patrons have been known to drive several hours for them.

Accommodations

Several chain hotels have representation in Cumberland including the **Fairfield Inn & Suites Cumberland** (21 N. Wineow St., 301/722-0340, www.marriott.com, $156-179), which has 96 rooms in downtown Cumberland, and the **Ramada Cumberland Downtown** (100 S. George St., 301/724-8800, www.ramada.com, $92-99), which offers 130 rooms and is also downtown.

There are also a few good inns and resorts in the Cumberland area. The **Bruce House Inn** (201 Fayette St., 301/777-8181, www.brucehouseinn.com, $109-175) is one of the oldest homes in Cumberland, having been built in 1840. The house is a federal Italianate-style home with a brick exterior, high ceilings, and a pretty curved staircase. It sits on a hill with a view of the church steeples Cumberland is known for and welcomes guests with a simple but elegant charm. The inn has five guest rooms with private bathrooms. A full gourmet breakfast is served each morning, and wine and tea are offered each afternoon. The inn has modern amenities such as Internet access, but maintains an old-world charm.

The Inn on Decatur (108 Decatur St., 301/722-4887, www.theinnondecatur.net, $138) has two immaculate rooms, delicious full breakfast, and a wonderful innkeeper. This federal-style bed-and-breakfast (circa 1870) offers a relaxing atmosphere with modern amenities and a location just two blocks from the downtown pedestrian area. The knowledgeable host is also a tour operator and provides complimentary tours of Cumberland to her guests. There are no televisions in the rooms.

Rocky Gap Casino and Resort (16701 Lakeview Rd., Flintstone, 301/784-8400, www.rockygapcasino.com, $179-219) is on Lake Habeeb in **Rocky Gap State Park,** in nearby Flintstone. There are 220 guest rooms, a casino, an 18-hole golf course, a restaurant, and meeting facilities. The exterior and grounds of the lodge are lovely, and the location right in Rocky Gap State Park is hard to beat. The interior is pleasant but could use some updating. Rooms have a lake or golf course view, and there are many hiking and biking trails in the park. The lodge is a bit isolated, but extremely convenient to I-68. Drink prices at the lodge are very reasonable.

Information and Services

Additional information on Cumberland can be found at www.explorecumberland.com or by stopping by the visitors center in the **Western Maryland Railway Station** (13 Canal St., Rm. 100, 301/722-8226, daily 9am-5pm).

Getting There

Cumberland is best reached by car and is located off I-68. It is 90 miles west of Frederick (1.5-hour drive) and 138 miles from Washington DC.

FROSTBURG

Frostburg is eight miles west of Cumberland on I-68 and U.S. 40. It is a small city with a population of just under 8,000 and home to Frostburg State University. Frostburg has a small downtown area with local shops, pizza parlors, and other casual restaurants that are patronized mostly by students from the university.

Sights

★ THRASHER CARRIAGE MUSEUM

The **Thrasher Carriage Museum** (19 Depot St., 301/689-3380, www.thethrashercarriagemuseum.com, May and Sept. Fri.-Sun. 12:30pm-2:30pm, June-Aug. Thurs.-Sun. 12:30pm-2:30pm, Nov.-Dec. Sat.-Sun 12:30pm-2:30pm, closed Jan.-April, $2) is a fantastic little museum next to the railroad station on Depot Street (at the bottom of the big hill). The museum has one of the best collections of horse-powered carriages in the country (more than 50 vehicles) and features everything from milk carriages to funeral wagons. Visitors can learn from interpretive guides about carriages used for pleasure, work, and even sleighs in their renovated 19th-century warehouse. The museum offers a rare glimpse into the everyday lives of Victorian Americans and represents vehicles from all economic segments of the local community. It is a great site to visit when taking the Western Maryland Scenic Railroad.

OLD DEPOT

Across Depot Street from the carriage museum is the **Old Depot.** This historic station was built

Thrasher Carriage Museum

in 1891 by the Cumberland & Pennsylvania Railroad Company, a local railway. It was originally a passenger and freight depot, but service subsided in 1942 when car travel became more popular. The station was renovated in 1989 and is now the turnaround point for the Western Maryland Scenic Railroad. A restaurant and shops are located in the depot, as is the large turntable used to turn around the steam engine for its return trip to Cumberland.

Food

The **Hen House Restaurant** (18072 National Pike, 301/689-5001, www.henhouserestaurant.com, Wed.-Fri. 5pm-9pm, Sat. noon-9pm, Sun. noon-7pm, $12-38) seven miles west of downtown Frostburg off Alternate Route 40 is known for seafood (especially crab), even though it is named after the staple of the first menu back in 1961, chicken. They are, in fact, the largest seafood restaurant in Maryland west of Frederick. The menu includes crab dip, crab cakes, blue crab ravioli, and other non-seafood items such as burgers and "damn fine chicken wings." The business has been owned and operated by the same family from the very beginning.

Good Italian food can be found just off Main Street in an old brick building. **Guiseppe's** (11 Bowery St., 301/689-2220, www.giuseppes.net, Sun. 4:30pm-9pm, Tues.-Thurs. 4:30pm-11pm, Fri.-Sat. 3pm-11pm, $11-33) serves traditional Italian dishes, a number of good house specials, and pizza. The ambience is warm and inviting, and they have a nice bar area.

Among the multiple choices for pizza in Frostburg, one place stands out. **Fat Boy's Pizza Shack** (116 E. Main St., 301/689-2727, Mon.-Sat. 11am-10pm, Sun. 11am-8pm, under $15), although unremarkable in ambience and decor, makes a great pizza. They also offer a nice pizza buffet for under $10.

Accommodations

The **Trail Inn Bed and Breakfast** (20 Depot St., 301/689-6466, www.trailinnatfrostburg.com, rooms $79-129, camping $15-25) offers basic accommodations in 12 rooms next to the Old Depot and near the Great Allegheny Passage. Queen rooms and bunk rooms are available. There is also a campground on-site. The Trail Inn is a pleasant, no-frills kind of place with reasonable prices. There is a café on-site. Downtown Frostburg is a steep hike up Depot Street (or five flights of stairs).

The ★ **Savage River Lodge** (1600 Mt. Aetna Rd., 301/689-3200, www.savageriverlodge.com, $235-280) is 10 miles from downtown Frostburg, or about a 30-minute drive.

Spruce Forest Artisan Village

Tucked into the 750-acre Savage River State Forest, the lodge is constructed of spruce and fir. Its 18 luxurious and private white pine cabins offer rustic but comfortable accommodations with upscale amenities. The beautiful lodge sits on 45 private acres and has a three-story multiuse area with 10,000 square feet of space. It also houses a library and meeting space. An on-site restaurant serves breakfast, lunch, and dinner. It has seating for 75 people and serves American cuisine. They provide a splendid, carefully selected wine list. There is a gift shop and ski shop at the lodge.

The guest cabins are stunning two-story log structures with beautifully appointed interiors. Each has a sleeping loft with a queen or king bed, a luxurious bathroom, a downstairs living area, a gas fireplace, and a kitchenette. Luxury yurts are also available for rent ($255-$280). The lodge is pet friendly.

Additional lodging in Frostburg includes the **Hampton Inn Frostburg** (11200 New Georges Creek Rd., 301/689-1998, www.hamptoninn3.hilton.com, $144-169) with 72 guest rooms and an indoor pool, and the **Days Inn Frostburg** (11100 New Georges Creek Rd., 301/689-2050, www.daysinn.com, $76-90), a pet-friendly hotel convenient to I-68.

Information and Services

For additional information on Frostburg visit www.frostburgcity.com.

GRANTSVILLE

Grantsville is a very small town in northern Garrett County with a population of less than 1,000. It is 14 miles west of Frostburg on U.S. 40. It was founded as a Mennonite and Amish settlement and was originally located in the middle of a tract of land owned by Daniel Grant (circa 1796).

Sights
★ SPRUCE FOREST ARTISAN VILLAGE

As you approach Grantsville from the east on U.S. 40, you will pass the **Spruce Forest Artisan Village** (177 Casselman Rd.,

301/895-3332, www.spruceforest.org, hours vary by artisan, free). It is a half mile before Grantsville near the **Casselman Bridge** (a 354-foot-long stone arch bridge beside U.S. 40 that dates back to 1811). The artisan village was founded in 1957 and now has a dozen log and frame cabins. Many of the structures are historic and were relocated to the artisan village from other sites (some even date back to the Revolutionary War). The cabins house artist studios that sell items such as carvings, stained glass, handloom weaving products, baskets, teddy bears, and pottery. Visitors can stroll through the village and see the artists at work. This place is very cute and feels like a Bavarian village. It is worth a stop, especially when combined with a meal at the Penn Alps Restaurant.

★ SAVAGE RIVER STATE FOREST

The **Savage River State Forest** (127 Headquarters Ln., 301/895-5759, www.dnr2.maryland.gov, daily 24 hours, free day use) protects the watershed in Garrett County and encompasses more than 54,000 acres. The forest is part of the Appalachian Plateau, the western section of the Appalachian Mountains, and offers the 360-acre Savage River Reservoir, a boat launch, 100 miles of multiuse trails (hiking, biking, cross-country skiing, horseback riding, etc.), picnicking, and a shooting range ($5 permit required). Trail maps are available at the forest office.

There are 70 primitive campsites in the forest. Campers must register for their campsites within the first hour of occupancy at the Headquarters Office or at one of six self-registration sites. Pets are allowed in the forest but must be under control at all times.

There are two state parks within the boundaries of the Savage River State Forest. The 455-acre **New Germany State Park** (349 Headquarters Ln., 301/895-5453, www.dnr2.maryland.gov, daily 8am-sunset, free day use) is five miles from downtown Grantsville. It has a 13-acre lake with swimming and fishing and also offers 10 miles of multiuse trails for hiking, running, biking, and cross-country skiing. **Big Run State**

Park (10368 Savage River Rd., 301/895-5453, www.dnr2.maryland.gov, daily 8am-sunset, free day use), at the mouth of the Savage River Reservoir, also offers access to the reservoir for boating and other recreation as well as trails and picnic areas.

Food

The **Penn Alps Restaurant** (125 Casselman Rd., 301/895-5985, www.pennalps.com, Mon.-Thurs. 11am-7pm, Fri. 11am-8pm, Sat. 8am-8pm, Sun. 8am-6pm, $8-14) is next to the Spruce Forest Artisan Village, housed in the "last log hospitality house on the National Pike." It offers a variety of menu items, but is best known for its soup and salad bar and weekend buffet. They serve salads, sandwiches, and entrées with a German flair, such as roast pork and sauerkraut. There is a craft shop on-site that sells some items from the artisan village as well as from other local crafters. It is a great place to find one-of-a-kind gifts.

The **Casselman Inn** (113 E. Main St., 301/895-5055, www.thecasselman.com, Mon.-Thurs. 7am-8pm, Fri.-Sat. 7am-9pm, $8-14) has a charming restaurant serving breakfast, lunch, and dinner. The menu contains simple country food influenced by the Pennsylvania Dutch and the Amish. Sample dinner entrées include honey-dipped chicken, rib eye steak, and chopped sirloin. Homemade baked goods are prepared in the in-house bakery, and visitors are welcome to watch the bakers in action. There are two dining rooms: one in the original historic inn, and one in an addition that was built in the early 1970s. Both are cozy and comfortable.

Accommodations

The **Casselman Inn** (113 E. Main St., 301/895-5055, www.thecasselman.com, $195) is right on Alternate U.S. 40, the main road through Grantsville. Guests can be accommodated in the historic inn (which has one suite and two guest rooms, each with private bathrooms) or in the **Casselman Motor Inn** ($68-74), which is also on the property and offers 40 guest rooms.

The inn was built in the mid-1840s to serve travelers passing through the area. It is a pretty, three-story, federal-style brick home with a fireplace in each room. Many original features remain in the house today, including a stunning cherry railing on the third-floor staircase. A charming restaurant services both the inn and motel as well as visitors not lodging at the Casselman.

The **Comfort Inn** (2541 Chestnut Ridge

Casselman Inn

Rd., 301/895-5993, www.comfortinn.com, $114-139) is right off I-68. It has 96 standard, clean rooms and efficient service. Guests get a free hot breakfast with a room, and there is a fitness room and indoor pool at the hotel.

Camping

There are 70 primitive camping sites in the **Savage River State Forest** (127 Headquarters Ln., 301/895-5759, www.dnr2.maryland.gov, open all year, $10 per night). Guests can self-register for the sites at the Headquarters Office (127 Headquarters Ln.) or at one of six self-registration sites (a map is available on the website) within one hour of occupying the site. No more than six people are allowed at one site and no more than two tents or camping units (RVs, campers, etc.). No more than two vehicles are allowed at each site. Backpack camping is allowed throughout the forest. Backcountry campers must also self-register ($10 per night).

New Germany State Park (349 Headquarters Ln., 301/895-5453, www.dnr2.maryland.gov, Apr.-Oct., starting at $23.10 per night for tent sites, cabins $82-122 per night) features 63 sites total, including 11 cabins (2-8 people), as well as a bathhouse with restrooms and showers. Pets are permitted in nine sites.

Big Run State Park (10368 Savage River Rd., 301/895-5453, www.dnr2.maryland.gov, open all year) offers 29 primitive campsites ($10), two large group campsites ($56), and one pavilion for rent ($82). Each site has a picnic bench and fire ring. Leashed pets are permitted.

Information and Services

For additional information on Grantsville, visit www.visitgrantsville.com.

Getting There

Grantsville is best reached by car. It is off I-68 on U.S. 40.

DEEP CREEK LAKE

Deep Creek Lake forms the heart of Garrett County. It is 18 miles southwest of Grantsville (via Route 495) in the Appalachian Mountains and is 161 miles from Washington DC and 178 miles from Baltimore. Deep Creek Lake is a former logging and coal-mining area turned all-season vacation area, with mild summer temperatures and low humidity, and enough snowfall for winter sports.

Deep Creek Lake is a hydroelectric project that was constructed on Deep Creek in the 1920s. It was developed by the Youghiogheny Hydroelectric Company. The lake covers almost 4,000 acres and is the largest artificial lake in Maryland. In recent decades it has become *the* spot for vacation homes for many people from the busy Washington DC area.

Several small towns dot the shoreline of Deep Creek Lake, including **McHenry, Oakland,** and **Swanton.**

Sights

★ **DEEP CREEK LAKE STATE PARK**
Deep Creek Lake State Park (898 State Park Rd., Swanton, 301/387-5563, www.dnr2.maryland.gov, daily 8am-sunset, $5) sits along one mile of shoreline on beautiful Deep Creek Lake. It is 10 miles northeast of Oakland on the east side of the lake. It is also west of the Eastern Continental Divide and inside the Mississippi River watershed. The land was part of the historic Brant coal mine.

Wildlife is abundant in the park. Some of its residents include black bears, bobcats, white-tailed deer, wild turkeys, raccoon, skunks, red-tailed hawks, and great horned owls.

Public access is available for launching motorized and cartop boats (additional fees apply), beach swimming, fishing, canoeing, hiking, picnicking, and snowmobiling. There are trails in the park on Meadow Mountain that are open to hiking, mountain biking, horseback riding, wildlife viewing, hunting, snowmobiling, and snowshoeing. More than 100 campsites can also be reserved at the **Meadow Mountain Campground** spring through fall.

The park is home to the **Deep Creek Discovery Center** (898 State Park

Rd., Swanton, 301/387-7067, www. discoverycenterdcl.com, Memorial Day-Labor Day daily 10am-5pm, Labor Day-Memorial Day Fri.-Sun. 10am-4pm, included with park admission). The center is an interpretive resource for people of all ages and offers hands-on exhibits focusing on local flora and fauna and the area's historical heritage.

The Deep Creek Lake State Park headquarters is located at the intersection of Brant and State Park Roads.

WISP RESORT

Wisp Resort (296 Marsh Hill Rd., McHenry, 301/859-3159, www.wispresort.com, year-round) is a popular all-season recreation resort at the northern end of Deep Creek Lake. It is the only ski resort in Maryland (peak season lift tickets $29-59). They offer 34 slopes on 172 acres of terrain with an elevation of 3,115 feet. The vertical drop is 700 feet. There is night skiing on 90 percent of the slopes. Other winter activities include snowboarding, a terrain park, snowmobiling, and ice-skating.

Wisp also offers activities at all other times of the year. They have an 18-hole golf course and a partnership with a summer sports center that includes waterskiing, kayaking, wakeboarding, knee boarding, and tubing. The resort also has a canopy tour, a skate park, a paintball field, day camps, and disc golf. A mountain coaster is also available for kids of all ages. This hybrid coaster is a mix of a roller coaster and a mountain slide. It is 3,500 feet long and glides downhill for more than 350 vertical feet.

SWALLOW FALLS STATE PARK

Swallow Falls State Park (222 Herrington Ln., Oakland, 301/387-6938, www.dnr2. maryland.gov, Mar.-Oct. 8am-sunset, Nov.-Feb. 10am-sunset, $5) is a very popular recreation area a few miles west of Deep Creek Lake and nine miles northwest of Oakland. The Youghiogheny River passes along the border of the park through stunning rock gorges. The park has fantastic scenery and wonderful waterfalls, including **Muddy Creek Falls,**

which is the highest waterfall in Maryland at 53 feet tall. A choice of pleasant, well-marked hiking trails can be found in the park, including a short, 1.5-mile hike that takes nature lovers past four waterfalls. Visitors can hike, mountain bike, and picnic in this gem of a park that features woods, rivers, and some of the most breathtaking scenery in Western Maryland. Camping is also available.

Sports and Recreation

Outdoor recreation is what Deep Creek Lake is all about. Bike, stand-up paddleboard, and kayak rentals are available from **High Mountain Sports** (21327 Garrett Hwy., Oakland, 301/387-4199, www. highmountainsports.com, kayaks $16 per hour, stand-up paddleboards $25 per hour, bikes $16 for two hours).

If the lake, area parks, and Wisp Resort don't satisfy your recreational itch, try participating in one of the many athletic events held in the area such as the **SavageMan Triathlon Festival** (www. savagemantriathlon.com) in September, or the **Garrett County Gran Fondo** (www. garrettcountygranfondo.org) bike ride, which comprises five rides of varying distances in June.

Those interested in horseback riding can take a trail ride at **Circle R Ranch** (4151 Sand Flat Rd., 301/387-6890, www. deepcreeklakestable.com, $25-50). They offer relaxing trail rides on well-cared-for and well-behaved horses. Trail rides are available for 30 minutes, 60 minutes, or 90 minutes. The minimum age is seven.

Food

McHENRY

The **Mountain State Brewing Company** (6690 Sang Run Rd., McHenry, 301/387-3360, www.mountainstatebrewing.com, Mon.-Thurs. 11am-10pm, Fri.-Sat. 11am-11pm, Sun. 11am-10pm, $7-24) sits alone off Sang Run Road across from a cornfield. Don't let the drab exterior fool you—this is a fun place to eat with good food and even better brew. The rustic interior with wooden tables and chairs is the perfect setting for delicious homemade brick-oven pizza and craft-brewed beer. There are nice mountain views, and the patio is dog friendly.

DC's Bar and Restaurant (296 Marsh Hill Rd., McHenry, 800/462-9477, www.wispresort.com, breakfast daily 7am-11am, lunch daily 11am-4pm, dinner Mon.-Sat. 4pm-10pm, dinner entrées $10-28) in Wisp Resort offers a nice ambience with a cozy lodge decor and outstanding food. The menu has enough variety to please most tastes, and the food is fresh and well prepared. The breakfast menu has reasonably priced favorites such as pancakes, omelets, and eggs Benedict, and the dinner menu has salads, sandwiches, and entrées such as duck, prime rib, and pasta. The lunch menu is a modified version of the dinner menu with a focus on soups, salads, and sandwiches. Save room for dessert. They have three trays of goodies to show you, and they are as delicious as they look.

Canoe on the Run (2622 Deep Creek Dr., McHenry, 301/387-5933, Mon.-Fri. 8am-2:30pm, Sat.-Sun. 8am-3:30pm, under $10) serves breakfast, lunch, and espresso and coffee drinks. Breakfast is 8am-noon and includes sandwiches, cereal, breakfast burritos, and scones. Lunch is sandwich-oriented with wraps and original specialty sandwiches. Carryout is available.

No vacation spot is complete without a local ice-cream shop, and in Deep Creek the **Lakeside Creamery** (20282 Garrett Hwy., McHenry, 301/387-2580, www.lakesidecreamery.com, mid-Apr.-fall Sun.-Thurs. 11am-11pm, Fri.-Sat. 11am-midnight, under $10) fits the bill. This old-time ice-cream parlor makes more than 90 flavors of homemade ice cream and sherbet using milk from local dairy farmers. Arrive by car on Garrett Highway or by boat (it's about a mile south of the Route 219 bridge).

OAKLAND

The place for pizza at Deep Creek Lake is **Brenda's Pizzeria** (21311 Garrett Hwy.,

Oakland, 301/387-1007, www.brendaspizzeria.com, opens daily at 11am, $8-19). They are easy to find in a little shopping strip on Garrett Highway and dish out delicious and large pizzas. A great place for a group and also for kids, they offer a friendly atmosphere and tasty food made with fresh ingredients.

Good coffee and breakfast are served each morning downstairs from Brenda's Pizzeria at **Trader's Coffee House** (21311 Garrett Hwy., Oakland, 301/387-9246, www.traderscoffeehouse.com, opens daily at 7am, under $10) They have fresh baked goods and some interesting breakfast options such as a protein wrap with bananas, peanut butter, granola, and honey, as well as traditional breakfast sandwiches and waffles.

Waterfront dining can be found at the **Ace's Run Restaurant & Pub** at the **Will O' the Wisp Condominiums** (20160 Garrett Hwy., Oakland, 301/387-6688, www.acesrun.com, daily 11am-10pm, $9-27). They serve an American menu of burgers, salads, and entrées such as turkey pot pie, meat loaf, and steak. Large windows provide a view of the lake, and there is a dock for visitors coming by boat.

Accommodations

Carmel Cove Inn (105 Monastery Way, Swanton, 301/387-0067, www.carmelcoveinn.com, $175-195) in Swanton is a renovated monastery with 10 individually decorated guest rooms. This pretty little inn is lakeside on Deep Creek in a very pleasant, private setting. It is away from the main highway but close to restaurants and activities. Each guest room has a private bathroom, wireless Internet, and a flat-screen television with DirecTV and HBO. The inn provides fishing poles, canoes, inner tubes, paddleboats, mountain bikes, and snowshoes. There is also a tennis court on-site.

★ **The Lodges at Sunset Village** (23900 Garrett Hwy., McHenry, 301/387-2227, www.dclhotel.com, $229-379) provide a delightful stay in one of 20 individual log cabins for a reasonable price. The property is located close to skiing options and in the heart of the Deep Creek Lake area. There are five floor plans (for one and two levels) to choose from and all are nicely appointed with cozy yet modern log furnishings. Each cabin has free Wi-Fi, a flat-screen TV, a kitchenette, and a fireplace. Hot tub cabins are also available. The staff is very helpful and accommodating and the cabins are pet friendly.

Lake Star Lodge (2001 Deep Creek Dr., McHenry, 301/387-5596, www.lakestarlodge. com $149-299) offers 20 guest rooms and one three-bedroom suite on the north side of Deep Creek Lake in McHenry. The lodge is lakefront, and all rooms have a lake or mountain view. The lodge is near Wisp Resort and Deep Creek Lake State Park, so winter and summer activities are close at hand.

Wisp Resort (290 Marsh Hill Rd., McHenry, 301/859-3159, www.wispresort. com, $139-239) is a popular destination in the Deep Creek Lake area. It is a four-season resort with a ski area, mountain coaster (a hybrid mountain slide and roller coaster), summer adventure park, canopy tour, and golf course. The hotel offers traditional guest rooms close to the activities. Although the facility is a bit dated, it has nice amenities such as an indoor lap pool, fitness room (accessed at the far end of the pool), and a wonderful restaurant. The resort also operates a beach area at Deep Creek Lake State Park where it offers kayak rentals ($44 per day), canoe rentals ($64 per day), and paddleboard rentals ($59 per day). The staff is very friendly, and the lovely lobby is the perfect place to relax in front of the gas fireplace. The hotel is dog friendly.

The **Inn at Deep Creek Lake** (19638 Garrett Hwy., Oakland, 301/387-5534, www. innatdeepcreek.com, $194-274) has five types of spacious guest rooms with queen or king beds. The inn is right on Garrett Highway but sits back from the road for privacy. It is well maintained and has a warm and inviting decor. Rooms offer flat-screen televisions and free wireless Internet. Some rooms have fireplaces.

There are many private homes for rent in the Deep Creek Lake area. A good starting place to find the perfect rental is at www. deepcreek.com.

Camping

Camping is available in **Deep Creek Lake State Park** (898 State Park Rd., Swanton, 301/387-5563, www.dnr2.maryland.gov, spring-fall) at the **Meadow Mountain Campground.** There are 112 campsites and the complex includes heated restrooms with hot-water shower facilities. They offer primitive sites ($26.10), sites with electrical hookups ($32.10), an Adirondack-style shelter ($41.36 per night), two mini-camper cabins ($70.10 per night), and a yurt ($51.36 per night). Pets are allowed in designated sites.

Swallow Falls State Park (222 Herrington Ln., Oakland, 301/387-6938, www.dnr2.maryland.gov, mid-Apr.-mid-Dec., $21.49-32.49 per night) offers 65 wooded campsites and modern bathhouses with hot water. Each site has a fire ring, lantern post, and a picnic table. Three sites are available with electric, water, and sewer ($37.10) and there are several camper cabins ($55.10). Call 888/432-2267 for reservations. There is a two-night minimum on weekends and a three-night minimum on holiday weekends. Up to six people are allowed at one site.

Information and Services

Additional information on Deep Creek Lake can be found at www.deepcreek.com.

Getting There and Around

It is best to travel to Deep Creek Lake by car, as there is no public bus or train route to the area. Deep Creek Lake is on Route 219 (Garrett Highway). It is a three-hour drive from Baltimore and Washington DC; follow I-70 to I-68, and then take exit 14 onto Route 219 south. Follow Route 219 approximately 13 miles.

There is also no local public transportation system in the Deep Creek Lake area, so once you arrive, you will also need a car to get around.

Background

The Landscape

GEOGRAPHY

The Atlantic coastal plain (also called the Tidewater), is the easternmost portion of Maryland, bounded on the west by Washington DC. It includes salt marshes, coastal areas, the Eastern Shore, and the Atlantic beaches. The Piedmont is the low, rolling, fertile central region. The far westernmost reaches of Maryland are part of the Appalachian Plateau. This area is known for its forests, rivers, and streams. Maryland's highest peak, Backbone Mountain (3,360 feet) in Garrett County, is located in this region.

CLIMATE

Maryland has what many residents feel is the perfect climate. There are four distinct seasons, and the weather is seldom extreme. Having said this, most of the region—eastern and central Maryland—is considered subtropical, which is defined by hot, humid summers and mild, cool winters. The western portions of the state has a humid continental climate, which is defined by large seasonal temperature fluctuations with warm to hot summers and cold to severely cold winters.

The abundance of water to the east, which includes the Atlantic Ocean, the Chesapeake Bay, and many large rivers and their tributaries, helps fuel the humidity commonly associated with the region. It's no surprise that the humidity is much higher on the coast. The western mountains are typically 10 degrees cooler throughout the year and considerably less "sticky."

Springtime in Maryland is fragrant and colorful. There are flowering fruit trees, blooming dogwoods, spring bulbs, and wildflowers. Rivers swollen from melted winter snow rush by blankets of blooming bluebells, and azaleas explode throughout suburban neighborhoods. Temperatures in the spring can vary greatly, but overall offer comfortable warm days with chilly nights.

Summer brings ample sunshine with frequent afternoon thunderstorms. The humidity can be far more uncomfortable than the heat, but there are days, especially in August, where both seem unbearable and the air is so thick you'll think you can swim through it. The good news is that there are rarely washout days in the summer when it rains continuously, and when it does, it's a welcome break from the heat. The shore areas offer refuge during the summer as do the mountains, but neither can match the comfort of modern air-conditioning.

Fall is brilliant. Temperatures are cool, the humidity recedes, and the landscape explodes from exhausted greens to vibrant reds and yellows. The autumn foliage is some of the best in the country, especially in the mountainous areas to the west. Peak foliage is normally in mid-October, but will vary year to year. The local news broadcasts usually keep tabs on the foliage and let people know the best days for leaf peeping. This spectacular natural display, coupled with crisp sunny days and chilly nights, make fall the best time to visit the region.

When the leaves finally fall and the pumpkins are ripe on the vine, winter is approaching. For most of Maryland, winter temperatures usually set in sometime in December and don't thaw until early March. Even so, the area receives minimal snowfall, normally a handful of snow events each season. Although it is possible to get a large snowstorm, it does not happen every year. Likewise, temperatures can dip into the single digits, but

Previous: Baltimore skyline; tractor on a Maryland farm.

Tree Trivia

- Black walnuts give off a toxic chemical that inhibits other tree species from growing near them.
- The popular weeping willow is related to the black willow, but is native to Asia.
- Early settlers extracted the oil found in bitternut hickory nuts and used it as fuel for their oil lamps.
- Vessels in white oak wood are plugged with a substance that makes the wood watertight. This is why whiskey and wine barrels are made from the wood.
- The northern red oak is one of the most popular timber trees in the Atlantic region.

that is not the norm. The thermometer normally rests somewhere between 25 and 40 degrees during the day in winter, but cold spells and also warm spells aren't unheard of. The exception to all of this is western Maryland, which can receive between 100 and 200 inches of snow annually and has temperatures on average of about 10 degrees cooler than the central and eastern parts of the state.

ENVIRONMENTAL ISSUES

One of the biggest environmental issues in Maryland is the health of the Chesapeake Bay. The bay faces many problems including nutrient and sediment pollution from agriculture, storm water runoff, wastewater treatment plants, and air pollution; contamination from chemicals; overharvesting; invasive species; and the effects of development on its shores and tributaries. All of these threats impact the health of the bay and its ability to maintain a viable aquatic ecosystem.

Excess nutrients are the primary pollutant in the Chesapeake Bay. They increase algae bloom growth, which blocks vital sunlight to aquatic grasses. These grasses are crucial to the bay's ecosystem since they provide food and habitat to aquatic animals, reduce erosion, and produce oxygen. In addition, when the algae die and decompose, it depletes the water of the oxygen that all aquatic animals need.

The issues facing the bay are not localized

problems. The Chesapeake Bay's watershed covers 64,000 square miles through six states and DC. There are 17 million residents living in this area.

Mass media attention in recent years has led to a greater awareness of the issues facing the bay and its tributaries, but there is still a very long way to go before the problems are solved.

The **Chesapeake Bay Foundation** (www.cbf.org), headquartered in Annapolis, Maryland, is the largest conservation organization dedicated to the well-being of the Chesapeake Bay watershed. Its famous "Save the Bay" slogan defines the continued quest to protect and restore the bay's natural resources.

Another environmental issue is the need for healthy farming. Unsustainable farming practices have contributed to water and air pollution and have also resulted in soil erosion, animal abuse, and poor human health. Organizations such as **Environment Maryland** (www.environmentmaryland.org) are looking for ways to expand opportunities for sustainable farmers that grow food in ways that don't pollute the environment.

PLANTS

Maryland's central location on the East Coast means it boasts both southern and northern flora. Visitors can see northern tree species such as spruce and fir in the western mountain areas and then drive east to visit cypress swamps in the coastal regions.

Trees

Forest covers roughly one-third of Maryland. Much of the mountainous regions in the western portion of the state is heavily forested and contains dozens of species of trees such as the eastern white pine (which can grow to 200 feet), Virginia pine, pond pine, eastern hemlock, and even red spruce. Forested areas can also be found in the coastal regions. Maryland is the northern reach of the loblolly pine's territory, and the same is true for the bald cypress. Other common trees found throughout the region include the eastern red cedar, black willow, black walnut, bitternut hickory (swamp hickory), American beech, American elm, yellow poplar, sycamore, northern red oak, and white oak (which is the Maryland state tree). Many ornamental trees are also native to the region such as holly, red maple, magnolia, and the flowering dogwood.

Plants, Shrubs, and Flowers

Because of the mild climate, there are many flowering shrubs and 85 species of ferns in Maryland. Nothing announces the arrival of spring like the bright yellow blooms of the forsythia. This sprawling bush is a favorite of homeowners since it provides pretty blooms in the spring and a good screen in the summer. Several varieties of azaleas are native to the region, and in May residential neighborhoods are painted in their vibrant red, pink, purple, and white blooms. Rhododendrons are also native to the region as well as the butterfly bush (sometimes referred to as summer lilac) and the stunning hydrangea.

Spring and summer yield thousands of wildflowers. Shenandoah National Park alone has 862 species, providing a breathtaking display from early spring through summer. Species include hepatica, violets, trillium, wild geraniums, mountain laurel, columbine, and wild sunflowers. In the coastal areas, wildflowers grow among marsh grasses and over sand dunes.

Although many native flowers grow quite well, such as the woodland sunflower, hibiscus, lupine, lobelia, and phlox, some species are partial to the eastern and western sides of the state. At least two types of asters are found primarily in the mountains: the smooth blue aster and the New England aster. The American lily of the valley is also partial to the mountainous region. The coastal region has its own share of plant species that exclusively call the area home such as the New York aster and seaside goldenrod.

ANIMALS

Maryland is full of wildlife. Its mild climate and varied geography allow for many types of animals to flourish. Since the mountainous

More Than Tasty Bivalves

Oyster lovers flock to the Chesapeake Bay region to feast on the famous eastern oyster. For more than 100 years, this delectable bivalve flourished in the bay and was one of the most valuable commercial fishing commodities. However, in recent decades, overharvesting, disease, and pollution have severely reduced its numbers. This is more than just a bummer for oyster eaters; oysters are a vital piece of the Chesapeake Bay's ecosystem.

Oysters provide habitat for many aquatic animals. Their hard shells with many nooks and crannies act as much-needed reefs and are relied on by hundreds of underwater animals such as sponges, crabs, and fish. Oysters and their larvae are also an important food source for many aquatic residents and some shorebirds. In addition, oysters are filter feeders, which means they pump large amounts of water through their gills when they eat. This filters the water, removing chemical contaminants, nutrients, and sediments, which helps keep the water clean. One oyster can filter more than 50 gallons of water in a single day.

areas are heavily forested and less populated, they are home to the most animals. Although most are shy, there are often sightings of foxes, skunks, raccoons, rabbits, chipmunks, squirrels, and white-tailed deer. In some of the park areas, the deer have become too friendly with humans and will literally walk right up to you. Under no circumstances should you feed the wildlife, no matter how cute and convincing they are. Other animals that live in the western regions include the coyote, bobcat, and black bear.

The central region provide shelter for many species of animals that have learned to coexist well with nearby human populations. Raccoons, opossums, squirrels, chipmunks, beaver, and more recently, coyotes, can be found.

The coastal regions' wetlands, marshes, and rivers entice populations of lizards, muskrats, butterflies, and snakes.

There are three types of venomous snakes in Maryland and 31 nonvenomous. The most common type of venomous snake is the northern copperhead having dark-colored cross bands shaped like an hourglass. Next comes the timber rattlesnake, which is found in the mountains. It also has a patterned back with wavy cross bands.

Birds

A huge variety of birds live in Maryland, from migratory shorebirds to tiny songbirds—and even bald eagles. Maryland has 222 native bird species, but you will often see many more seasonal species that do not actually nest in the state. In spring and early summer, the woods are alive with the happy calls of songbirds, but during winter, many migrate south. On the flip side, some northern birds, such as snow geese, come down from Canada since the winters are milder here.

Many hawks live throughout the region and the red-tailed variety can frequently be spotted (although they will surely see you before you see them). Another impressive, and often seen, bird is the turkey vulture, also known as a buzzard. They are huge and can have a wingspan up to six feet. Wild turkeys are also prevalent and look like they walked out of a children's Thanksgiving story. Game birds such as the grouse are residents of the area and sometimes startle hikers by launching themselves in the air when they see someone approach.

Migratory birds such as warblers and jonquils frequent the mountain regions during the winter. The coastal areas are prime for bird-watching. More than 40 types of ducks, geese, and swans alone have been documented in water-rich areas. This area is also home to osprey, oystercatchers, plovers, peregrine falcons, black skimmers, and dozens of other shorebirds.

History

PREHISTORY

It is believed that the first humans arrived in the Maryland region approximately 18,000 years ago. They were hunter-gatherers most likely organized into seminomadic bands. As time went on, hunting tools became more efficient, and delicacies from the Chesapeake Bay such as oysters became an important food source. With new developments came the first Native American villages and the formation of social structures. Successive Native American cultures continued for thousands of years prior to the arrival of Europeans.

THE COLONIAL PERIOD

After many failed attempts at establishing a permanent settlement, in 1607 the first English settlers arrived at the mouth of the Chesapeake Bay in three ships and traveled 30 miles up the James River under the guidance of Captain John Smith. The settlers disembarked and promptly began to build a settlement at what later became Jamestown.

They found the coastal area inhabited by Algonquian natives (called the Powhatan Confederacy) who controlled land stretching from what is now North Carolina to the Potomac River. These native settlements included approximately 10,000 people who relied on hunting, fishing, and farming for survival. Another native group controlled what is now Maryland and the regions into the Allegheny Mountains.

The settlers were met with rich lands, many game animals, and initially friendly natives. Even so, they were not prepared for the physical labor and inevitable problems that came with starting a new settlement, and the colony nearly failed in the first few years. Around 1612, a colonist named John Rolfe brought in the first tobacco seeds which he had gathered from an earlier voyage to Trinidad. The first tobacco crops were planted and were soon in high demand back in England. This provided an instant boost to the New World's economy.

Put mildly, life was very difficult for the early settlers. Disease, famine, and attacks from Native Americans wiped out much of the early population. Although the Native Americans were initially friendly, it didn't take long for their feelings to change when they realized the settlers intended to stay permanently. It became unsafe for the settlers to venture past their settlement fences.

Meanwhile, in 1609, an Englishman named Henry Hudson, arrived in the Delaware Bay. Working on behalf of the Dutch West India Company, Hudson was pleased with the wonderful conditions he found in the region. As a result, in 1631, a group of Dutch West India traders established a small whaling port and tobacco-growing center in what is now Lewes, Delaware. At the same time, the first European settler, William Claiborne, came to Maryland and established a fur trading post on Kent Island.

In 1632, Charles I of England granted approximately 12 million acres north of the Potomac River to Cecilius Calvert, second Baron Baltimore. The area was substantially larger than today's Maryland, and Maryland later lost some of the land to Pennsylvania. The first full settlement was established in 1634 on St. Clement's Island.

Maryland was established as a refuge for religious freedom for Catholics, although many Protestants moved there also. This caused religious feuds for years in the colony. At the same time, its economy relied on tobacco fueled by African slave labor and indentured servants. Farming, tobacco, and the abundance of land slowly brought prosperity to the early colonies.

As land along the coast filled up, pioneers began to move farther inland toward the mountains. New immigrants continued to arrive, including people from other countries such as Germany and Scotland.

In 1649 a settlement called Providence was founded on the north shore of the Severn River and was later moved to a more protected harbor on the south shore. It was then called Town at Proctor's, which changed to Town at the Severn, and later Anne Arundel's Towne. The city became very wealthy as a slave trade center. In 1694, the town became the capital of the royal colony and was renamed Annapolis for the future queen of Great Britain, Princess Anne of Denmark and Norway. Annapolis was incorporated in 1708 and flourished until the Revolutionary War.

Maryland was a region of large plantations and minimal urban development. Since much of the plantation labor was supplied by indentured servants, few women came to the area. This, combined with a high rate of disease, made for the slow growth of the local population.

By 1700, most Native Americans had been driven out of the area. At the same time, the number of African slaves had grown rapidly in the region as the number of indentured servants declined. Throughout the first half the century, tensions between the colonies and their European motherland grew as England tried to squeeze as much money as possible out of the colonists through taxes while extending them far fewer rights than held by those living in the home country. One of the final straws came in 1763 with the passing of a law prohibiting westward expansion of the colonies, which angered many colonists. A passionate and heated speech delivered by Patrick Henry in Williamsburg in 1765 implied publicly that the colonies might be better off without King George III. Tension between England and the colonies continued to grow, and rebellious outbreaks such as the Boston Tea Party in 1773 began to grow more frequent. Maryland had its own tea party in Chestertown in 1774, when colonists burned the tea-carrying ship *Geddes* in the town's harbor. In 1775 Henry delivered his famous speech at St. John's Church in Richmond where he was quoted as saying, "I know not what course others may take; but as for me, give me liberty or give me death." Although no major Revolutionary War battles were fought in Maryland, it was the first colony to adopt a state constitution.

EXPANSION

The city of Baltimore incorporated in 1797 and experienced rapid growth as a shipbuilding and industrial center. By 1800, its population outnumbered that of Boston, and the development of Maryland's resources became a priority. Baltimore was spared seizure during the War of 1812, but suffered a 25-hour attack at Fort McHenry (during which Francis Scott Key wrote "The Star-Spangled Banner"). British troops went on to burn the young capital city of Washington DC.

After the war, steam locomotives and clipper ships were developed, greatly expanding trade possibilities. A series of canals was built, including the Chesapeake & Ohio Canal along the Potomac River, and railroads such as the Baltimore & Ohio Railroad were constructed. This greatly increased access between East Coast ports and land west of the Appalachians. By the mid-1800s, railroad lines ran through Maryland bringing wealth and prosperity to many agricultural-based businesses.

THE AMERICAN CIVIL WAR

In 1859, a raid on the federal arsenal in Harpers Ferry led by an American abolitionist named John Brown resulted in the death of 21 people—both free African Americans and whites—and the realization by the country that slavery opponents were willing to kill and die themselves for their cause.

In 1860, Abraham Lincoln was elected president and pledged to keep slavery out of the territories. In December that same year, South Carolina seceded from the Union and was followed shortly thereafter by Mississippi, Alabama, Georgia, Florida, Louisiana, and Texas. Although technically still a slave state in 1860, Maryland was one of the border states that stayed with the Union during the Civil War. However, Maryland soldiers fought on both sides.

Four years of bloody fighting took place on soil passionately defended less than a century before in the Revolutionary War. More than 600,000 Americans lost their lives in the war, more than those lost in both World Wars combined. Maryland hosted several well-known battles, including its most famous Battle of Antietam, the Battle of South Mountain, and the Battle of the Monocacy.

The Confederate city of Richmond was burned on April 3, 1865. Six days later, General Robert E. Lee asked General Ulysses S. Grant for a meeting. Terms of the surrender were drafted and signed at Appomattox Court House, and the Confederate army turned over arms in a formal ceremony on April 12. Both armies saluted each other, and the Civil War was history.

MODERN TIMES

The 1900s brought a diversification of industry to Maryland. Baltimore suffered a devastating fire in 1904, but recovered quickly. World War I gave a boost to Maryland by increasing the demand for industrial product. The Great Depression slowed growth in some markets. As American industry diminished,

Maryland turned to agriculture and U.S. government-related research and services.

In recent decades, the Washington DC area has experienced an economic and technological boom, resulting in an increase in population, housing, and jobs in the capital region of Maryland. By the early 1990s, Maryland had a population of 4.7 million.

The early part of the new millennium was scarred by the terrorist attacks on 9/11 and by sniper shootings in the DC area in 2002 that left 10 people dead. The resilient communities of DC and Maryland were actually united by these events, and today, they work together to tackle common issues such as rapid suburban development, economic downturns, and environmental preservation.

Government and Economy

Maryland is traditionally a liberal state. Maryland has a state constitution and three branches of government. Maryland is unique in the sense that it allows each of its counties to have significant autonomy.

There are five principal executive branch officers in Maryland: the governor, lieutenant governor, attorney general, comptroller, and treasurer. With the exception of the treasurer, all are elected statewide, with the governor and lieutenant governor running on one ticket. The treasurer is elected by both houses of the General Assembly on a joint ballot.

The legislative branch is a General Assembly made up of two houses with 47 senators and 141 delegates. Members of both houses are elected to four-year terms. Each house establishes its own rules of conduct and elects its own officers.

Maryland's judiciary branch consists of four courts. Two are trial courts (the District Court and Circuit Courts), and two are Appellate Courts (the Court of Special Appeals and the Court of Appeals). The Court of Appeals is the highest court.

Maryland is a small but wealthy state

Maryland State House in Annapolis

whose economy has traditionally been heavily weighted toward manufacturing. Two Maryland counties, Howard and Montgomery, are consistently listed in the nation's top 10 richest counties.

In recent years, Maryland's economic activity has included a strong focus on the tertiary service sector, which is largely influenced by its proximity to Washington DC. Technical administration for the defense and aerospace industry and bioresearch laboratories is also key in its economy. In addition, many government agencies have satellite headquarters in Maryland for which they need staffing.

Transportation is another major revenue maker for Maryland, thanks to the Port of Baltimore. The port is the second largest automobile port in the country, but also accommodates a large variety of other goods including bulk commodities such as petroleum, sugar, iron ore, and fertilizers. These goods are distributed on land in trucks and by rail, further adding to the transportation influence.

A third major contributor to the state's economy is educational and medical research. Several key institutions are located in the state, the largest being Johns Hopkins University. Johns Hopkins is currently the largest single employer in the Baltimore area.

Maryland is also known for its food production thanks mostly to commercial fishing in the Chesapeake Bay and offshore in the Atlantic Ocean. Prime catches include blue crab, striped bass, menhaden, and oysters. Dairy farming in the Piedmont region also contributes to the economy.

People and Culture

Historically, Marylanders were fishers and farmers. Although southern and western Maryland are still mostly rural, the rest of the state is now primarily urban with dense populations, especially in Baltimore and near Washington DC. This makes for a unique blend of both southern and northern American culture and a melding of ideals from both regions.

Maryland was founded as a place for Roman Catholics to escape religious persecution since the Catholic religion was repressed in England following the founding of the Anglican Church. The Catholic faith is still the most prevalent in Maryland, although it only makes up approximately 15 percent of the population.

During colonial times, groups of Quakers moved into Maryland from Pennsylvania, and in the mid-17th century a group of conservative Protestants called Puritans settled south of Baltimore. Although Puritans are not defined as such today, another conservative Protestant group, the Old Order Amish, is still strong in some areas of southern Maryland and the Eastern Shore. Their horse-drawn wagons can be seen on many roads throughout those areas.

Other religions quickly made their way into Maryland with the first Lutheran church being built around 1729 and the first Baptist church in 1742. Methodists came to the state as well, and a large Jewish population settled in Baltimore in the early part of the 1800s.

Today Maryland is widely accepting of religious diversity, and people from all faiths (and of no faith) can be found within its borders.

Maryland has always had a large African American population. During the time of slavery, Maryland had the largest population of free African Americans of the northeastern slave states. Today, African Americans make up 30 percent of Maryland's population.

Unfortunately, race relations have traditionally been strained in Maryland, and many neighborhoods are strictly delineated by race.

Baltimore is the most diverse area of the state, while western Maryland (Garrett County) is the least.

THE ARTS

Maryland offers numerous opportunities for residents and visitors to not only enjoy the arts but to become part of them. In fact, the arts are an important part of many people's lives in this region, whether they realize it or not. Access to top-rated performances, historic architecture, quality handicrafts, and literature is often taken for granted by the people who live there. A recent survey in Maryland, for instance, showed that 90 percent of the state's residents engaged in art in some form or another over the past year, whether by attending a musical performance, taking part in a festival, or visiting a museum or gallery. A stunning 84 percent said they create art in some form or another themselves. The state's long history, diversified population, proximity to the nation's capital, and relative tolerance for religious and social beliefs open it to many traditional and forward-thinking expressions of art, which in turn, has created a thriving artistic community open to everyone who passes through the area. Countless theatrical venues throughout the region, including world-renowned venues in Washington DC, invite the highest-quality performances to the doorstep of many local communities, and specialized venues provide access to cutting-edge artistic advances.

Essentials

Transportation

AIR

Most major airlines serve the three primary airports in the region. The first is **Ronald Reagan Washington National Airport (DCA)** (703/417-8000, www.metwashairports.com), just outside Washington DC in Arlington, Virginia. It is a 15-minute drive from the airport to downtown Washington DC. The airport is serviced by the Blue and Yellow Metrorail lines. Taxi service is available at the arrivals curb outside the baggage claim area of each terminal. Rental cars are available on the first floor in parking garage A. A shuttle to the rental car counter is available outside each baggage claim area.

The second is **Washington Dulles International Airport (IAD)** (703/572-2700, www.metwashairports.com), 27 miles west of Washington DC in Dulles, Virginia. It is a 35-minute drive to downtown Washington DC from Dulles. Bus service between Dulles Airport and Metrorail at the Wiehle Avenue Station in Reston (Silver Line) is available through **Washington Flyer Coach Service** (888/927-4359, www.flydulles.com, $5 one way). Tickets can be purchased at the ticket counter in the Main Terminal at Arrivals Door #4 or at the Metrorail station at Wiehle Avenue. Buses depart approximately every 30 minutes. Passengers going from the Wiehle Avenue Metrorail station should follow signs for the Washington Flyer bus stop. Tickets can be purchased from the bus driver. At the time of publication, **Metrobus** (202/637-7000, www.wmata.com) operates an express bus (Route 5A) between Dulles Airport and the L'Enfant Plaza Metrorail station in Washington DC. Passengers can board the bus at the airport at the Ground Transportation Curb (on the Arrivals level) at curb location 2E. Metrobus has proposed the elimination of this route several times since the opening of the Metrorail Silver line, so check their website before relying on this route.

The third is **Baltimore Washington International Thurgood Marshall Airport (BWI)** (410/859-7040, www.bwiairport.com), 32 miles from Washington DC near Baltimore, Maryland. It is approximately 50 minutes by car from BWI to Washington DC and 15 minutes to downtown Baltimore. BWI is serviced on weekdays by MARC commuter trains at the BWI Marshall Rail Station. Free shuttles are available from the station to the airport terminal. Shuttle stops can be found on the lower-level terminal road. Metrobus service is available between BWI and the Greenbelt Metrorail station (Green Line) on the **BWI Express Metro.** Bus service is available seven days a week with buses running every 40 minutes.

The **Washington Dulles Taxi and Sedan** (703/554-3509, www.washingtondullestaxisedan.com) provides taxi and sedan service for passengers at all three airports. Shuttle service is also available from all three airports through **SuperShuttle** (800/258-3826, www.supershuttle.com).

The **BayRunner Shuttle** (www.bayrunnershuttle.com) provides daily, scheduled shuttle service between the Eastern Shore of Maryland and BWI and Western Maryland and BWI. Areas serviced on the Eastern Shore include Kent Island, Cambridge, Easton, and Ocean City. Areas serviced in Western Maryland include Frederick, Cumberland, Frostburg, and Grantsville. Shuttle service is also available to the Baltimore Bus Terminal.

CAR

Maryland, like most regions of the United States, is easiest to explore by car. It can take nearly four hours to drive from Western Maryland to the Eastern Shore. Thankfully, a large network of interstate highways provides access throughout the entire area, even in the more rural areas on the western sides of the state.

I-95 is the main north-south travel route along the East Coast and connects Baltimore, Washington DC, and Richmond. This highway is a toll road in Maryland. I-81 cuts through a narrow portion of Maryland at Hagerstown before continuing into Pennsylvania.

I-70 is the primary east-west route and links Baltimore to Frederick and runs out to Western Maryland before swinging north into Pennsylvania, at which point I-68 becomes the primary highway running east-west in the western corner of the state. I-270 is another primary route that runs north-south between Bethesda and Frederick. U.S. 50 is the major route through the Eastern Shore in Maryland. It starts in Ocean City, runs west to Salisbury, then turns north to Cambridge, across the Bay Bridge (where there is a toll), past Annapolis, and continues west into Washington DC. It then continues into Virginia as a minor route.

Washington DC is circled by I-495, also called the Beltway, which runs through both Virginia and Maryland as part of I-95. This massive highway has access points to many suburbs and can have extreme rush hour traffic. Baltimore has a similar beltway, I-695, which is not part of I-95 but has a toll at Key Bridge.

Speed limits are posted throughout Maryland. The maximum allowable speed limit is 65 miles per hour, although most roads have speed limits posted much below their maximums. Keep in mind that state-maintained roads can have both a name and a route number.

In Maryland, text messaging and handheld cell phone usage are banned for all drivers. Drivers under 18 are prohibited from all cell phone use. Seatbelt laws are enforced.

The Washington area is not known for its efficiency at clearing snow off the roads in winter, but for the most part, state-maintained roads are plowed fairly quickly. The biggest hazard is ice, specifically black ice, especially when above freezing temperatures during the day melt ice and snow and then below freezing temperatures at night cause a refreeze. Fog can sometimes be an issue when driving in the mountains, especially in western Maryland.

The department of transportation is a good resource for maps, toll rates, webcams, road conditions, and details on HOV restrictions. Visit www.mdot.maryland.gov.

TRAIN

Amtrak (800/872-7245, www.amtrak. com) offers rail service to eight stations in Maryland. There is also one station in Washington DC—Union Station. Although a train ticket can rival the cost of airfare, it can also be more convenient and more comfortable to travel by train.

Amtrak connects to the **Maryland Area Rail Commuter (MARC)** (410/539-5000, www.mta.maryland.gov) train in Maryland. MARC operates on weekdays only and provides service to areas such as Harford County, Baltimore, Brunswick, Frederick, and Washington DC.

BUS

Many cities in Maryland can be reached by **Greyhound** (800/231-2222, www.greyhound. com). Tickets are less expensive when purchased in advance and often discounts are available to students, seniors, and military personnel.

Local bus service is available in many cities, with the most extensive being the **Metrobus** (202/637-7000, www.wmata.com/bus) service in and around Washington DC and its suburbs. Metrobus has an incredible 11,500 bus stops on 325 routes throughout Washington DC and Maryland and is the sixth busiest bus service provider in the nation. They have more than 1,500 buses.

Tourist-friendly bus systems exist in both Washington, DC with the **DC Circulator** (www.dccirculator.com, $1) and Baltimore with the **Charm City Circulator** (www. charmcitycirculator.com, free).

SUBWAY

Washington DC and the surrounding area has a clean, reliable, and generally safe subway system called **Metrorail** (202/637-7000, www.wmata.com/rail) that is run by the **Washington Metropolitan Area Transit Authority (WMATA).** The Metrorail system is commonly known as the Metro and provides service to more than 700,000 customers a day. The system is number two in the country in terms of ticket sales and serves more than 80 stations throughout DC, Maryland, and Virginia.

There are six color-coded rail lines, the Red, Orange, Blue, Yellow, Green, and Silver. The system layout is easy to understand as most stations are named for the neighborhood they serve and getting from one station to another normally requires no more than a single transfer. Metrorail stations are marked with large "M" signs at the entrance that have colored stripes around them to show which line they serve. A complete list of fares and a map of each train line can be found on the website. Metrorail opens at 5am on weekdays and 7am on weekends. It closes at midnight Sunday-Thursday and 3am Friday and Saturday. Bicycles are permitted during non-peak hours.

WATER

If you're lucky enough to cruise into Maryland on a private boat, you'll have options for docking in marinas along the Chesapeake Bay, the Intracoastal Waterway, and the Potomac River. Most towns on the water offer marina slips, but making plans ahead of time is advised, especially during the prime summer months and in popular areas such as Annapolis.

Recreation

If you can dream it, you can do it in Maryland. People in this region are crazy about getting outside, and with the mountains and seashore just a few hours apart, the opportunities are endless.

HIKING

Hiking trails are available throughout Maryland. You only need a good pair of trail shoes or hiking boots and you're on your way. The **Potomac Appalachian Trail Club** (www.potomacappalachian.org) is a wonderful resource for hikers throughout the area and offers maps, books, and trip information.

BIKING

Whether you like to road bike, mountain bike, or just toddle along on a cruiser enjoying the scenery, Maryland is the place to do it. From the flat Eastern Shore to the challenging mountains of Western Maryland, there are endless choices for getting out and pedaling. For those who are competitive, the racing scene is thriving in the region, and road races are held most weekends April through October. Mountain bike races are also very popular and run even later in the year.

Road Cycling

Many organized rides take place in Maryland, including the famous **Seagull Century** (www.seagullcentury.org), held each October on the Eastern Shore. Wide, flat roads with little traffic make the Eastern Shore a favorite place to bike almost any time of the year. The terrain is nearly pancake flat, although there is often a headwind. A more challenging ride is the fierce **Garrett County Gran Fondo** (www.garrettcountygranfondo.org) in Western Maryland.

Not all roads are conducive to road cycling, given the extreme traffic conditions in many urban areas. Be wise about choosing a biking route; accidents do happen, and usually the bike is on the worse end of it.

Mountain Biking

Mountain biking is big in the mid-Atlantic. Mountain bike trails can be found near the cities, in the rural areas, and throughout the mountains. Fat-tire races are also held throughout the year. **Singletracks** (www.singletracks.com) is a good resource for mountain biking in the region.

CANOEING AND KAYAKING

Canoeing is one of the most popular ways to enjoy the multitude of rivers, creeks, and lakes. Dozens of outfitters and liveries rent canoes and many offer guided trips.

Flat-water kayaking has become extremely popular in Maryland over the last decade. This part of the country may have lagged behind other water-influenced regions in the adoption of this sport, but it has fully caught on. Kayak tours and instruction are now available on many eastern rivers, lakes, the Chesapeake Bay, and at the beaches.

White-water kayaking is a much more specialized sport. A training center for racing is located on the Potomac River. Additional information can be obtained from the **Potomac Whitewater Racing Center** (www.potomacwhitewater.org).

BOATING AND SAILING

Salt water, lakes, marinas, dock and dine restaurants, Maryland has them all. The Chesapeake Bay alone has 11,684 miles of shoreline, which is more than the West Coast of the United States. Every town on the bay has a marina and access can also be gained from public boat ramps in many locations.

Many visitors even arrive from other regions by water. Take a look at the boats in Annapolis Harbor and where they're from; there's a good reason Annapolis is called the "Sailing Capital of the World." It's a sailor's dream. Commercial and recreational powerboats must be registered in Maryland if that is where they are primarily used.

FISHING

Whether you prefer fishing in a quiet lake, fly-fishing in a mountain stream, surf fishing, or taking a deep-sea fishing charter, you can do it all in this region. Most state parks offer fishing, and some areas are stocked through breeding programs.

Some favorite fishing spots in Maryland include the Chesapeake Bay (bluefish, flounder, and drum), Sandy Point State Park (striper, white perch, and rockfish), Deep Creek Lake (bass), Point Lookout State Park (rockfish, bluefish, and hardhead), and Assateague Island (surf fishing for stripers).

Licenses are required in Maryland and Washington DC. Maryland fishing licenses can be purchased online from the **Department of Natural Resources** (www.dnr.state.md.us/service/license.asp) or by calling 855/855-3906. Non-tidal licenses are $20.50 for residents and $30.50 for nonresidents. Chesapeake Bay and coastal sport fishing licenses are $15 for residents and $22.50 for nonresidents. Licenses are valid from January 1 to December 31 of the same year. Fishing licenses in Washington DC can be purchased from the **District Department of the Environment** (www.green.dc.gov). Licenses are $10 for residents and $13 for nonresidents and are valid from January 1 to December 31 of the same calendar year.

Crabbing and clamming are free in Maryland if you are doing so for personal use only. Beaches and marsh areas are publicly accessible, but keep in mind that limits and regulations apply. Current regulations can be found at http://dnr.maryland.gov/service/fishing_license.asp.

GOLF

Hundreds of public golf courses are located in Maryland. A listing of courses can be found at www.golfmaryland.com.

ROCK CLIMBING

Carderock Recreation Area in Maryland, located near Washington DC, has more than 100 climbing routes.

WINTER SPORTS

It's no surprise that winter sporting opportunities are concentrated in western Maryland. A handful of ski resorts such as **Wisp Resort** in the Deep Creek Lake area are open during the winter months. Cross-country skiing and snowmobiling are available on a limited basis when the weather cooperates on designated trails. Ice-skating and hockey, however, are available in indoor and seasonal outdoor facilities.

Travel Tips

FOREIGN TRAVELERS

Visitors from other countries must present a valid passport and visa issued by a U.S. consular official unless they are a citizen of a country eligible for the Visa Waiver Program (such as Canada) in order to enter the United States. A foreign national entering the country by air that is a citizen of a country eligible for the Visa Waiver Program must present an approved Electronic System for Travel Authorization and a valid passport. A list of exceptions can be found on the Department of Homeland Security website at www.cbp.gov.

ACCESS FOR TRAVELERS WITH DISABILITIES

Accessibility is in the eye of the beholder. Despite the Americans with Disabilities Act, it is unfortunate that universal access in public places is still not a reality in most parts of the country. Maryland is no exception. Although many restaurants, theaters, hotels, and museums offer ramps or elevators, some smaller, privately owned establishments (such as bed-and-breakfasts) do not always provide these necessities. It is best to call ahead and verify the type of access that is available. A list of state and public lands in Maryland that offer accessible amenities can be found on Maryland's Department of Natural Resources website at www.dnr.state.md.us/publiclands/accessforall.asp.

SENIOR TRAVELERS

Numerous hotels, venues, and attractions offer discounts to seniors, all you have to do is ask when making your reservations or purchasing your tickets. The **American Association of Retired Persons (AARP)** (www.aarp.org) is the largest organization in the nation for seniors. They offer discounts to their members on hotels, tours, rental cars, airfare, and many other services. Membership in AARP is just $16 a year, so it's worth joining.

GAY AND LESBIAN TRAVELERS

Washington DC, Baltimore, and Rehoboth Beach have large LGBT populations and readily accept same-sex couples and families. Most other parts of Maryland welcome business from everyone, so unless you need specialized accommodations, travel shouldn't be a concern. The **Gay and Lesbian Travel Center** (www.gayjourney.com) is a great resource for travel.

TRAVELING WITH CHILDREN

Although most places don't make specific accommodations for children, in general, most tourist attractions throughout Maryland are

Maryland has become more pet-friendly.

family-friendly (except for obvious exceptions where noted). Baltimore offers museums devoted specifically to children and many other sights have a children's component to them.

TRAVELING WITH PETS

In recent years more and more pet-friendly establishments have been popping up. Many higher-end hotels (such as the Kimpton hotel chain) allow four-legged family members, and some establishments even host doggie happy hours. It's not uncommon for attractions, stores, historical sites, campgrounds, outdoor shopping malls, parks, beaches, and even the patios at some restaurants to welcome dogs with open arms. It is always best to call ahead before assuming an establishment is pet-friendly. Service and guide dogs are welcome nearly everywhere with their human companions.

TIPPING

A 15-20 percent tip is standard throughout Maryland on restaurant bills. Other service providers, such as taxi drivers and hairstylists, typically receive 10-15 percent. Bellhops and airport personnel normally receive $1-2 per bag.

Information and Services

TOURIST INFORMATION

For information on tourism in Maryland, visit the **Maryland Office of Tourism site** (www.visitmaryland.org). For information on tourism in Washington DC, visit the official **DC tourism site** (www.washington.org).

COMMUNICATIONS AND MEDIA
Cell Phone Coverage

Cell phone coverage is generally available in most parts of Maryland. As with any state, there are scattered pockets of spotty coverage even near large cities, but overall, coverage is reliable. As a rule, the more rural the region you are traveling through (such as Western Maryland), the less coverage is available, but for the most part, the major highways have fairly consistent coverage. Once you leave the major highways, coverage can be a concern. Any time you head into the backcountry, be sure to bring supplies in case of an emergency instead of relying on your cell phone.

Internet Access

Internet access is readily available in hotels throughout Maryland and is very commonly included with the price of a room, or else as an add-on. A list of free Wi-Fi hotspots can be found at www.openwifispots.com.

Media

Major city newspapers and magazines are available throughout Maryland. The most widely circulated daily newspaper in the Washington DC area (including the Capital Region of Maryland) is the *Washington Post* (www.washingtonpost.com). The paper features world news and local news and places an emphasis on national politics. The *Washington Times* (www.washingtontimes.com) is another daily newspaper that is widely circulated. Weekly and specialty newspapers include the *Washington City Paper* (www.washingtoncitypaper.com), an alternative weekly newspaper, and the *Washington Informer* (www.washingtoninformer.com), a weekly newspaper serving the DC area's African American population.

The most widely read paper in Baltimore is the *Baltimore Sun* (www.baltimoresun.com). It is Maryland's largest daily newspaper and covers local and regional news. The Baltimore *City Paper* (www.citypaper.com) is a free alternative weekly paper that is distributed on Wednesdays. It is known for having good coverage of clubs, concerts, restaurants, and theater. It also has political articles and covers subjects not featured in mainstream publications.

Health and Safety

For emergencies anywhere in Maryland, dial 911 from any telephone at no charge. From a cell phone, the state police can be reached by pressing #77. Generally speaking, hospitals are very good, and excellent in the larger cities. Emergency room treatment is always costlier than a scheduled appointment, but emergency care facilities can also be found in most areas to treat minor conditions.

LYME DISEASE

Maryland is in prime tick area, so **Lyme disease,** which is transmitted through the bites of deer-tick bites, is a risk. Use insect repellent, and check yourself thoroughly after spending time in the woods or walking through tall grass. If you are bitten, or find a red circular rash (similar to a bull's-eye), consult a physician. Lyme disease can be life-threatening if it goes untreated.

INSECTS

Mosquitoes are common throughout Maryland and aside from being annoying can carry diseases. Damp, low areas can harbor large populations of these little vampires, so use insect repellent and steer clear of stagnant water. **Bees, wasps, yellow jackets,** and **hornets** are all permanent residents of the region and are particularly active (and aggressive) in the fall.

Female **black widow spiders** are also found in the region and can be identified by a small red hourglass shape on their black abdomens. They live in dark places such as rotting logs and under patio furniture. Symptoms of their bite include severe abdominal pain and should be treated. The males are harmless. The **brown recluse spider,** contrary to common belief, is not native to this region. They can on occasion be found here, but only as a transplant.

ANIMALS

There are three types of venomous snakes in Maryland. The most common is the northern copperhead. This snake has dark-colored cross bands shaped like an hourglass. The second type is the timber rattlesnake, which is found in all the mountainous regions. It also has a patterned back with wavy cross bands.

Swimming in the Atlantic Ocean or the Chesapeake Bay could put you in contact with stinging **jellyfish** or **sea nettles** (especially in the Chesapeake Bay). **Sharks** are also found occasionally in both bodies of water and have even been spotted in the Potomac River near Point Lookout.

PLANTS

Poison ivy, poison oak, and **poison sumac** are all native to the region and should be avoided even if you have never had a prior allergic reaction (you can develop one anytime). As the saying goes, "Leaves of three, let it be." Local mushrooms and berries can also be poisonous, so don't eat them unless you are 100 percent sure of their identification.

WEATHER

In addition to the obvious presence or prediction of a tornado, tropical storm, hurricane, or snowstorm (all of which are possible but rare in the region), be aware that **lightning** is a greater danger on exposed ridges, in fields, on golf courses, on the beach, or anywhere near water. Thunderstorms can pop up quickly, especially during the summer months, so check the weather before venturing out and be prepared with a plan B. Hypothermia can also be an issue. Being wet, tired, and cold is a dangerous combination. Symptoms include slurred speech, uncontrollable shivering, and loss of coordination.

CRIME

As in many states, downtown areas of larger cities such Baltimore and Washington DC can be unsafe, especially at night. Ask hotel staff about the safety of the area you're staying in, lock your doors, take a cab instead of walking, and don't leave valuables in your car.

Resources

Suggested Reading

HISTORY
General History

Barbour, Philip, and Thad Tate, eds. *The Complete Works of Captain John Smith, 1580-1631.* Chapel Hill: University of North Carolina Press, 1986. Three volumes of Captain John Smith's work.

Doak, Robin. *Voices from Colonial America: Maryland 1634-1776.* Washington DC: National Geographic, 2007. First-person accounts, historical maps, and illustrations tell Maryland's history.

McWilliams, Jane W. *Annapolis, City on the Severn.* Baltimore, MD: The Johns Hopkins University Press, 2011. The story of Annapolis.

Civil War History

Catton, Bruce. *America Goes to War: The Civil War and Its Meaning in American Culture.* Middletown, CT: Wesleyan University Press, 1992. An interesting study on the Civil War.

McPherson, James. *Battle Cry of Freedom: The Civil War Era.* New York: Ballantine Books, 1988. Perhaps the best single-volume history of the war.

SCIENCE AND NATURE

Fergus, Charles. *Wildlife of Virginia and Maryland: and Washington, D.C.* Mechanicsburg, PA: Stackpole Books, 2003. Provides details on the animals in the diverse habitats throughout Virginia and Maryland.

RECREATION

Adams, Scott, and Martin Fernandez. *Mountain Biking the Washington, D.C./ Baltimore Area.* 4th Edition. Guilford, CT: Falcon Guides, 2003. A great guide to mountain biking around Washington DC and Baltimore.

Adkins, Leonard. *Explorer's Guide 50 Hikes in Maryland.* Woodstock, VT: The Countryman Press, 2007. A good resource for hiking in Maryland.

Blackinton, Theresa Dowell. *Moon Take a Hike Washington DC: 80 Hikes within Two Hours of the City.* 2nd edition. Berkeley, CA: Avalon Travel, 2013. A terrific resource for hiking the Washington DC area including hikes in metropolitan DC, the Shenandoah, Western Maryland, Eastern Maryland, and Virginia's Piedmont and Coastal Plains.

Eltringham, Scott, and Jim Wade. *Scott & Jim's Favorite Bike Rides.* Arlington, VA: S&J Cycling, 2007. A fun guide to biking in Northern Virginia and central Maryland.

High, Mike. *The C&O Canal Companion.* Baltimore, MD: Johns Hopkins University Press, 1997. A well-written guide to the C&O Canal National Historical Park.

Horst, Eric, and Stewart M. Green. *Rock Climbing Virginia, West Virginia, and Maryland*. Helena, MT: Falcon Press, 2013. Detailed information on climbs in Shenandoah National Park, Great Falls, and Carderock.

Moore, Steve. *Maryland Trout Fishing: The Stocked and Wild Rivers, Streams, Lakes and Ponds*. Calibrated Consulting, 2011. An informative guide to trout fishing in Maryland.

Internet Resources

STATE RESOURCES
www.maryland.gov
The official Maryland website.

www.visitmaryland.org
The official tourism website for Maryland.

WASHINGTON DC
www.washington.org
www.visitingdc.com
Visitor information on Washington DC.

www.si.edu
Information on the Smithsonian Institution.

www.wmata.com
Information on Metrorail and Metrobus service.

HISTORY
www.mdhs.org
Information on historical Maryland.

www.dchistory.org
The interesting and helpful website of the Historical Society of Washington DC.

RECREATION
www.nps.gov
The National Park Service website, a comprehensive guide to national parks throughout the country.

www.dnr.maryland.gov
Information on the Maryland Department of Natural Resources.

www.baydreaming.com
Offers an excellent list of marinas and boating facilities in the Chesapeake Bay area.

www.thebayguide.com
A guide to boating in the Chesapeake Bay area.

www.findyourchesapeake.com
The Chesapeake Bay Gateways Network website provides information on public access parks around the bay.

LOCAL RESOURCES
www.hometownfreepress.com
A guide to local newspapers.

www.chesapeakeboating.net
Chesapeake Bay Magazine is full of interesting articles on the bay area.

www.baydreaming.com
A guide to Chesapeake Bay events.

Index

List of Maps

Photo Credits

Also Available

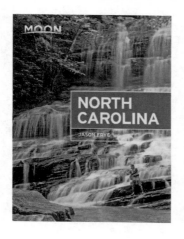

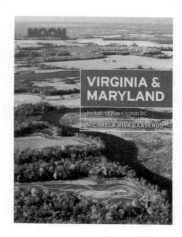

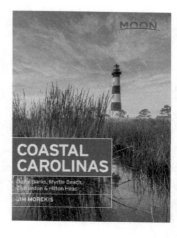

MAP SYMBOLS

▦▦▦ Expressway	★	Highlight	✗	Airfield	⚓	Golf Course
═══ Primary Road	○	City/Town	✈	Airport	🅿	Parking Area
─── Secondary Road	◉	State Capital	▲	Mountain	⬟	Archaeological Site
┄┄┄ Unpaved Road	⊛	National Capital	✛	Unique Natural Feature	✚	Church
┄┄┄ Trail	★	Point of Interest				
⋯⋯ Ferry	•	Accommodation	🗲	Waterfall	⛽	Gas Station
▬▬▬ Railroad	▼	Restaurant/Bar	▲	Park	◎	Glacier
▨▨ Pedestrian Walkway	▪	Other Location	⊟	Trailhead	🗺	Mangrove
▥▥▥ Stairs	Λ	Campground	⛷	Skiing Area	▦	Reef
					▤	Swamp

CONVERSION TABLES

$°C = (°F - 32) / 1.8$
$°F = (°C \times 1.8) + 32$
1 inch = 2.54 centimeters (cm)
1 foot = 0.304 meters (m)
1 yard = 0.914 meters
1 mile = 1.6093 kilometers (km)
1 km = 0.6214 miles
1 fathom = 1.8288 m
1 chain = 20.1168 m
1 furlong = 201.168 m
1 acre = 0.4047 hectares
1 sq km = 100 hectares
1 sq mile = 2.59 square km
1 ounce = 28.35 grams
1 pound = 0.4536 kilograms
1 short ton = 0.90718 metric ton
1 short ton = 2,000 pounds
1 long ton = 1.016 metric tons
1 long ton = 2,240 pounds
1 metric ton = 1,000 kilograms
1 quart = 0.94635 liters
1 US gallon = 3.7854 liters
1 Imperial gallon = 4.5459 liters
1 nautical mile = 1.852 km

°FAHRENHEIT	°CELSIUS	
230	110	
220	100	WATER BOILS
210	100	
200	90	
190		
180	80	
170		
160	70	
150		
140	60	
130		
120	50	
110		
100	40	
90	30	
80		
70	20	
60		
50	10	
40		
30	0	WATER FREEZES
20		
10	-10	
0		
-10	-20	
-20	-30	
-30		
-40	-40	

MOON MARYLAND

Avalon Travel
An imprint of Perseus Books
A Hachette Book Group company
1700 Fourth Street
Berkeley, CA 94710, USA
www.moon.com

Editor: Rachel Feldman
Series Manager: Kathryn Ettinger
Copy Editor: Brett Keener
Graphics Coordinator: Elizabeth Jang
Production Coordinator: Elizabeth Jang
Cover Design: Faceout Studios, Charles Brock
Interior Design: Domini Dragoone
Moon Logo: Tim McGrath
Map Editor: Mike Morgenfeld
Cartographers: Austin Ehrhardt and
  Mike Morgenfeld
Indexer: Greg Jewett

ISBN-13: 978-1-63121-467-7
ISSN: 2374-7714

Printing History
1st Edition — 2015
2nd Edition — June 2017
5 4 3 2 1

Front cover photo: wild horses on Assateague Island
  © Michael Rickard/Getty Images

Back cover photo: interior dome of the Capitol
  Building in Washington, DC © Cynthia Farmer |
  Dreamstime.com

Printed in Canada by Friesens

KEEPING CURRENT

If you have a favorite gem you'd like to see included in the next edition, or
see anything that needs updating, clarification, or correction, please drop
us a line. Send your comments via email to feedback@moon.com, or use the
address above.